Time and Timelessness in Victorian Poetry

Edinburgh Critical Studies in Victorian Culture

For a complete list of titles published visit the Edinburgh Critical Studies in Victorian Culture web page at www.edinburghuniversitypress.com/series/ECVC

Also Available:
Victoriographies – A Journal of Nineteenth-Century Writing, 1790–1914, edited by Diane Piccitto and Patricia Pulham
ISSN: 2044-2416
www.eupjournals.com/vic

Time and Timelessness in Victorian Poetry

Irmtraud Huber

EDINBURGH
University Press

Edinburgh University Press is one of the leading university presses in the UK. We publish academic books and journals in our selected subject areas across the humanities and social sciences, combining cutting-edge scholarship with high editorial and production values to produce academic works of lasting importance. For more information visit our website: edinburghuniversitypress.com

Edinburgh University Press Ltd
The Tun – Holyrood Road
12(2f) Jackson's Entry
Edinburgh EH8 8PJ

Typeset in 11/13 Adobe Sabon
by Manila Typesetting Company

A CIP record for this book is available from the British Library

ISBN 978 1 3995 1181 0 (hardback)
ISBN 978 1 3995 1183 4 (webready PDF)
ISBN 978 1 3995 1184 1 (epub)

Contents

Acknowledgements

The first draft of this manuscript was completed while the rules of the world were being reshuffled by a tiny virus, and I write these words while Europe as I thought I knew it is being turned on its head by massive human violence. Meanwhile, the greater part of humanity, or at least the part in power, continues to watch sedately the destruction of our planet. It is a tough time for optimism, and for maintaining the worth and importance of the kind of work this book results from and hopes to inspire. Yet it is my firm conviction that this is precisely the kind of work that we have dire need of: a critical and historical engagement that challenges our own presumptions and certainties, that allows us to encounter and inhabit alternative, even contradictory perspectives, that makes us see that the world can be thought differently and can be made different.

I have had the great luck and privilege to encounter, work with and learn from many people who cherish and pursue this kind of work and who have been endlessly generous in sharing their thoughts and experience. My former colleagues at the English Department of the Universität Bern have provided me with a fertile ground in which the seeds of this project could begin to grow. Particular thanks go to Virginia Richter, without whom I would not be the literary scholar I am, and Ursula Kluwick, who has been a steadfast friend and formidable critic of my work since the beginning. At a crucial moment, Tobias Döring from the Ludwig-Maximilians-Universität München offered me the position which allowed me to finish this book, and I am deeply grateful for the immense support he has given and continues to give me. I thank him, Ingo Berensmeyer, Inka-Mülder Bach, Anne-Julia Zwierlein and Virginia Richter for the valuable feedback they have provided on earlier drafts of this book, and I thank my long-standing partner in crime, Wolfgang Funk, for his unflagging optimism and moral support. Special thanks go to Ewan Jones, who has not only welcomed me incredibly generously at Cambridge when I knew no one and had little to offer, but who has also given invaluable feedback on my manuscript, always asking the questions that hurt most (and are therefore most helpful).

This book would not exist had I not had the full support of my family: thank you, Philipp, for believing in me and appreciating my work; thank you, Madeleine and Dominic, for the joy you bring and for forcing me away from the screen, and thank you to their grandparents, for being available whenever they are needed. I want to thank my mother, in particular, for her willingness to follow me across several national borders to support me and the family.

Parts of this book have been previously published as journal articles. A part of Chapter 1 shares significant material with the article 'Competing for Eternity: Tracing the Relation between Poetry and Science in Victorian Discourse', *Journal for Literature and Science* 12.1 (2019), 1–20. A part of Chapter 3 has been previously published as 'Idle Singers, Idle Songs – the Birth of Poetry from the Spirit of Idleness', *Victorian Poetry* 58.4 (2020), 409–31 (republished by permission of West Virginia University Press). I am grateful for the permission to reuse this material. During some of my research for this book I have received generous support of the Swiss National Science Foundation.

Introduction – Time, History and the Lyric

A Sonnet is a moment's monument,
Memorial from the soul's eternity
To one dead deathless hour. Look that it be,
Whether for lustral rite or dire portent,
Of its own intricate fulness reverent:
Carve it in ivory or in ebony,
As Day or Night prevail; and let Time see
Its flowering crest impearled and orient.

A Sonnet is a coin: its face reveals
The soul, its converse, to what Power 'tis due:
Whether for tribute to the august appeals
Of Life, or dower in Love's high retinue,
It serve; or, 'mid the dark wharf's cavernous breath,
In Charon's palm it pay the toll to Death.[1]

Dante Gabriel Rossetti wrote this programmatic poem early in 1880. Adding an illuminated drawing, he gave it to his mother as a birthday present some months later and finally used it as a proem to his sonnet sequence *The House of Life*, as it was published in his collection *Ballads and Sonnets* in 1881. The aesthetic ideal which this sonnet brilliantly both describes and performs is that of the poem as a wrought artefact in which transitory time is captured, aesthetically elevated and memorialised for eternity, a prime example of what Herbert Tucker has called '[t]he spacetime magic of poetry' (1997: 277). Beyond its immediate claims about the poetic form of the sonnet, Rossetti's poem appears to crystallise an understanding of lyric poetry that thinks of it as resisting time or, more drastically phrased, as timeless.

Yet, as soon as we look beyond the opening line and turn to the poem in its entirety, we necessarily become aware of the various temporalities involved even in its programmatic attempt to solidify and freeze time into poetic form. Indeed, one may well ask in what sense Rossetti's poem can be called timeless at all. To start with the most banal observation, as a text, the poem is necessarily temporal since, short as it may be, its words have to be taken in successively; its sense can only be established in a temporal sequence of before and after. If Sharon Cameron, in a rare study of lyric time structures, points out that 'lyric meaning gives the illusion of not having to wait upon time for its completion' (1979: 196), she is careful to insist that this can never be more than, precisely, an illusion. Indeed, she acknowledges a 'crucial relationship between the ability to speak at all and an indispensable sense of time' (20). But the sonnet is not only a piece of language; it is a piece of rhythmical language in rhyme: in spite of its numerous foot substitutions, the sonnet's iambic pentameter establishes a basic recurring beat, a succession of pulses which make time audible. The phonological repetitions structuring the poem, not only in its recurring rhyme sounds, but also in the almost tongue-twisting assonances and consonances it revels in, further shape the experience of reading as a temporal one of successive echoes, of raised, extenuated and satisfied expectations. Moreover, the poem is, of course, centrally concerned with time thematically. It specifically addresses the sonnet's (indeed, so it claims, any sonnet's) relationship with time. 'Moment', 'Memorial', 'eternity', 'hour', 'Day', 'Night', 'Time': nouns directly relating to time abound in the octave. The sonnet does not escape time, time is its essence; personified Time is even, explicitly, a sonnet's ideal audience ('let Time see' l. 7). The moment is memorialised precisely because it is fleeting and as a memorial the poem attests to the moment itself as much as to its passing, to death as much as to deathlessness.

With the sestet, then, the poem itself enters as a third term into an equation which was popular among the Victorians (even more so, perhaps, than it still is today): 'time is money'. The sonnet is a moment's monument, that is solidified time, and it is also a coin, that is money, in a circular logic that undermines the common wisdom of the popular proverb by substituting both terms: 'a sonnet is a sonnet'. The octave and the sestet thus oppose two different approaches to time in two different conceptualisations of the sonnet: either as unique, individual and fully self-contained ('of its own intricate fulness reverent'), or as ex- and interchangeable in a market economy of tributes, dowers and tolls. The significant, beautiful moment memorialised in a sonnet is contrasted to the uniformity and commodification of clock-time, but the sonnet, intriguingly, is associated with both.

It is also worth bearing in mind that Rossetti gave this poem as a birthday present to his mother. With this action it enters into another kind of economic system as a gift, but is also given another temporal dimension: as a token for the regular recurrence of a particular day, thus combining linear and circular temporal aspects, marking the passing of a life as much as the revolving of the year. As a birthday present, the poem can be seen to ironically undermine the logic of both its octet and its sestet. A birthday marks the return of a day much more than a specific moment, and a gift escapes from the economic logic of coins.

Finally, this poem serves as an introductory poem to Rossetti's sonnet sequence *The House of Life* and thus acknowledges further temporal relationships. Each moment, memorialised in the individual sonnets in the sequence, is framed as a part of a larger temporal progression, a life, while the astrological connotations of the title emphasise the contrasting temporality of recurring cycles of stellar constellations. The importance of time for the sequence is further established by the titles of its two parts: 'Youth and Change' and 'Change and Fate'.[2] Thus, Rossetti's sonnet is, on the one hand, a programmatic formulation of an influential ideal of lyric timelessness which still reverberates in characterisations of the lyric today. On the other hand, it enters into a complex network of different temporalities. To characterise this poem as 'timeless' must risk losing sight of such multiple and intricate temporal relations.

And yet the position that timelessness is an essential feature of the lyric is by no means rare in literary criticism. Northrop Frye, for example, argues that '[i]n the lyric [. . .] we turn away from our ordinary continuous experience in space and time, or rather from a verbal mimesis of it' (1985: 31). Even more drastically, Karol Berger claims in his ambitious *Theory of Art* (2002), that the lyric 'can be defined at first only in negative terms [. . .]. The lyric is nonnarrative, that is, it is the atemporal form, the kind of form in the constitution of which time plays no essential role' (195). Similarly, Monique Morgan distinguishes between lyric and narrative modes in a study of nineteenth-century British long poems primarily on the basis of their respective relation to time, suggesting that the lyric 'creates a timeless present, an indefinitely suspended moment, which contrasts with narrative's past progression of events' (2009: 9). As Heather Dubrow (2006) has noted, such generalisations are especially frequent in discussions about the relation between narrative and the lyric, and often suggest a conflict. This, she points out, fails to take account of the various ways in which the two modes can intermingle and interact (254). Eva Zettelmann goes further in exposing the underlying logic of such antitheses. She suggests that '[b]y constructing poetry as an exclusively atemporal, non-spatial, non-sequential, non-specific, non-experiential, and anti-illusionist mode, narratology has been able to elevate the antitheses of these features to the rank of generic narrative properties' (2017: 137). Meanwhile, professed lyricologists have also contributed to this critical misconception. Rüdiger Zymner, for instance, assembles a collage of statements of various contemporary poets, which, in his opinion, all point to 'an experience of stalled or suspended time as an essential experience of the lyric process and a central condition for the function of the lyric' (2013: 69; my translation) and his own contribution to a 'lyricology of time' from a cognitive science perspective focuses on what he calls 'the problem of the "suspension of time" in or by means of the lyric' (2016: 34; my translation; see also Zymner 2020). Even Sharon Cameron's *Lyric Time* (1979), one of the most sustained and sophisticated considerations of the subject to date, can easily be misread as making the same claim when she speaks variously of the lyric's 'recoil from temporality' (24), or its 'attempt to stall time to a stasis' (260).[3]

This book offers a sustained rebuttal to such a critical commonplace and highlights the importance that questions of time play in an understanding of poetry, including lyric poetry. If such a rebuttal seems unnecessary, it remains the case that, as Zymner notes, 'compared with the critical treatment of the temporal dimension in narrative literature [. . .], lyricological research on time is to date limited in historical reach and highly selective as well as theoretically underdeveloped' (2016: 32; my translation; see also von Ammon 2020). Since the turn of the millennium, there has been an increasing push towards developing more sophisticated theoretical concepts for the structural analysis of poetry, including its relationship to time, among German scholars in particular (see Hillebrandt et al. 2020 for an up-to-date overview, as well as specific contributions dealing with the question of time). As the term 'lyricology' already suggests, however, such work, like the earlier one by Cameron, tends to focus on the lyric genre, rather than on poetry more broadly. Thus Zymner, for example, considers the briefness of the lyric poem as key (2016: 44; 2020: 327). This fails to adequately account for the way longer poetic texts, even longer lyric poems, shape time. At the same time, German scholarship in particular tends to appropriate figures and concepts from narratology to approach time in poetry (see, for example, von Ammon 2020; Hempfer 2014; Hühn 2016; Mahler 2006). While productive to a degree, this approach often struggles to clarify specificities of poetry and tends to reduce poems to their narrative elements. I want to begin to redress such theoretical lacunae. In the final chapter of this book, I therefore propose a conceptual framework for the analysis of time in poetic texts which casts a wider net, claiming applicability to the broad diversity of genres and forms that poetry, in fact, offers.

Beyond this aim to provide a better vocabulary to address time structures of poetry than is at present available, the question I ultimately seek to answer is why and how it came to seem reasonable or perhaps even inevitable to characterise the lyric as timeless in the first place. Indeed, a historical perspective, I maintain, is essential for an understanding of the way both literary forms and theoretical concepts take shape in time. Only a historically informed theoretical position can begin to realise its own preconceptions. It is therefore no surprise that historical, as opposed to theoretical, studies of (lyric) poetry have much more frequently shown an interest in temporal structures. Such studies often focus on a particular poetic genre, like Christopher R. Miller (2006), who also rejects definitions of the lyric as timeless in his investigation of Romantic evening poems, Jennifer A. Wagner (1996), who explores the nineteenth-century sonnet as a record of an 'engagement [. . .] with the relationship of poetic form to temporality' (12), or Marion Thain (2016), whose argument that 'the very generic conventions of the lyric were brought into crisis [in the nineteenth century] by larger-scale theoretical shifts in the conception of time' (55) will be repeatedly corroborated by my broader argument about poetry beyond the lyric. Others develop a thematic focus on aspects of time, like Marcus Tomalin's study of representations of various timekeeping devices in the long eighteenth century (2020), or Emily Rohrbach's exploration of the Romantics' fraught relation to an uncertain future (2016). Such historical perspectives may offer important correctives to the ideal of the brief and timeless lyric, which so often governs the theoretical reflections mentioned above.

I therefore propose to bring the historical focus of such studies in conversation with theoretical efforts to understand and define poetry. I turn to the poetic practice and theory of the Victorian age to argue that the current conception of lyric as timeless is a result of nineteenth-century reconsiderations and redefinitions not only of the lyric, but of poetry in general, in response to radically changing experiences and conceptualisations of time. I follow Thain's observation that the temporal logic of poetry which the Victorians inherited from the Romantics came under increasing pressure in the course of the nineteenth century (2016: 4) but explore further the reason for and consequences of this change: poetry's claims to eternal truths and validity were undermined by a spreading historical awareness and loss of religious certainties, as well as by the growing authority of science; idle contemplation as a condition for poetic production was challenged by the increasing cultural prevalence of a relentless work ethic; a traditionally celebrated balance between freedom and restriction in the form of metrical composition threatened to collapse into the monotonous rhythms of the machine. I thus concur with Thain's observation that poetry 'responded to some of the key conceptual shifts of the nineteenth century because it had to: some of its core generic conventions were deeply challenged by changing ways of thinking and being' (2016: 230). Thain's study focuses on the lyric and on Aestheticist responses to these challenges in particular, but her general arguments, I believe, have a broader relevance for the way in which the very concept of poetry changed in the course of the nineteenth century. To put these changes under scrutiny, highlighting the role of time, is to begin to account for the conceptual distance that lies between today's critical commonplace about lyric's timelessness and early nineteenth-century voices like those of Georg Wilhelm Friedrich Hegel, who maintained in his lectures on aesthetics (1835–8) that 'the outpouring of lyric stands to time, as an external element of communication, in a much closer relation than epic narrative does' (1975: 1136), or Eneas Sweetland Dallas, who, in his *Essay on Poetry* (1852), called metre, which for most Victorians was still one of the essential elements of poetry, 'time heard' (164). If we take the sometimes arcane and seemingly outdated Victorian deliberations about poetry, about prosody and about genre seriously, they can begin to teach us something about our own conceptual blind spots.

Timeless? Lyric?

In order to begin to tackle these issues, one might note that to call a poem 'timeless' can mean fundamentally different things. There are at least four kinds of timelessness.

First, if Shakespeare, in sonnet 18, celebrates art as a way to immortalise love – since, famously, 'So long as men can breathe or eyes can see, / So long lives this, and this gives life to thee' – the timelessness of the poem depends largely on its continuing reception.

In effect, the poem's claims rest on an astounding confidence in the everlasting fame of the poet's work. Michael Clune calls this the 'Aesthetics of the Enduring Word' and notes that, in the sonnets, 'Shakespeare argues that poetry stakes its claim to immortality not on the finitude of a given material instantiation, nor on the compromised reproducibility of the copy, but on the infinite reproducibility of the human species' (2018: 18). This is a confidence which is on the wane in the nineteenth century, in face of an increased historical awareness, and new scientific insights like deep time, evolution theory and the second law of thermodynamics, all of which suggested that human reproducibility is by no means a timeless guarantee. In contrast to Shakespeare's bravado claims for immortality, Alfred Tennyson, in *In Memoriam A.H.H.* (1850), dares only hope for his 'modern rhyme' to end up as a bookbinding or a hair curler, or, perchance,

> A man upon a stall may find,
> And, passing, turn the page that tells
> A grief, then changed to something else,
> Sung by a long-forgotten mind. (LXXVII, ll. 9–12)

Even the chance future reader is no guarantee for timelessness as time works its change both on the grief expressed in the poem and on the poet, who has been forgotten. It no longer seems very likely that art will indeed guarantee eternal survival, eternal memory. There is little hope for 'modern rhyme' precisely because it is 'modern'; it is not timeless but changeable and doomed to final irrelevance.

Second, a poem can be called timeless in quite a different sense, if it addresses what are perceived to be timeless topics, which never lose their relevance. Echoing Clune, we might call this an 'Aesthetics of Eternal Essence'. As we will see in Chapter 1, it is this sense of timelessness that dominates much Victorian discourse on the question, as poetry is understood as elevated speech, dealing with elevated topics and often associated with the divine. The still ongoing debate around the relationship of the lyric to historical circumstances relates to this aesthetic premise, as lyric timelessness, by its detractors, is understood as synonymous with blindness to, or a deliberate evasion of, history.

Third, a poem can be timeless in the sense suggested by Rossetti (the sense which is also most prevalent in Cameron's study of the subject), in that the poem may variously strive to resist, halt or transcend time, encapsulating a moment in its poetic form. As Cameron puts it: 'Novels and dramas stylize temporality; lyrics transform it' (1979: 242). Rossetti's poem helps to suggest that this depends on a high degree of formal patterning, creating what Tucker has called 'poetic spacetime', in which a poem's 'measured pace and its crafted shape become each other's meaning, here and now in the monumental textual moment' (Tucker 1997: 275). It is the form of the artwork itself which grants it timelessness, regardless both of its referential content and its future reception. Rossetti's memorial does not rely on future readers. The only reader it imagines is Time itself. I will call this the 'Aesthetics of Self-sufficient Form', and will trace its ascendancy in the course of the nineteenth century.

Finally, a poem can be understood to be timeless in the sense in which the term is frequently used today: as a feature of the lyric mode in particular, predominantly taken simply as a lack of sequences of action (that is, of plot) and thus set in contradistinction to the specific temporal structure ascribed to narrative. Timelessness in this sense can hardly be called a properly developed aesthetics. Rather, it is understood to be a marker of a fundamental difference of genre or mode.

It is worth dwelling on the differences between these kinds because, although they are not incompatible, they are by no means interchangeable and because they pose different kinds of challenges and problems. Note, for example, that the first two senses apply not just to poetry but to all art and even beyond. Eternal fame or eternal relevance are aims which a scientist or philosopher might strive for, as well as any artist and, as I will argue in Chapter 1, scientific claims to truth played a pivotal role in the gradual displacement of the Aesthetics of Eternal Essence for poetry. At the same time, both the Aesthetics of the Enduring Word and the Aesthetics of Eternal Essence are based on an implicit belief in an eternal, unchanging nature and existence of human beings. The resistance to time celebrated in Rossetti's sonnet seems at a first glance closely related to both the former, but in fact develops a different logic. Its claim to eternity lies neither in its enduring fame and reception, nor in its subject matter. The sonnet is not a monument to eternity, but to a fleeting moment. The accent has shifted from content to form. Poetry is not understood to express or transmit general, eternal truths, but rather takes the (arbitrary, even insignificant) individual moment and enshrines it in eternal poetic formal relations. It is a monument to a dead hour made deathless only by its poetic reification. As pure poetic form, it becomes a symbolic currency like a coin, divested of its temporal and spatial context. In this ideal, eternity is not poetry's premise, but its value. This value, however, is entirely self-contained and, at least rhetorically, independent of the poem's reception. The poem enshrines the moment, even if it is never read again. It aims to create a poetic spacetime which resists change just as it derives its urgency from an understanding of change as radical and omnipresent. No longer based on extrinsic factors like reception or reference, the timelessness of the poem is entirely intrinsic. Finally, the recent outgrowth of these aesthetics takes the Aesthetics of Self-sufficient Form as foundational but empties it of its element of struggle as well as of its specific historical valence. If timelessness is claimed for the lyric as opposed to narrative temporality, the previous meanings of timelessness often implicitly resonate but remain generally unacknowledged, while the binary opposition itself is fraught with contradictions. While I will maintain (especially in Chapters 2 and 5) that narrative and lyric modes can be differentiated on the basis of their different temporal structures, this difference is emphatically not that of the temporal versus the atemporal.

While the different aesthetics of poetic timelessness mentioned above are not mutually exclusive and all continue to resonate today, they do follow a certain chronology and I will trace various conceptual shifts that contributed to this transformation over the course of this study. In particular, I explore the question how and why a dominant Aesthetics of Eternal Essence was gradually displaced by an Aesthetics of Self-sufficient Form in the course of the nineteenth century. Thus I emphasise that Rossetti's famous definition of the sonnet as 'a moment's monument' is a child of its time; it is, first and foremost, a monument to its own historical moment. Indeed, it has been widely discussed as such by critics who place the sonnet in its historical context, like Jennifer Wagner (1996), John Holmes (2005) or Marion Thain (2016). Building on such work, my aim is to situate Rossetti's signature sonnet in a wider literary and cultural context in which general attitudes towards time underwent major changes and in which the literary landscape saw new developments which radically and lastingly reshuffled practices and hierarchies. Rather than hoping to go much beyond the expert readings of Rossetti's work mentioned above, however, in these pages I trace a larger conceptual shift in the relationship between time and poetry in which Rossetti's sonnet takes part. Such an undertaking reveals present-day critical commonplaces about the timelessness of the lyric in contrast to the temporality of narrative as unproductive, since these lose sight of the complex temporal concepts and commitments which inform Victorian poetry and poetics. In fact, I will argue, such a contemporary position is the result of the historical developments I am tracing here. As I will elaborate further in my final chapter, the temporal structure of the lyric is more productively understood as an alternative temporality, rather than as atemporality.

Any clear and dichotomous distinction between lyric and narrative is notoriously difficult to uphold, especially in a historical context. After all, the contrast between lyric and narrative, though commonly evoked nowadays, is neither logically inevitable and clear-cut nor historically deeply rooted. It is often connected to the classic Goethean distinction between 'epic, lyric and drama' as basic 'natural forms of poesy' (Goethe 1827: 120), and David Wellbery, in fact, assigns Goethe's early work a pivotal role in establishing what he calls 'the myth of the lyric voice' (Wellbery 1996). The way the distinction is used these days, however, tends to cut across such earlier genre distinctions (some of Goethe's early lyrics which Wellbery discusses, for example, are ballads and thus take narrative form). Recently, the new lyric studies heralded in particular by Virginia Jackson and Yopie Prins have highlighted the difficulties of establishing the lyric as a transhistorical genre and have criticised what they call 'lyrical reading' as a result of twentieth-century reading practices which restrict our understanding of the historical reception of poems (2014; see also Jackson 2005). Part of the problem which Jackson and Prins identify lies in a widespread tendency to treat the lyric as the poetic per se on the one hand, and to associate narrative predominantly with prose on the other. Even an ambitious attempt at providing foundational theoretical approaches to poetry like Eva Müller-Zettelmann and Margarete Rubik's essay collection *Theory into Poetry: New Approaches to the Lyric* (2005) is premised on such an equivocation, as the substitution of 'lyric' for 'poetry' in its subtitle already indicates. In their introduction, in which they lament the lack of a consistent theory of the lyric, they likewise use 'poetry' and 'lyric' synonymously. That they do so deliberately becomes clear once one turns to Werner Wolf's contribution to their collection. Although his aim is to establish a definition of the lyric, he seeks to base this definition on an understanding of the lyric in its broadest sense, claiming that in view of the general usage of the word 'no distinction between "the lyric", "poetry" and "poems" seems to be appropriate any longer' (2005: 23).[4]

If poetry is thus conflated with the lyric, either term's relationship to narrative becomes even more difficult to navigate, a difficulty which is amply reflected in recent criticism. Thus, while Müller-Zettelmann and Rubik lament the absence of a theory of (lyric) poetry, which would be on a par with narratological approaches, Brian McHale regrets the absence of poetry from contemporary narrative theory and feels the need to remind us that '*most* poems before the nineteenth century, and many since then, have been narrative poems' (2009: 12). He also recognises, however, that a purely narratological approach which treats poems like prose texts fails to take account of the specificities of poetic narration. According to McHale, the relevant distinction is not between poetry and narrative, but between verse and prose. Conversely, Rubik questions precisely this distinction, arguing that '[t]he borderline between poetry and the short story, in particular, is difficult to draw' (Rubik 2005: 194). At the same time, the premise that much poetry, even lyric poetry, contains narrative material – in her contribution to Zettelmann's and Rubik's collection Monika Fludernik calls this a poem's 'residual narrativity' (2005: 99) – encourages approaches like that of Peter Hühn, who analyses lyric poems within a narratological framework and argues that lyric 'poems do use narrative devices and they even do so pervasively and extensively' (2016: 3). The concomitant transferral of narratological vocabulary to the analysis of lyric texts always runs the danger of obscuring essential differences, as has been repeatedly remarked (Hempfer 2014: 28–9; McHale 2009). Jonathan Culler has most decisively rejected such a tendency to treat narrative 'not as one possible literary form but as the very condition of experience, which is made intelligible by narrative form that traces causal sequence and represents experience as something accomplished and able to be narrated' (2008: 201). This widespread assumption, according to Culler, has led to an approach to non-narrative poetry which 'adopt[s] the model of the dramatic monologue as the way to align poetry with the novel: the lyric is conceived as a fictional imitation of the act of a speaker, and to interpret the lyric is to work out what sort of person is speaking, in what circumstances and with what attitude or, ideally, drama of attitudes' (2008: 201).[5] Culler argues against such a practice and for the specificity of the lyric genre 'as discourse addressed, a rhetorical transaction' (2008: 213). He therefore speaks of the lyric in terms of a 'Western tradition of short, nonnarrative, highly rhythmical productions, often stanzaic, whose aural dimension is crucial' (2018: 89). Calling the lyric 'nonnarrative', however, he downplays a fact he acknowledges elsewhere: that even among the prototypical lyric poems on which he bases his inductive approach to a definition there are some which indeed are essentially narrative. Discussing Goethe's poem 'Heidenröslein', for example, Culler notes that '[t]he poem is a brief anecdote recounted in the past, a very common lyric structure' (2018: 23). Far from non-narrative, it seems that narrative is 'very common' in the lyric. Indeed, in his *Theory of the Lyric* Culler clarifies that he considers the central tension to lie not between narrative and lyric modes, but rather between what he calls fictional elements and ritualistic aspects. '[W]e need a model', he argues, that is capable of 'acknowledging the tension in lyric between story and character, on the one hand, and song on the other, but the ultimate dominance of song as distinctive of lyric' (2018: 122). It must be emphasised at this point that Culler understands precisely the tension between these elements to be central to the lyric and therefore does not simply identify the lyric with its songlike, ritualistic aspects.

These different positions are bewildering in their various theoretical investments, their juxtapositions and equations of poetry and lyric, narrative and prose, fiction and ritual, and their internal contradictions. Müller-Zettelmann and Rubik suggest that poetry is distinct from narrative, since their aim is to establish a theoretical approach to poetry that would be on par with (but different from) theories of drama and narrative. At the same time, they acknowledge the presence of narrative in (lyric) poetry and question the difference between poetry and prose. McHale points out that most poetry *is* narrative but argues that verse narration is distinct from prose narration and that narrative theory needs to find ways to address the specific 'poeticity' of verse narratives (2009: 14). Hühn and Schönert, in turn, argue that even most lyric poems include narrative sequences and can therefore be approached with narratological tools of analysis; and Culler evokes a difference between narrative and lyric, only to replace it with another set of terms that come with their own baggage: fiction and ritual.

I wager in this book that a historical perspective can provide a new and productive perspective on such fundamental theoretical disagreements. In fact, the very terms of the discussion are bound to the contemporary historical moment. For the Victorians, the fault lines ran rather differently (though with scarcely less dissent). If today there is a tendency to equate poetry with the subgenre of the lyric, for the Victorians, the former term was generally much more encompassing. Some Victorians, most prominently John Stuart Mill (1860: 125) and Walter Pater (1888: 143), indeed considered lyric poetry the purest form of poetry, but even they did not go so far as to subsume all poetry under the lyric. Moreover, epic poetry was still widely considered the highest poetic achievement. Indeed, poetry was often understood in terms of Platonic, rather than literary, form. Poetry, in this conception, is universal in that it appertains to anything in which Truth and Beauty (always capitalised) manifest themselves in emotion. Poetry transcends its form as poem; or, as minor playwright and critic J. Westland Marston put it in a lecture delivered in 1838 at the Grimsby Mechanics' Institute: 'What is Poetry? We reply Love, Beauty, and Truth. What is a Poem? The lovely, the beautiful, the true. It is essential that we distinguish between the Poetry, and the Poem; Poetry is the Cause, the Poem, the Effect; Poetry is the active Life which manifests itself in various forms, the Poem is its manifestation in one' (6).[6] Other definitions, still broad, use 'poetry' in the sense we would use 'literature' today, as imaginative (and fictional) language.[7] In this sense poetry embraces dramatic and narrative genres. Indeed, Shakespeare's drama and Milton's epic poetry are the most frequently mentioned poetic paradigms in Victorian poetics. Even the novel is occasionally subsumed under the term 'poetry', since, as psychologist and critic Alexander Bain notes in his handbook *On Teaching English* (1887), '[i]f we do not stretch the definition of poetry so as to include the prose romance, that peculiar form of composition is without a place in any known classification of literature' (254). In a narrower sense of the word, for the Victorians poetry depends on versification, or at least on some sense of rhythm. In the ninth edition of the *Encyclopaedia Britannica*, published in 1885, Theodore Watts attempts to reconcile these different meanings, offering the following definition: '*Absolute poetry is the concrete and artistic expression of the human mind in emotional and rhythmical language*' (Watts 1885: 257).

Thus, three meanings of 'poetry' with different scopes are current (and frequently confused) in Victorian discourse: 1. poetry as an abstract, idealised force and feeling which is essentially associated with beauty, truth and passion; 2. poetry as imaginative literature; 3. poetry as verse, or rhythmical language. Even where the word is used in a narrow sense, however, it almost inevitably involves an implicit or explicit quality judgement: 'just as there is an impassable abyss between the music-hall song of the hour and the symphony of a great master, so there are many kinds of verse which are not in the slightest degree poetical', says poet and critic Edmond Holmes at the turn of the century (1900: 4). From these definitions arise different pairs of opposition which are constantly debated by the Victorians: 1. poetry versus science; 2. fiction (imaginative literature) versus truth; 3. verse versus prose.

Several points should already have become clear from these observations: the distinction between poetry and narrative, as it is commonly made today, would have made little sense to the Victorians, nor would they have generally understood poetry primarily as lyric. Conversely, before the rise of free verse and prose poetry, the association of poetry and verse was much stronger. Timothy Steele pertinently remarks that 'the verse–poetry distinction reflects a difference between earlier literature and the literature of our time. In earlier periods, there is an abundance of metrical composition, not all of which is considered poetry. In our time, there is an abundance of composition that is considered poetry, much of which is not in meter' (1990: 112). Finally, the novel played a pivotal role in disturbing accepted classifications, and the various attempts to differentiate poetry from the novel still inform genre concepts today.

All this is relevant to the present discussion because a study of the temporal commitments of Victorian poetry must take such changes in the meaning of its central term into account. If it seems counterintuitive nowadays to pick out poetry for a study of time in literature, it is worth highlighting that the very definitions of poetry which are common today in fact derive their meaning partly from a historical process of negotiating and redefining poetry's relationship to time.[8] The historical focus of this study brings the interrelatedness of the theoretical debates outlined above into sharp relief, tracing connections between the process of lyricisation of poetry criticised by Prins and Jackson, attempts to differentiate poetry from the modern phenomenon of the novel, and changing concepts of poetic timelessness. All of these, this is my main contention, need to be understood within the broader context of historically changing ways of conceptualising time. Moreover, this perspective maintains the important role of Victorian poetry in any historically informed understanding of the development of poetic concepts still prevalent today.

The basic claim I will develop throughout this study is that the lyric became identified as the purest poetry in the nineteenth century because it offered a way to continue to define poetry as timeless in face of crumbling certainties. The Victorians, who found themselves constantly confronting new intellectual, social and cultural developments, began to lose faith in the viability of an Aesthetics of Eternal Essence. An alternative was found in projecting the principle of durability onto a specifically lyric voice – a voice that attempts to escape the threat of solipsism by becoming appropriable: 'a drained and reinhabitable voice not tied to an identifiable character or concerned with historical topicality', in the words of Veronica Alfano (2017: 5). As lyric event, poetry could continue to maintain its associations with timelessness, independent of the kind of transcendent beliefs on which this timelessness used to be based. Moreover, as others have argued (Schlaffer 2015: 84–5; Thain 2016: 62–3), the typically tight formal structuring of the lyric lends it a recursive element as well as tying the individual lyric instance back to a long tradition of poetic form. However, this redefinition of poetic timelessness as lyric form comes with a price. Not only does it promote an inadmissibly narrow concept of poetry, but it also, eventually, can lead to the kind of blindness for poetic and lyric temporal structures that afflicts critical discourse today.[9] It is a mistake to decouple aspirations to lyric timelessness from their historical grounding in an ideology which continues to define poetry as transcendent, elevated and elevating. Timelessness is not a generic feature of the lyric. Rather, it is a historically contingent ideal which individual poems may, or may not, pursue and always, necessarily, fail to reach. To the degree that such elevated ideas of poetry's nature have been superseded today, I argue, an ascription of timelessness to the lyric clings to the husk of prior allegiances, whose continued usefulness may be called in question.

Victorian Time

Why, however, should the Victorians have felt the need to redefine poetry's relationship to time in the first place? This claim needs to be situated in the wider social and cultural context of the Victorian age, which saw fundamental and pervasive changes in temporal regimes. That temporal conceptions are not only culturally but also historically variable has been stressed by a wide range of cultural critics.[10] Societies do not only frame a way to experience time but also produce time (Castoriadis 1987 [1975]: 202–11). Many factors contributed to unsettle time concepts during the reign of Victoria. The main changes Victorian ideas about time underwent could be summarised under the following key terms: regulation and commodification; standardisation and mechanisation; extension and historicisation. Each of these merits, and has received, extended scholarly scrutiny, and I will here restrict myself to pointing briefly to some of the most significant developments in order to set the scene for my further argument.[11] For one, the accelerating industrial revolution forced an ever larger percentage of the lower strata of society into precisely timed, monotonous and relentless work routines under the regime of machine and clock (Thompson 1967).[12] Time thus enters as a central variable into Karl Marx's analysis of the logic of capitalism, in which the time of the labourer, rather than the product of his or her work, is bought and sold. In this logic, time needs to be uniform, quantifiable and precisely measured. In tandem with this temporal logic of labour, all strata of society were affected by the strict temporal logic of the railways. Abstract and standardised time was introduced on a national level by the spread of the railway network, which first brought so-called 'railway time' into the rural areas, effectively abolishing a multiplicity of local times.[13] In spite of occasional local resistance, by the middle of the century most local times in Britain had been effectively displaced by Greenwich Mean Time as the railway standard, although it was only legally affirmed as Britain's national time in 1880.[14] Moreover, according to Jack Simmons's history of the Victorian railway, the timetable was a conceptual innovation directly resulting from the unprecedented temporal rigidities imposed by the railway (2009: 183–4). Time was not only abstracted and standardised, but visualised as a homogeneous, regular and regularised spatial grid. Soon commerce, news, communication and travel adapted themselves to the regular fixed departure and arrival times of the trains, turning punctuality into a key Victorian virtue, and Lewis Carroll's White Rabbit into a paradigmatic Victorian character.

As Simmons suggests, '[i]t was not a mere accident of taste that the erection of a public clock came to be a fashionable civic gesture from about 1850 onwards' (2009: 347). Indeed, quite fittingly, one of the age's most emblematic architectural monuments is a clock tower and was celebrated for bringing reliable time to the Londoners: the tower housing Big Ben, installed in May 1859. While still functioning as a symbol of social status, clocks were no longer the sole privilege of the mighty and wealthy. While the eighteenth century saw immense progress in the precision of timekeeping, only in the nineteenth century, with incipient mass production in Switzerland and the United States, did ownership of clocks and pocket-watches gradually turn from a luxury good into a more widely affordable necessity (Landes 1983: 287, 318). It was a necessity not only because railways enforced a punctual schedule on everyday life as more and more people commuted, or because labour was put under an increasingly rigorous time regime, but also because, in a rapidly urbanised society, the coordination of daily life generally depended more strongly on punctuality and the adherence to timetables, schedules and deadlines. As Sally Mitchell has shown, the extension of the mail system, with several daily deliveries, the wider availability of daily newspapers (both of which of course depended on the railways), as well as, later in the century, the spread of the telegraph further contributed to make a new concept of time and the importance of temporal coordination ever more widely felt throughout the country (2009: 71–83; see also Wright 1968: 154–9).

Work was timed with increasing precision, but so was leisure. Thorstein Veblen early diagnosed the rise of the 'leisure class', a wealthy middle class which paraded its social status not only by means of 'conspicuous consumption', but also by 'conspicuous leisure' (1998 [1899]). '[M]odern leisure', claims Peter Bailey, 'made its début in Victorian England, the first mature industrial society' (1987: 4). Extensive studies of the history of leisure like Hugh Cunningham's *Leisure in the Industrial Revolution* (1980) show how the conception and use of 'free' time changed throughout the century, and also that the issue of how to spend one's leisure time became the subject of much concern among nineteenth-century intellectuals and pedagogues. Male middle-class authors devoted much thought to the proper use of free time by members of the working class and middle-class women in particular. The problem of the proper use of their free time by the latter, who were largely restricted in their activities to the home, gave rise to the publication of numerous manuals and became a contested issue in discussions of the so-called 'Woman Question' (Maynard 2009: 20–7).

Beyond these everyday practicalities, time was also redefined by nineteenth-century scientific achievements. If scientists and intellectuals of the eighteenth century discovered history and turned their attention to processes of genealogy, cause and effect, as Michel Foucault (2018 [1966]) has influentially argued, this dynamic redefinition of knowledge came into its own in the nineteenth century with the publication and publicity of the theories of Charles Lyell and Charles Darwin, with the work of Karl Marx and Friedrich Engels and with critical theologians like David Friedrich Strauss. Living in an 'era more strenuously devoted than any earlier one to the historical record and the historical method' (Buckley 1966: 15), the Victorians were obsessed with the past (Chapman 1986; Colley 1998; Parker and Wagner 2020; Rosenberg 2005). Victorian scientists not only immensely extended the range of time many million years into the past, discovering what is now commonly referred to as 'deep time' and realising that, as Martin J. S. Rudwick puts it, *'nature has had a history of its own'* (Rudwick 2014: 2). The theories of evolution and uniformitarianism also brought Victorians face to face with the transformative potential of time, beyond teleology (Haber 1972: 384–5). The present face of the earth and its inhabitants could no longer be taken for granted as a fact of creation, and it became harder to rationalise change as teleological, the whole of creation moving towards some higher aim; rather, the natural environment they had previously perceived as relatively stable presented itself as the result of dynamic and contingent processes, continually changing and open-ended.[15] The question whether time was infinite or finite became of central importance to influential scientific debates, with Lord Kelvin attempting to put limits on the enormously long time periods assumed by uniformitarian geologists and by evolution theory (Brush 1977: 33). If evolution theory made the past dynamic, the discovery of the second law of thermodynamics appeared to close down the future. Both undermined concepts of a stable return of the same and introduced radical change.[16]

A sense of dynamic flow in which human knowledge and truth no longer transcend time but are necessarily conditioned by circumstance and therefore subject to change lies at the heart of the strong current of relativist thinking which Christopher Herbert has identified in Victorian thought (2001). On different scales and with different emphasis, Herbert argues, the existence of time-transcending absolutes was denied by Victorian thinkers like Alexander Bain, Herbert Spencer, Walter Pater and even John Ruskin (see also Garratt 2010). Coupled with a strong interest in history, such thought led to a degree of moral relativity. Jerome H. Buckley suggests that '[s]ince to understand is usually in some degree to condone, the deepening knowledge of other times and places engendered an increasing relativity of judgment. [. . .] Once men asked whether an idea was true, whether a policy was sound and good; now they asked how the idea came to be credited, how the policy was adopted and developed' (1966: 19–20; see also Altick 1973: 99–101). Most disturbingly for the Victorians, such relativism also began to erode the foundations of religious belief (Newsome 1997: 195). With human existence restricted to the historical, 'time pressed more heavily upon man', as 'the only medium in which human life unfolded and fulfilled itself' (Meyerhoff 1955: 95). The influence of time's arrow became ubiquitous, whether this awareness of historical change led to a belief in progress or, more pessimistically, in the inevitability of a gradual dispersion of energy suggested by the second law of thermodynamics. On all these fronts, a growing awareness of historical change and developments in time threatened to undercut a trust in eternity as '[t]ruth itself became a function of time, or the historical process, no longer a reflection of an "eternal" order of things' (Meyerhoff 1955: 94). Carol Christ even goes so far as to diagnose a wholesale 'collapse of the dimension of eternity within the framework of religious belief, within the philosophical framework of verities and values, and within the social

framework of apparently permanent, fixed social and political structure' (1975: 108).

Moreover, the redefinition of time through science contributed to
the spread of a scientific, abstract idea of time throughout Victorian
culture. According to Helga Nowotny, in the nineteenth century,
'[t]he time-structure of the linear, homogenized, arbitrarily divisible
continuum is transferred through the machine from the realm of
nature to that of society' (1994: 83). Scientific concepts of time
gained relevance at the expense of other systems of temporal ordering. While the competition between 'merchant's time' and 'sacred
time' had already emerged in the Middle Ages (Le Goff 1980), the
nineteenth century saw an acceleration of a process in which a religious regulation of time, typically characterised by bells marking
important moments (the time for prayer, the time for work and for
rest, the time for religious feasts), is gradually replaced by a time
of the machine that runs continuously and evenly. The importance
of machine time for an increasingly industrialised, urbanised and
secularised capitalist society led Lewis Mumford to announce that
'[t]he clock, not the steam-engine, is the key-machine of the modern industrial age' (1946: 14). However, for the particular situation
of the Victorians, the implications of these two key machines must
be understood to be inextricably interwoven. The temporal regimes
which increasingly spread throughout Victorian society, informing
both its material conditions and its structures of knowledge and
thought, are thus emblematically realised in these two machines:
the regularity, punctuality and abstraction of the clock, and the uni-
linear acceleration of measurable temporal progression which the
Victorians saw materialised in the railway engine.

Towards the end of the Victorian age and with the beginning of
the new century, time came prominently on the agenda. The importance of time for Modernism is indisputable as the theorisation of
new time concepts gathers momentum (Friedrich Nietzsche's eternal
recurrence, Henri Bergson's *durée*, John McTaggert's philosophical
arguments about the unreality of time, fourth dimension theory,
and Albert Einstein's relativity theory are only the most prominent
examples), and time is addressed as a central aesthetic challenge (as
in the Modernist *Zeitroman*). But the time regimes the Modernists
pitched their alternatives against were in the process of gaining their
influence in the course of the nineteenth century and were then still
contending with other (especially religious) understandings of time.
For the Victorians, the challenge of time is thus both less monolithic
and less theoretical. No full-scale philosophical theories of time were

developed by them; rather certain temporal assumptions underwrote their thoughts and theories, often tacitly (deep time and evolutionary time, for example), or introduced very practical changes into their everyday lives (railway time, labour time). The relevance of changing temporal concepts for Victorian poetry is thus not revealed in a wealth of poetic meditation on the nature of time, but conversely in their continual struggle to understand and redefine the nature and role of poetry and its relation to their historical moment.

Chapter Overview

My explorations of Victorian poetry unfold against the backdrop of this array of cultural and intellectual developments, all of which affected the way time was conceived and experienced. As Marcus Tomalin notes in the conclusion to his study *Telling the Time in British Literature, 1675–1830*, 'the impact of this diachronic temporal shift on the literature of the Victorian period is something that still awaits focused critical consideration, despite the existing plethora of research into time measurement and time telling in the nineteenth century' (2020: 196). This is the research lacuna which this study is setting out to fill, at least with regard to poetry. Far from being aloof from temporal concerns, I demonstrate, time and renegotiations of temporal concepts are pervasive concerns of Victorian poetry, lying at the heart of debates about the definition and role of poetry in society. Reading Victorian poetry against the background of the cultural history of time throws a new light on the forces behind some of the most striking developments in poetry of the time. As the individual chapters of this study will suggest, changing temporal concepts can be seen to play a part not only in the gradual privileging of the lyric and the Aestheticist withdrawal into art for its own sake, but also in the loss of cultural prominence of poetry; in the popularity of mixed poetic genres like the poetic sequence, the dramatic monologue and the novel; and in the eventual turn towards free verse.

Provocatively, one could say that the temporal regimes outlined above correlate with the two key rivals by which poetry finds itself challenged in the nineteenth century: science and the novel. The terms of and reactions to this challenge will be my topic in Chapter 1, in which I focus on the way in which poetry's relation to time was understood and rethought by the Victorians in the face of their experience of accelerated change and unsettled eternal guarantors like religion. In particular, I am interested here in the relation between the claims to a timeless validity of scientific truth and poetic truth on the one hand, and, on the other, in the controversial question of poetry's relation to the Victorian present. Whether or not poetry should refer to contemporary reality was a matter of serious debate for Victorian poets and reviewers, especially during the 1840s and 1850s. At the same time, critical opinion and poetic practice were highly heterogeneous and divergent. Putting these discourses and practices under scrutiny reveals their underlying temporal investments. To this end, I draw on Victorian discussions of the nature of poetry in reviews, lectures and articles, as well as on metapoetical statements that abound in poems themselves.

In Chapter 2, my focus is on solutions found to the challenges discussed in Chapter 1, in particular in the form of generic experimentation. The dramatic monologue, the verse novel and the poetic sequence take centre stage as paradigmatic sites of Victorian genre innovation. I read such combinations of narrative, dramatic and lyric elements as attempts to redefine poetry's temporal affinities, arguing that the appeal of these mixed genres to the Victorians can be, at least in part, accounted for by the perceived need to rethink the temporal structure of poetry. The Victorians tested formal affordances and boundaries in answer to the challenge omnipresent change posed to an understanding of poetry that sought its foundation in eternal truth.

Chapter 3 addresses the consequences of Carlyle's influential 'gospel of work' as well as the acceleration of print culture. For the Romantics, poetry was strongly and influentially associated with rest and reverie, the creative distillate of a Wordsworthian recollection in tranquillity. In an age governed by the spirits of utilitarianism and progress, and which witnessed an increasing organisation of labour and a professionalisation of literature, such idle time becomes not only rare, but also to some extent suspicious. In this chapter, I trace ambiguous Victorian stances towards idleness, which the poets continue to value as well as to condemn. The issue of idleness, in particular, reveals some of the privileges and power structures that manifest in socially sustained time regimes, especially along the lines of class and gender. Thus, I relate the ambiguous status of idleness primarily to a capitalist ideology of success through endeavour. In the final part of this chapter, however, I turn to the poetry of Christina Rossetti in order to explore an alternative stance, firmly rooted in Rossetti's religious faith.

Chapter 4 is devoted to the rich Victorian prosodic debates. I argue that the innovations in prosodic theory of the time can be fruitfully connected to a conceptual process in which time is increasingly split into a regular, abstract and public time which stands in constant tension with a flexible, embodied personal time. This chapter traces the conditions under which metre and rhythm were reconceptualised in the complex nexus between mechanism, abstraction, body and mind. I propose that the mechanisation and standardisation of time contributed to an increasingly restrictive perspective on metre from which only free verse measures seemed to offer an escape. To this aim, I revisit Victorian prosody, particularly the work of Coventry Patmore, but also consider the attitude poets took towards an increasingly mechanic regulation of time by looking at the way poems about railway travel dramatise (and metrically negotiate) the conflict between natural and mechanic rhythms.

My final chapter leaves the historical focus behind to pose fundamental and systematic questions. What light does the historical perspective throw on today's discussions about poetry, and the lyric in particular? In what ways does it challenge us to rethink or historicise conceptions of the temporality of the lyric? In this chapter, I argue that the concepts of time we have inherited from the Victorians are fundamentally narrative and therefore make us blind to other kinds of temporality. It is with the aim to make such temporal alternatives visible that I develop a methodological framework for the analysis of the time structures of poetry; a framework which, I hope, will prove useful beyond the limited historical remit of Victorian literature.

Notes

1. All references to Dante Gabriel Rossetti's poems are to Jerome McGann's edition of Rossetti's *Collected Poetry and Prose* (2003) unless otherwise indicated.
2. I will return to Rossetti's sequence and its complex relationship to time and the moment in Chapters 2 and 5.
3. Morgan, for example, misreads her in this way (2009: 10). I will draw on Cameron's much more complex and sophisticated argument in my final chapter.
4. This claim is perhaps more easily justifiable in German than in English. Modern German indeed commonly uses *Lyrik* to designate poetry in general, while *Dichtung* and *Poesie* are more rarely used and have other connotations. This practice, however, loses sight of important differentiations, and I believe it is a mistake to follow common practice here, instead of insisting on the value of distinctions offered by critical language.

5. This reads, indeed, like a fairly adequate summary of what Hühn and his colleagues Jörg Schönert and Jens Kiefer set out to do, in spite of their repeated protestations that they do not intend to 'blur the distinction between poetry and prose fiction and treat poetry indiscriminately as a narrative genre' (Hühn 2016: 5; see also Hühn and Schönert 2005: 2).

6. While there is a political angle to this approach, in which poetry becomes the property of everyone, regardless of class and education, such a broad and idealised concept of poetry was by no means exceptional. Thus Theodore Watts's entry for 'poetry' in the ninth edition of the *Encyclopaedia Britannica* begins by stating that '[i]n modern criticism the word poetry is used sometimes to denote any expression (artistic or other) of imaginative feeling, sometimes to designate one of the fine arts' (1885: 257).

7. 'Literature', in turn, was commonly used in a much broader sense to include a wide variety of genres like historical and theological studies, biographies, pamphlets, sermons, philosophy and even scientific and economic writings. For an illustration of this one might take a look at the table of contents of Charles L. Craik's *Compendious History of English Literature*, published 1863, in which he lists entries on Newton, Darwin, on political and theological writings, on political economy and historical writings next to those on poets and writers of prose fiction.

8. There has recently been an increase in critical interest on issues of time, temporality and literature and the research field is both rich and diverse. There is a tendency to focus on narrative texts, however, as well as on the historical period of Modernism, and an attempt at an overview seems unproductive to me in this context. Tomalin provides a brief summary of important texts and trends, which remains necessarily cursory but might offer a good starting point for the interested reader (2020: 15–21).

9. Veronica Alfano's study of memory and forgetting and the Victorian lyric is a striking example. Alfano repeatedly speaks of the lyric as 'atemporal' (2017: 2, 14, 33 and *passim*), though her main concern is to trace its relation to remembered or misremembered pasts. She apparently sees no contradiction in claiming, within the same paragraph, that Victorian lyricists 'pursue timeless stasis' and that 'the simultaneity of remembering and forgetting [. . .] is conspicuous in Victorian lyric' (2017: 15). But are not remembering and forgetting insistently temporal processes (as, for that matter, is the concept of simultaneity)? In consequence, her observation that the lyric resists progression or narratable teleology is frequently couched in the language of failure or betrayal, in which stable narratable identity appears to feature as the healthy alternative to lyric temporal displacements, which 'can place speakers in a disconcertingly inertial and reiterative mode of unplotted

atemporality' (2017: 31; see also 34–5). Her insistence on framing her generally insightful observations on the workings of lyric memory as atemporal constantly threatens to turn the lyric into an unhealthy or escapist resistance to an allegedly more rational time of plot.

10. Though not new, the interest in historically changing time conceptions has in the last few decades led to a proliferation of important publications, for example Adam 2004; Assmann 2013; Nowotny 1994. In the German context, this interest was fuelled in particular by Reinhart Kosellek's seminal study of the rise of a historical consciousness in the eighteenth century (1979; in English translation 2004) and Hartmut Rosa's work on social acceleration (2005; in English translation 2013). See also the work of the German research cluster on 'aesthetic temporalities' (Ästhetische Eigenzeiten), which explores what they call 'polychronic modernity' (Gamper and Hühn 2014; see also Detmers and Ostermeier 2016; Gamper et al. 2016).

11. For more detailed overviews of these developments, see Buckley (1966); Ferguson (2013); Murphy (2001: 10–30); Zemka (2012: 70–91).

12. As Thompson points out, this has to be understood as an uneven process fraught with struggles between employers and the labourers, who had to be painstakingly socialised into an acceptance of the rule of abstract, standardised machine time. See Sue Zemka (2012) on the consequences this had for the cultural relevance of the moment.

13. The history of the railway and its immense influence on Victorian life and culture has been the subject both of specialised scholarship (Hylton 2007; Perkin 1971; Simmons 2009) and of works directed at a wider audience (Wolmar 2008). In the context of the influence of the railways on perceptions of time and space, see Wolfgang Schivelbusch's *The Railway Journey* (2014 [1977]).

14. The story of the increasing standardisation of time has been told with varying degrees of detail by Bartky (2007), Howse (1997: especially 91–7, 114–15) and Wright (1968: 143–9).

15. As Stephen Gould illustrates, Lyell himself long resisted this unsettling logic of time's arrow and only accepted it late in his career (1987: 132–79).

16. Literary reactions to evolution theory have been a particularly rich field of scholarship in the last couple of decades, following seminal work by Gillian Beer (1983) and George Levine (1988); see, for example, Carroll (2004); Glendening (2007); Holmes (2013); Richter (2011). The importance of theories of thermodynamics has not yet drawn a similar amount of attention, in spite of Barri J. Gold's reminder that '[t]he discourse on energy is at least as prevalent as Darwinian biology in Victorian sensibilities, and perhaps even more important to us' (2010: 29), but see also Gold's most recent book (2021) as well as Jones (2013) and Jones (2018).

Chapter 1

'Utterly vain is, alas! This attempt at the Absolute, – wholly!' – Poetry's Changing Relation to Timeless Truths

In a lecture delivered at the Wolverton Mechanics' Institute in 1853, the speaker, James Henry Powell, confidently asserts that, '[s]ociety [. . .] feels through all its connecting, all its necessary and indispensable parts, either directly or indirectly, something of the influence – something of the blessings of poetry. It permeates our whole intellectual, moral, and social being' (Powell 33). Twenty years later, in 1873, a contributor to *The St. James's Magazine* acknowledges poetry's beleaguered state, but nonetheless makes the astonishing claim that '[f]ew will be disposed to quarrel with the truism that "the condition of poetry is a matter of public concern"' (D. C. L. 261). Fast-forward another twenty years, to 1893, and literary critic Edmund Gosse asks in all seriousness and with strikingly diminished optimism:

> is poetry, in its very essence, an archaic and rudimentary form of expression, still galvanised into motion, indeed, by antiquarianism, but really obsolete and therefore to be cultivated only at the risk of affectation and insincerity; or is it an art capable of incessant renovation – a living organism which grows, on the whole, with the expansion of modern life? (159)

In other words, is poetry immutable and therefore obsolete in a world governed by change? Or is it protean, adaptable, contemporary? Is it an archaic form, a fossil, timeless only in death; or is it a living organism, capable of evolution in time? Many Victorian controversies and definitions of poetry revolve around such issues of temporality. In this chapter, I will interrogate Victorian concepts of poetic permanence, and the struggles to define and redefine its meaning in the face of the challenge to poetry from science on the one hand, and from the novel on the other.

My main argument in this chapter is that this double challenge required a renegotiation of poetry's relationship to time; a renegotiation which hinges on the paradoxical role of embodied permanence in an age whose temporal concepts come increasingly under the double aegis of the abstract, regular, 'timeless' logic of the clock – a logic which underlies scientific truth claims – and the progressive, accelerating logic of the railway, which finds aesthetic expression in the novel. Victorians struggled to reconcile an idealistic idea of poetry rooted in a firm belief in permanent values and truths with an increasing awareness of relativism and change. In what follows, I set out by probing Victorian definitions of poetry before exploring how such definitions were challenged by the novel and how poetry was contrasted to or related with science. I trace various strategies of response to these challenges, all of which involve fundamental reconsiderations of what poetry is and which form(s) it should take. These range from the pessimistic denial of a future for poetry in the modern world, to ardent calls for new poetic forms which are adaptable to the present, to a withdrawal from the world (and time) into ideas of self-contained and self-sustaining aesthetic form. Eventually, I argue, the developments which I trace in this chapter were significant factors in shifting definitions of poetry towards the lyric, since the lyric offered a way to hold on to a specific kind of timelessness rooted in aesthetic form and the epiphanic moment, even while relinquishing the kind of commitments to transcendent and permanent truths presupposed by an Aesthetics of Eternal Essence.

Victorian poetic theory and practice shows distinctive traces of a struggle with cherished Romantic ideas, which become increasingly untenable in the course of the century. In his famous 1802 preface to the second edition of the *Lyrical Ballads*, William Wordsworth asserts that poetry's 'object is truth, not individual and local, but general, and operative; not standing upon external testimony, but carried alive into the heart by passion' (1992: 73). In a nutshell, this one sentence comprises elements of definition which are reiterated, with varying emphasis, throughout Victorian poetics, but it also opens the door to the challenges such a definition must suffer. Poetry's object is defined as truth, but truth, in the nineteenth century, is increasingly understood to belong to the realm of science and scientific prose. Poetry is supposedly concerned with what is general and permanently valid in human experience, but Victorian reality is dominated by an experience of encompassing and radical change. The most direct and apt literary expression of this reality is generally thought to be found in the novel, which concerns itself with what is individual and local.

This double challenge – from science's claim to universal and fundamental truths on the one hand and the novel's agility in representing
the changing present on the other – leaves defenders of poetry in
a double bind: attempts to distinguish poetry from, and elevate it
above, the novel put their stakes on claims for permanence and universal concerns beyond individual embodiment and circumstance.
Faced with the universal and permanent validity of abstract scientific
laws, however, poetry is frequently justified as impassioned, embodied and concrete. Romantic attempts to root poetry in permanence –
like Wordsworth's emphasis on the 'permanent forms of nature'
incorporated in simple rural men and women, which should be poetry's subject (1992 [1802]: 60), or Percy Bysshe Shelley's famous definition of poetry as 'the very image of life expressed in its eternal truth'
and his rejection of story as too much circumscribed by time, place
and circumstance (2002 [1840]: 515) – should ironically contribute
to make poetry appear as not timeless, but out of time, outdated, in
an age of accelerating urbanisation, industrialisation and seculari-
sation. 'In the old times', Arthur Henry Hallam remarks already in
1831, 'the poetic impulse went along with the general impulse of the
nation; in these it is a reaction against it, a check acting for conservation against a propulsion towards change' (2005: 545). Poetry was
commonly defined precisely via its resistance to change. Matthew
Arnold went even further in heralding poetry as the one true stronghold of permanent value in the face of crumbling religious certainties (1888: 2).[1] The poetry in religion and the religion in poetry lies
precisely in a relation to infinite and eternal transcendence. Being
thus upheld as a bulwark against change and modernity – a term
which Charles Baudelaire, famously, defined precisely as 'the ephemeral, the fugitive, the contingent' (1964 [1863]: 13)[2] – poetry came
under increasing pressure in a time which John Stuart Mill called
an 'age of change'. In an age in which '[m]ankind have outgrown
old institutions and old doctrines, and have not yet acquired new
ones' (Mill 1831: 20) – 'Wandering between two worlds, one dead, /
The other powerless to be born' in Matthew Arnold's evocative
words from the 'Stanzas from the Grande Chartreuse' (ll. 85–6)[3] –
Victorian poetics struggled to reconcile its Romantic inheritance
of poetical transcendence with a cultural and historical context in
which Romantic convictions became ever harder to uphold.

Faced with such challenges, perhaps more than ever before and
since, Victorians were struggling with the question: 'What is poetry?'
Attempts to provide an answer date from across the century and
take the form of book-length treatises, essays, prefaces, reviews

and miscellaneous contributions to periodicals. The answer, however, proved elusive, and the difficulty of defining poetry became
a Victorian commonplace. In a short article entitled 'Poetry in All
Things', published in the popular *Chambers's Edinburgh Journal* in
April 1846, the anonymous author puts the dilemma in the following
terms:

> [M]ust we [. . .] suppose that poetry has no clear and definable char-
> acter? Is it conceivable that a power which has in all ages exercised so
> mighty and so direct an influence upon men's minds, is in its own nature
> so vague, or so uncertain, that it cannot be brought within the grasp of
> human intelligence; or that its essential qualities cannot be expressed in
> the compass of a definition? (209)

With admirable confidence, the author answers, '[s]urely not' and
goes on to offer his own dexterous but contradictory solution to the
riddle: there has been so much disagreement about poetry's essential
nature because 'poetry is the voice of the Infinite, and can accommodate itself to the capacities of all'. The many different definitions
that have been offered highlight various, finite aspects of the infinite
ideal. In effect, the definition offered here is thus paradoxically that
poetry cannot be defined, because it shares in the divine; its 'essential
nature [. . .] is not based upon human imaginations'. Although such
a non-definition ostensibly accounts for protean possibilities, the
author simultaneously asserts the immutability and universal validity of the ideal: 'The highest poetry is a living reality – universal and
immutable; it is coeval with creation; for it is the likeness of God,
reflected in his works' (209).

   In its panegyrical idealisation as well as in its frustratingly contradictory vagueness, this definition is perhaps an extreme example of
early Victorian poetological discourse. But it is neither an exception,
even among more sustained attempts at theorisation, nor do such
opinions disappear entirely later in the century. Compare Francis T.
Palgrave, arguably a more circumspect and sober critic, who nonetheless asserts in an article published in 1886 that '[a]nalyse and
define how we may, no one has ever caught and imprisoned in words
the volatile vital element which makes poetry. Could we define it,
it would be that magical thing which we call poetry no longer; the
spell would be broken by the word; – the fairy gift would fly' (644).
This does not deter Palgrave from comparing poetry to the other
fine arts, to assert an ideal of unity of form and matter and to maintain the importance of metre (a controversial question ever since the

publication of Walt Whitman's *Leaves of Grass* in 1855). At the turn of the century, school inspector and educationalist Edmund Holmes still asks the same question with a hyperbolic emphasis on its difficulty and magnitude in his short book *What is Poetry?* (1900): 'I am setting myself a task that "far exceeds man's might". I am inviting myself to solve, by implication, all the master problems of human thought' (1–2). His own answer, too, is still typically Victorian, in being both vague and restrictive at the same time and in conflating poetic form, content and effect, as he bases his definition on the following two rather tautological assumptions: '1) that poetry is the expression of strong and deep feeling; 2) that wherever there is feeling there is something to be felt' (2).[4]

What ails such definitions is, on the one hand, the widespread Victorian conceptualisation of poetry as a spirit, mood or passionate feeling. Such a definition is usually charged with highly idealised but equally vague values of absolute (capitalised) Truth, Beauty and Moral Good and necessarily transcends any more narrow understanding of poetry as a specific artistic form, or effect. On the other hand, Victorians do take 'poetry' to mean, in the narrower sense, primarily a verbal artefact in rhythmical language, notwithstanding the common hyperbolic generalities. Even the author of 'Poetry in All Things' quoted above refers to Burns and Shakespeare as his main examples of 'true poet[s]' (1846: 209).[5] Ideal and formal aspects are inextricably interwoven in Victorian poetological discourse. An awareness of such entanglements is necessary to an adequate understanding of the challenges posed to poetry by the widespread social, cultural and literary changes during Queen Victoria's reign. True to the double meaning of the word 'poetry' current at the time, as spirit on the one hand and literary form on the other, poetry finds its main contesters on two fronts: as an ideal, a spirit and a kind of truth, poetry's authority is challenged by science; as a literary form, its market share and cultural primacy are threatened by the novel.

As I will argue in this chapter, these two challenges converge on the question of temporality. They come to a head in debates about the nature of poetic truth in relation to scientific truth on the one hand and on the other in the lively controversy about poetry's relation to the 'unpoetical' present which occupied Victorian poets and critics during the 1840s and 1850s. These debates may seem quaint and somewhat arcane from today's perspective, but they go to the heart of what poetry meant for the Victorians and stand witness to the profound changes the concept of poetry underwent during the nineteenth century.

'A truth looks freshest in the fashion of the day' – Poetry and the Contemporary Moment

Shelley's 'eternal truths' and Wordsworth's 'permanence' would reverberate throughout Victorian poetological discourse, in which it was a widely accepted critical commonplace that poetry concerns itself with what is elevated, eternal, universal, divine. Explicitly and implicitly, this assumption underlies much Victorian criticism: 'Poetry is derived from heaven [. . .]. Preachers of the religion of the beautiful, great poets go forth to indicate eternity shining through time' (Bedingfield 1847: 142); to the poet 'is given to hear the far-off movement of an Eternal Harmony' (Allingham 1867: 535); 'In proportion to the poet's grasp of the essential, and therefore universal significance of his subject; [. . .] will be the degree of essential poetry, or imaginative truth attained, and the vitality of his creation for all time' (Noel 1876: 479) – such statements can be found in abundance in the periodical literature of the time, particularly, but not exclusively, among early Victorian voices. The contemporary, the transitory, change and the everyday were, in contrast, often considered prosaic, fit topic only for news and novels. Such belief found an influential formulation in John Stuart Mill's essay 'What is Poetry?', first published in 1833, and famous for its contentious definition of poetry as soliloquy: 'The truth of poetry is to paint the human soul truly: the truth of fiction is to give a true picture of life' (2005: 564).

This is the background against which arose, in the 1840s and 1850s, a hot debate on the question whether poetry could and should address the realities of the contemporary world. To many, the contemporary world seemed an exceedingly unpoetical age. An anonymous reviewer of Elizabeth Barrett's collected *Poems*, published in 1844, aptly summarises this position:

> The present, we are told, is an unpoetical age; and truly, when we give heed to the sounds that most frequently enter our wearied ears, and consider the chief pursuits and engagements of that aggregate humanity, which is rushing past us in breathless chase of what it holds to be the chief good, we are half inclined to believe the affirmation, and despairingly enunciate that this is the age of *sense*, as opposed to intellect, of understanding, rather than reason, – an age in which, with rude hands, we analyse and dissect what we once worshipped, heedless of our impotence to re-unite, and reanimate [. . .] – that it is an age of share-markets and steam-whistles, and of travelling swifter than the wind [. . .]. Life is so much all hurry and hot haste [. . .] and it cannot be denied that the feverish excitements, vivid anxieties, and ceaseless turmoil that prevail

are exceedingly unfavourable to the development of the poetic faculty. A priori, one would say that steam-engines and poetry must flourish in inverse proportions. (*'Poems*. By Elizabeth Barrett' 1845: 337)

Clearly, this reviewer rehearses a position that he or she understands to be widely held and to be already familiar to the reader. The four main reasons which are named for the age's alleged incompatibility with poetry are the prevalence of science and scientific investigation, an economy of speculation, a sense of haste and acceleration and, finally, technological progress, exemplified in the railway. And although the essay, as is already suggested by the passage above, goes on to question such a judgement, the terms on which it does so are striking. Precisely because the age is so unpoetical, the writer argues, the need and demand for poetry grows, because 'eagerly do we seek to escape out of ourselves into the ideal world which the poet opens to us [. . .]. And contrast heightens the charm' ('*Poems*' 1845: 338). Instead of denying that the contemporary world is unpoetical and provides no fit subjects for poetry, the reviewer maintains that poetry must offer a contrast to and an escape from contemporary prosaic realities.

Acceleration and the new time regime of the railway are identified repeatedly as one cause for the demise of poetry. The anonymous author of *The Poet of the Age. A Satirical Poem* (1842), for instance, offers the following diagnosis:

> Motion, the ruling spirit of the hour, has unpoetised our generation. The public mind is in a perpetual whirl. Everything is looked at; nothing is seen. [. . .] Hence the universal encouragement of ephemeral literature – novels without meaning, poetry without vigour, books of travel without instruction, dramas without plot. (16)

An age of change and perpetual motion brings forth a literature of the ephemeral and transitory, a poetry which has lost its transcendent aims and thus, to the mind of many Victorians, scarcely deserves the high name of poetry anymore. Such pessimism did not remain uncontested, however. A reviewer of Sydney Dobell's epic poem *The Roman*, for example, opined in 1849:

> Surely our age, too, abounds in the element of poetical excitement, awaiting only fit utterance. [. . .] The railway carriages of this mechanical age are the conductors of the fire of intellect and passion—and its steamboats may be loaded with thunderbolts as well as with bullocks or yarn. [. . .] Mechanism, indeed, may be called the short-hand of poetry, concentrating its force and facilitating its operations. ('Art. II. *The Roman: A Dramatic Poem*. By Sydney Yendys.': 675)

In such discussions, the railway becomes the symbol for deeper concerns about the nature and role of poetry which touch not only the more obvious question of fit topics, but also the question of form, of 'fit utterance'. Those Victorians who believed in the possibility of modern poetry were on the lookout for a 'poet of the age' who would give apt expression to contemporary reality (Moore 2015: 3–10).

I will return to the railway as both a symbolic and a material challenge to poetry in Chapter 4, but here I want to highlight the more fundamental underlying debate about modern poetry: the question to what degree poetry could or should change in the face of modernity, and the related question how much poetry might be able to change without becoming something else entirely. This question, debated by critics and reviewers, also surfaces in some of the major poetry of the time. In what follows, I trace the two sides of the debate as they arise in works by Alfred Tennyson, Matthew Arnold, Arthur Hugh Clough and Elizabeth Barrett Browning.

Defending the mastodon – Tennyson and Arnold

With a healthy dose of self-irony, Alfred Tennyson makes an early contribution to this debate in 'The Epic', published in his poetry collection of 1842. The poem recounts a meeting of four friends on Christmas Eve, among them the poet Everard Hall, who voices decided opinions about the issue at hand:

> 'You know,' said Frank, 'he burnt
> His epic, his King Arthur, some twelve books' –
> And then to me demanding why: 'O, sir,
> He thought that nothing new was said, or else
> Something so said 't was nothing – that a truth
> Looks freshest in the fashion of the day;
> God knows; he has a mint of reasons; ask.
> It pleased me well enough.' 'Nay, nay,' said Hall,
> 'Why take the style of those heroic times?
> For nature brings not back the mastodon,
> Nor we those times; and why should any man
> Remodel models? these twelve books of mine
> Were faint Homeric echoes, nothing-worth,
> Mere chaff and draff, much better burnt.' (ll. 27–40)[6]

Hall, it is suggested, has not only destroyed his Arthurian epic, but also seems to have been silenced as a poet altogether. No longer able to claim lasting relevance and eternal truth but subject to changes in times and styles, poetry finds itself in the midst of an evolutionary struggle in which it needs to adapt or die out like the mastodon. Tennyson, however, obviously did not entirely share Hall's opinion. After all, 'The Epic' serves as an introductory frame for the Arthurian fragment 'Morte d'Arthur', allegedly the only one of Hall's twelve books which Frank had been able to save from the flames. Indeed, the fact that Tennyson later republished 'Morte d'Arthur', renamed 'The Passing of Arthur' (1870), without the framing poem and as a part of his own twelve-book epic *The Idylls of the King* stands testimony to his belief that epic poems in a chivalric setting can indeed speak to a modern age. Moreover, there is little formal difference between 'The Epic' and 'Morte d'Arthur', the latter being composed in the same frequently enjambed rolling rhythms of hypotactic blank verse as the former, albeit using a greater number of archaisms. Stylistically, there is a sense of continuity between the modern frame poem and the epic fragment that serves to undercut their contrasting subject matter. What 'The Epic' amply demonstrates, then, is Tennyson's awareness of, and engagement with, the question of poetry's relation to modernity, a question which emerges repeatedly within his oeuvre.

Critics clearly expected from Tennyson an epic poem of the age. When he published his first long poem, *The Princess. A Medley*, in 1847, reviewers were accordingly puzzled and disappointed. They looked for an epic poem that would make sense of their age, but what they got was a poem 'so bizarre, indeed grotesque, as this correctly enough named "medley", in which grave matter of fact and wild fancies, solemn disquisitions, and sportive ridicule, all mingled with much sweet poetry, are so strangely jumbled together' ('The Princess. A Medley' 1848: 20). Once again, Tennyson seems unwilling to commit to an epic representation of the contemporary world, though the poem's frame has a contemporary setting. A group of young men and women meet in a country house park, where common people have gathered for a sort of science festival. The poem's main tale, in contrast, combines highly topical issues like women's education and new scientific knowledge with a medieval fairy-tale setting of royal courts and jousting knights. Allegedly a collaborative product of several (male) storytellers, interspersed with lyric songs sung by women, this fantastic tale is introduced as a 'Seven-headed monster [. . .] only made to kill / Time', part serious, part satire, 'But something made to suit with time and place' (Prologue ll. 200–1, 224).

The contemporary setting is thus both emphasised (as the story is triggered by the narrators' environment and circumstances) and trivialised as idle pastime.

The frame tale goes in fact some way to showcase the incongruent contiguity of widely diverse cultural, temporal and social elements in the medley that is contemporary life, thereby turning the poem's formal inconsistencies into the basis for its claim to contemporariness:

> A Gothic ruin and a Grecian house,
> A talk of college and of ladies' rights,
> A feudal knight in silken masquerade,
> And, yonder, shrieks and strange experiments
> For which the good Sir Ralph had burnt them all,—
> This were a medley! (Prologue ll. 225–30)

It is precisely the poem's mottled form, then – its mixture of medieval and modern thematic elements as well as its combination of epic narrative and lyric songs – which suits the contemporary moment, in which past and present elements constantly clash, mingle and collapse into each other. And yet there is something evasive in this poem's attempt to reconcile inconsistencies. Its idyllic country house setting, for example, is careful to emphasise harmony and to show no hint of conflict or tension. Class differences are played down in the benevolent procedures of a country fair, in which the grounds of the landed gentry are open to the populace, 'sown / with happy faces and with holiday' (Prologue ll. 55–6); scientific inquiry is turned into entertainment, as where 'a group of girls / In circle waited, whom the electric shock / Dislinked with shrieks and laughter' (Prologue ll. 68–70); and the steam engine, which proved such a testing rod to the ability of poetry to address the present, is infantilised into a mere toy:

> round the lake
> A little clock-work steamer paddling plied
> And shook the lilies: perched about the knolls
> A dozen angry models jetted steam:
> A petty railway ran: (Prologue ll. 70–4)

All conflict is relegated to the safely distant space of the fairy-tale setting, where it can be happily resolved in the poem's conservative ending, in which the Princess gives up her aims of independence and education, consenting to marry the Prince. While Tennyson clearly took the role of poet of the age to heart, he seems doubtful about a poetry which addresses the present head on. He has his speaker say in the conclusion to the poem

> ourselves are full
> Of social wrong; and maybe wildest dreams
> Are but the needful preludes of the truth:
> For me, the genial day, the happy crowd,
> The sport half-science, fill me with a faith. (Conclusion ll. 72–6)

The poet's role, in face of the multitudinous present, Tennyson seems to suggest, may be to harmonise, even if such harmony can only take the form of a wild dream. His recurrence to the past becomes the prelude to a future, in which the present incongruities and tensions will dissolve again in genial faith.

The Princess is clearly ambivalent about the ability of epic poetry to represent the present directly,[7] but Tennyson begins to suggest here that new genre mixtures may provide a solution. He was to emphasise the lyric element by adding lyric interludes to the third edition of *The Princess*, but, for the most part, lyric and epic voices remain clearly separated (and clearly gendered). This stands in contrast to the more closely intertwined and unstable genre affiliations in dramatic monologues, poetic sequences and verse novels which I discuss in the next chapter and which Tennyson was to experiment with further in *In Memoriam* (1850) and *Maud* (1855). In such mixtures, I go on to suggest in the next chapter, Victorian poets sought formal answers to modernity's temporal challenge.

Meanwhile such mixtures, and especially the inward turn taken by a poem like *Maud*, were strongly rejected by Matthew Arnold, who most vociferously and most influentially defended the position that the past provided the best models and the best material for poetic production. Notoriously he rejected his own earlier poetic practice as unhealthily focused inwardly on the mind, excluding his poem 'Empedocles on Edna' from the second edition of his poems. Arnold's rejection of contemporary subject matter gathers force in view of the marked emphasis on content, not form, in his definition of great poetry. In his preface to the 1853 edition of his poems, in which he justifies the exclusion of 'Empedocles on Edna' outlining his poetic ideals, he argues that 'the eternal objects of Poetry, among all nations and at all times [. . .] are actions; human actions' (1979: 656). Clearly developing an epic ideal, for Arnold action is the essential poetic element. The question of a suitable setting gains central relevance because action usually takes place within more or less clearly defined limits of time and space. With his preface, Arnold enters a debate that was clearly well established and takes exception to 'the opinion which many critics of the present day appear to entertain against subjects chosen from distant times and countries: against the choice, in short, of any subjects but modern ones' (656). Against this, Arnold claims that '[t]he date of an action [. . .] signifies nothing: the action itself, its selection and construction, this is what is all-important' (659). Excellent actions, according to his definition, are those

> which most powerfully appeal to the great primary human affections: to those elementary feelings which subsist permanently in the race and which are independent of time. These feelings are permanent and the same; that which interests them is permanent and the same also. The modernness or antiquity of an action, therefore, has nothing to do with its fitness for poetical representation; this depends upon its inherent qualities. (657)

While, in theory, this repeated emphasis on permanence and universal truth, on what remains untouched by external change in human nature, 'independent of time', should make the setting irrelevant, in practice Arnold repeatedly voices his conviction that the present age is inimical to the production and appreciation of great actions: 'an age wanting in moral grandeur can with difficulty supply such, and an age of spiritual discomfort with difficulty be powerfully and delightfully affected by them' (669). Indeed, Arnold's investment in the permanence and timelessness of poetry is so strong that he only admits the ancients as fit models for poetry. Taking the ancients' 'intense significance, their noble simplicity, and their calm pathos' as their ideal, poets will 'escape the danger of producing poetical works conceived in the spirit of the passing time, and which partake of its transitoriness' (668). In Arnold's view, then, true poetry cannot be modern, if only because transitoriness is part of the very definition of modernity. While others call for a change in poetry, not only in terms of content, but also in terms of form, Arnold maintains that the only legitimate and successful poetic form is that developed by the ancient Greeks. He heralds precisely those 'faint Homeric echoes' which Hall had condemned in Tennyson's 'The Epic'.

For Arnold, too, one main factor which made the present age so 'deeply *unpoetical*' (1968: 99 [Feb. 1849]), as he was to lament in a letter to his friend Arthur Hugh Clough, was its temporal logic of acceleration, change and progress. This much can clearly be seen in Arnold's own poetry. After all, Arnold did write poetry about the present age. In fact, William Buckler even suggests that 'on the whole and despite notable exceptions, the dominant impression that Arnold's poetry gives to one who knows something of his age is of a representation of that age' (1982: 196). Notably, though, this poetry predominantly takes the form of lyric elegy, suffused by a nostalgic yearning for the past.[8] Repeatedly, Arnold blames the haste and hurry of the present day as well as a sense of constant strife and accelerated change for an impaired poetic vision. If in his essay 'The Function of Criticism' (1864) he names the 'epochs of Aeschylus and Shakespeare' as truly creative epochs comparing unfavourably with the 'wilderness' of the present day (2005: 631–2), in the 'Stanzas in Memory of the Author of "Oberman"' (1852) he suggests that even the previous generation of Wordsworth and Goethe had had an easier poetic task:

> But we, brought forth and rear'd in hours
> Of change, alarm, surprise –
> What shelter to grow ripe is ours?
> What leisure to grow wise?
>
> Like children bathing on the shore,
> Buried a wave beneath,
> The second wave succeeds, before
> We have had time to breathe.
>
> Too fast we live, too much are tried,
> Too harrass'd, to attain
> Wordsworth's sweet calm, or Goethe's wide
> And luminous view to gain. (ll. 69–80)

Again, it is the change in the pace of life as much as the sense of perpetual change, perpetual surprise, that robs the poet of the necessary detachment and wholeness of vision, of that 'sad lucidity of soul', as Arnold puts it elsewhere, which enables the poet to 'see Life unroll, / A placid and continuous whole' (in 'Resignation: To Fausta' [1849], ll. 198; 189–90). Thus Arnold warns the 'Scholar Gipsy' (1853) against the 'strange disease of modern life, / With its sick hurry, its divided aims, (ll. 203–4), in which all 'clear aims be cross and shifting made' (l. 228).

A similar lament underlies the structure of Arnold's most famous poem, 'Dover Beach' (1867). The first two stanzas emphasise calmness and the unchanging nature of the sea, suggesting continuity and the endlessly recurring and uniform rhythms of nature: 'The sea is calm to-night' (l. 1), 'the cliffs of England stand, / Glimmering and vast, out in the tranquil bay' (ll. 4–5), and one can hear the waves

'Begin, and cease, and then again begin / With tremulous cadence slow' (ll. 12–13). There is already a hint of violence, perhaps, in the 'grating roar' and the drawing and flinging of pebbles on the beach (ll. 9–10) but it is only the final line of the first stanza, which definitely gives this serene scene a sinister turn, as the waves 'bring / The eternal note of sadness in' (ll. 13–14). The second stanza at first universalises this subjective impression by establishing continuity between the speaker and Sophocles, who has heard the same sound 'long ago' (l. 14) and has likewise been inspired by it. The temporal and spatial distance separating Arnold's speaker from Sophocles is dissolved in an experience that is not only common, but supposedly universal and of timeless validity.

But from the third stanza onwards, this commonality is increasingly undermined by the inexorable modernity in which the speaker finds himself. Rather than establishing continuity, the second stanza retrospectively turns out to stress difference, namely the impassable gulf of time and change that lies between Sophocles and the speaker. As Alan Grob notes, the poem turns 'from the Sophoclean mode of analysing significant human events in terms of a supposedly direct and immediate metaphysical determination to an emerging nineteenth-century predisposition to interpret them as the varied effects of an ongoing historical causality' (2002: 178). If the sound of the waves suggested to Sophocles the 'turbid ebb and flow / Of human misery' (ll. 16–17), the poem's speaker can only hear the 'melancholy, long withdrawing roar' (l. 25) of the 'Sea of Faith' (l. 21), 'Retreating, to the breath / Of the night-wind, down the vast edges drear / And naked shingles of the world' (ll. 26–8). While Sophocles' experience and thought is described in terms of a perpetual and unchanging ebb and flow, the speaker can conceive of time only as a linear, historical succession. Even the sea, which the poem initially establishes as a site of eternal return, is appropriated by the modern mind into a lament of constant decline. The inappropriateness of this appropriation – the fact that Arnold's speaker chooses to ignore the necessary return of the tide in the development of his analogy – enforces the point. The modern consciousness imposes its temporal concepts on the vehicle of the metaphor even in spite of their unsuitability.

The last stanza, then, contrasts the calm night scene with which the poem began with the tumultuous 'darkling plain / Swept with confused alarms of struggle and flight / Where ignorant armies clash by night' (ll. 35–7). Returning to the rhyme words of the poem's beginning ('night' and 'light'), the final stanza reveals the beautiful calm of the first lines to have been an illusion. Estranged from the calm eternity of the ancients, subject to the linear time concepts of modernity, the speaker rejects the salvation that might be found in subscribing to a belief in progress: 'the world, which seems / To lie before us like a land of dreams, / So various, so beautiful, so new, / Hath really neither joy, nor love, nor light, / Nor certitude, nor peace, nor help for pain' (ll. 30–4). In face of the changefulness of modernity, of its haste and struggle, its uncertainty and transitoriness, even the speaker's anguished call for faithful love can hardly serve as a safe haven in a world with no faith, no love and no certitude.

That poetry, too, fails to offer a solution is suggested by the way the poem undermines its own use of the sea as metaphor, not only in its temporal logic. The latent violence of the waves in the first stanza and its association with 'human misery' (l. 18) in the second rub strangely with the image of a bright 'Sea of Faith'. Moreover, the poem's setting at Dover and explicit reference to the French coast bring associations of conflicts and national rivalries. Even the insistence on the calmness of the bay in the first stanza by exclusion hints at the sometime destructive force of the sea. The poetic image fails to provide clarity. It partakes in the confusion and struggle with which the poem concludes. Thus, when Arnold returns to a tight rhyme scheme and metre in the final stanza, after increasingly varying both over the course of the previous stanzas, this appears to be the formal equivalent of his apparently hopeless appeal to love. Poetic form, like the 'brave new world' of technological, cultural and social progress, is a beautiful mirage, but in a modern world it lacks the deeper, eternal truth and certainty poetry aims for.

In the drawing-rooms of the present – Clough and Barrett Browning

It is precisely the lack of such stable truths which Arnold criticises in the poetry of his friend Clough, to whom he writes: 'You are too content to *fluctuate* – to be ever learning, never coming to the knowledge of the truth' (1968: 146 [30 Nov. 1853]). In contrast to Arnold, Clough deliberately chose contemporary settings and topics for his poetry, in particular his two long narrative poems *The Bothie of Tober-na-Vuolich* (1848) and *Amours de Voyage* (written in 1849, but only published in 1858). He plunges willingly into the 'Time Stream' that Arnold found so distasteful and from which he desired to remain aloof (Arnold 1968: 95 [Nov. 1848]). As Joseph Bristow has argued, these well-known differences between Arnold and Clough 'point to one of the major divisions in middle-class poetic practice in the late 1840s and 1850s' (1995: 32). They arise not from mere personal idiosyncrasies but are representative of a wider cultural debate, deeply rooted in a cultural context in which new temporal regimes began to threaten traditional concepts of poetry.

That Clough turns to contemporary topics with a clear sense of the pressure under which poetry finds itself is suggested in his 1853 review of the poetry of Arnold and Alexander Smith, in which he admits that '[t]here is no question, it is plain and patent enough, that people much prefer Vanity Fair and Bleak House' to poetry (2005: 583). The reason, Clough proposes, is precisely that poetry, in decided contrast to the novel, has misguidedly refrained from addressing the present:

> is it, that to be wildly popular, to gain the ear of multitudes, to shake the hearts of men, poetry should deal more than at present it usually does, with general wants, ordinary feelings, the obvious rather than the rare facts of human nature? Could it not attempt to convert into beauty and thankfulness, or at least into some form and shape, some feeling at any rate, of content – the actual, palpable things with which our every-day life is concerned; [. . .] intimate to us relations which, in our unchosen peremptorily-appointed posts, in our grievously narrow and limited spheres of action, we still, in and through all, retain to some central, celestial fact? (583)

Poetry, according to Clough, does wrong to leave the field of contemporary life to the novel. Still faithful in these lines to an ideal of poetry rooted in the revelation of deeper meaning and divine ('celestial') truth, Clough exhorts poets to reveal such truths in the sordid circumstances of a modern setting.

His own poetry, however, seems somewhat doubtful about such an endeavour. Certainly, he invokes the 'Muses and Graces, who love the plain present, / Scorning historic abridgement and artifice anti-poetic' in the *Bothie* (Section VI, ll. 99–100), and makes use of both epic and pastoral conventions in this tale of an Oxford reading party, which gradually morphs into a story of happy love. In fact, by writing in his own version of an epic hexameter, he intervenes in a controversial prosodic debate about the possibility to adapt this classical quantitative verse form to the accentual-syllabic metres of the English language; a controversy which I will address in Chapter 4. But while Natasha Moore argues that such strategies convey heroism on the everyday (2015: 30), there is something deliberately absurd in lines such as: 'Be it recorded in song who was first, who last, in dressing' (Section I, l. 12). While the contemporary story it tells and many of the contemporary issues it touches are not merely playful, the *Bothie* thrives on the humour derived from the incongruity between its form and content. Rather than effecting a successful merger of traditional poetic form with contemporary content, the *Bothie* could be seen to prove precisely the opposite, namely that ancient form and contemporary content cannot be reconciled without becoming to some degree ludicrous. The effect of Clough's long dactylic lines, which he combines with contemporary and even colloquial diction is, more often than not, wryly ironic or openly humorous in tone. The point is not that traditional and contemporary elements are necessarily irreconcilable, but that the *Bothie* deliberately foregrounds their incongruity to humorous effect (cf. Moore 2015: 158).

For the somewhat less light-hearted, though still ironical and satirical, *Amours de Voyage* (1858), Clough maintains the dactylic hexameter but writes the poem in epistolary form. This form of narration references the novel – with Samuel Richardson as an influential model – rather than the epic and establishes proximity between event and representation. Opening with protagonist Claude's disenchantment with Rome, the first few letters further emphasise a rejection of the past as either model or inspiration. 'Rome disappoints me much', Claude exclaims, 'Ye gods! what do I want with this rubbish of ages departed, / Things that nature abhors, the experiments that she has failed in?' (Canto I, ll. 40–1). Rejecting an Arnoldian reverence for the clarity and unity of ancient ideas, Claude asks deprecatingly: 'Doubtless the notion of grand and capacious and massive amusement, / This the old Romans had; but tell me, is this an idea?' (Canto I, ll. 45–6). Thus Claude's letters soon turn to contemporary issues and the stalled love plot of the poem develops against the background of the turbulent political situation of the 1849 siege of Rome. But by giving up the superior perspective of the epic voice, Clough makes the poem's insights dependent on the limitations of his characters. Claude is a singularly unlikely source for intimations of 'some central, celestial fact'. He is perceptively characterised by contemporary reviewer Walter Bagehot as

> a hesitating young gentleman, who was in Rome at the time of the revolution of 1848 [*sic*]; who could not make up his mind about the revolution, who could not make up his mind whether he liked Rome, who could not make up his mind whether he liked the young lady, who let her go away from him without him, who went in pursuit of her, and could not make out which way to look for her, who, in fine, has some sort of religion, but cannot himself tell what it is. (1862: 318)

One of the main currents running through the poem is precisely Claude's inability to commit to any conviction or truth, or even to rely on and communicate his own experience. 'Utterly vain is, alas! This attempt at the Absolute, – wholly!' (Canto V, l. 63) he exclaims in despair at the end of his abortive would-be love affair. Nor does he find a Romantic faith in the truth of subjective vision viable:

> What with trusting myself, and seeking support from within me,
> Almost I could believe I had gained a religious assurance,
> Formed in my own poor soul a great moral basis to rest on.
> Ah, but indeed I see, I feel it factitious entirely;
> I refuse, reject, and put it utterly from me;
> I will look straight out, see things, not try to evade them;
> Fact shall be fact for me, and the Truth the Truth as ever,
> Flexible, changeable, vague, and multiform, and doubtful.
>   (Canto V, ll. 95–102)

Instead of absolute and stable truths, Claude seeks his salvation in a commitment to mere facts, and thus turns from the transcendent ideal, to an experience of the contemporary.

Such a project, again, is called into question from the very first lines of the poem. In the short lyric preface to the first canto, an encouragement to go on a journey is directly countered with scepticism: ''Tis but to prove limitation, and measure a cord, that we travel; / Let who would 'scape and be free go to his chamber and think; / 'Tis but to change idle fancies for memories wilfully falser; / 'Tis but to go and have been' (Canto I, ll. 7–10). The truth of direct experience – of looking straight at the facts and reporting them in the near-contemporary representation promised by the epistolary form – is here denied as illusory from the outset. The poem does not privilege a realist agenda over an idealist one, but constantly questions to what degree the contemporary can be represented, or indeed experienced, at all. Claude's description of the battle in Canto II is characteristically vague and studded with qualifications (Canto II, l. 97–134), and even the one properly sensational experience that he admits to having had is immediately called into question: 'So, I have seen a man killed! An experience that, among others! / Yes, I suppose I have; although I can hardly be certain, / And in a court of justice could never declare I had seen it' (Canto II, ll. 164–6). Scrupulously self-interrogatory, Claude leaves scarcely any of his observations, opinions or thoughts without qualification or flat contradiction. Far from being able to reach some 'central, celestial fact', Claude is uncertain about his own most direct experiences and most intimate feelings.

Characteristically, he even realises his love for fellow traveller Mary Trevellyn only once it is too late.

No less than Arnold, Clough feels the 'infinite jumble and mess and dislocation' of the present, which, if it is a battle, ''tis battle by night' (*The Bothie*, Section IX, ll. 64, 51). But, as Moore has argued, '[f]or Arnold, the "multitudinousness" of the world in which the poet finds himself, the unceasing flow of matter that pressed upon him, is a threat to the ideal truth poetry seeks to embody', while 'Clough, in complete contrast, cannot accept as truth any version of reality that averages out or smooths over inconsistent and inconvenient actuality' (2015: 34). Indeed, I would go further to suggest that Clough's poetry can itself be read as a site of struggle to redefine poetry in face of the loss of a certainty in ultimate, transcendent truths, a loss that is closely connected to religious doubts. Though Clough's poetry still evinces a yearning for 'central, celestial facts', in its failure to establish 'the Absolute' it submits to the world.

Visible both in the *Bothie* and in *Amours*, this struggle becomes central to the Faustian story of *Dipsychus* (1850). Where Arnold retreats from the world that overwhelms him into the idealised silence of the cloister (in 'Stanzas from the Grande Chartreuse') and eventually gives up writing poetry altogether, Clough grants the last words and the final victory in the fragmentary *Dipsychus* to the Mephistophelian worldly Spirit, who commits Dipsychus to the present:

> O goodness! won't you find it pleasant
> To own the positive and present;
> To see yourself like people round,
> And feel your feet upon the ground!. (Scene IX, ll. 74–7)

This is certainly an ambivalent testimony, as Dipsychus reluctantly enters a pact with the devil. But Dipsychus's idealism has led him into a dead end and the Spirit has in the course of the poem too often successfully debunked Dipsychus's lofty ideals for the latter to truly seem like the better alternative. 'O the misery', Dipsychus exclaims, 'That one must truck and pactise with the world / To gain the 'vantage-ground to assail it from' (Scene VIII, ll. 5–7). Instead of fleeing from the contemporary world, the poem suggests, it has to be faced if anything is to be achieved. But to face the world is to be grounded in the transitory present and to resign an idealism that strives for the eternal.[9]

Three years after the publication of Clough's review and Arnold's preface, Elizabeth Barrett Browning published *Aurora Leigh* (1856), as if in answer to Clough's challenge. In her attempt to merge the novelistic with the epic, she turns to the contemporary with mission- ary force and has her eponymous heroine exclaim, in a deliberate refutation of the aesthetics of Poet Laureate Tennyson:

> Nay, if there's room for poets in the world
> A little overgrown, (I think there is)
> Their sole work is to represent the age,
> Their age, not Charlemagne's, – this live, throbbing age,
> That brawls, cheats, maddens, calculates, aspires,
> And spends more passion, more heroic heat,
> Betwixt the mirrors of its drawing-rooms,
> Than Roland with his knights, at Roncesvalles.
> To flinch from modern varnish, coat or flounce,
> Cry out for togas and the picturesque,
> Is fatal, – foolish too. King Arthur's self
> Was commonplace to Lady Guenever;
> And Camelot to minstrels seemed as flat,
> As Regent Street to poets.
>
> Never flinch,
> But still, unscrupulously epic, catch
> Upon the burning lava of a song
> The full-veined, heaving, double-breasted Age:
> That, when the next shall come, the men of that
> May touch the impress with reverent hand, and say
> 'Behold, – behold the paps we all have sucked!
> This bosom seems to beat still, or at least
> It sets ours beating: this is living art,
> Which thus presents and thus records true life.' (Book V, ll. 199–221)[10]

If Arnold despairs of modern poetry, Barrett Browning is exultant about the full-veined present, which will lend its life to the art that represents it truly. Poetry, according to this view, can turn to the transient without losing its permanence, because it retains not merely a moment, but an entire age for the contemplation of future genera- tions. In evoking a future readership, this recurs to an Aesthetics of the Eternal Word with a confidence in art's endurance that some of Barrett Browning's contemporaries had already lost – Tennyson, for example, who asks in *In Memoriam*, 'What hope is there for modern rhyme?' (LXXVII, l. 1). Moreover, these lines claim for art the power not only to memorialise, but to keep alive, or at least to retain the semblance of life in an ideal of poetry that is fully epic, not lyric. At the same time, though, this apparent embrace of historical relativism merely leads to a deeper acknowledgement of the spiritual force that lies beneath mere material transience, which poetry aims to access and communicate:

> If a man could feel,
> Not one day, in the artist's ecstasy,
> But every day, feast, fast, or working-day,
> The spiritual significance burn through
> The hieroglyphic of material shows
> Henceforward he would paint the globe with wings,
> And reverence fish and fowl, the bull, the tree,
> And even his very body as a man (Book VII, ll. 857–64)

Once again, this echoes Clough's review, committing to an Aesthetics of Eternal Essence in which a sort of pantheistic 'spiritual significance' (l. 860) that permeates everything becomes poetry's aim and reason. Indeed, Aurora fully adheres to high claims for poetic truth as she heralds poets as 'the only truth-tellers, now left to God, – / The only speakers of essential truth, / Opposed to relative, comparative, / And temporal truths' (Book I, ll. 859–62). Inverting the Shelleyan rejection of transitory relations as unsuited for poetry, however, Aurora claims that a recognition of essential truths leads to a proper appreciation of the material and transient, of 'even his very body as a man'. Her version of the Aesthetics of Eternal Essence thus paradoxically comes with a promise of fundamental change. 'The world waits / for help' (Book IX, ll. 923–4), Aurora's cousin Romney exclaims in the final verses of the poem,

> The world's old
> But the old world waits the hour to be renewed:
> Toward which, new hearts in individual growth
> Must quicken, and increase to multitude
> In new dynasties of the race of men, –
> Developed whence, shall grow spontaneously
> New churches, new œconomies, new laws
> Admitting freedom, new societies
> Excluding falsehood. HE shall make all new. (Book IX, ll. 941–9)

Poetry is instrumental for bringing this change about while at the same time, it remains firmly rooted in providence. Through the voice of Aurora, Barrett Browning thus answers the changeable times with a breathtakingly ambitious programme for poetry, in which it somewhat paradoxically serves as a force both of conservation and of innovation, emphasising the contemporary but always pointing towards the eternal divine. While the poem thus turns emphatically to transient facts in depicting its contemporary setting and plot, Aurora aims at the celestial central truths which Clough called for, but which his poetry is deeply doubtful about.

Thus, as I explore in more depth in the next chapter, for both Clough and Browning, a commitment to the contemporary *theme* of novels led simultaneously to an approximation of its *form*, creating hybrids between novel and poem. As the autobiographical account of the formation of a poet, *Aurora Leigh* reads on the one hand like a feminine answer to Wordsworth's *The Prelude*;[11] on the other, its plot and its social commitment are reminiscent of a Condition of England novel. Its blank verse and language are often elevated and lyrical, but also cover passages of vapid society chatter. While *Aurora Leigh* was generally well received, this hybridity was deeply felt by contemporary reviewers, who would criticise it for being too realistic for a poem and too improbable for a novel and who would complain about the prosaic quality of some passages on the one hand and castigate the dialogue between the two main protagonists as too poetically elevated to be realistic on the other.[12] Clough, for his part, is most effectively contemporary in *Amours de Voyage* for which he appropriates the tradition of the epistolary novel and the travel account. Thus, for Barrett Browning and for Clough one answer to the challenge of change seems to lie in making poetry look more like novels. Nevertheless their hybrid genre experiments essentially work to retain and confirm the genre distinctions between novel and poetry. What is contemporary in their poetry is generally novelistic while poetry's task in this merger is to elevate the everyday into lasting beauty.

My discussion of these poets is necessarily selective, but it is not my aim to affix them to set positions in the debate. Rather, I merely want to illustrate the serious consideration that was given to these questions by some of the century's most prominent poets. After the 1850s, the debate about the suitability of contemporary topics and issues in poetry gradually subsided. In his overview of *English Poetic Theory, 1825–1865*, Alba H. Warren would brush the debate aside entirely and conclude that, on the whole, an agreement was established that '[a]ny subject is fit for poetry if it is treated imaginatively. This includes ordinary feeling, steam engines, and the "grand subject"' (1966: 7). But, in turning to contemporary topics, Victorian poetry struggles to maintain its hold on permanence and timeless truths, which are no longer simply rooted in supposedly timeless subject matter. *Aurora Leigh* is symptomatic in the sense that poetry generally continued to claim deeper insights (its 'soul') and to evoke them in order to elevate itself over the merely transient novel (mere 'body'). It is this Romantic elevation of poetry, granting it privileged epistemological insight into permanent, absolute truths, which comes under pressure from another direction, that of the increasingly confident truth-claims of science.

Poetic Truth, Scientific Truth

In thinking about the relationship between poetry and science, the Victorians were strongly influenced by Wordsworth's and Samuel Taylor Coleridge's assertion that the two are antithetical. Coleridge's posthumously published lecture on 'The Definition of Poetry' (1836), in which he claims that '[p]oetry is not the proper antithesis to prose, but to science' (7), appears to have been a particularly popular reference, possibly helped by the fact that it is quoted by both George Moir's entry on poetry in the seventh edition (1842) of the *Encyclopaedia Britannica* (140) – the entry was reprinted in the eighth edition of 1854 – and Theodore Watts's entry on the same topic in the ninth edition (1885: 261). In his lecture, Coleridge goes on to characterise the antithesis he postulates in the following terms: 'The proper and immediate object of science is the acquirement, or communication, of truth; the proper and immediate object of poetry is the communication of immediate pleasure' (1836: 7–8). Poetry and science are assigned different aims or effects, truth and pleasure respectively, and are thus conveniently kept apart. On this basis, however, it remains unclear what the antithesis between poetry and science really consists of, since truth and pleasure are by no means logical opposites. In fact, Coleridge almost immediately proceeds to blur his own neat distinction when he speaks of poetry as 'a more vivid reflection of the truths of nature and of the human heart, united with a constant activity modifying and correcting these truths by that sort of pleasurable emotion, which the exertion of all our faculties gives in a certain degree' (10). Even while he highlights pleasure as poetry's main aim, such pleasure is firmly rooted in the revelation of truths.

Coleridge's juxtaposition gains additional urgency in the context of Wordsworth's definition of poetry as truth. For Wordsworth, poetry and science share their principal aim and he responds to science's increasingly self-confident claims to a monopoly on truth.

The answer he gives in the 1802 preface to the *Lyrical Ballads* is two-pronged. Poetry, at least the variety of poetry to which he commits himself, is concerned with tracing 'the primary laws of our nature: chiefly, as far as regards the manner in which we associate ideas in a state of excitement' (1992: 61). Thus, poetry is essentially concerned with what is human; its truths are subjective and psychological. As Wordsworth later added in the 'Essay supplementary to the Preface' (1815), its business is 'to treat of things not as they *are*, but as they *appear*; not as they exist in themselves, but as they *seem* to exist to the *senses* and to the *passions*' (1974a: 192). Notwithstanding their subjective nature, these truths are by no means restricted to individual experience. Quite the contrary. It is the man of science whose knowledge is 'personal and individual'. He 'seeks truth as a remote and unknown benefactor; he cherishes and loves it in his solitude'. The truth of the poet, in contrast, is general, shared by all human beings. His knowledge is 'a necessary part of our existence, our natural and unalienable inheritance' (1992: 76). His truth is not solipsistic, remote and elitist like the scientist's, but communal, social and immediately intuited: 'The Poet binds together by passion and knowledge the vast empire of human society, as it is spread over the whole earth, and over all time' (77). Thus poetry is on the one hand justified as a branch of science, precisely a 'science of feelings' as Wordsworth calls it elsewhere (1974b: 97). On the other hand, Wordsworth makes for poetry the much more ambitious and embracing claim to be 'the first and last of all knowledge – it is as immortal as the heart of man' (1992: 77). Individual man might be mortal, but poetry is concerned with the 'essential passions of the heart', with our 'elementary feelings', which Wordsworth assumes to be permanent and immutable (1992: 60). Since all knowledge is necessarily human and addressed to humans, poetry, as the knowledge of the essentially human, stands first and last and incorporates scientific knowledge: it knows the observer and the receiver of scientific facts.

It is well worth dwelling on Wordsworth's position in this context, because, as Gregory Tate has argued, the nineteenth-century discourse on poetry and science is largely continuous, with no clearly discernible shift from Romantic to Victorian positions (2017: 104). Indeed, Victorian approaches to the problem of the relation between science and poetry generally arrange themselves on a spectrum of possibilities very similar to those implied in Wordsworth's preface: by some Victorians, poetry and science are perceived to be related activities, sharing the same aim in their search for universal and eternal truth, but reaching for it by different methods (and, perhaps, with different success). Others see poetry's strength in its psychological acuity. If the natural sciences contribute to the knowledge of natural phenomena, the poet contributes to the knowledge of human nature and mind. Their objects of investigation and therefore their truths are of a different kind. The most pessimistic, but today perhaps the most familiar view, sees poetry and science not only as antithesis but as antagonists. In this view, poetry is not associated with truth, but in the best case with either the unknowable or art for art's sake, and in the worst case with harmful lies.[13]

Just as Romantic thought continued to hold sway and to influence Victorian positions, the three main conceptions of the relationship between poetry and science which I trace in what follows coexist as much as they succeed each other. While I do mean to imply some sense of chronology – from endeavours to uphold poetry's privileged access to all kinds of universal truths, to a focus on its psychological acuity, to finally, a retreat (or liberation) into an Aestheticist doctrine of art for art's sake, which renounces the essentiality of poetry's relationship to truth – such a chronology can at best be one of emerging and receding tendencies.

All these juxtapositions generalise broadly and inadmissibly about both science and poetry. Indeed, 'science' is no less complex and contested a term than 'poetry'.[14] As the general editors of the anthology *Victorian Literature and Science* caution:

> in Victorian Britain there was little consensus as to what the terms 'science' and 'literature' actually meant. [. . .] [I]t makes little sense to impose retrospectively our own more clearly defined sense of what constitutes the scientific and the literary [. . .] onto the considerably more complex circumstances of the nineteenth century. (Dawson and Lightman 2011: ix)

Victorian juxtapositions of the two thus always involve reductive and misleadingly monolithic constructions of the terms of comparison. It is partly for this reason, as we will see, that the contrast between poetry and science proved to be so resilient to attempts to resolve it and so productive of new negotiations of what poetry and science might mean in the first place. While these common juxtapositions of science and poetry therefore cannot tell us anything about the complexity of a Victorian scientific or poetic practise, they do attest to ideological and conceptual positions current at the time. Further, my main point in the following discussion will be that conceptions of time play a crucial role in all these negotiations.

Common end, different means – synthesis versus analysis

One common way to distinguish science and poetry was to say that science analyses and poetry synthesises, a view unsurprisingly popular among poets themselves: 'The Man of Science, the Man of Business, break up the whole into little bits, for analysis, for calculation, for sale; the Poet reconstructs the shattered world, and shows it complete and beautiful' – thus wrote William Allingham in 1867 (525). Science is associated in such oppositions with the practice of diligent description and classification characteristic of the naturalist, whose search for facts deafens his (it is inevitably 'his' for the Victorians) ears to higher harmonies. Science, in this characterisation, may supply enduring facts, but the higher, permanent and universal truths that lie beyond scientific descriptions are accessible only to the poetic imagination.

That is the root of the tragedy of Theophilus in the poem 'A Man of Science or the Botanist's Grave' (1868) by Edward Robert Bulwer-Lytton (whose pseudonym was 'Owen Meredith'). As a young boy he is eager to know nature, 'Not [. . .] the *act*, which I see, but the *thought*, which I cannot discern: / I stand in the centre, gaze round me, see everywhere action alone, / And find nowhere the source of the thought found in action wherever I turn' (ll. 38–40). But his teacher tells him that nature can only be perceived piecemeal: 'The thought may be one, once for all, / All at once; but the action is many and diverse, to unity brought / In the mind by slow aggregates growing alike from the great and the small' (ll. 42–4). Theophilus longs for the permanent truths of nature but can only access its changeable materiality. He turns to botany, only to be taken aback:

> But O what a hopeless confusion doth Order at first sight appear!
> Unwearied Theophilus, sitting, and conning the grammar of Nature,
> Thro' the whole of the humming hot noon with the cuckoo's note
> cleaving it clear,
> Is it knowledge thou seekest? Then patience, and master, meanwhile,
> nomenclature. (ll. 77–80)

The ridiculous rhyme of nature with nomenclature forgetfully passes over the natural as well as poetical beauties of the alliterative intervening line and overlooks the clarity promised by the cuckoo's call. Over the dry practice of naming and classifying, in the attempt to find order in nature's chaos and to gain knowledge, Theophilus is both blind and deaf to nature as well as to the passing of his life.

The problem, the poem suggests, is that the kind of knowledge Theophilus longs for lies beyond the reach of science, in the realm of poetry. Buried among his books he sighs:

'Ah, but all this, after all, is not what I pined for! Up there
The veilèd Mystery sits on the solemn mountain peak:
The vast clouds form and change at her feet: and my heart's despair
Cries aloud where no answer is heard: for this Silence never will speak.

'Yonder, up there, as of old, when he play'd on my heart's harp-strings,
The wind, with a surly music, is moaning aloof in the tree:
Yonder, up there, in the blue and the breezy mid-sky swings
The lanneret Hawk, as of old, when my heart went higher than he.

'Could one leap all at once to the end! not doom'd, like a grub, to grope
About in the blinding earth, looking up never more from one's load!
Well, never mind! One is laying up knowledge, at least, one must hope;
And one cannot afford to leap over the knowledge that lies in one's
road.' (ll. 133–44)

It is no coincidence that the heart, which is so closely associated with poetry for the Victorians that Kirstie Blair called it 'the most vital cliché of nineteenth-century poetics' (2006: 102), is mentioned three times in these lines, whose language, diction and imagery draw heavily on the poetical register and whose musical cadences contrast distinctly with the harsh sounds and awkward rhythm of the scientific jargon employed in lines like: 'a manuscript newly begun // On the carbonaceous compounds found in botanical tissues, – / Cellulose, glucose, lignine, dextrine, inuline, starch, —' (ll. 12–14). The leap Theophilus longs for cannot be made by scientific knowledge, but only by poetic imagination.[15]

However, the difference between an analytical science, which is immersed in details, and synthesising poetry approaching eternal truths breaks down where science sets out to discover fundamental laws, as it would do with increasing success throughout the century. This turns out to be the core of the argument put forward by Robert Hunt in his popularisation of scientific advances, *The Poetry of Science* (1848). Confessedly indebted to Romantic thought, Hunt opens *The Poetry of Science* with an allusion to Keats's much-quoted conclusion to the 'Ode to a Grecian Urn' (1819), in order to emphasise the common ground of scientist and poet: 'The True is the Beautiful. [. . .] To be forever true is the Science of Poetry, –

the revelation of truth is the Poetry of Science' (Hunt 1850: 19). Hunt, too, admits that the (analytic) scientific labour of gathering facts may seem inimical to poetry: 'The fumes of the laboratory, its alkalics and acids, the mechanical appliances of the observatory, its specula and its lenses, do not appear fitted for a place in the painted bowers of the Muses' (17). But the grander truths which scientific study aims at, the 'elementary principles, and [. . .] the laws which these obey' which inductive science strives to discover – these are deeply poetical, because they connect 'common phenomena with exalted ideas' (18). Hunt clearly conceives of poetry not in its more restricted sense as a literary form but in terms of an idealised spirit, and it is as such that he understands it to be compatible with science. Science is not poetical in its study of dry facts but in its illustration of fundamental natural laws. The poetry of science lies, precisely, in its universal, eternal truths:

> The regulation which disposes the arrangements of matter on this earth, must exist through the celestial spaces, and every planet bears the same relation to every other glittering mass in heaven's o'erarching canopy, as one atom bears to another in the pebble, the medusa, the lion, or the man. An indissoluble bond unites them all, and the grain of sand which lies buried in the depth of one of our primary formations holds, chained to it by these all-pervading forces, the uncounted worlds which, like luminous sand, are sprinkled by the hand of the Creator through the universe. Thus we advance to a conception of the oneness of creation. (Hunt 1848: 313)

Of course, Hunt deliberately uses the imagery and vocabulary of poetic diction in such an evocation of the poetry of science. Though Hunt will not admit it, it is the language of such passages as the one above which aligns them with poetry at least as much as the natural theology expressed in them. Nonetheless, the exalted subjects do matter in a context in which poetry was commonly defined in terms of its content and imbued with religious significance. The passage above can count as a nearly perfect example of poetry if the latter is defined in terms like those used by Reverend Thomas T. Lynch in 1853: 'To unite earthly love and celestial [. . .]; to reconcile Time and Eternity; [. . .] to harmonise our instinctive longings for the definite and the infinite in the ideal Perfect; to read creation as a book of the human heart both plain and mystical and divinely written: such is the office fulfilled by the best-loved poets' (19). Unfortunately for such an exalted conception of poetry, science increasingly appeared to be in a much better position to establish universally and eternally valid truths and to communicate the harmony of nature's laws. Hunt even suggests that the 'high inferences to which the analysis of the subtle agencies of creation leads us, render science, pursued in the spirit of truth, a great system of religious instruction' (1850: 63). In effect, poetry as an aesthetic form is superseded by science, which gives rise to poetic and religious feeling precisely by its evocation of eternally valid truths more effectually than a poem ever could: 'The vigorous mind of that immortal bard who sang "of man's first disobedience," never, in the highest rapture, the holiest trance of poetic conception, dreamed of any natural truths so sublime as those which science has revealed to us' (Hunt 1850: 313).

Fifteen years later, John Tyndall was to conclude his *Heat Considered as a Mode of Motion* (1863) in remarkably similar terms:

> Presented rightly to the mind, the discoveries and generalizations of modern science constitute a poem more sublime than has ever yet been addressed to the intellect and imagination of man. The natural philosopher of to-day may dwell amid conceptions, which beggar those of Milton. (2014 [1863]: 433)

The sublimity of this poetic science, it should be noted again, lies primarily in its realisation of eternal truths, as it teaches us 'to detect everywhere, under its infinite variety of appearances, the same primeval force' (434). Tyndall's lectures on heat are centrally concerned with the first law of thermodynamics, the law of conservation which 'rolls in music through the ages, and all terrestrial energy, – the manifestations of life, as well as the display of phenomena, are but the modulations of its rythm [*sic*]' (434). What necessarily disappears from this analogy of scientist and poet is the act of individual creation as the poetry of science is a poetry of representation rather than of creation. Thus the spirit of poetry (perhaps even its rhythmic form) is preserved within science, but at the cost of creative literature. The understanding of poetry widely held among the Victorians, which privileged mimesis over creation and spirit over language and which rooted the nature of poetry in timeless truths, could hardly hold its own in face of such scientific advances. Conceptions of poetry had to change.

The abstract natural laws established by science thus usurp poetry's claim to convey deeper, eternal truths. A striking example of the consequences of this loss of authority, in particular with reference to the role of religion, can be found in the poem 'Science of Things Outward' (1858), by classical scholar and philosopher Francis William Newman (John Henry's younger brother). Like Hunt,

Newman recognises the religious potential of scientific truths, which lies precisely in their timeless stability:

> The Science of things quantitative gives at once this vast advantage,
> (Peculiarly precious for religion and for practical faith,)
> An absolute confidence of the mind in the certainty of Truth,
> That it is unchangeable, and cannot be tampered with. (ll. 23–6)

Newman recognises science as the new guarantor of eternal, immutable truths, and thus as a most important ally of religion, which depends on a faith in 'absolute Law' (l. 39). Science also combats pagan superstition, insisting on truth, and confronts the mind with thoughts of infinity, revealing 'how measureless is God's world great and small': 'And imagination spreads wide to clasp ideas so mighty, / And clothes with new grandeur the Ruler of the Universe' (ll. 52; 54–5). Imagination, truth, permanent validity, and close relation to the divine – all aspects which Newman's contemporaries commonly associate with poetry – are here assigned to science. While Hunt called this aspect of science its poetry, Newman drives a different point. In contrast to science, Newman aligns poetry with change:

> Whereas those whose culture is from Poetry alone and Fine Art,
> And from History and from Oratory and from practical Politics,
> Are prone to believe in the universal virtue of compromise
> And in the absence of fixed laws and in the anarchy of genius,
> And to explode as *Platitudes* all broad moralities.
> And their virtue is too superficial, based on shifting opinion
> Or on partial expediency, all pliant and unrigid. (ll. 31–7)

Newman's position is intriguing, because it showcases the conditions under which the common claims for an eternal and transcendent validity of poetry became increasingly questionable and difficult to uphold. Whereas science's latest advancements pointed to the uniformity of natural laws, absolute and unvarying over an ever-extending abyss of deep time, a growing interest in history led to an awareness of historical difference and to increasing moral relativism.[16] Once poetry is associated with change, rather than timelessness, however, its previously close allegiance with religion and the divine weakens. Conversely, where divinely ordained eternal truth is called into question, poetry can no longer hope for an access to a deeper mimetic truth. As Lawrence J. Starzyk notes, 'without prior paradigms to repeat, the artist operated without antecedent facsimile. "Making the same" or repeating the Truth by God first spoken became an impossibility' (1992: 23; see also Wasserman 1959: 10–12). For those who maintained that transcendence is part of poetry's essence, an association with change must have meant that poetry betrays itself and becomes, strictly speaking, impossible.

Head and heart – natural versus human truth

In face of the impossibility of truthful mimesis, 'without an external lodestar to guide him on his way', Starzyk goes on to suggest, quoting from Carlyle, 'the artist was necessarily dependent upon his own inner resources, that "imbroglio of Capabilities", those thousand uncomposed faculties and interests' (1992: 23). This turning inward did not necessarily mean, however, that poetry would relinquish its claims to truths, even eternal, universal truths. If poetry soon had to concede to science a more rigorous hold on the truths of nature, it managed to maintain much longer its claims to a deeper knowledge of the human mind and subjectivity, and in particular human sensibility and emotion. A widely accepted commonplace held that poetry 'is rooted rather in the heart than the head', in the words used by Oxford poetry professor John Campbell Shairp in 1881 (3).

In fact, poetry could once more claim superior authority through embodiment, since this adds subjective (poetic) to objective (scientific) knowledge, as Leigh Hunt proposes in his 'Answer to the Question "What is Poetry?"' (1844): 'Poetry begins where matter of fact or of science ceases to be merely such, and to exhibit a further truth: that is to say, the connexion it has with the world of emotion, and its power to produce imaginative pleasure' (1891: 4). In this conception, emotions do not lead to a distortion of facts. By understanding the relation of the object to the emotional state of the human observer a higher truth is recognised, a truth that is more relevant to humans because it centres on the human being and its emotional response. In this sense, the Wordsworthian distinction between scientists representing things as they are and poets representing things as they appear privileges poetic truth as the higher and fuller truth.

Thus, for many Victorians, the universality and permanence of poetic truth was still guaranteed since poetry was assumed to be concerned with what is essential in human nature, with soul and spirit, which are universal and unaffected by change: 'the nearer we get to the springs of poetry, the nearer also do we get to those dormant passions and unformulated thoughts which seem to be potentially common to all men, and which constitute a secret bond of sympathy between man and man' (Holmes 1900: 12). As Isobel Armstrong notes in *Victorian Scrutinies*, the appeal to common bonds and to sympathy were absolutely central to Victorian conceptions of the effect and value of poetry (1972: 9). Sympathy, which depends on the imaginative faculty, was assumed to be the basis of a kind of idealised human community which is all-embracing and timeless and plays an important role for peaceful human cohabitation. As Armstrong explains, '[i]t was assumed that [. . .] poetry would appeal to the sympathies and the affections of the reader, to those impulses which are aroused by the essentially "human" ties and feelings which we can all share' (10). In 'What is Poetry?', Mill exemplifies this logic of eternal poetic truth ratified by sympathy. The truth of the human soul which he assigns to poetry is entirely dependent on the notion of sympathy: 'poetry, which is the delineation of the deeper and more secret workings of the human heart, is interesting only to those to whom it recalls what they have felt, or whose imagination it stirs up to conceive what they could feel, or what they might have been able to feel, had their outward circumstances been different' (2005 [1833]: 564). In this conception, poetry can only speak intelligibly, or at least interestingly, at all if it is true to the bonds of common human nature, presumed to have eternal and universal validity.

In face of an increasing awareness of deep time and its transformative potential in the wake of Lyell and Darwin, rooting poetic timelessness in human nature faces some serious challenges, however. Once the time of the earth no longer coincides with the existence of human beings, poetry can hardly be any longer considered a timeless constant. Moreover, psychologists like Alexander Bain and George Henry Lewes as well as philosopher Herbert Spencer began to draw on evolutionary thinking in order to argue for the essential changeability of human nature and consciousness (Garratt 2010: 33–4, 189). What happens to this conception of poetic truth and value, when the universal validity and permanence of general laws of human nature are being called into question? When the poet can no longer rely on those bonds of sympathy which would turn a subjective expression into a timeless truth? When the individual human being is individualised to the extent that its individuality becomes opaque, unsharable? When change reaches into the depths of the human self, as in the image of the individual which Walter Pater develops in his famous conclusion to *The Renaissance* (1873):

> To such a tremulous wisp constantly re-forming itself on the stream, to a single sharp impression, with a sense in it, a relic more or less fleeting, of such moments gone by, what is real in our life fines itself down. It is with

this movement, with the passage and dissolution of impressions, images, sensations, that analysis leaves off – that continual vanishing away, that strange, perpetual, weaving and unweaving of ourselves. (1998 [1873]: 151–2)

Constant change is ascribed to the very essence of the self, that last stronghold of poetry's claim to eternal truth. This becomes even more explicit in a paragraph following the above in the earlier version of this text, which Pater had published as part of a review on the poetry of William Morris: 'Such thoughts [. . .] bring the image of one washed out beyond the bar in a sea at ebb, losing even his personality, as the elements of which he is composed pass into new combinations. Struggling, as he must, to save himself, it is himself that he loses at every moment' (1868: 311). Especially in contrast with the success of the natural sciences in reducing natural phenomena to general laws, human nature seemed increasingly protean, unpredictable, inexact. In *The Gay Science* (1866), E. S. Dallas writes: 'The most certain thing in human life is uncertainty. We are most struck with its endless changes, and cannot be over-confident that we shall ever reduce these to the unity of science' (2011: 105). The concepts of fragmentation and change, according to Gregory Tate, became central to Victorian psychology, which 'draw[s] attention to the mutability of the mind and to the way in which the ostensibly unified psyche fragments under the pressure of analysis' (2012: 7).[17] Such a focus did not necessarily mean that psychologists no longer believed in general laws of human nature. However, such laws became inaccessible by self-reflection and introspection, the main basis of earlier psychological inquiry (see Faas 1988: 35–8). In *Problems of Life and Mind*, George Henry Lewes writes:

> An inquiry into the genesis of his [the introspective psychologist's] sentiments and opinions would assure him that his mind was the product of a history; and with this assurance he must conclude that, since his history has not been precisely that of other men, their minds cannot be precisely like his own. His consciousness, therefore, cannot be the standard; it is only material for science in so far as it is in general agreement with the consciousness of fellow-men. By striking off what is individual in each, we may get at a conception of what is common to all. (1879: 96–7)

Lewes's general laws are thus pursued on the basis of scientific abstraction, not poetic concreteness. He aims to 'reach the solid data for a general science', which needs a more 'objective' basis than mere self-conscious introspection. This threatens to invalidate poetic approaches to universal truths of human nature, which are intuited from individual experience, rather than distilled from a mass of comparative data, and it should not surprise that Lewes had already some decades earlier called for a literary criticism that is aware of historical change. Great poets, according to Lewes, 'are *not* "mirrors of eternal truth", but mirrors of their age'. With this realisation, 'a new torch is placed in our hand whereby we may penetrate into much of the darkness and obscurity of the past, and also penetrate into certain unexplained regions of Art itself' (1842b: 33). In this conception, poetry no longer reveals eternal truths, but provides evidence for historical change.

A fascinating essay by critic John Addington Symonds, 'On Some Principles of Criticism', first published in 1890, brings some of these issues to a head, as Symonds shows himself torn between the appeal of reliable scientific laws, an endeavour to maintain the fundamental and permanent truth of poetry, and an awareness of the importance of history for a worldview that acknowledges the ubiquity of change. The law of evolution, according to Symonds, 'forces us to dwell on the inevitable conditions of mutability and transformation'. Paradoxically, this law itself 'is of permanent and universal application' (Symonds 1907: 56). Nonetheless, Symonds still strives to maintain the 'abiding relations' (an expression he takes from Goethe) that give worth to art. These 'abiding relations' are not to be found 'in evolution, but in man's soul – his intellectual and moral nature' (57). At this point, he seems to suggest that the evolutionary law which he had previously described as universal does not apply to those 'abiding relations' which he lists as relevant for the judgement of art. At the same time, he values evolution too much to remain quite content with this exception. No judgement, he admits, can ever be final 'for no one is wholly free from partialities, due to the age in which he lives and to the qualities of his specific temperament' (58). Thus, Symonds ultimately turns aesthetic judgement itself into a historical process of canon formation. Only by a historical consensus, 'after many processes of sifting, the cumulative voice of the wise men' – the only ones he deems morally and intellectually positioned to pronounce judgement – decides (58). Turning aesthetic judgement into a historical process, however, subordinates it with a vengeance to an evolutionary law which evokes precisely those spectres of the relativity and changeability of aesthetic judgements which Symonds is trying so hard to ban. In the next section of the essay, declaredly composed three years later, Symonds then partly seems to reconsider his earlier claims by putting even more emphasis on the critic as 'natural historian of art and literature'. As such, the critic

> must study each object in relation to its antecedents and its consequents, must make himself acquainted with the conditions under which the artist grew, the habits of his race, the opinions of his age, his physical and psychological peculiarities. Only after having conscientiously pursued this method, may he proceed to deliver judgments; and these will invariably be qualified by his sense of relativity in art and literature. (60)

Reading like an early version of Fredric Jameson's directive to 'always historicize' (1981: 9), this emphasis on historical relativity of both the production and the reception of works of art seems to leave little room for those abiding relations which Symonds yet cannot quite relinquish.

An awareness of the ubiquity of change, in particular the changing nature of the human mind not only undermined poetry's hold on universal and unchanging laws of human nature as on a par with, or even superior to, science's laws of nature, but posed even more fundamental challenges to poets' confidence in their ability to communicate. As Carol Christ notes, quoting from Pater's conclusion:

> The growing fear of a solipsism in which each mind keeps 'as a solitary prisoner its own dream of a world' poses difficult problems for poetry. If man can know nothing but his own experience, if personality composes a barrier between the self and the world, the very self-consciousness which had been for the Romantics the source of poetry's divine truth became for later poets the burden which limited its significance to incommunicable personal impressions. (1984: 30–1)

If the self is in perpetual flux and if the poet can no longer rely on sympathy based on a common essence of human nature, poetry's truths can hardly hope to strive for universal, permanent validity. Instead of serving as a common bond, binding together all human beings, subjectivity is reframed as the hallmark of solipsistic individuality. Poetry's subjective truths can no longer claim superiority to objective truths because there can be no certainty that subjective impressions are shared, or even shareable. I will be concerned more closely in the next chapter with various reactions to these challenges by the poets themselves, who were looking for answers in formal innovations, in particular by means of those generic experiments in mixing narrative, lyric and dramatic elements which are so characteristic of Victorian poetry. While Christ describes such reactions as an 'attempt [. . .] to objectify the materials of poetry' (1984: 3), I suggest that such genre experimentations can also be understood as ways to encounter and incorporate change into poetry. Where poetry is no longer sure of its access to essential and universally valid truths, neither about nature, nor about the human mind (or soul); where it definitively turns from Aurora's 'essential truths' to those 'relative, comparative and temporal truths' which she denigrates, the terms of its relationship to science have shifted. It no longer contests with science for a higher truth but finds its justification in its own aesthetic and form.

Modern scientific truth versus archaic beautiful illusion

Of course, the position that poetry is rooted in illusion, not truth, indeed that it is antithetical to truth, dates back at least as far as Plato. From this perspective, every attempt to reconcile science and poetry must be futile. As John Henry Newman puts it, poetry 'is always the antagonist to *science*. As science makes progress in any subject matter, poetry recedes from it' (1858: 72). Science's mission, Newman maintains, 'is to destroy ignorance, doubt, surmise, suspense, illusions, fears, deceits', but poetry resides in the mysterious and unknowable: 'It implies that we understand [its objects] to be vast, immeasurable, impenetrable, inscrutable, mysterious; so that at best we are only forming conjectures about them, not conclusions, for the phenomena which they present admit of many explanations, and we cannot know the true one' (72). The essence and aim of poetry is thus not truth and knowledge, but wonder and awe. For Newman, it is precisely this awe that allies poetry once again to religion.[18]

Since science, in the nineteenth century, indubitably made progress in every subject matter, such a view could only lead poets to despair. 'The poetry of earth is fading fast', writes Alaric Alexander Watts in his poem 'Egypt Unvisited. Suggested by Mr. David Roberts's Egyptian Sketches' (1851), because 'Science, with eye of microscopic power, / And disenchanting lamp, from land to land, / With railroad speed continues still to scour, / Till scarce a spot on earth remains unscanned' (ll. 5–8). Railway lines replace lines of verse, scientific scanning of geographical space replaces the scanning of metrical verse. In influential progressivist philosophical positions like that of Auguste Comte, poetry, instead of being timeless, was given a date of expiry. Once science had taken over the present and the future, poetry became a thing of the past, a mastodon unfit to survive in the evolutionary struggle, a victim of progress and modernisation. Judith Plotz's book *Ideas of the Decline of Poetry: A Study in English*

Criticism from 1700 to 1830 (1987) amply attests to the long legacy of this logic. Reverence for the ancient poets came into conflict with the ideal and indeed the perceived reality of progress in knowledge and civilisation, since few found themselves willing to claim that modern poetry was an improvement upon the poetry of the cultural heroes Homer, Virgil, Shakespeare or Milton. Because it seemed to be an exemption from the law of progress, poetry was given no place in a progressive age. In its most drastic manifestation, this position could lead into the kind of anti-progressivism and nostalgic hostility towards science expressed in the poetry of George Barlow, who exclaims in 'Poetry and Science' (1884):

> Give me the days of faith, and not of Science!
>   Give me the days of faith in unseen things!
> The days of self-doubt, not of self-reliance:
>   Days when the rainbow flashed from fairy wings.
>
> Knowledge hath little worth, if dreams are going.
>   Let me watch in the stream the Naiad's hair;
> Or wander forth when balmy winds are blowing
>   Through sunlit groves, and find sweet Daphne there.
>
> To know is well, but not to know is better.
>   'Tis ignorance that makes the child sublime.
> To learn new facts adds fetter unto fetter
>   For all the already weary sons of time. (1902–14a: ll. 37–48)

In Barlow's and John Henry Newman's conception, poetry does not strive for truth but for uncertainty, for a Keatsian negative capability that cherishes wonder and mystery. While Newman in his work explicitly rejects 'so heartless a view of life' as Comte's philosophy of evolutionary stages, and insists on the coexistence of all stages in the all-embracing present of the Catholic Church (1858: 71), Barlow's position is more conventional in associating poetry most closely with the mythical and medieval past and, accordingly, in lamenting its disappearance in an age which was widely understood to be unpoetical. At the beginning of the twentieth century, he concludes:

> The twentieth century's doom's exceeding dismal!
>   It has to march, with stern-browed Truth to lead,
> Towards moonless plains and forest-depths abysmal,
>   Past many a cold, once fairy-haunted, mead.
>   [. . .]

Nothing to break the dreary desolation;
  All secrets probed, all mystery solved at last!
In truth ours is a luckless generation:
  Happier, I think, was almost all the past. (1902–14b: ll. 101–12)

The allegiance of beauty and truth evoked by Keats's ode, is here dissolved. Truth and science have become synonymous, joint antagonists to poetic wonder and beauty.

Notwithstanding Barlow's prevailing pessimism, his apparent willingness to eschew any claims to poetic truth and knowledge, his nostalgic turn to the past and his escapist rejection of the poet's role as unacknowledged legislator of the world are not unrelated to late-Victorian attempts to re-empower poetry in a doctrine of art for art's sake. When the 'standard of merit' for poetry is declared to be 'not the truth, but the poetry' (Garnett 1898: xxxiii) – as it was, in this case, by Richard Garnett, in his introduction to an edition of Coleridge's poems, 1898 – poetry claims a self-sufficiency which refuses to be judged according to extraneous measures. This, crucially, is a self-sufficiency which casts off the referential ties and epistemological concerns which had governed conceptions of poetry throughout the century and instead roots itself firmly in an ontology of form.[19] By 1901, when the newly appointed Oxford Professor of Poetry Andrew C. Bradley titled his inaugural lecture 'Poetry for Poetry's Sake' and argued that a poem's 'poetic worth as a satisfying imaginary experience [. . .] is to be judged entirely from within' (1901: 8), this formal aesthetics had arrived at the centre of the poetical establishment. Becoming a means and an end in itself, poetry retreats from the conflict with science but also turns the question of past or present setting moot. Thus, Pater praises William Morris's medieval and Hellenic poetry precisely for being 'neither a mere reproduction of Greek or medieval life or poetry, nor a disguised reflex of modern sentiment'. Rather '[t]he atmosphere on which its effect depends belongs to no actual form of life or simple form of poetry' (Pater 1868: 300). While fifty years earlier poets and critics had heatedly debated the question of appropriate subjects, Bradley would feel free to dismiss it cavalierly: 'it is surely true that we cannot determine beforehand what subjects are fit for Art, or name any subject on which a good poem might not possibly be written' (1901: 15).[20] Art creates its own realm of transcendent reference, still a truth, but one in and of itself, timeless no longer because it refers to timeless truths, but because it presents a closed self-referential system. If the Aestheticist doctrine freed poetry from its heavy moral fetters and opened exciting new aesthetic possibilities, it also largely surrendered the terrain of material reality, social conditions and the search for knowledge to science and to the novel.

Conclusion – The Lyric Ideal

In terms of the ideal of poetic timelessness, the developments I have traced in this chapter, while by no means linear or universal, combine to suggest a gradual replacement of a previously dominant Aesthetics of Eternal Essence with an emergent Aesthetics of Self-sufficient Form.[21] From this perspective, Dante Gabriel Rossetti introductory sonnet may stand paradigmatically for a broader conceptual shift, in which it is no longer the content, the respective moment as such, that has eternal validity, but it is the poetic *form* which eternalises the moment. Poetry's value is no longer located in its relation to supposedly permanent ontological givens, but in the effects of its own formal intricacies. It is timeless in that it is formally self-referential, and its form, rather than its subject matter, lends it durability. The aestheticist doctrine of art for art's sake, I propose, is propelled by the need to rethink poetry's relation to time. Rooting poetic timelessness in aesthetic form serves to detach poetry from its former commitments to a given set of moral and ontological certainties and thus impregnates it against pervasive perceptions of change. Due to this shift discussions about the proper subjects for poetry could eventually subside towards the end of the century.

Considering that Rossetti chooses the sonnet in particular to express this formal aesthetics, a clarification of my argument in this point seems to be in order. Rossetti's turn to form, I would insist, is not primarily a recourse to a poetic tradition, in the sense of *imitatio* (the imitation of poetic predecessors), in the attempt to contextualise the individual poetic production in a supposedly transhistorical context of poetic forms. This is what Christoph Reinfandt has suggested as the primary role of traditional poetic forms: to connect a poetic utterance to a 'social idiolect' which makes it generally accessible, by tying it to tradition. In his study Reinfandt traces the relationship between form and utterance from the seventeenth century to Modernism. In this context, he reads the preoccupation with and proliferation of forms among Victorian poets as an attempt 'to stabilise subjectivity by means of all culturally available forms' and considers the resulting increasing flexibility and new contextualisation to be an unintended loss (2003: 141; my translation). But his argument can easily be turned on its head. Thus Marion Thain suggests that a pervasive historical awareness has made such a 'timeless' recourse to form impossible by the late nineteenth century. Commenting specifically on the Parnassians' recourse to medieval forms, she stresses their performance of historical difference and calls it 'a dialectics of collision between past and present rather than a quest for an eternal time out of time'. Formal continuity thus marks, rather than obscures, historical difference: 'Far from a retreat into lyric history, it might be seen to engage with concerns about our ability to reach back for continuity with the past, offering instead a kind of deracinated, simultaneous, but not historically transcendent iteration of the past' (Thain 2016: 108). Considering the manifold ways in which Victorian poets took up traditional forms to deliberately highlight historical difference – for example in Clough's use of the hexameter as seen above, in revisionary uses of the sonnet sequence, or in the adaptation of prosopopoeia and monodrama that characterises the dramatic monologue – Thain's argument seems rather more convincing than Reinfandt's. Consequently, the sonnet, for Rossetti, does not per se provide stabilisation in a timeless tradition. Rather, the individual sonnet must meet his high formal expectations, it must in itself provide the justification of its own formal mastery (it must be 'of its own fulness reverent'). As we shall see in the next chapter, the inevitable reference to the historical dimension of the sonnet form in fact stands in some tension to this elevation of formal timelessness.[22]

This shift in the meaning of poetic timelessness is inseparably related to another conceptual shift that progressed in the course of the nineteenth century: the conceptual narrowing of 'poetry' to coincide with 'lyric'. The discussion above testifies to a variety of broader conceptions of poetry, which include and are frequently – as in the case of Arnold – even primarily based on narrative and dramatic forms.[23] The indisputable poetic geniuses of the English language mentioned by Victorian critics are almost invariably Shakespeare (as dramatist, not as the author of the sonnets) and Milton. Nonetheless, Shelley's rejection of story as a possibility for poetry and John Stuart Mill's assertion that lyric poetry is 'more eminently and peculiarly poetry than any other' (1860: 125) prefigure a general nineteenth-century trend in which the lyric became increasingly identified with poetry per se. Thain suggests that 'the growing importance of the lyric genre within poetry is a result of the [. . .] erosion of the importance of poetry within the literary marketplace as a whole. The more poetry was defined in relation to and in opposition with the novel, the more it was equated with lyric as its quintessential form' (2013: 157).

In the light of my discussion in this chapter, I would add the pressures on poetry from the growing authority of science as another factor. The lyric mode abetted a redefinition of poetry's timelessness via a withdrawal into form and into what Emily Harrington calls the 'paradoxically impersonal intimacy' of the lyric (2014: 177). The highly crafted short lyric can claim timelessness in its formal self-sufficiency, since 'the high degree of internal patterning and complexity in these forms offers the potential for an illusion that, at a formal level, no time passes over the course of the poem' (Thain 2016: 62; see also Zymner 2016: 44). For *this* endeavour, at *this* historical moment, rather than for the lyric more generally, Rossetti's 'moment's monument' indeed provides 'the most iconic statement' (Thain 2016: 62). The point here is, then, that the lyric as such neither is nor isn't 'timeless', but rather that what it means for the lyric and for poetry more generally to be 'timeless' changes, as timelessness is differently understood and justified. Furthermore, we can see a sort of division of labour, in which narrative – and the novel in particular – is given the task to represent the increasingly pervasive awareness of time and change, while only the brief moment, which becomes associated with the lyric, offers the hope of an epiphanic glimpse of eternity.[24]

As the discussion above serves to suggest, lyric timelessness could therefore take three different, though overlapping and interrelated forms: a focus on the moment as a privileged, potentially epiphanic nucleus of meaning; interiorisation, that is, betting on the transcendence of the soul; and an elevation of the formal dimension of art as transcendent in itself, that is, art for art's sake. Claims to timelessness are thus variously projected onto what David Wellbery has described as the 'myth of lyric voice', in which the voice itself becomes absolute: 'The lyric is the voice set free ("autonomous"), no longer an instrument, no longer the accident of idiosyncrasy, but rather a unique form of spiritual-corporeal life.' This myth, whose emergence Wellbery locates at the end of the eighteenth century and connects specifically with the early lyric work of Johann Wolfgang Goethe, posits the transcendental voice as 'a medium that vibrates forth from the irreplaceable singularity of the speaking body but at the same time merges with conceptuality (thought) such that the utmost in tonal personality coincides with a universality' (1996: 188). The lyric voice performs the singularity of subjectivity, but by virtue of being a performance, it can be appropriated by anyone. As I will go on to argue in the next chapter, these possibilities for lyric transcendence all arise from what can be described as a basic lyric temporal structure: not 'timelessness', but an iterative performativity.

The notion of the lyric, as it merged with the notion of poetry, became highly idealised even while actual poetic practice was prolific and heterogeneous. Virginia Jackson and Yopie Prins have argued that '[t]he immense social currency of so many verse genres seems to have inspired nineteenth-century thinkers to imagine a transcendent poetic genre ever more abstracted from that currency, a genre ever more a perfect idea rather than an imperfect practice' (2014: 3). Thus, in contrast to the discursive endeavours to retain poetry's hold on transcendence – albeit at the cost of narrowing it down to only one of its modes, namely the lyric – the period's poetical practice was highly diverse and open to experiments which would welcome change, transience and relativity. Indeed, much of Victorian poetic output can be understood as precisely an attempt to merge and mix dramatic, narrative and lyric elements. Turning from poetic ideals to poetic practice in my next chapter, I will pay specific attention to those mixed genres which the Victorians particularly favoured: the dramatic monologue, the verse novel and the poetic sequence.

Notes

1. That religion and poetry were closely intertwined and frequently treated as almost synonymous by Victorians, especially under the influence of Tractarian aesthetics, has been amply demonstrated and discussed by Kirstie Blair (2012: 9–10) and G. B. Tennyson (1981: 40).
2. On the importance of the ephemeral as an experience of modernity and a central motif in both art and science of the long nineteenth century, see Bies, Franzel and Oschmann (2017). They make the valuable point that this focus on the ephemeral can be read as a reworking of pre- and early modern ideas of transience and mortality. The decisive difference lies in replacing concepts of cyclical return with those of an open future.
3. All line references to Arnold's poems in this and subsequent chapters are to the Longman's annotated edition of *The Poems of Matthew Arnold*, edited by Kenneth and Miriam Allott, 2nd edn (1979).
4. In his *The Science of Poetry and the Philosophy of Language*, published in 1910, Maxim Hudson offers an amusingly irate estimate of the inconclusiveness and heterogeneity of Victorian definitions of poetry, showcasing and discussing a broad variety of definitions and proposing, of course, his own more formally minded one.
5. The author's rather surprising conclusion from the necessary disparity of high ideal and actual poetic practise is that 'the highest kind of human poetry', namely poetry which would 'reveal the deeper

mysteries of our being [and] show the great purpose of life as consisting in conquering self, and striving after conjunction with the All-
perfect' has never yet been written ('Poetry in All Things' 1846: 211).
Perhaps a necessary consequence of the almost limitless elevation of the
poetic ideal, such an opinion seems to have been not entirely eccentric.
William Allingham suggests the same some twenty years later in his
article 'On Poetry' (1867: 531). Matthew Arnold's position (on which
I comment below) that the only truly great poetry is that of the ancients
is barely less exigent.

6. All line references to Tennyson's poems in this and subsequent chapters
   are to the Oxford World's Classics edition of *The Major Works*, edited
   by Adam Roberts (2009).
7. See also Moore (2015) who recognises this ambivalence – which she
   calls, quoting from *The Princess*, Tennyson's 'strange diagonal' – in all
   of Tennyson's longer poems, 74–9.
8. Alan Grob suggests that it is the pessimism of Arnold's poetry which
   constitutes its peculiar modernity, that it 'seems modern in its unspar-
   ingly deep and pervasive bleakness' (2002: 17). It is worth emphasising, though, that such pessimism stems, at least in part, from an acute
   perception of the incongruity of modernity with the understanding of
   poetry which Arnold wished to uphold. Thus, Arnold's 'affinity with
   modernity' (Grob 2002: 16) lies partly in the realisation that the possibility for poetry changes under modern conditions and in a rejection of
   such change.
9. Clough's use of rhymed tetrameters for the Spirit while Dipsychus
   speaks mainly in blank verse also turns this into a debate between a
   popular poetry appealing through its use of rhyme and easy rhythms
   and the kind of philosophical poetic meditation associated with a
   Romantic use of blank verse.
10. All line references to *Aurora Leigh* in this and subsequent chapters are
    to the Penguin Classics edition *Aurora Leigh and Other Poems*, edited
    by John Robert Glorney Bolton and Julia Bolton Holloway (1995).
11. For a comparative reading of these two poems, see Blake (1986); Reeds
    (2019).
12. See, for example, the review in the *Athenaeum* ('Aurora Leigh' 1856).
13. It is worth pointing out that several Victorians were both scientists and
    poets, Charles Dodgson (aka Lewis Carroll), James Clerk Maxwell and
    John Tyndall being probably the most famous examples. As a rule, how-
    ever, it seems these activities were largely separated. Charles Dodgson
    and poet and scientific philosopher Constance Naden, for instance,
    published their poetry and their scientific contributions under different
    names, and Maxwell's and Tyndall's poetry remained largely unpub-
    lished during their lifetime. On Maxwell's, Dodgson's and other scien-
    tists' poetry, see also Brown (2013); on Naden, see Stainthorp (2019).
    John Tyndall's poetry has recently been published in a collected edition

with a substantial introduction by Roland and Nikola Kacjson and Daniel Brown (2020).

14. See, for example, Lorraine Daston and Peter Galison's study of the rise of objectivity as an epistemological virtue in the course of the nineteenth century (2007). Their discussion highlights fundamental changes in the way scientific truths were established and understood.

15. On the ways this differentiation is complicated by Victorian scientist's insistence on the importance of imagination for science, see Huber (2019) and Shaw (1987).

16. Ironically, Newman's stark opposition of the stable, eternal laws of science and the changing laws of human history was concurrently undermined from within empirical and relativist traditions within science. See Christopher Herbert's work on Victorian relativity (2001), Peter Garratt's *Victorian Empiricism* (2010) and Philipp Erchinger's discussion of the time-bound understanding of scientific insight developed by prominent Victorian scientists like T. H. Huxley. For Huxley, Erchinger points out, 'people's experience of the present can never be a sufficient basis for the inference of certain knowledge about the future' (2018: 64). On this empiricist basis, all scientific truth is potentially changeable and subject to transformation in time. Indeed, Daston and Galison identify an increasing sense of vertigo among scientists from the mid-nineteenth century onwards. The accelerating pace of scientific discovery increasingly destabilised previously acknowledged truths to the point that 'scientists themselves seemed sickened by the speed of it, and to have lost their bearings and their nerve' (Daston and Galison 2007: 213).

17. See also Garratt, who notes that 'change and adaptation became key determinants in empiricist notions of subjectivity' (2010: 33) and points to the importance of evolutionary thought for Victorian empiricist 'resistance to the metaphysical idea of the mind as a fixed entity or substance' (34).

18. The idea of reserve, that is, the inscrutability of God, lies at the heart of a Tractarian aesthetics which 'insists above all on the religious character of poetry' (Tennyson 1979: 8). See also Blair (2012: 21–50).

19. Of course, the rejection of truth as the basis of poetry found earlier proponents, too, notably Arthur Henry Hallam, who writes, in his review of Tennyson's first poetry collection (1831) that 'a man whose reveries take a reasoning turn, and who is accustomed to measure his ideas by their logical relations rather than the congruity of the sentiment to which they refer, will be apt to mistake the pleasure he has in knowing a thing to be true, for the pleasure he would have in knowing it to be beautiful'. Beauty, not truth, Hallam claims, is poetry's first aim. 'Whenever the mind of the artist suffers itself to be occupied during its periods of creation, by any other predominant motive than the desire of beauty, the result is false in art' (2005: 541). In spite of this early

Aestheticist intervention, however, many Victorians continued to hold with Keats's urn that 'Beauty is truth, truth beauty'.

20. Bradley does qualify this radically 'formalist' position, as he calls it, by insisting that some subjects are more amenable to poetic treatment than others. A subject which 'exists in the general imagination' like the Fall of Man, so he claims, is 'an inchoate poem or the débris of a poem' (1901: 16).

21. Raymond Williams's description of shifting cultural paradigms as dominant, residual and emergent is useful to conceptualise the fluid coexistence of different paradigms and the gradual changes in cultural balance I have traced here (1997).

22. As a further clarification, it might be worth stressing that the Rossettean elevation of formal timelessness which I have called the Aesthetics of Self-sufficient Form is not necessarily correlated with ideas about form in twentieth-century formalist criticism. Rather, it offers a historically conditioned attempt to retain a received poetic value (timelessness) by new means (form, rather than subject matter).

23. In the preface to the second edition of his *Poems* in 1854, Arnold freely admits that in the first preface he 'leaves [. . .] untouched the question, how far, and in what manner, the opinions there expressed respecting the choice of subjects apply to lyric poetry' (1979: 671–2), but he does not endeavour to rectify this omission.

24. Sue Zemka shows that the epiphanic moment also gains importance in nineteenth-century fictional prose: 'Over the course of the nineteenth century, temporal mimesis in fiction increasingly treats momentariness as a sublime precipitate of duration, or as the only meaningful means of accessing duration' (2012: 207). In fact, the moment is already charged with significance in the work of Johann Wolfgang Goethe, the most obvious instances being the role the perfect moment plays in Faust's wager and the conclusion of *Wilhelm Meisters Lehrjahre* (1796). See also Nicholas Rennie's discussion of the importance given to the moment as an element of resistance to the chaos and flux of modernity in the work of Goethe, Leopardi and Nietzsche (2005). My suggestion is that here lurks a logical fallacy: as the lyric is associated with transient glimpses of eternity, the epiphanic moments in novels or dramas can, in turn, appear to be 'lyric' moments.

Chapter 2

Negotiating Time in Victorian Genre Innovations

After Elizabeth Barrett Browning's eponymous heroine Aurora Leigh has dedicated herself to a poetry of the present age, she off-handedly dismisses the question of form:

> What form is best for poems? Let me think
> Of forms less, and the external. Trust the spirit,
> As sovran nature does, to make the form;
> For otherwise we only imprison spirit,
> And not embody. Inward evermore
> To outward, – so in life, and so in art,
> Which still is life.
> [. . .]
> Keep up the fire
> And leave the generous flames to shape themselves. (Book V, ll. 222–5)

Clearly indebted to Romantic ideals of organic form, Aurora evokes the existence of a pure poetic spirit that may not be dissociable from its embodiment (the flames cannot be distinguished from their shape) but that brings forth its own form. Form is here determined by content, body by spirit. However, the quoted passage appears in the middle of a long discussion of the advantages and disadvantages of different poetic genres. Before Aurora defends the possibility of a modern epic (see Chapter 1), she has already dismissed the ballad for moving too quickly to express weighty thoughts, the descriptive poem for being 'too far and indistinct' in its prospects (Book V, l. 91), the pastoral for showing mere pretty 'surface-pictures' (Book V, l. 131) and the sonnet for forcing the poet to 'stand still, nor take a step' (Book V, l. 89). Thus formal considerations clearly do play a role; indeed, they appear to be central to Aurora's struggle to find an adequate expression for her poetic ambition. At the same time, the traditional genres Aurora reviews cannot provide her with an adequate form for her poetic intuition, in part precisely because their temporal structure is not suitable (the ballad moves too fast, the sonnet is too static). She defends the epic and praises the drama, but these, too, do not fit her poetic needs.

Aurora's struggle and her solution, the generically undefined (indefinable?) book with which she finally succeeds, are the same as those of her author. As early as December 1844, in a letter to her friend Mary Russell Mitford, Barrett Browning states her intention 'to write a poem of a new class' (1991: 305), a poem which would be able to address the contemporary in a way that common critical opinion of the day reserved for the prose novel. Nor was she the only one who self-consciously and deliberately set out to explore new genre formations in the attempt to adapt poetry to the modern age. In her discussion of what she calls 'the long narrative poem of modern life', Natasha Moore remarks that Victorian authors often frame such work by evoking the 'pioneer-poet trope' (2015: 2). Though, as she shows, such claims were usually overstated, the sense of treading new generic ground was clearly pervasive.

The verse novel was not the only generic experiment tried by the Victorians. Much more lastingly influential, Victorian poetry helped the dramatic monologue to unprecedented popularity. The simultaneous invention of this genre by Robert Browning and Alfred Tennyson in the early 1830s is both a critical commonplace and a most striking coincidence. Even if Tennyson and Browning were not the first to have ever written dramatic monologues, as some critics suggest with an eye on the poetry of women like Letitia Elizabeth Landon and Felicia Hemans (Armstrong 1993: 325–6; Byron 2003: 46–56; Flint 1997), as well as on the tradition of the monodrama and prosopopoeia (Culler 1975), it still remains true that dramatic monologues proliferated after the successes of Browning's and Tennyson's early work.

If, at least in the English context, the genres of the verse novel and the dramatic monologue are particularly associated with the Victorians, the third genre which interests me in this chapter, the poetic sequence, has a long and venerable history. The sonnet sequence in particular carries not only a specific formal potential, but also a historically determined semantic burden. To write sonnet sequences is to necessarily engage with a powerful literary tradition. Like dramatic monologues and verse novels, poetic sequences were highly popular among the Victorians who found striking ways of adapting the form to their poetic needs and the term 'sonnet sequence' is in fact a Victorian invention. The *OED* lists as its first occurrence the subtitle of Dante Gabriel Rossetti's 1882 publication of *The House of Life*, although the term may have been suggested to Rossetti by Algernon Charles Swinburne's review of the 1870 publication of his poems (which included an earlier version of *The House of Life*), where Swinburne talks of the series as 'this sequence of sonnets' (1870: 554).

What do these different genres have in common? Clearly, each promises an answer to some kind of poetic need of the age. While the affordances of each of these forms (in Caroline Levine's sense of the term; 2015: 6–11) offer different possibilities which each individual text develops in its own, specific way, I argue in this chapter that in choosing and developing these three genres, Victorian poets react to the same kind of pressure: the pressure to readjust poetry in a cultural environment in which its temporal allegiances (to eternity, the unchanging, the universal and the past) have come under threat. This is not to say that this temporal aspect is the only factor in the development of these favourite Victorian genres. The rise of the dramatic monologue for instance has been convincingly explained in relation to the increasing importance of the study of the human mind (Faas 1988), as an attempt 'to objectify the materials of poetry' in reaction against Romantic subjectivity and threatening solipsism (Christ 1975: 3), or as an 'appropriate form for an empiricist and relativist age' (Langbaum 1957: 108). What a focus on the temporal aspects of these forms can add is a broader perspective which sees different Victorian genre developments as interrelated. Although the verse novel, the poetic sequence and the dramatic monologue each have their own generic specificities (and, as with all genres, these specificities have fuzzy boundaries), all of them merge different temporalities – and all of them, I argue, can be understood as complex combinations of narrative, dramatic and lyric temporal elements.[1] Different as these poetic forms may be, they thus share a certain family resemblance, which becomes particularly evident in the significant number of Victorian poems in which they are combined or blurred. Historically, of course, these different poetic genres have been amenable to a variety of poetic needs before and after the nineteenth century. But I argue that an important part of their specific appeal to Victorian poets lies in their potential to reframe and redefine poetry's temporal allegiances. In discussing my examples in this chapter, I thus limit myself to exploring their temporal complexities, paying little attention to other aspects. I therefore take the liberty to address with unabashed brevity texts about which whole books have been (or could be) written. My aim in this chapter is not to present fresh readings of individual works, but rather to offer them as instances for different kinds of solutions for a central temporal puzzle: how to negotiate or redefine poetry's claim to eternity in a cultural context in which change has become a central paradigm.

I need to clarify, though, what I mean in this context by narrative, dramatic and lyric elements. For my discussion, I want to narrow these terms to describe three essentially different though interconnected and rarely isolated temporal possibilities of poetic mediation. I am fully aware that such a use of these terms is reductive in that it does not take into account some of the qualities by which they are usually identified and differentiated. Moreover, to use the terms 'lyric', 'narrative' and 'dramatic' in a purely temporal sense and to restrict them to describe different kinds of mediation, is to understand them neither as genres nor as more broadly conceived modes, but as different forms of temporal organisation on the level of communication. A restriction to temporal aspects is justified, I hope, in avoiding some of the terms' ambiguities and some of the pitfalls of a historically retrospective application. Narrative, for example, is all too often used as a synonym for story or, more recently, for the novel, and we have already seen the problems that arise from a failure to differentiate between poetry and the lyric. Moreover, drama is usually neglected in juxtapositions of the apparent binary of lyric and narrative. For example, where scholars are interested in the different temporalities of genre, they usually juxtapose narrative time to lyric time, or timelessness (see, for example, Culler 2018: 226; Markovits 2017: 8; Morgan 2009: 11). By including dramatic temporality, I hope to avoid some of the problems that arise from such binary models.

I understand these three different kinds of temporality to operate on the level of mediation; that is, they describe different communicative situations of a text. Of these, narrative temporality may be the most familiar. I take it to depend on the implied distance between story time and discourse time and to involve what Frank Kermode (1967) has called the sense of an ending, that is, a retrospective emplotment which results from a specific narrative perspective. Such narrative emplotment involves an active configuration of past events into a causal sequence, an ordering that can only be established retrospectively and produces a specifically narrative sense of time (sequential, causal, retrospective) just as much as it tells a story. I thus take narrative temporality to be, essentially, the temporality of narrative plot, understood with Peter Brooks as 'a structuring operation elicited by, and made necessary by, those meanings that develop through succession and time' (1984: 12). Narrative time is shaped in retrospection, ordering events, summarising some and dwelling on other aspects. It also implies a temporal continuity between the moment of experience and the moment of narration; narrative revisits events that have happened in the past and brings them into a continuous causal sequence. What Brooks's definition highlights and what is worth stressing here is that narrative temporality (just like the other kinds of temporalities, lyric and dramatic) is an *operation*; that is, these generically different temporalities are different ways of actively structuring (rather than merely passively representing) time. Time is not represented as a prior given but emerges from the ordering processes enacted by the text.

Some more detailed elucidation will be necessary to explain my understanding of dramatic and lyric temporality, which follows that of Roman Ingarden (1968). Like narrative, drama usually develops a plot, but generally it does not foreground a representation of the act of emplotment itself, as narrative does. Instead of the retrospective ordering and evaluation of events in narrative temporality, dramatic temporality always unfolds in the present (though its unfolding present may, of course, be set in the past). If narrative time is a double time, in which there is a temporal distance between narrator and character, dramatic time is double in the sense that audience and characters do not share the same *hic et nunc*, as Manfred Pfister has pointed out (2001: 327). But in contrast to narrative time, in which temporal doubleness takes the shape of chronological extension, in dramatic time two times and places overlap, one fictional (dramatic situation) and one real (theatrical situation). In a narrative temporal logic, a narrator recounts events that have happened for the audience, who may share the moment of telling but not of experience. Drama necessarily presents events as they are happening (even in cases in which such events are framed as flashbacks or prolepses): the characters speak from a present that is always in the moment of unfolding, embedded within a continuity of plot and resonating with the memory of previous events and the expectation of future developments (Ingarden 1968: 142). Nonetheless, dramatic temporality introduces a distance between the speaker and the reader or audience: I witness its unfolding present, but I do not share it. However much I might be drawn into the action by pity and sympathy, my part remains that of an audience, removed from the represented world and thus external to its time (Ingarden 1968: 142).[2]

In lyric time, in contrast, speaker and reader ideally coincide. Lyric, too, unfolds in the present, but in contrast to dramatic temporality that present is decontextualised and iterable. In a lyric temporal logic, the speaking voice merges with my own, or addresses myself, in my own (or every other) present. The specific feature of lyric time, as I want to suggest here, can thus not be simply understood as a coinciding of the temporal levels of énonciation and énoncé, as Hempfer proposes (2014: 34–5). I agree with Hempfer (and Culler) that lyric time is performative in the sense that it becomes its own event. But to say that lyric time is 'a special temporality which is the set of all moments at which writing can say "now"', or that it 'is a time of discourse rather than of story' (Culler 2018: 226), is potentially misleading. After all, arguably any direct reader address, indeed, any metafictional moment in a novel, would fit this definition. Rather, this kind of evocation of and in the present becomes specifically lyric, I would insist, because it asks for the reader to appropriate it as *their own* present. As Ingarden puts it, the reader of a lyric poem is invited to merge with the lyric voice, to 'become the lyric speaker *in fictione*' (1968: 139; my translation). Thus, temporally speaking, 'the "now" of the poem and the "now" of the reader coincide fully, as if they were one and the same' (Ingarden 1968: 142; my translation). Moreover, poetic form plays a crucial role in enabling such appropriation. 'Language and form of the poem', Heinz Schlaffer writes, 'are aiming for appropriation by anyone, rather than for individual expression' (2015: 117; my translation). Instead of being an individual spatio-temporally determined and limited utterance, the lyric poem is thus rooted in collectivity and repeatability. It partakes, as Culler argues with Roland Greene, in a ritualistic mode (Culler 2018: 7), stressing repeatable utterance and eventfulness – lyric poems are speech acts that are performative in the sense of being 'both iterable and inaugural, that live by repetition but seek innovating effects' (Culler 2018: 122). Like ritual time, lyric time is a time of heightened significance – it is charged with meaning. However, in contrast to ritual time, lyric time does not necessarily derive its significance from being embedded in a larger network of beliefs and narratives. Lyric time can and often does performatively establish its own significance.

In contrast to Ingarden, however, who ascribes these different temporalities to the novel, the drama and the lyric poem respectively, I understand them to be available as possibilities for shaping literary texts more generally. Thus a text can be more or less lyric, dramatic or narrative in temporal structure, regardless of whether it is a poem, a play or a piece of prose fiction (though, in the specific context of my study, I speak about poems in particular). My approach thus ties the underlying temporal logic of a poem to its speech situation, but it also suggests that, to some degree at least, these different temporal possibilities are interpretive offers, different 'identit[ies] for apprehension' (Greene 1991: 10). Indeed, the fact that Culler can lament a current tendency to read all lyric poetry as dramatic monologues while Virginia Jackson concurrently criticises the prevalence of 'lyric reading', which reads all poetry as lyric, is an apt illustration of such potential possibilities of reading (Culler 2018; Jackson 2005). Instead of criticising either or both approaches to a poem as misguided, however, it seems to me to be more fruitful to understand them as potentialities, with some texts leaning one way or the other, and some profiting from full ambiguity. Thus, if the distinctions I have suggested are to be of any heuristic use, it needs to be kept in mind that I understand these different temporalities as a field of tension in which individual texts situate themselves (or indeed are situated by their readers). They can combine and fuse, or be present as alternative, even contradictory, interpretive possibilities. At the same time, my contestation is that genre differences and developments can be understood and described in terms of various kinds of combinations of these different temporalities.

For the analysis of Victorian poetic experiments in particular, the value of this terminological framework is threefold: first of all, the fundamental temporal structure of mediation I identify as lyric can be seen to provide the condition for all three venues which are exploited to claim lyric transcendence as I have outlined them in the previous chapter. It affords interiorisation by making its emotional signatures available in reiteration; in its performative eventfulness it offers itself as a moment charged with meaning; its ritualistic form makes it self-sufficient in its iterability. Rather than promoting lyric transcendence, however, the Victorian mixed genres often serve to call it into question. Secondly, my terminological framework allows me to untangle and address the underlying temporal assumptions that arise directly from genre designations like dramatic monologue, novel in verse and poetic (or lyric) sequence. My argument is that the potential for temporal complexity of these mixed genres constituted one of their strongest appeals for Victorian poets who would or could no longer rely on the validity of an Aesthetics of Eternal Essence. Finally, the terminological structure I have suggested also enables me to address poetry as involving a combination of and sometimes a tension between narrative, dramatic and lyric temporalities without implying a fall from poetical grace. My terminology is thus meant to resist common equations of poetry with lyric, narrative (and fiction) with the novel and the dramatic with the play. Finally, the distinction between narrative, dramatic and lyric kinds of mediation I employ in this chapter will return as one cornerstone of the conceptual framework for addressing poetic temporality which I develop more fully in Chapter 5.

Beyond a 'Moment's Monument' – The Poetic Sequence

The popularity of sonnets among the Victorians has been noted by recent critics, who draw attention to the 'sonnettomania' which pervades the nineteenth century, culminating in its last two decades. Natalie Houston is doubtlessly correct in reminding us that '[m]ost Victorian sonnets were not published in sequences' (2003: 148), but it is in their sequences that Victorian poets most explicitly engage with and depart from the sonnet tradition. Indeed, Alison Chapman maintains that 'the revival of the sonnet sequence' was '[a]rguably the most significant contribution of the Victorians to the sonnet renaissance' (2002: 105).

The central contention I want to put forward is that the form of the poetic sequence offered Victorian poets a viable solution for their time-troubles. It allows them to have their cake and eat it. They tentatively continue to invest in permanence and eternal truth, thus upholding ideals of poetic timelessness rooted in an Aesthetics of Eternal Essence, but do so by pitching everything on the specific temporal effect of an appropriable lyric voice. At the same time they incorporate and acknowledge change, narrative trajectory, relativity and the Paterian isolation of the individual subject 'keeping as a solitary prisoner its own dream of a world' (Pater 1998 [1873]: 151). In other words, poetic sequences allow for multiple combinations of lyric, narrative and dramatic temporalities and can simultaneously shape different, even contradictory temporal constellations.

Temporal complexity is an inherent formal potential of the poetic sequence. Addressing the affordances of its form, Janine Rogers has concisely described the poetic sequence as 'a whole constructed from distinct parts, each one of which has its own individual status and yet simultaneously contributes to the larger entity' (2015: 88). Its 'integrity [. . .] is tenuous – it might first appear to be indivisible, a unit, but it is easily broken down, as poems are often read in isolation'. Furthermore, she remarks, 'the poetic sequence, as a poem of poems, puts pressure on the materiality of poetry; as a composite object, it emphasizes the composite nature of poems generally' (88). The poetic sequence foregrounds the play of contradictory elements which are at least subliminally present in all poems and provides an ideal site for a renegotiation of what poetry can do and mean. In the dialectical play between individual poem and its place in the sequence, between the specific poetic moment and the accumulative repetition arising from their succession, between fragmentation and continuity, the sequence inevitably brings different temporalities into dialogue (or conflict). The isolable, individual poem can mark a specific moment, or be uttered in a gnomic mode of iterable assertion. Connected in a sequence, however, such specific moments are always put into a dynamic relation of repetition with a difference. While in a sequence individual parts do not necessarily follow directly from and build upon each other, simple accumulation already involves a sense of time at least on the level of reader experience, if not always in terms of content. Moreover, particularly in the case of sonnet sequences, the form inevitably carries its own history with it and thus always invokes an intertextual temporal depth. The rich history of a lyric form such as the sonnet, as Marion Thain has recognised, allows the poetic voice to be 'highly individual' and yet to 'speak from a historically collective position that acknowledges a lyric community with which the poet inevitably writes' (2016: 185). For all its construction of individual subjectivity, the sonnet thus always, formally, speaks with a collective voice.

The year 1850 was an important one for the Victorian poetic sequence, seeing the publication of two poems with lasting influence: Alfred Tennyson's *In Memoriam A.H.H. OBIIT MDCCCXXXIII* and Elizabeth Barrett Browning's *Sonnets from the Portuguese*, the first an elegiac poem, mourning the death of a beloved friend, the other a courtship sequence culminating in marital bliss. Both are 'Post-Petrarchan' (to use Greene's term) in that they inscribe themselves into a tradition of Petrarchan sequences with which they enter into dialogue. This is perhaps more obvious with regard to *Sonnets from the Portuguese*, which more closely engages with its Petrarchan heritage, in form, topic and tropes, and indeed poses as a translation of a non-existent Portuguese example of the Renaissance tradition. Yet critics have also remarked upon the structural similarity of the *In Memoriam* stanza with the quatrain of the Petrarchan sonnet and have pointed out Tennyson's indebtedness to the male-to-male erotic of Shakespeare's sonnets (Campbell 2011: 208; Zuckermann 1971).

Indeed, in its handling of time, *In Memoriam* shares much with the Petrarchan model. Greene identifies Petrarch's central temporal strategy as what he calls a retrospective topos, confronting a *then* and a *now*. The insistent repetition of this temporal structure, Greene explains, 'confers a sense of temporal movement on the entire lyric sequence' (1991: 49). This sense of temporal movement depends on the fixity of its limits, with the first sight of Laura and the speaker's anticipated death as ultimate boundaries, within which there can be a sense of accumulating past and moving present (52). In the *Canzoniere*, this process does not rely on a logic of plot development, 'but on the sheer additive force of the *then-now* poems, each trailing an illusory thread of retrospection behind it' (49). While certain events do structure the development of the sequence (like Laura's death), and some of the poems are self-dating, most of the poems within the sequence could easily change place. *In Memoriam* is similarly framed by two ultimate temporal limits within which the poem progresses, or rather accumulates: the death of the loved one and the anticipated reunion in afterlife. Along the same lines as the *Canzoniere*, the temporal process of Tennyson's elegy is anchored by sparse calendrical references (three Christmases, the passing seasons, the anniversary of Arthur Henry Hallam's death. . .), but it is primarily the sheer number of the individual sections that produces an effect of passing time and lasting grief. Moreover, Tennyson emphasises the temporal trajectory of his sequence by frequently referring back to, contradicting or adjusting the lyric statements of earlier poems. He does so as early as section XVI, which interrogates sections XI and XV:

> What words are these have fall'n from me?
> Can calm despair and wild unrest
> Be tenants of a single breast,
> Or sorrow such a changeling be? (ll. 1–4)

Directly addressing the contradictions between individual previous sections, these lines emphasise a dramatic reading that sees the previous parts of the poem not as isolated lyric expressions, but as (seemingly incompatible) psychological stages, aspects of a specific mind in grief. Retrospectively, the temporal relationship between the previous sections is emphasised, as they emerge as successive states of mind through which the speaker has passed. Instead of so many offers for ritualistic re-utterance, the previous lyrics become interpretable as facets of a fictional character. These retrospective comparisons do scarcely constitute a narrative, however, because they do not develop the kind of linear, causal connectivity characterising acts of narrative emplotment. They recall but do not recount the previous moments. Indeed, the speaker at this point rejects the possibility of narrative control, not only rhetorically by casting the whole section as a series of questions, but also explicitly: 'fancy fuses old and new, / And flashes into false and true, / And mingles all without a plan' (Section XVI, ll. 14–16).

Thus, most of the individual sections of the poem can stand alone as lyric evocations of powerful emotion, performatively appropriable into any present and thus banking on the ritualistic aspect of the lyric in order to lend their statements transindividual validity. But in the accumulation of sections, in the movement from one to the other and in their shifts in moods, a dramatic structure is established. If we are able to ritualistically inhabit the present of the individual lyric moment, we become spectators of a dramatic development in watching the speaker shift his stance from one section to the next, even to the point of direct contradiction. In following the speaker's argument, he is individualised in a dramatic process which turns him into a character, rather than a universal lyric 'I'. The reiterable lyric present is turned into a specific moment, its eventfulness becomes an aspect and a stage in the development of a character. The lyric temporality of performative actuation is not destroyed by such an extension into the dramatic, but held in abeyance as a potentiality of the individual section.

Meanwhile, the proem to the poem establishes a narrative framework. The speaker of the proem looks back to the sequence as 'these wild and wandering cries, / Confusions of a wasted youth' (ll. 41–2). He thus implies a retrospective distance and frames the poem as a sort of *Bildungsroman* plot of youthful confusion overcome by mature faith. Thus, the individual sections emerge as stages of a psychological development whose end point (recovery and redemption) is already implied by retrospective assessment. The sections constitute events in a plot in which grief is overcome and faith is renewed. If this narrative temporality were to take precedence, its retrospective perspective would turn the sequence into an ordered series, in which all sections were brought into a relation of causal necessity. However, the poem lyrically resists such a strict emplotment, and many of the sections could take different places in the sequence.

An example might be in order to illustrate this simultaneous presence of lyric, dramatic and narrative possibilities. For this, I turn to one of the most frequently discussed sections of the poem, which I quote in its entirety:

LIV
Oh yet we trust that somehow good
Will be the final goal of ill,
To pangs of nature, sins of will,
Defects of doubt, and taints of blood;

That nothing walks with aimless feet;
That not one life shall be destroy'd,
Or cast as rubbish to the void,
When God hath made the pile complete;

That not a worm is cloven in vain;
That not a moth with vain desire
Is shrivell'd in a fruitless fire,
Or but subserves another's gain.

Behold, we know not anything;
I can but trust that good shall fall
At last—far off—at last, to all,
And every winter change to spring.

So runs my dream: but what am I?
An infant crying in the night:
An infant crying for the light:
And with no language but a cry.

This powerful example of lyric temporality calls for re-utterance and is performative in several senses. Its numerous phonetic, morphologic and syntactic repetitions turn it into a chant that is compelling in itself, even beyond its semantic content. It demands to be given voice, to be appropriated into the reader's present, in particular through its self-referential emphasis on language as a desperate cry. Its introductory inclusive gesture, 'Oh yet we trust' (l. 1), by using the plural pronoun further claims a ritualist communal voice. Speaking both to and for us, the section's main gesture is gnomic, offering both its trust and its doubt as, in principle, available to any subject position. This gesture is particularly powerful because the poem performatively produces the doubt it voices. Setting out from a statement of trust, it proceeds in the next two stanzas to rephrase this trust in ways which make it ever more untenable. Once the initial trust that good will eventually come of all ill is rephrased in terms of the extreme claim that not even a single worm or moth ever dies in vain, it is hardly tenable. The imperative 'Behold' (l. 13) both emphasises the performative lyric present and marks a double point of rupture. It calls for a reassessment of the argument, leading to the acknowledgement that 'we know not anything' (l. 13), but it also drives a wedge between the speaking subject and the community for which the poem had originally spoken confidently. The trust can thus only be reiterated as the trust of an individual, much more haltingly and with qualifications: 'At last – far off – at last' (l. 15). The final image offered in this stanza is moreover much less hopeful than the initial trust. After all, the seasons are cyclical, with winter eventually following spring again just as inevitably. The image of the seasons thus can at best suggest a balance between good and evil, but not confirm good as the final end of all. In the final stanza, even this trust threatens to dissolve into a mere dream and the confident voice of the communal plural we encountered in the first stanza disintegrates into the inarticulate cry of an isolated infant. The point is, though, that the section not only voices its doubt, but develops it. The section itself *is* this cry, highly articulate indeed, albeit painfully inadequate to provide the light and assurance it yearns for.

Read not in isolation as a lyric utterance, however, but in its context in the sequence, section LIV becomes part of both a dramatic and a narrative process. The doubt that is expressed in section LIV is further developed in the following two sections culminating in the famous outcry of section LVI:

> O life as futile, then, as frail!
> O for thy voice to soothe and bless!
> What hope of answer, or redress?
> Behind the veil, behind the veil. (ll. 25–8)

Together, these three sections provide a powerful lyric moment in the sequence, evident also in the frequency with which critics have turned to them. In terms of the sequence's dramatic and narrative development, however, it is precisely their lyric intensity which leads to an impasse. For individual poems, the emotional intensity of these lyrics and their gesture of language's failure is sustainable, because lyric temporality asks only for repetition, not for continuance. The lyric can thus performatively posit the breakdown of language and meaning without self-contradiction and without withdrawing the grounds on which its own existence is based. But both a dramatic and a narrative process develop sequentially and thus depend on a continuing

belief in the possibilities of verbal expression. The next two sections of
In Memoriam, then, do primarily dramatic and narrative work, recu-
perating the previous moments of lyric intensity into a climax of plot
development:

> Peace; come away: the song of woe
> Is after all an earthly song:
> Peace; come away: we do him wrong
> To sing so wildly: let us go.
>
> Come; let us go: your cheeks are pale;
> But half my life I leave behind:
> Methinks my friend is richly shrined;
> But I shall pass; my work will fail. (LVII, ll. 1–8)

With this gesture of (self-?)address readers turn from participants
in a ritualistic moment into spectators of a dramatic development.
The gnomic claims of the lyric despondency of the previous sections,
which made further articulation seem impossible in the face of the
immensity of doubt, are here mitigated, by being no longer assigned
to the universal, ritualistic lyric 'I', but to a specific character. His
failure is the failure of an individual from whom I, as reader, can
distance myself.

The next section then, incorporates this dramatic process insistently into a narrative retrospection:

> In those sad words I took farewell:
> [. . .]
> The high Muse answer'd: 'Wherefore grieve
> Thy brethren with a fruitless tear?
> Abide a little longer here,
> And thou shalt take a nobler leave.' (LVIII, ll. 1, 9–12)

One of the few occasions of past tense in *In Memoriam*, this section
offers a way out of the impasse reached in both lyric and dramatic
terms in the previous sections, by introducing a retrospective perspective that can accommodate despair as a difficulty overcome, without having to offer solutions to the problems the previous sections
raised. Moreover, the narrative acts as a double promise because the
prophetic words of the Muse are ratified by the retrospective point
of view of the narrative voice. Opening a distance between narrated
time and time of narration, the past tense suggests that the Muse's
prophecy has already come true from the retrospective point of view

of the narrator. This allows the poem to account for the otherwise seeming incongruity of its apostrophe to sorrow in the next section (LIX), with which the sequence returns to an apostrophic lyric temporality (which Culler defined as 'a special temporality which is the set of all moments at which writing can say "now"' (2018: 226)), and even stresses continuity as if the previous crisis had never happened ('My centred passion cannot move', l. 9). Again, section LIX works independently as a lyric expression of a sorrow that is always present but not always obvious. Read in its dramatic context, it expresses one further aspect of the speaker-character's specific grief (especially since it rephrases and reconsiders a similar address to sorrow from section III). But, in its immediate context, the section can also be read narratively, retrospectively constituting the next step in a psychological process, resignation following climactic doubt.

The retrospective narrative turn of section LVIII cannot undermine the ritualistic power of lyric presentification of the previous sections, however. Such ritualistic power is still effective in each fresh reading, and the subsequent narrative incorporation offers no solution or consolation to the doubts that are raised. When the poem retrospectively returns to the desperate outcry of section LIV towards its hopeful ending, it can only reiterate trust (a trust which section LIV still effectively questions) by calling on the intuition of faith as something felt in the heart, not known or understood. The narrative retrospection in which this assurance is offered only makes it available to this particular speaker-character, in this particular situation, however, but not necessarily to the reader.

I have picked out just one of the many complex interactions between dramatic, narrative and lyric temporalities that could be traced in *In Memoriam*, in order to give more substance to my basic claim that such combinations allow Victorian poets to juggle contradictory exigencies: on the one hand, the desire to address and express some universal and eternal truth; and on the other, the suspicion that everything is subject to change, that even 'The hills are shadows, and they flow / From form to form, and nothing stands' (CXXIII, ll. 5–6) and that the individual self is too isolated and too unstable to offer more than a solipsistic version of truth at best: 'But in my spirit will I dwell, / And dream my dream, and hold it true' (CXXIII, ll. 9–10). Its simultaneous investment in lyric, dramatic and narrative processes allows *In Memoriam* to offer its many gnomic utterances as truths, while at the same time qualifying them by making them assignable to a specific (autobiographical) character and a specific narrative situation and trajectory, with little epic pretensions. Balancing narrative, dramatic and lyric expression, *In Memoriam* thus manages to combine a story of personal grief and recovered peace and faith with powerful statements of dejection and doubt. The answers proposed in the narrative and dramatic process of the poem (the larger lay) can be accepted, but do not have to be. They are not presented as ultimate truths (which might be scorned), but merely as possible truths. The poem thus affords various kinds of reading: readers can lyrically appropriate isolable sections, get a sense of the unfolding of a complex speaker-character, or follow a (supposedly autobiographical) narrative trajectory, or indeed do all of this at the same time. It is this versatility and temporal complexity, I argue, which made the form of the poetic sequence particularly attractive to Victorian poets, and a deliberate exploitation of this formal affordance is notable in many Victorian poetic sequences.

Barrett Browning's *Sonnets from the Portuguese*, for example, similarly merge lyric, narrative and dramatic temporalities. More explicitly than Tennyson, Barrett Browning draws on a Petrarchan sonnet tradition while reversing the gender of speaker and addressee. The extent to which this gesture proves empowering or debilitating has been controversially discussed by critics over the last few decades (see, for example, Billone 2007: 63–80; Phelan 2005: 34–60; van Remoortel 2011: 90–6). However, I am more interested here in the various narrative, dramatic and lyric gestures the sequence performs. While its temporal complexity might not always have been the prime appeal of the sonnet sequence over the long history of the form, I would like to suggest that the way Barrett Browning exploited its temporal potential provided an influential model which helped boost the form's subsequent popularity among the Victorians.

Compared with *In Memoriam*, the *Sonnets* are much more tightly plotted. Only a few of the individual forty-four poems could exchange places, and many of the sonnets are directly connected by conjunctions or verbal references, which suggest a continuation of argument. Indeed, this strong interconnection of the individual poems makes it harder to dissociate them easily from their context within the plot of the poem, with some notable exceptions like the frequently anthologised sonnet XLIII ('How do I love thee? Let me count the ways'). Moreover, if *In Memoriam* throughout puts emphasis on the continuity of grief, in spite of the gradual development it traces, the *Sonnets* display a life-changing transformation. The speaker at the end of the *Sonnets*, after having accepted and come to rely on love, is a different person from the speaker at the beginning, who is full of doubt and sorrow and does not allow herself to trust in love. The sequence thus centres on a dramatic process. As readers, we are witnesses to the gradually unfolding story of a strengthening love in which individual sonnets mark decisive steps. This dramatic aspect is further strengthened by the type of address that predominates in the poems, as a large majority directly addresses the lover. In most cases, however, this address is not a lyric apostrophe, that is, it does not seek to verbally bridge a distance that is implied to be unbridgeable. Instead, the sequence frequently suggests the actual presence and reaction of an auditor. To give but one of the most obvious examples, sonnet XXXIII begins with 'Yes, call me by my pet name!' (l. 1), indicating a previous speech act by the addressee. Rather than working as a lyric apostrophe which, as Culler has argued, 'can in fact be read as an act of radical interiorization and solipsism' (1981: 146), the kind of address in most of the sonnets is dramatic in the sense that it suggests an underlying dialogue (though, as in the dramatic monologues to which I will turn later, one part of the dialogue is merely implied by the speech of the other). Moreover, the accumulation of sonnets serves to flesh out both speaker and addressee as specific characters with their specific pasts and present situation, instead of universal lyric pronouns. Both speaker and addressee, for example, are clearly identified as published poets, emphasising not only a dramatic, but indeed an autobiographical dimension.

The dramatic plot of the poem becomes particularly evident and compelling, however, because it is continually recuperated into a narrative retrospection, which summarises, orders and gives a sense of teleological direction. Providing the speakers with a past already establishes a tenuous narrative continuity. More explicitly, sonnet XXVII looks back on the struggle of the earlier sonnets from a distance 'As one who stands in dewless asphodel, / Looks backward on the tedious time he had / In the upper life' (ll. 10–12), to conclude 'That Love, as strong as Death, retrieves as well' (l. 14). Even more strongly suggestive of a retrospective construction of linearity is sonnet XXXVIII. One of the few sonnets which forgo direct address for a more obviously narrative perspective, the poem retraces the speaker's emotional development in response to the lover's first kisses, the first on her hand, the second on her brow, the third on her lips, sealing their love. Instead of leaving the reconstruction of the dramatic plot to the reader, such narrative gestures integrate the earlier sonnets into a retrospection that establishes a clear narrative progression in causal connection. Moreover, as was the case with *In Memoriam*'s prologue, the sequence's initial sonnet is retrospective and already suggests the trajectory that the rest of the sequence realises, as the 'mystic Shape' (Barrett Browning 1850: l. 10) which, in a gesture of disquieting violence, draws the speaker 'backwards by the hair' (l. 11) is already identified as 'Not Death, but Love' (l. 14).

The emphasis I have laid on the dramatic and narrative aspects of the *Sonnets* should not detract from the fact that they also contain very powerful lyric poems. The sequence unfolds in a series of iterable lyric moments. But by their insistent integration into a dramatic development and a narrative retrospection, the individual lyric moments are recuperated into a continuity that is no longer performative and universal, but specific and singular, part of an individualised character's experience. Thus, the sequence packages its lyric events in a dramatic process and a narrative construction which, once more, offer alternative ways of reading: as a lyric love poem, as the dramatic development of a character in a given situation or as the (autobiographical) narrative of a specific courtship. This might suggestively be related back to the gender issues that have been so much at the focus of critical discussions of this sequence, by arguing that narrative and dramatic gestures qualify the vatic lyric authority which may have been difficult to maintain as a woman poet (though women were generally allowed some authority on questions of love). However, the fact that similar combinations of dramatic, narrative and lyric aspects characterise so much of Victorian poetry seems to point to a broader unsettling of lyric authority, beyond gender concerns. Once they are narratively or dramatically embedded, lyric utterances are qualified as specific rather than universal. And yet, because they can often be easily dissociated from their immediate context, they may retain much of their lyric authority at the same time. Lyric, narrative and dramatic temporalities are, as often as not, simultaneously at work in the same text passage and offer different potentialities of reading.

Discussing the *Sonnets from the Portuguese*, Dorothy Mermin has called their combination of what she refers to as lyric and novelistic elements 'the most important generic innovation of the Victorian age' (1993: 65). Many of the Victorian poetic sequences that were to follow *In Memoriam* and *Sonnets from the Portuguese* decidedly develop a storyline, either narratively (for example George Eliot's short sequence *Brother and Sister* (1869)) or dramatically (for example Augusta Webster's incomplete *Mother and Daughter* (1895) or Christina Rossetti's *Monna Innominata* (1881)), or both, sometimes even to the point of sidelining the lyric independence of the individual sonnet or section. In this sense, the introductory sonnet of Dante Gabriel Rossetti's sonnet sequence *The House of Life* (1881) states what has, indeed, become a prominent practice in the aesthetics of the sonnet: 'The sonnet is a moment's monument'. Developing narratively or dramatically, many Victorian poetic sequences use their individual sections or sonnets as moments of charged lyric intricacy that are integrated as important steps in a continually unfolding story. The importance they are given in this narrative or dramatic process can provide circumstantial justification for their lyric relevance, which might otherwise no longer be taken for granted. The sonnets thus become monuments to moments indeed, since the sequence in which they are embedded involves both dramatic specificity and narrative retrospection. At the same time, lyric iterability, lyric universality and the lyric's formal intricacy all are focused on the individual moment, a highly charged, but specific and per definition ephemeral small increment of time. Veronica Alfano suggests that 'Victorian praise of brevity is frequently connected to a desire for textual purification', reaching for an idealised and lyric concept of pure poetry that hopes to establish in 'monuments to ecstatic instants' a 'mood of static timelessness [. . .] in order to safeguard or recover or remember evanescent loveliness' (2017: 11).[3] Thus the transient moment could become not eternity's opposite, but its realisation and guarantee. In the face of a world which has lost its certainties, in which change is the only constant and in which faith in religious guarantees of eternity is waning, paradoxically, transcendence may appear to be achievable in the momentary.

I have already suggested in the previous chapter that Rossetti's introductory sonnet reinterprets poetry's transcendent claims by rooting them in form, instead of content. By its focus on the moment, however, the introductory sonnet suggests a tension between the specific and individual relevance of the moment on the one hand and art's endeavour to enshrine it and give it universal import on the other. To imagine the sonnet as a moment's monument is to link it to a particular instance of time, to which only art can grant eternity. The tension between the octet and the sestet of Rossetti's sonnet strikingly expresses this contradictory endeavour, which we have also seen to be at play within the other poetic sequences I have discussed above. If the octet invokes the sonnet as a monument to a specific moment, the sestet calls the sonnet a coin, that is, a generic, interchangeable token, valuable not because of its individuality, but because of its role in a symbolic system of exchange, emptied of the specific point of reference which is necessary to the monument.

Rossetti's introductory sonnet is particularly intriguing, because it seems to fit sequences like the ones I have discussed above – sequences in which the individual sonnets refer to specific moments that are given relevance in the context of a narrative or dramatic development – better than his own. Indeed, many of the 102 sonnets of *The House of Life* (counting the repressed 'Nuptial Sleep') refer less to a specific moment than to a temporal process, or a general state; others are argumentative or, like the Willowwood group, they develop little allegorical narratives; others again refer to moments that have never happened, chances that have been missed. Thus, not only do 'the individual sonnets persistently *fail* in their effort to become eternal moments', as Jennifer Wagner has argued, since the 'sequence as a form thematizes the loss of every "intense" or "special moment" in progressive temporality' (1996: 141; original emphasis), but many of the sonnets never even attempt to monumentalise a moment at all. Indeed, Alison Chapman quotes from a note Rossetti added to the manuscript of *The House of Life* held in the Fitzwilliam Museum, in which the poet asserts: 'these emotional poems are in no sense "occasional". [. . .] Whether the recorded moment exist [*sic*] in the region of fact or of thought is a question indifferent to the Muse, so long as her touch can quicken it' (Chapman 2002: 104). In spite of the tendency of earlier critics to impose an autobiographical narrative on the work,[4] *The House of Life* decidedly resists the dominant trend towards story which marks so many Victorian poetic sequences. Accordingly, John Holmes describes Rossetti's innovations in the following terms:

> Firstly, he pared down the narrative element which had characterised the earlier revivals, in doing so decreasing both the text's and the reader's dependence on structural linearity. In Rossetti's sequence the movement from one sonnet to another, the relationship between them and their relative importance is left much more in the hands of the reader. Secondly, Rossetti extended the thematic breadth of the form, which in English had tended to prioritise either sexual love or religion rather than according equal centrality to both. [. . .] Thirdly [. . .] *The House of Life* is not limited, as *Sappho to Phaon*, *Sonnets from the Portuguese* and *Modern Love* largely are, to the fictionalisation of the poet's own experience. Instead it invites the reader to trace aspects of his/her own self-perceptions in the sequence as it develops. (Holmes 2005: 3)

While Rossetti thus popularises the term 'sonnet sequence' with his subtitle and while he provides a programmatic sonnet on the sonnet with his proem, *The House of Life* resists the broader trend towards story and character development, towards narrative and dramatic modes. Rather than resolving the tensions that arise from claims for poetry's transcendence by containing lyric appeal within the limits of narrative and dramatic specificity, Rossetti's sequence displays and probes precisely these tensions.

It does so not only by refusing to tell a story, but also by consistently unsettling its subject positions. Neither speaker nor addressee remain stable throughout the sequence. Even among the sonnets of the first section of the poem ('Youth and Change'), which is often considered to be the more coherent part, there are sonnets which switch to third or second person (like 'VIa: Nuptial Sleep', 'XIII: Youth's Antiphony', 'XXI: Love-Sweetness', 'XLVI: Parted Love') while the addressee changes even more frequently. In the second part of the sequence, the positions of speaker and addressee become still more fluid and even contradictory. Consider, for example, the three alternative imperatives offered in the group 'The Choice': 'Eat thou and drink; to-morrow thou shalt die' (LXXI, l. 1); 'Watch thou and fear; to-morrow thou shalt die' (LXXII, l. 1); 'Think thou and act; to-morrow thou shalt die' (LXXIII, l. 1). The parallel rhetorical structure of these poems establishes a similar communicative situation, but clearly speaker, and perhaps also addressee must be different for each, since their respective calls to hedonism, repentance and action are incompatible. While it is conceivable to read them as three different positions taken up by the same speaker successively, in any case the sonnets offer the reader different subject positions to inhabit. Indeed, elsewhere in the sequence, like in the sonnet 'Lost Days', it becomes clear that any such subject position is provisional and subject to change over time, as the speaker imagines himself meeting his lost days after death: 'Each one a murdered self, with low last breath. / 'I am thyself, – what hast thou done to me?' / 'And I – and I – thyself,' (lo! each one saith,)' (LXXXVI, ll. 11–13). Moreover, the sonnet 'He and I' suggests that such multiple, incompatible selves do not merely follow each other in time, one replacing the other, but coincide: 'Even in my place he weeps. Even I, not he' (XCVIII, l. 14). Subject positions and personal pronouns in *The House of Life* are thus continually in flux. David Riede has argued that therewith Rossetti 'has masterfully recorded a personal sense of the fragmentation of personality widespread at a time when people began to find themselves without a unifying idea of God, of a traditional stable society, or of anything else' (1992: 141–2). However, I would argue that the sequence goes beyond showing a fragmented self. Rather than adding up to a sense of character, even a fragmented one, each sonnet in the sequence challenges its readers to revaluate its communicative situation. By resisting appropriations into coherent character constellations, the accumulation of sonnets in the sequence retains the lyric universality, or rather versatility, of speaker and addressee. At the same time, however, precisely because the lyric subject positions *The House of Life* offers are so various and provisional, even incompatible, the sequence resists a vatic stance. While nearly all of its sonnets can be voiced lyrically and can thus be ritually appropriated by the reader, by making so many and so various offers for lyric appropriation, the sequence avoids monolithic truth claims. Instead, as Jerome McGann has argued, in Rossetti's work '[e]very vantage point is provisional, relativity is the permanent rule of order' (2000: 43).[5] If the narrative and dramatic sequences discussed above contextualise and relativise their lyric stance by a process of serialisation, developing the specifics of story and character even while retaining lyric force for their individual, potentially isolatable sections, Rossetti's sequence qualifies lyric claims by accumulative contradiction.

Therewith, Rossetti's example opens further ways of developing the poetic sequence to later Victorians, beyond narrative and dramatic solutions. Acknowledging Rossetti's influence, John Holmes even provocatively speaks of the generation of (male) sonneteers that succeeded the publication of *The House of Life* as 'sons of Gabriel' (2005: 36). It was this flexibility of the sequence, I argue, and the possibilities it offers to retain lyric authority and make it provisional at the same time, which contributed to its Victorian popularity. Thus, if Holmes is correct to say that the poetic sequence was 'a profound contribution to the attempts of the late Victorians to comprehend and articulate themselves' (2005: 5), I would add that it helped not only to explore the self, but to comprehend the role and nature of poetry at a time in which both concepts were undergoing fundamental changes.

I would like to conclude this section with one of these 'sons of Gabriel', John Addington Symonds, whose metatextual comments on his own sonnet sequences show that the Victorians themselves were very alive to the generic ambiguities which I have discussed. Symonds published two volumes of sonnets, *Animi Figura* (1882) and *Vagabunduli Libellus* (1884). Each book contains some individual sonnets, but most of the sonnets are gathered into groups. In the preface to *Animi Figura*, Symonds avers that '[t]his book cannot claim strict unity of subject. Connecting links between its sonnet-sequences are wanting'. Indeed, most of the sonnets are meditative or speculative, rather than mimetic, and although Symonds suggests that they present the 'Portrait of a Mind' (1882: vii), they scarcely individualise a character in a dramatic sense and develop no temporal or spatial specificity. In this aspect, *Animi Figura* shows most resemblance to its Rossettean model, in favouring a lyric temporality – though, in contrast to the proliferating ambiguities of *The House of Life*, this remains largely unqualified. Yet two years later, in the preface to *Vagabunduli Libellus*, Symonds claims that the amatory sequence 'Stella Maris' included in that work was written because '[t]he portrait of a beauty-loving and impulsive but at the same time self-tormenting and conscientious mind, which I attempted to display in *Animi Figura*, was incomplete and inexplicable without the episode of passionate experience set forth in "Stella Maris"' (1884: viii). Retrospectively, Symonds thus posits a continuous development that supposedly underlies *Animi Figura*, and 'Stella Maris' is assigned a specific place within that development. 'Stella Maris' itself does dramatically present the story of a love-episode, individualising speaker and addressee to a much larger degree than the sonnets of *Animi Figura*.

Symonds explicitly addresses what is at stake in such genre hybridisations. He acknowledges that 'the problem of solving human difficulties by communion with the divine idea is complicated in our age' (1882: viii). There is no certainty, neither religious, nor scientific:

> famed religions, systems, creeds,
> Sciences, shapes of knowledge, social laws,
> Deductions from the universal cause, –
> Are but the symptoms and effects of deeds.
> Having expressed wither the world's life leads,
> Summed past results, flourished with brief applause,
> They perish. (1882: 'Yggdrasil' II, ll. 1–7)

Because, that is, everything is subject to change and the individual can rely neither on God, nor on the self, nor on tradition, religion or other systems of knowledge to communicate something universal and lasting, the poet may only seek, more humbly, 'to adumbrate the form which feelings common to all men assume in some specific and perhaps abnormal personality constructed by his fancy' (1884: ix). The dramatically and narratively constructed individual replaces the performative universality of the lyric voice, the progression of plot replaces lyric repetition, though the commitment to common feelings shared by all 'men' continues to resonate.

'So many utterances of so many imaginary persons, *not mine'* – The Dramatic Monologue

If the lyric sequence in its long history has often hovered between an appropriable lyric voice and the construction of a fictional speaker-character, Symonds's reference to an 'abnormal personality' gestures towards the 'flagship genre of Victorian poetry' (Slinn 2002: 80): the dramatic monologue. While there is much disagreement on what precisely are the elements that are necessary for a poem to count as a dramatic monologue, there seems to be a general agreement in recognizing it as a mixed genre, which combines lyric, dramatic and narrative elements. I do not want to enter here into a lengthy discussion of genre definitions and delineations, of essential features and Wittgensteinian family resemblances. I use the designation dramatic monologue for convenience's sake but am mainly interested in shared temporal features. My central contention is that, for the Victorians, the kinds of poem that are nowadays often called 'dramatic monologues' offered another possibility to engage with and attempt to solve the same kinds of temporal tensions the Victorian poetic sequences are exploring. This is not to say that their potential temporal complexity is their only appeal, but that it is one feature that essentially contributed to the genre's popularity among the Victorians.

I have argued that the poetic sequence allowed Victorian poets to balance different kinds of temporality and thus to offer lyric appropriation while at the same time suggesting dramatic distance and narrative perspective. The dramatic monologue, in contrast, tends to invoke but undermine lyric appropriation. For lyric performativity it substitutes dramatic performance, often crucially involving narrative retrospection. It does so by deliberately focusing on the construction of a fictive character. The main point of this construction, however, as I see it, is not the distance it creates between the speaker and the poet – a distinction which definitions of the dramatic monologue have tended to highlight (see Byron 2003: 11–20). Rather, it is the obstacle such a construction of a speaker-character sets for a lyric appropriation of the poetic utterance, that is, the distance from the speaking 'I' which it enforces on the reader. I thus share Elizabeth Howe's view, who notes that '[t]he reader of a lyric poem may identify closely with its speaker, who is not necessarily particularized or identified in any way; whereas the "I" of a dramatic monologue is experienced as separate from both poet and reader, as "other"' (1996: 7).

This distancing gesture, I would argue, can be confirmed and further intensified by the introduction of an auditor.[6] The more the auditor appears as an agent, or even an individual, the less likely the reader is to feel directly addressed as the poem's 'you'. In dramatic monologues which lack an auditor, which are presented as soliloquies that are overheard, this distancing often works precisely by emphasising the absence of an addressee.[7]

Dramatic monologues discourage readers from identifying either as speaker or as audience, by filling those positions with more or less clearly delineated fictional characters. Moreover, I would argue that there is a tendency in dramatic monologues to play down what Culler and Greene call ritualistic elements, that is, patterns of repetition and sound which call for re-utterance. Of course, this is not to say that dramatic monologues are not highly crafted texts or forgo phonetic patterning like metre and rhyme. However, such patterning in principle tends to work against the development of character because it foregrounds sound, not sense. As Mutlu Konuk Blasing argues, '[i]f sounds dominate, sense is compromised; if sense is too fixed, sounds are not free to do their kind of affective signifying work' (2007: 29). To put it differently and in the terms of Roman Jakobson (1960), the more the poetic function of a text highlights language's materiality, the more do the other functions – emotive, conative and referential in particular – recede from view. Thus, as has often been observed, the phonetical patterning of dramatic monologues frequently serves to highlight the difference between the speaker and the shaping poet. The Duke of Ferrara does not speak in rhyming couplets, Robert Browning does. Such a personality split within the very shape of the poem, which plays sense against sound, adds a further obstacle to lyric appropriation. Finally, the means by which dramatic monologues individualise their speakers are frequently narrative. In many dramatic monologues, the speaker narrates something of his or her past. This serves to establish once again a distance between the reader and the speaking 'I', which is no longer an indeterminate indexical signifier, but given a specific personal history which goes far beyond the usually much more generalisable references to past events to be found in the lyric (like falling in or out of love, experiencing some kind of loss, and so on). Moreover, this emphasises retrospective narrative construction and a kind of temporality that is based on a linear sequence of causal connections, thus highlighting the way in which a textual 'I' can only become individual by filling the empty signifier with a constructed narrative of the past. As Marion Thain has noted, '[t]his breaks the bond of the lyric's "impersonal sub-jectivity"', identifying the subject with a specific character in a spe-cific transaction' (2016: 179). If the lyric sequence allowed poets to maintain, though qualify, lyric iterability, the dramatic monologue tropes a kind of temporality that emphasises uniqueness – a specific utterance, in a specific situation, with specific rhetorical aims.

Some of these poems are dramatic in that they are transformative: the rhetorical aim of their utterances is to make something happen in the fictional world they evoke. Ulysses wants to convince the sailors to set out with him, Fra Lippo Lippi wants to appease the soldiers who detain him, Bertha wants to punish her sister for her betrayal (Mermin 1983: 16; Pearsall 2000; 2008). Though Pearsall has argued for the centrality of this transformative aspect, there are numerous dramatic monologues in which any transformative impulse is clearly doomed to fail. In such cases, as Robert Langbaum has noted, the situations described are habitual rather than singular, or they are at least suggestive of possible repetition (1957: 157). They reveal a character in so far as they are *in* character, typical, and thus likely to recur. What the dramatic monologue retains in lyric iterability is thus, as it were, projected onto a specific speaker. Instead of the freely appropriable lyric 'I', the 'I' becomes a trap in the dramatic monologue, as iterability no longer suggests plurisignification but repetition compulsion and monotony. The speakers of dramatic monologues usually struggle, and often fail to escape their present moment.

'[I]f the speaker in a dramatic monologue were to enter a novel,' Dorothy Mermin suggests, 'he would have to be a minor figure whose nature does not change, or a Dickens grotesque, or a hero who has gotten stuck at the beginning of his career and never achieved his education' (Mermin 1983: 10–11). The reason, according to Mermin, is that 'the monologue lacks the resources to develop the temporal dimension, the notion of life as a continuing process of growth and change, that pervades Victorian thought and is essential to the Victorian novelist's sense of character' (10). This comparison to the novel, I think, is revealing, because it overlooks the rich temporal possibilities of the dramatic monologue. Though the speakers are often stuck and though the restricted length of the dramatic monologue can only depict their present, many dramatic monologues in fact show us their speakers at the end point of a development that has significantly failed to fulfil the developmen-tal promise of the *Bildungsroman* which Mermin evokes. Speakers in Webster's 'A Castaway', Amy Levy's 'Xanthippe', Tennyson's

'Ulysses' or 'Tithonus', Browning's 'Porphyria's Lover' or 'Andrea del Sarto', to name but a few examples, are not 'stuck at the beginning of [their] career' but find themselves at a dead end. Though the temporal extension of the dramatic monologue itself may be limited, such poems frequently at least sketch the past development of their speakers in narrative retrospection. In fact, 'the notion of life as a continuing process of growth and change' is, I would argue, the basic underlying premise for the entire genre. A sense of time as a process of growth and irreversible change (not repetition and recurring types) lies at the heart of the generic innovations of the dramatic monologue. The characters of the dramatic monologue are trapped in themselves as much as in their present, but the reader looks on that present from a critical distance as something that has passed, or might pass, as a specific moment in a specific process. Much of the tensions developed in these poems derive from reading their present against the background of the possibility, even the necessity, of change. A temporality of process and development thus informs not only the narrative retrospection on which characterisation so often hinges in these texts, but, more crucially, it is realised in the distance between speaker, auditor and reader.

These different temporal structures – lyric iterability, dramatic unfolding, narrative retrospection – are realised in various ways and are variously interrelated in individual dramatic monologues. In this, the bulk of Victorian dramatic monologues fall into three major groups, each of which develops different, though to a degree analogous, premises. The first group features speech acts that are explicitly or implicitly situated in a more or less clearly identified historical context. Some of the well-known early dramatic monologues fall in this group, like Tennyson's 'St. Simeon Stylites' (1842) and Browning's 'Johannes Agricola in Meditation' (1836) and, most famously, 'My Last Duchess' (1842). Browning had a penchant for historical speakers, and many others were influenced by him in this, most prominently perhaps Algernon Swinburne in poems like 'Anactoria' (1866) and 'Hymn to Proserpine' (1866). The second group features mythical or (quasi-)literary characters like Browning's 'Caliban upon Setebos' (1864). Such speakers are favoured by Tennyson but also appeal to female poets like Augusta Webster and Amy Levy. The third group features speakers who are identified as roughly contemporary. While the prolific Browning wrote some examples of this category, too, it is more closely associated with the work of women. For instance, most of the poems in Augusta Webster's collection *Portraits* (1872) feature contemporary speakers.[8]

Partly due to the prominence of Robert Browning's work in later criticism, discussions of the genre have made much of the characteristic historical distance in his dramatic monologues. Herbert Tucker, for example, argues that 'historical contextualisation' is 'the generic privilege of the dramatic monologue and [. . .] one of its indispensable props in the construction of character' (2007 [1985]: 544). For Langbaum, too, historical distance is essential to the effect created in the dramatic monologue. Indeed, it lies at the heart of Langbaum's notion of judgement: 'judgment [in the dramatic monologue] is largely psychologized and historicized. We adopt a man's point of view and the point of view of his age in order to judge him – which makes the judgment relative, limited in applicability to the particular conditions of the case' (1957: 107). Thus, according to Langbaum, we derive pleasure even from the Duke of Ferrara's villainy because we view it with the assuring retrospection of the historian (97). This historically contextualised judgement makes the dramatic monologue, Langbaum argues,

> an appropriate form for an empiricist and relativist age, an age which has come to consider value as an evolving thing dependent upon the changing individual and social requirements of the historical process. For such an age judgment can never be final, it has changed and will change again; it must be perpetually checked against fact, which comes before judgment and remains always more certain. (108)

Piquantly, Langbaum's own discussion of 'My Last Duchess' may serve as a prime example of such changing and relative judgements. His argument that the dramatic monologue works by balancing sympathy and judgement and his confident claim that 'the reader' is seduced by the Duke, feeling admiration for his power of eloquence and his proud elegance (83, 85), has puzzled later critics. Langbaum's uncritical universalisation of his own reader response has become untenable in a later critical environment, more aware of the heterogeneity both of the original text basis (Langbaum's work is based exclusively on the poems by male authors) and of reader reaction (see Byron 2003: 21–2; Scheinberg 1997).

An awareness of historical process thus doubly informs the historical dramatic monologue. On the one hand, Browning's monologues in particular were praised by contemporaries for their awareness of 'local colour'. They give us 'the tone of each particular age', and it was considered 'certain that Mr. Browning is not only a poet but a subtle historian' ('Robert Browning's

Poems' 1863: 310). On the other hand, awareness of the historical (and, in most cases, also geographical) distance to the speaker
influences the reader's judgement. It is at least partly on the basis
of an awareness of historical change that readers can judge the
speakers from a moral high ground or see dramatic irony resulting from their own retrospective knowledge (as, for example, in
the Christian context of Robert Browning's 'Karshish' (1855) or
Charlotte Brontë's 'Pilate's Wife's Dream' (1846)). Thus, the historical dramatic monologue, as Carol Christ has pointed out, offers a
way to negotiate between historical relativism and the desire for an
ahistorical perspective: 'the form can at once display the historical
conditions of the speaker's understanding and maintain the fiction
that the poet does not suffer similar limitation' (Christ 1984: 114).
Still, the choice of historical speakers can affect readings in a range
of different ways and can stress continuity as much as difference.
Indeed, the question whether a poem highlights historical difference or transhistorical similarity is one which lies, at least partly,
in the eye of the beholder, as Langbaum's and Cynthia Scheinberg's
different readings of 'My Last Duchess' serve well to illustrate.
If Langbaum (along with some Victorian reviewers) emphasises
historical distance and difference, Scheinberg prefers to consider
Browning 'a proto-feminist' who 'demonstrates [. . .] how deeply
women have been oppressed by male language' (1997: 178), an
argument that derives its force from being transhistorical, not limited to the sixteenth-century Italy of the poem's setting. My point
is that both these possibilities are in principle available to a reader
of historical dramatic monologues and that this ambiguity forms
part of the genre's appeal. The reception of Swinburne's notorious
collection *Poems and Ballads* (1866) provides the most obvious
Victorian example of the dynamics of this ambiguity. Reviewers
who felt scandalised by the collection's attack on Victorian morals
and beliefs chose to ignore the poet's somewhat disingenuous insistence on them being mere dramatic and historical studies.[9] Thus,
in the words of Tucker, '[c]haracter in the Browningesque dramatic
monologue emerges as an interference effect between opposed yet
mutually informative discourses: between an historical, narrative, metonymic text and a symbolic, lyrical, metaphoric text that
adjoins it and jockeys with it for authority' (2007 [1985]: 545).
Arguably, what made Swinburne's monologues so provocative is
their tendency to lyricise their speakers, who are never individualised to a similar degree as Browning's characters are, and whose
highly sensual use of language seduces into lyric appropriation,

by privileging sound over sense. In the historical dramatic monologue, dramatic presentation thus becomes the nucleus of tension
between narrative retrospection and lyric iterability, both in its conception and in its reception.

Narrative of a different kind becomes important in dramatic
monologues whose speakers are mythical or fictional characters. In
those cases, temporal distance to the speakers also plays a role, but
even more than the historical speakers, mythical and literary characters bring their own stories with them. The appreciation of these
monologues depends on the knowledge of the narratives in which
the speakers are embedded and by which their trajectory is already
predetermined. From the moment a familiar character is named in
a title, the poem enters the logic of narrative retrospection which
judges the dramatically presented moment of speech as significant
within a larger causal development, a plot. This strategy removes
some of the burden of narrative from the poems themselves, since
they can rely on the reader's prior knowledge of the narratives they
refer to. In some cases, notably in poems by Tennyson, this can
lead to a relyricisation of the dramatic monologue, as for example
in the final verses of 'Ulysses' (1842), which can easily be divorced
from their specific context within the poem as an appeal to Ulysses'
sailors,[10] or the beginning of 'Tithonus' (1860), whose first lines,
uncharacteristically for a dramatic monologue, lack deictics, personal pronouns or direct address. More frequently, however, an
acknowledgement of historical change underwrites the narrative
commitments of this kind of dramatic monologue, too, though in a
different sense. Many dramatic monologues featuring mythical or
literary speakers provide a revisionary perspective on the respective
narratives they refer to. Tennyson's Ulysses is shown to be driven
by boredom and distasteful condescension to his 'aged wife' (l. 3),
'decent' son (l. 40) and 'savage' people (l. 4). His egotistical desire
to 'drink / Life to the lees' (ll. 6–7) drives him to abandon his kin
and his people, convincing his sailors to accompany him to their
deaths. Browning's Caliban is presented as a primitive creature, but
not devoid of poetic graces and a warped kind of rationality, and
he is more likely to elicit sympathetic reactions than Shakespeare's
character (see Moy 2018: 381–2). Maligned female figures like
Medea, Circe or Xantippe are revisited by women poets to offer
justifications for their acts, presenting them as victims or products
of patriarchal suppression: 'I live what thou hast made me', says
Webster's Medea to Jason's ghost ('Medea in Athens', l. 188).[11]
These poems offer alternative narratives, new ways of approaching

old stories, and thus rely no less on a historical change of perspective than the dramatic monologues featuring historical personages as speakers.

Indeed, in these poems the yearning for change, for an escape from the present situation, is a strikingly recurrent topic. Tithonus, Tiresias and Ulysses are all tired of their present existence and long for death, or a journey that amounts to death. Caliban chafes against Prospero's yoke. Medea and Xantippe are trapped in love–hate relationships from which they cannot extricate themselves and Webster's Circe, obviously influenced by Tennyson's monologues, experiences her island dominion as a stifling prison and exclaims desperately: 'Give me some change' (l. 48). In spite of the prominence of the narratives in their background, with the partial exception of 'Ulysses', the predominant sense of time in these poems is that of time stalled, arrested in its flow rather than progressing, recurrent rather than variable.

Indeed, Webster's 'Circe' and Tennyson's 'Tithonus' offer striking examples of how lyric iterability can be reinterpreted as stifling monotony in the extended dramatic context of the monologue. 'Tithonus' begins with what sounds initially like a lament for the workings of time:

> The woods decay, the woods decay and fall,
> The vapours weep their burthen to the ground,
> Man comes and tills the field and lies beneath,
> And after many a summer dies the swan. (ll. 1–4)

In the next lines, however, this lyric lament is reframed as the tragic background to Tithonus's inability to die: 'Me only cruel immortality / Consumes' (ll. 5–6). Tithonus's plea to Aurora to take back her gift of immortality and let him die is hopeless, doomed to be repeated incessantly, just like the process of dawn itself. By being set into the specific dramatic context of an immortal man addressing the goddess who granted him immortality, the lyric iterability of the first lines, no longer impersonal, becomes terrible in its relentlessness.

In the beginning of 'Circe', similarly, the speaker's own perspective only begins to emerge after nine lines of lyric description of the sunset and an approaching storm:

> The sun drops luridly into the west;
> Darkness has raised her arms to draw him down
> Before the time, not waiting as of wont

> Till he has come to her behind the sea;
> And the smooth waves grow sullen in the gloom
> And wear their threatening purple; more and more
> The plain of waters sways and seems to rise
> Convexly from its level of the shores;
> And low dull thunder rolls along the beach:
> There will be storm at last, storm, glorious storm. (ll. 1–10)

As in 'Tithonus', the speaker's perspective offers a revaluation of the foregoing lines. The ominous rising of the storm turns out to be welcome rather than feared, and the violent erotic charge of the lines is highlighted. The final line of this first stanza begins to turn the description of the approaching storm into an event of individual significance to the speaker, something to finally break 'the sickly sweet monotony' (l. 32) of her days. Circe welcomes the storm and the ship it wrecks as something that will 'bring [her] change' (l. 31), but her monologue continues to reveal that this apparently decisive event is only an extension of her sense of repetition and monotony. On seeing the ship coming to the isle, her anticipation of the outcome is decidedly jaded. First the shipwrecked sailors will be grateful for their survival and weep for home, the next day they will revel in their new-found ease and enjoy their stay, 'Then the next day the beast in them will wake' (l. 159):

> One will grow mad with fever of the wine,
> And one will sluggishly besot himself,
> And one be lewd, and one be gluttonous;
> And I shall sickly look and loathe them all. (ll. 165–8)

The parallelisms and anaphors of these lines lend the process a sense of inevitability. Circe has seen all this before. Her claim that when she turns men into beasts there is no true change – 'Change? There was no change; / Only disguise gone from them unawares' (ll. 188–9) – jars strikingly with her former wish for change. The sorceress best known for her transformative powers is, in fact, unable to effect any transformation at all, least of all in her own situation.

There is irony, of course, in presenting a mythical figure notorious for the transformations she causes long for a change which she cannot bring about herself and whose premise is, in fact, that her ability to cause change fails. After all, the true lover she expects will be the one who is able to drink from her cup without being transformed into an animal. She believes that a resistance to her powers would be due to the inherent quality of the man:

> had there been one true right man of them
> He would have drunk the draught as I had drunk,
> And stood unharmed and looked me in the eyes,
> Abashing me before him. (ll. 191–3)

As we know from the *Odyssey*, however, Circe's hope is bound to be disappointed. Odysseus only withstands her powers with the help of an antidote and he will eventually leave her alone on her island. While the poem depicts Circe as waiting for her true lover, 'him whom fate will send / One day to be my master utterly' (ll. 110–11), and the ship about to arrive might possibly be that of Odysseus, knowledge of Circe's story does little to relieve the sense of stifling repetition the monologue dwells on.

At the moment of their dramatic present, these speakers either yearn to begin their narrative ('Circe') or to end it ('Tithonus', 'Medea in Athens', 'Xantippe' – Ulysses arguably fits both descriptions); they look towards the future or hope to leave the past behind. All of them yearn for change. Lyric iterability and privileging of repetition over succession is the prison from which these speakers are striving to escape into narrative progression, an attempt that necessarily fails to be realised within the circumference of the poem. Indeed, the form traps the speakers forever in their present, as they are doomed to repeat their utterance in each new reading.

The final group of dramatic monologues I want to discuss features speakers set within a recognisably contemporary context. Historical distance, which Langbaum and Tucker found to be so central to the workings of the dramatic monologue, seems to play no role here. Nonetheless, I argue, such dramatic monologues often arise from a sense of the possibility, even the necessity of historical change. Instead of distancing the speaker historically from the reader, however, turning all judgement relative, dramatic monologues with contemporary speakers generally gesture towards the possibility of future change. It may be for this reason that contemporary speakers appealed particularly (though, of course, not exclusively) to women writers, who were identifying much that was amiss in their own situation and in society in general. Many of the dramatic monologues featuring contemporary speakers can be read as more or less direct social criticism, a criticism which does not grant the reader an escape to the high moral ground of historical retrospection. At the same time, the very fact that speakers are clearly identified or identifiable as contemporary demonstrates historical awareness, while the act of criticism implies a belief in the possibility of change. In other words, social criticism in dramatic monologues with contemporary speakers on the one hand, and the irony and scepticism which historical distance can lend to dramatic monologues by speakers from the past on the other, are two sides of the same coin. They both arise from, and are predicated on, a sense of historical change. Thus, dramatic monologues featuring contemporary speakers turn the critical gaze of historical awareness on the contemporary present.

Such poems draw on the Romantic dramatic lyric, but to contemporary speakers, even more consistently than in the poems discussed above, lyric iterability turns into a trap, as it pre-empts the possibility of escape from their situation. At the same time, it puts weight on the poem's criticism, since contemporary speakers are often generic characters, determined by their role and situation in society (this is reflected in titles like Browning's 'Any Wife to Any Husband' (1855) or 'A Woman's Last Word' (1855), Barrett Browning's 'The Runaway Slave at Pilgrim's Point' (1848), or Webster's titles in *Portraits* (1870/1893), like 'A Painter', 'A Preacher', 'The Happiest Girl in the World'). Thus what they retain of lyric iterability serves to suggest that their situation is not purely individual, but typical and repeatable. Their predicaments are not individual, but social. In dramatic monologues featuring contemporary speakers, narrative, lyric and dramatic temporalities can thus be played off against each other: we encounter a speaker in a specific dramatic situation, who often provides a narrative account of his or her past which serves to establish a retrospective causal chain of events that accounts for the dramatic situation of the speaker's present. These individualising gestures, however, are counterbalanced by lyric iterability as the speakers are turned into types and their situation becomes endlessly repeatable. Lyric iterability is here associated not with freedom of appropriation and reinterpretation but with the social restrictions which circumscribe the speakers. Precisely because the speakers cannot become fully individualised in a narrative and dramatic process, precisely because the relatively short form 'lacks the resources to develop the temporal dimension' (Mermin 1983: 10), the form serves so well to expose the social mechanisms which make the speakers' situation not unique, but repeatable. In such dramatic monologues, lyric iterability is troped as confinement in static social structures which call for change.

I have suggested that the dramatic monologue engages with changing temporalities, pitching narrative causality and dramatic process against lyric iterability, where the former are often valued above the latter. Thus, in contrast to the lyric sequence, in which lyric iterability is maintained as a possibility, coexistent and in balance with narrative or dramatic readings, the dramatic monologue exploits tensions between the modes and, repeatedly, tropes the lyric as stifling, and deeply problematic.

'A plain tale of naked fact, unconscious of design' – The Novel in Verse

In 1868–9 Robert Browning published *The Ring and the Book*. The poem consists of an epic twelve books, ten of which offer dramatic monologues from different perspectives, by different actors in the same criminal case, the trial of Count Guido Franceschini, which took place in 1698. This monumental work takes the dramatic monologue and turns it into a novel in verse. While *The Ring and the Book* is unique in its extension of dramatic monologues to epic dimensions, many other Victorian verse novels show close affinities to the other two genres I have discussed in this chapter. Alfred Tennyson's *Maud* (1855), for example, combines aspects of all three genres, as a sequence of partly lyric, partly dramatic soliloquies of a disturbed mind, which develops a plot, sometimes in novelistic detail. The first book of Coventry Patmore's *Angel in the House* (1862) precedes its first-person narrative parts with short lyric introductory preludes, while the second part is, like Clough's *Amours de Voyage* (1849) (which also contains lyric introductions to each canto), an epistolary poem in which the plot unfolds sequentially in a dramatic process, quite similarly to the way it does in plot-driven poetic sequences. Even beyond such hybrid combinations, the verse novel is no less problematic to define as a genre than the dramatic monologue, though it has attracted much less critical attention and therefore less controversy. Recent scholarship has begun to recognise, however, that one is mistaken to consider the novel in verse, as some still do, as a 'small genre [. . .] primarily represented by Elizabeth Barrett Browning's *Aurora Leigh*' (Najarian 2013: 589).[12] What seems clear, moreover, is that this 'peculiar and peculiarly perverse genre' (Felluga 2002: 171) is peculiarly Victorian.[13] It has important forerunners, of course, in the work of Lord Byron, Walter Scott and in Wordsworth's *Prelude*, but its interest in the psychological development of convincing characters and its frequent turn to modern settings seemed innovative to contemporaries.[14] Certainly, as I have already mentioned above, Victorian authors themselves frequently gave explicit expression to their sense of novelty when they embarked on their verse novels. In their own view at least, they were exploring new generic possibilities.

It is tempting to see the verse novel in terms of a rear-guard action, an attempt to rescue poetry from being overwhelmed by the success of the novel, 'play[ing] to that market as best it could by exploring those characteristics that made the novel such a popular success (narrative sequentiality, realistic description, historical referentiality, believable characters, dramatic situations, fully realized dialogism and, above all, the domestic marriage plot)' (Felluga 2002: 171). As Clough somewhat cynically admitted in his 1853 call for a new poetic practice, in contrast to poetry which is no longer widely read at all, the novel 'obtains one reading at any rate; is thrown away indeed tomorrow, but is devoured today' (2005: 583). Instead of aiming any longer for eternity, poetry should therefore dare to become as ephemeral as the present itself. It is also tempting to see this attempt as abortive. The common critical story, Dino Felluga suggests, is that the verse novel 'arose in England only to disappear again by the 1870s' (2002: 171; see also Moore 2015: 197). While the verse novel has not disappeared without an afterlife and Felluga certainly has a point when he suggests that the specific conditions of academic professionalisation may have blinded critics to such hybrid forms, it is nonetheless true that the novel in verse did not fulfil the high hopes set into it by the Victorians. Instead of becoming a new poetic paradigm it entered literary history as a freak, while poetry became gradually reduced to an increasingly narrow conception of the lyric.[15]

Precisely this reduction of poetry to lyric, as well as that of narrative to fictional prose, especially the novel, can blur our perspective on the Victorian verse novel today. There is, for one, the danger of too easily associating verse with lyric and the novel with narrative in descriptions of the kind of hybridity that characterises the verse novel. There is, second, the danger of downplaying the complexity and heterogeneity of the (prose) novel itself, as well as the complexity of poetic heritage. For example, two recent studies of verse novels discuss the form as a mixture of narrative and lyric modes and temporalities (Markovits 2006; Morgan 2009).[16] While both these studies provide stimulating readings of a variety of long narrative poems of the time, their juxtaposition of lyric and narrative modes is fraught with problems. Morgan, as I have already had occasion to point out, understands the lyric explicitly and exclusively in terms of its supposed timelessness. Drawing on Culler's suggestion that the lyric present is 'the set of all moments at which writing can say "now"' (Culler 1981: 149), Morgan calls all those textual passages lyric in which the moment of enunciation comes to the foreground of the narrative. It seems debateable, however, if such gestures can usefully be characterised as lyric instead of calling them simply self-reflexive, or metafictional. After all, strategies which draw attention to the moment or the act of composition abound in prose novels, in which they would presumably not strike many readers as particularly lyrical.

Markovits bases her argument about the mixture of lyric and narrative modes in Victorian verse novels primarily on the frequent 'rough-mixing' of generic forms (she borrows this term from David Duff's work on Romantic genre hybrids) to be found in them. That is, she emphasises cases which 'intersperse blank-verse narrative sections with embedded or intercalary songs and short poems' (2017: 6), that is, non-narrative poetic forms which she identifies as lyric. One might object, though, that by no means all Victorian verse novels *do* include such lyric forms and thus any generalising definition from such a feature must prove misleading. Conversely, the rough mixing of narrative and lyric forms is not restricted to verse novels (see, for example, my discussion of Tennyson's 'The Lotos-Eaters' in the next chapter). Markovits's position seems to ignore the possibility that Victorian verse novels might deliberately avoid the lyric, in spite of the fact that they are composed in verse, a possibility I will dwell on. In fact, as I have already hinted at in my discussion of Tennyson's *The Princess* in the previous chapter, precisely the fairly frequent 'rough-mixing' of forms to be found in verse novels may point to the fact that the lyric is deliberately marked off from the narrative rather than more fully integrated within it.[17] Finally, the Victorian verse novel has itself taken so many different forms that it is hard to generalise broadly about it.

It is important to emphasise that the sense of innovation which Victorian authors of verse novels explicitly expressed again and again had little to do with the simple fact of narrating a story in verse form. It is worth recalling that Victorian readers were much more likely to encounter verse narratives with little affiliations or associations with the novel than readers commonly are nowadays. The simple fact that a long narrative is told in verse may be highly conspicuous, even alienating to readers today, but was surely much less so 150 years ago. Instead, the innovation lies in the *kind* of stories that verse novelists turned to and the kind of temporality they implied. What was considered to be peculiar in the form of the verse novel can thus only be understood in the context of the dominant concept of poetry I have discussed in my previous chapter, as well as the debate about poetic truth claims and contemporaneity. The verse novel is *not* first and foremost a combination of lyric (verse) and narrative (novel) but rather of the novel and the epic, the prosaic everyday and the transcendent poetic (see Moore 2015: 145–2).[18] It is in this sense that the verse novel differs also from most early Victorian verse narratives which, as Anne-Julia Zwierlein has pointed out, not only turned to the past for their subject matter but were not concerned with historical accuracy or probable representation, favouring instead the marvellous in the tradition of romance literature (Zwierlein 2015: 243). This strong tradition of poetic narrative is overlooked when the mere presence of narration is directly taken as a reference to the novel. In the context of the other two genres I have addressed in this chapter, the verse novel, I would argue, can be seen to reject lyric possibilities, to isolate them or to tie them firmly into larger narrative and dramatic structures.[19]

This plays out with particular clarity in the repeated insistence of verse novels on singular incidents and individual psychology instead of reiterable, performative truth. William Michael Rossetti's novella in verse 'Mrs. Holmes Grey' (1867–8) offers a striking example of such a poetics of facts, not truth. In an explanatory note to the poem, Rossetti closely links his poetic endeavour to a Pre-Raphaelite aesthetics, declaring his aim 'to approach nearer to the actualities of dialogue and narration than had ever yet been done' in poetry (1867–8: 459). Albeit short, the story has all the trappings of a sensation novel: secret adulterous infatuation, suicide and a gothic thirst for revenge, and, like sensation novels, it emphasises its factuality through reference to ostensibly reliable sources of information. Thus a major part of Rossetti's story of a domestic tragedy is taken up by a supposedly literal insertion of a newspaper report (a prosaic genre if ever there was one), while much of the rest consists of a dialogue between the husband of the deceased and a sympathetic friend, named Harling. Rossetti's note is telling in its emphasis on 'actualities' as well as on both narrative and dramatic features. What role, if any, the lyric plays in this endeavour, remains unspecified. Indeed, the poem seems to deliberately reject the lyric. Its two opening stanzas provide a potentially lyric setting of the scene, offering impersonal descriptions of typically lyric material: recurring natural processes of changing weather, the setting of the sun, the ebb and flow of the sea.

Almost immediately, however, details disturb the scene, turning it specific, prosaic even, in somewhat distasteful particularity. The beach is littered with 'profuse and pulpy sea-weed' (l. 2), among which 'there were the wonted tetchy and sidelong crabs, / With fishes silvery in distended death' (ll. 7–8), while the 'sun / Sank, a red glare, between two lengthened streaks, / Hot dun' (ll. 11–13). If these lines might still raise lyric associations, both by their evocation of a natural scene and by their conspicuous sound-patterning, the next stanza turns novelistic with a vengeance, referencing that most prosaic, most commonplace of British concerns, conversations about the weather:

> The townspeople, and, more, the visitors,
> Were passing to the sea-beach through the streets,
> To take advantage of the lull of rain.
> The English 'Rainy weather' went from mouth
> To mouth, with 'Very' answered, or a shrug
> Of shoulders, and a growl, and 'Sure to be!
> Began the very day that we arrived.' (ll. 15–21)

This emphatically prosaic and banal beginning sets the tone for the rest of the poem in which a frequently heavily enjambed blank verse mainly seems to speed up the pace of narration, as in the lines above, pressing towards an economical use of words.

The poem balances its main focus on the irrationally and insuperably strong love of the titular Mrs. Grey with the deliberately factual and sober report of the coroner's inquest and filters Holmes Grey's passionate sorrow and fury through the focaliser Harling. Strong passion, which the Victorians believed finds its natural expression in verse (see Chapter 4), and which is easily associated with the lyric in particular, is here held at bay. In fact, the poem makes much of the (male) control of emotion in contrast to the fatal (female) overflow of powerful feelings, emphasising repeatedly the endeavour of male speakers to control their passion (for example ll. 293–5, 433–5). And yet his passion overpowers Grey at the end of the poem which remains surprisingly inconclusive, pitched as it leaves Grey for enacting his revenge on his rival.

Only the poem's conclusion does, briefly, strike a lyric note again, with the powerfully evocative lines: 'Harling had seen the night / Equal, unknown, and desolate of stars' (ll. 809–10). Such use of the night as a symbolic comment concluding the poem resonates with lyric iterability and suggests a truth beyond facts, though this truth might amount, precisely, to a recognition of ignorance.[20] Even here, in this final evaluation of the emotional impact of the story, however, the lines are tied tightly to the perspective of the narrative's main focaliser, Harling. Their lyric potential seems to be deliberately curtailed.

Of course, Rossetti's use of blank verse – though often prosaic in its profusion of caesuras and enjambments, which go some way to mask the underlying iambic pentameter – contradicts the poem's insistence on direct, unmediated representation. There is even something slightly absurd in the notion of a coroner's inquest in blank verse. Such contrast between content and form was widely felt in the case of verse novels. Yet, the choice to tell a story in verse, according to John Holmes, 'elevates [a poem's subject] from single instances into an exemplary narrative' (2018: 95). The Victorian association of poetry with elevated subject matter and lasting significance may have helped to lend the singular, transient occurrences of narrative some trace of transcendent symbolic value. Conversely, one could also argue on a more formal level that the metrical shaping of narrative material constantly foregrounds the act of shaping, the act of narration. It thus highlights the kind of temporality which lies at the heart of narrative: the temporal distance between the events presented and their retrospective narrative construction. In verse narrative, so to speak, there can be no covert narration. Narration is always conspicuous. As Holmes notes with regard to 'Mrs. Holmes Gray', '[w]here prose might be a documentary account, blank verse can only ever be art, even if what we are reading is a newspaper report' (2018: 94).

Robert Browning addresses this issue directly in his metapoetic commentaries of the first and the last book of *The Ring and the Book* (1868/69). Browning's guiding metaphor evokes the equally metaphorical pure gold of historical fact, the truth out of which his poetical ring is ultimately fashioned. He emphasises repeatedly the materiality and actual existence of the yellow book from which he derives his materials, states meticulously where exactly he found it, how much he paid for it, what it contains, and mentions the further local research he has done on the case. In this book, he insists, 'lay absolutely truth, / Fanciless fact' (Browning 1961: Book I, ll. 140–1). Browning introduces his ring metaphor precisely to address his shaping agency as a poet. He takes the raw ingot of golden truth and adds the alloy necessary to give it form:

> To wit, that fancy has informed, transpierced
> Thridded and so thrown fast the facts else free,
> As right through ring and ring runs the djereed
> And binds the loose, one bar without a break. (Book I, ll. 459–62)

Browning suggests that it is precisely this shaping agency of the poet which can bring the dead past back to life, give it immediacy (Book I, ll. 752–65). But this is an immediacy that is highly aware of change and of relativity of judgement. The poem foregrounds retrospective narrative construction as every different monologue presents a different (and often contradictory) narrative of the same events, and it embraces dramatic process in taking the form of a series of dramatic monologues. But Browning deliberately rejects a lyric temporality of reiterated appropriation for one that thrives on particularity and change: 'See for yourselves, / This man's act, changeable because alive!' (Book I, ll. 1356–7). Browning suggests that he could make this 'novel country' (literally also the terrain of the novel) his own 'By choosing which one aspect of the year / Suited mood best, and putting solely that / On panel somewhere in the House of Fame' (Book I, ll. 1340–3), thus locking the story in a lyric time of repeatability rather than succession. Rejecting this possibility, he exclaims, 'Rather learn and love / Each facet-flash of the revolving year!' (Book I, ll. 1352–3). He justifies this choice not only by life's changeability, but, more importantly for the poem, by the changeability of human judgement. The truth he is eventually aiming for is 'This lesson, that our human speech is nought, / Our human testimony false, our fame / And human estimation words and wind' (Book XII, ll. 834–6). When Browning thus closes both the first and the final book of *The Ring and the Book* with an address to Elizabeth as 'lyric Love', this is not only a gesture of loving deference, but also one of differentiation. Associated with his deceased wife, the lyric is relegated to the realm of the elevated, the divine and the mythical (it is 'half angel and half bird'; Book I, l. 1383). It can preside over, but stands apart from, the throbbing, changeable life of historical fact which is the essence of Robert Browning's endeavour.

But, of course, Elizabeth Barrett Browning herself has written the most enduringly successful Victorian verse novel herself. Like her husband, Barrett Browning is centrally concerned with the question of the kind of truth art may offer but, as I have already suggested in the previous chapter, her answer is rather different. For Barrett Browning, art's truth is a decidedly spiritual, religious truth. The only aim and justification for poetry which Aurora allows and repeatedly calls for is to show the spiritual significance that suffuses all existence. Artists should witness 'God's / Complete, consummate, undivided work' (Book VII, ll. 838–9). In such a poetic programme, form may indeed be as inconsequential as Aurora suggests: 'Keep up the fire, / And leave the generous flames to shape themselves' (Book V, ll. 234–5).

However, the form which the poem does take carries significant aesthetic consequences. Once again, my argument is that it is misleading to parse the poem's governing logic of a marriage of the ideal and the real as a combination between lyric and narrative or even merely between lyric and narrative temporal structures. With its dual emphasis on retrospective narration and dramatic unfolding (in particular in the profuse dialogues and the inserted letters), the temporal structure of this verse novel strongly mixes narrative and dramatic features but, I would argue, avoids the form of the lyric – just as Aurora herself rejects the sonnet form. At no point does the poem aim to let the reader forget the *origo* of the speaking voice, be it Aurora herself or one of her numerous interlocutors. It even goes so far as to particularise the moment of speaking, as in the conspicuous nod to the dramatic monologue at the beginning of Book III, as Aurora interrupts her writing to reprimand her maidservant for disturbing her (ll. 25–35). And as much as the poem provides Aurora with poetic authority, tracing her own development in a clear analogy and female response to Wordsworth's project in *The Prelude* (1850), and confirming in its own form many of Aurora's aesthetic judgements, Aurora remains, emphatically, a fictional character and a narrator who is not entirely reliable. After all, she is embroiled in a plot which centrally revolves on her misunderstanding of others and her failure to know her own feelings. Her cousin Romney, too, who sketches the final vision of poetry as a world-renewing force, has proven himself throughout the poem as an idealistic dreamer, whose high plans tend to fail tragically. Aurora is often taken to be a mouthpiece for Barrett Browning, and I do not mean to deny that this might be the case. But the poem demonstrates strikingly what is at stake for poetry in the transformation of Victorian culture and belief systems. Only as long as the divine nature of poetry remains granted, poets can still hope, with Aurora, 'To speak my poems in mysterious tune / With man and nature' to the point

> That men shall feel it catch them on the quick,
> As having the same warrant over them
> To hold and move them, if they will or no,
> Alike imperious as the primal rhythm
> Of that theurgic nature (Book V, ll. 26–30)

Once the divine foundation of poetry is questioned, though, Aurora's and Romney's high hopes for poetry turn into fitting though somewhat ridiculously bombastic individual traits of these two fictional characters, whose story reveals them to be often wrong in their judgements and biased in their beliefs.

With *Aurora Leigh* then, Barrett Browning shows resistance to an Aestheticist solution which replaces the divine authority of poetry with the self-sufficient, performative moment of lyric utterance, in which general relevance is eschewed for individual iterability. Similarly, she rejects the redefinition of poetic truth as merely human and relative. Her poem embraces change but enfolds it within a concept of eternity – indeed claims the latter as necessary for a unified and unifying poetic vision. The poem also shows, however, how dependent its poetic vision is on something external to itself. If *Aurora Leigh* attests to Barrett Browning's belief that timeless truth can be found beyond a decontextualised and thus repeatable lyric utterance in the specific locatedness of an emphatically modern dramatic situation and in the lessons to be drawn from narrative retrospection, it also demonstrates how quickly the universal can collapse into idiosyncrasy once the belief in an underlying divine essence is no longer shared.

Dramatic Sonnet Sequence Novel – George Meredith's *Modern Love*

One poem which combines all the above-mentioned genres is George Meredith's *Modern Love* (1862). Though the individual poems of this sequence consist of sixteen lines in four quatrains, the work deliberately positions itself in relation to and in contrast with the Petrarchan sonnet tradition. Instead of the lover who eulogises his unattainable (because married) ideal woman, however, Meredith's sequence focuses on the husband, and his hate, or love–hate, rather than loving admiration. Meredith goes even further in transforming the tradition with his focus on 'change, as opposed to the eternalizing sacramental monument of marriage' or idealised Petrarchan love (Campbell 2011: 216) and on relative and specific, instead of universal, truths. *Modern Love* is a poem not about love, but about modern love, and the way it positions its speaking voice is central to this modernity.

The poem not only shifts from narration to dramatic presentation, but also from third- to first-person speaker. As Phelan notes, 'like the novelists, Meredith allows himself the luxury of an "inside view" of the principal character in order to allow us to share his perspective, while at the same time retaining for himself the novelist's privilege of omniscience' (2005: 110). Similar to other novels in verse, the focus of *Modern Love* is domestic, telling a story of marital disintegration, sometimes in novelistic details. But since the story is told in the form of a sequence of lyric moments, narrative continuity is constantly interrupted and any straightforward understanding of the plot is complicated. Thus, Phelan's comment is perhaps misleading if it suggests that an omniscient narrative perspective guides us through the sequence. The heterodiegetic narrative voice mainly emerges briefly at the beginning and in the conclusion of the sequence, while much of the plot has to be pieced together on the basis of the sonnets in the voice of the husband. Indeed, the narrative voices sometimes merge with each other, making clear distinctions difficult (for example, when the homodiegetic perspective first emerges suddenly in the middle of section 3). In fact, I want to argue, rather than providing authorial guidance, the narrative shifts in the text serve to destabilise the voice of the speaker, creating a critical distance to the reader typical for dramatic monologues. Intriguingly, in Meredith's sonnet sequence, we face a speaker in an ostensibly lyric setting whose reliability is highly doubtful.

The reliability of Meredith's speaker is called into question just as the narrative ground, provided only through his perspective and consisting of discontinuous momentary glimpses, becomes treacherous. We understand that the marriage is in trouble and that the husband believes that the wife has fallen in love with someone else. Yet, it seems, he knows that she has not betrayed him in the act: 'To know her flesh so pure, so keen her sense, / That she does penance now for no offence / Save against Love' (24, ll. 2–4). He himself, though, admits to having had lovers before (20) and takes a new lover to console him, making his wife miserable in turn. This double moral and his obviously wounded pride arguably make his judgements, even if presented in the form of formally sophisticated quasi-sonnets, questionable. He deliberately tortures his wife, evading her attempts to speak to him – 'With commonplace I freeze her, tongue and sense' (34, l. 15) – and is fully aware that he is pushing her towards suicide. He knows that 'She is no one / Long to endure this torpidly, and shun / The drugs that crowd about a woman's hand' and yet, his vanity prevents him from giving in: 'Save her? What for? To act this wedded lie!' (35, ll. 10–12, 16).

I want to stress how unusual this set-up is. Sonnets in particular tend to key us for lyric reading, and even in the case of those poetic sequences discussed above in which speakers are dramatically individualised, the single section can often be read lyrically in isolation.

In any case, the dramatic distancing of the speakers through the sequence rarely undermines their reliability. Even if the speaker of Tennyson's *In Memoriam*, for example, contradicts himself, this contradiction emerges as various subsequent stages of grief, all of which are sincere. Such contradictions do not undermine the credibility of the speaker's perspective. In *Modern Love*, in contrast, even sections which state ostensibly general truths are rendered relative in their context. Section 30, for example, recalls *In Memoriam*'s struggle with an evolutionary idea of nature 'red in tooth and claw' (*In Memoriam* LVI, l. 15):

> What are we first? First, animals; and next
> Intelligences at a leap; on whom
> Pale lies the distant shadow of the tomb
> And all that draweth on the tomb for text.
> Into which state comes Love, the crowning sun:
> Beneath whose light the shadow loses form.
> We are the lords of life, and life is warm.
> Intelligence and instinct now are one.
> But nature says: 'My children most they seem
> When thy least know me: therefore I decree
> That they shall suffer.' Swift doth young Love flee,
> And we stand wakened, shivering from our dream.
> Then if we study Nature we are wise.
> Thus do the few who live but with the day:
> The scientific animals are they. –(30, ll. 1–15)

The gnomic lyric stance taken here, claiming general relevance as a *conditio humana* and a pessimistic and materialistic precept for living is revealed as a self-serving apologetics with its concluding line, which I have omitted above: 'Lady, this is my sonnet to your eyes' (30, l. 16). The *carpe diem* rationale promoted by a reference to recent science serves merely to justify the speaker's predatory stance towards his lover. Since we are first animals, and since love is but a passing dream, pursuing carnal pleasure and living from day to day is 'wise' (l. 13). And yet this pessimistic materialism serves to characterise the speaker further rather than to encourage the lyric iterability which its form invites only to undermine.

In such ways, the speaker's judgements and pronouncements are repeatedly called into question by the context; and truth, whether lyric or merely factual, remains elusive. This culminates in the conclusion of the sequence. When the wife finally does kill herself, the husband implies that she has done so for his sake, to free him for a happy life with his new lover and yet his insistence on his own interpretation may itself raise doubts: 'Will the hard world my sentience of her share? / I feel the truth; so let the world surmise' (48, ll. 15–16). The readerly doubt that is invited by these lines finds further fuel in the next and penultimate section, in which the heterodiegetic narrative voice returns to provide a single, though brief and ambiguous, glimpse of the interiority of the wife:

> He found her by the ocean's moaning verge,
> Nor any wicked change in her discerned;
> And she believed his old love had returned,
> Which was her exultation, and her scourge.
> She took his hand, and walked with him, and seemed
> The wife he sought, though shadow-like and dry.
> She had one terror, lest her heart should sigh,
> And tell her loudly she no longer dreamed.
> She dared not say, 'This is my breast: look in.'
> But there's a strength to help the desperate weak.
> That night he learned how silence best can speak
> The awful things when Pity pleads for Sin.
> About the middle of the night her call
> Was heard, and he came wondering to the bed.
> 'Now kiss me, dear! it may be, now!' she said.
> Lethe had passed those lips, and he knew all. (49)

If the husband's vanity suggests to him that she has sacrificed herself for the sake of her love for him, this section is at least ambiguous about this interpretation. What is it that the wife has to hide in her breast? Why is his returning love a 'scourge' (l. 4)? What is the dream that has ended for her? Rather than dying for him, is she dying to escape from him? The brief glimpse we get of her perspective provides no answer to these questions, but it does cast the husband's assurance that he 'feel[s] the truth' into doubt (48, l. 16). That this doubt is programmatic is made clear by the final lines of the poem:

> Ah, what a dusty answer gets the soul
> When hot for certainties in this our life! –
> In tragic hints here see what evermore
> Moves dark as yonder midnight ocean's force
> Thundering like ramping hosts of warrior horse,
> To throw that faint thin line upon the shore! (50, ll. 11–16)

There is no truth on offer here, no certainties but only tragic hints thrown as the thin line of writing onto the page. The image Meredith chooses is apt, in that the waves are thrown on the shore individually and rhythmically, like the individual, intermittent sections of the poem. The thin line the text traces on the page scarcely manages to hint at 'what evermore / Moves dark' (ll. 13–14) and can only be pieced together and guessed at by the reader.

Meredith's poem thus achieves its radical textual instability by playing on a combination of lyric, dramatic and narrative time structures, which undermine each other's truth claims. Lyric iterability and condensation breaks up narrative continuity and transparency of causal relation and evades retrospection, dramatic distancing undermines lyric appropriation and prevents the establishment of the self-constituting event of the lyric voice, while the narrative's reliance on the husband's perspective and the quasi-sonnet form of the poem's sections complicate the distance necessary for the critical judgement on which the truth claims of dramatic monologues are based.

Conclusion – Reactions to a Temporal Impasse or the Fate of the Lyric

The temporal complexity of the genres discussed in this chapter offered Victorians ways to negotiate the changing conditions for poetry, as its association with and reliance on eternal and divine guarantees could no longer be taken for granted. The poems I have examined to varying degrees redefine poetry's relation to change by embracing the transient and relative, as well as the everyday and the banal, adjusting poetry to a reality governed by change, by scientific standards of truth and a comparative loss of (Christian) faith. At the same time, they can be seen as ways to resist the ongoing lyricisation of poetry by emphasising character and plot. One way for poetry to attempt an escape from change and to continue to claim transcendence was to redefine itself as (idealised) lyric. Where it embraced change it often turned to story.

And yet, the association between poetry and transcendence remained strong, and with it a sense that it is set apart from the banalities and bare exigencies of everyday existence. This is not only visible in Dante Gabriel Rossetti's introductory sonnet, but no less in Barrett Browning's religious idealisation of the poet as God's voice, or in Clough's hope that a poetry of the contemporary would 'intimate to us relations which, in our unchosen peremptorily-appointed posts, in our grievously narrow and limited spheres of action, we still, in and through all, retain to some central, celestial fact' (2005 [1855]: 583). This desire for transcendence, however, would turn into another complex temporal problem for poetry in a society which increasingly conceived of time as a scarce resource; a resource which needs to be wisely and pragmatically employed to ensure commercial and personal success in life, and cannot be squandered in the idle writing and reading of poetry.

Notes

1. These three genres are arguably the most prominent examples, but there are also other instances for the importance of such renegotiations between narrative, lyric and dramatic time structures in Victorian poetry. James Thomson's *The City of Dreadful Night* (1874), for example, alternates lyric descriptions with narrative passages which refuse progression and resolution in its nightmarish evocation of irremediable despair. See also Emily Harrington's discussion of lyric and narrative temporality in Augusta Webster's verse romance *Yu-Pe-Ya's Lute* (2013).
2. Where the theatrical situation entirely takes over, as in some performance pieces, the kind of double dramatic temporality I am concerned with here disappears.
3. It testifies to the influence of Rossetti's phrasing of this ideal that Alfano echoes the language of his introductory sonnet without mentioning it explicitly.
4. Some critics have read *The House of Life* as a consistent portrayal of character and story, often in an endeavour to argue for the artistic unity of the sequence. David Riede quotes several such autobiographical readings and agrees to the extent that he sees the sequence as an artistic expression of Rossetti's life. He notes, however, that 'if that life was not unified, the poem will reflect the fissures between experience and aspiration, flesh and spirit, life and art. And indeed the poem does reflect and even overtly describe such fragmentation of the selves' (1992: 118–19).
5. This is also the central argument of John Holmes' perceptive reading of the sequence, in which he argues for the centrality of the sonnet 'Inclusiveness' to the sequence's poetics: 'Philosophically, "Inclusiveness" suggests a vision of the world in which no vision of the world can claim primacy' (2005: 15).
6. Dorothy Mermin, in contrast, maintains that the auditor acts as the reader's foil or representative (1983: 8).
7. See, for example, Helen Luu on the pertinent absence of auditors from the dramatic monologues of Augusta Webster (2016).

8. For an extensive, though by no means complete, or entirely unproblematic list of Victorian dramatic monologues by 'minor poets' arranged in similar groups, see Faas (1988: 210–15).

9. In his defence of his work, the *Notes on Poems and Reviews* (1866), Swinburne emphasises that 'the book is dramatic, many-faced, multifarious; and no utterance of enjoyment or despair, belief or unbelief, can properly be assumed as the assertion of its author's personal feeling or faith' (4).

10. Tucker notes with regard to the poem's final paragraph the lyrical 'evanescence of its "I"' with which Tennyson is 'transgressing the generic boundary of the dramatic monologue' (2007 [1985]: 546). A striking recent example of the possibility of a lyrical appropriation of these lines would be their use in the James Bond movie *Skyfall* (2012), where these words of a king trying to evade his responsibility towards his people are, with unintentional irony, quoted by M to justify and celebrate the secret service.

11. All line references to Webster's poetry are to the Broadview edition of *Portraits and Other Poems* edited by Christine Sutphin (2000) unless otherwise indicated.

12. For recent work on the Victorian novel in verse, see, in particular, Felluga (2002); Markovits (2006); Moore (2015). See also Herbert Tucker's comprehensive study of the pronounced epic drive in the long nineteenth century, which encompasses numerous novels in verse in its survey (2008).

13. Adrian Kempton's study *The Verse Novel in English* (2018), with its focus on verse novels published from the 1980s onwards, implicitly contradicts such an assessment. However, Kempton's rather cursory view of the Victorian predecessors of the contemporary trend he is interested in seriously underestimates the number of verse novels written in the nineteenth century. If there is a revival of the form in the late twentieth century and early twenty-first century, there is little doubt that it saw its first wave of popularity during Victoria's reign. Novels in verse like Owen Meredith's *Lucile* (1860) or Coventry Patmore's *Angel in the House* (1862) were widely read bestsellers at the time.

14. In fact, one of the earliest 'Victorian' novels in verse may be said to be Alexander Pushkin's *Eugene Onegin*, a self-proclaimed novel in verse deeply inspired by the example of Byron's *Don Juan*. Russian poetry was not well known among the Victorians, however, and the earliest mention of a translation of the poem I have been able to locate dates from 1881; intriguingly, its subtitle proclaims the work to be a romance, not a novel, in verse. One review of this translation begins by asserting that 'Russian poetry remains all but unknown to Western Europe' ('Eugene Onéguine' 1881: 396). Reviewing the same translation, the *Athenaeum* agrees that, outside of Russia, 'little seems to be known of his [Pushkin's] works – at least, of those written in verse'

('Book Review' 1881: 361). It seems therefore rather unlikely that Pushkin's innovation had any direct influence on the somewhat later flourishing of the genre in Victorian Britain, though the importance of Byron's work to both is undeniable.

15. Perhaps this is about to change. Over the last couple of decades an increasing number of verse novels has been published and the form is slowly gaining visibility, most prominently with Bernardine Evaristo's *Girl, Woman, Other* winning the Man Booker Prize in 2019. However, both critics and the author herself seem to avoid calling this book a novel in verse.

16. Moore, too, suggests that the verse novel 'can be basically understood as the distinctive but highly flexible product of two opposing pressures: an influential lyricism inherited from the Romantics, and the increasingly pushy naturalism of the contemporary novel' (2015: 70). She avoids pitching narrative against lyric, however, specifying the contrast as one between 'a Romanticism that upholds the supremacy of emotional and subjective realities' and 'a novelistic realism that works primarily with actions, events, circumstances, and the social and physical details of daily life' (2015: 70).

17. See, for example, Moore's reading of the relationship between the lyric preludes and the narrative sections of Patmore's *The Angel in the House* (1862), for a convincing argument about their necessary difference as well as their productive interaction (2015: 93–101).

18. Tucker has little to say about the relationship between the epic and the verse novel, but his comprehensive discussion of the nineteenth-century epic includes many works that could equally count and have elsewhere been discussed as verse novels, and he comments occasionally on their relationship in passing. Tucker's work is relevant, though, in that it illustrates both the strong epic presence in the nineteenth century and remarks upon 'the categorical erasure of the epic genre from our working picture of the nineteenth century' (2008: 10). The reflex to think of prose novels when we think of narrative is historically biased.

19. In this I disagree with Stefanie Markovits's critique of what she calls a 'preferred focus on epic' in discussions of verse novels (2017: 5). Markovits suggests that one of the consequences of such a focus is that it 'has tended to obscure the generic implications of these poems' explorations of love' and argues that this should be 'viewed through the lens of love poetry, so often the close-bounded province of the lyric' (2017: 6). This suggestion obscures not only that the lyric can hardly be reduced to the topic of love, but, more relevantly, that the novel was the Victorian genre of choice for stories of love, much more decidedly than lyric poetry.

20. John Holmes comments on this that the poem insists on facts only to end on a note of a 'profound, even existential sense of ignorance' (2018: 93).

Chapter 3

Idle Poetry and Poetic Idleness – Poetry in the Age of the Gospel of Success

Is idleness indeed so black a crime?
What are the Busy doing, half their time?
(William Allingham 1884)

If the debate in the 1840s and 1850s which I delineate in Chapter 1 revolved around the question whether poetry could legitimately address the present without becoming something less than poetry, over the course of the century the challenge to poetry also takes a more fundamental turn. Rather than asking whether a poetry of the present is possible, the doubt is raised whether poetry is possible in the present. The problem with the age is not only that it is 'unpoetical' in the sense of providing unfit subject matter for poetry. The age is also unpoetical because the 'fretful stir / Unprofitable, and the fever of the world' (Wordsworth 'Tintern Abbey' ll. 53–4; 1992: 117), which seem to become ever more ubiquitous features of Victorian experience, are ostensibly inimical both to poetic production and to poetic reception.

A supposedly new sense of time's urgency characterised the Victorian age for many of its contemporaries, with change and acceleration as central features. Austin Dobson laments this perceived change in his rondeau 'On the Hurry of this Time' (1885):

With slower pen men used to write,
Of old, when 'letters' were 'polite';
In Anna's or in George's days,
They could afford to turn a phrase,
Or trim a struggling theme aright.

They knew not steam; electric light
Not yet had dazed their calmer sight; –

They meted out both blame and praise
With slower pen.

Too swiftly now the Hours take flight!
What's read at morn is dead at night:
Scant space have we for Art's delays,
Whose breathless thought so briefly stays,
We may not work – ah! would we might! –
With slower pen.

In a typically nostalgic tone, which is given formal expression by the choice of the rondeau, an old French poetic form, the poem specifically singles out the temporal changes brought about by technological advances like electric light and the steam engine as causes for the decline of poetry, but also blames the acceleration of print production, publishing and reception. This affects poetry in particular: 'Scant space we have for Art's delays / Whose breathless thought so briefly stays' (ll. 12–13). The placing of the line break and the choice of rhyme words suggests that it is first and foremost the delay of the poetic line, with its brief pause which encourages thought to 'briefly stay [. . .]', for which the current prosaic age has no patience. People are 'too busy for poetry', Andrew C. Bradley, later Oxford Professor of Poetry, complains in 1884 (26). The average man, as he grows older, 'puts poetry away with his other follies; and, once embarked on the business of life, he has, he fondly tells himself, "no time" for such things as these' (Bradley 1884: 4).

In other words, what both poets and readers are allegedly lacking in the accelerated circumstances of modernity is the requisite idleness to produce and to enjoy poetry. As I argue in this chapter, idleness is fraught with ambiguity and even anxiety for Victorian poets, who continue to appreciate its role as a source or even a condition for poetic creativity but at the same time acknowledge its resistance to a broader cultural context which values duty, exertion and ambition. This ambiguity emerges again and again from poems which contemplate idleness. Victorian poems about idleness frequently turn out to be, at heart, poems about the nature and possibility of poetry. At the same time, my discussion aims to further complicate matters by confronting common assumptions about both idleness and the ideology of work which condemns it, with issues of class, gender and religion.

Of course, Dobson's poem also suggests that the problem is not so much that poetry can no longer be written, but rather that poetic production, along with the rest of the age, has dramatically accelerated and proliferated. The role the periodical press played in the distribution of poetry at the time contributed to the increasing ephemerality of poetic production. Periodical poetry has only recently begun to receive sustained critical attention, with critics like Caley Ehnes (2019) arguing that most middle-class Victorian readers would have encountered poetry primarily in periodicals and newspapers, that is, in a publication format that is inherently transient. Periodical publication not only encouraged occasional, topical poetry, but also tends to undermine poetry's claims to lasting, eternal value. To contemporaries steeped in Romantic ideals of poetic permanence, a poetry which no longer outlives the moment in the protean Victorian age and is caught up in the whirl of the world may, however, have seemed to hardly merit its name. As Ehnes notes, this 'sets up a binary between the poetry published in the periodical press and that published in the traditional single volume format' (2019: 8).[1] True poetry is replaced by mere transient verse.

Curiously, arguments about the lack of time for poetry fail to confront the reality that more and more people apparently did have sufficient leisure time (as well as sufficient literacy) to read periodicals and novels. Indeed, for the middle classes and gradually as the century progressed for the labouring classes as well, leisure became significantly *more* widely available.[2] Cultural historians John Lowerson and John Myerscough point out:

> there was in Victorian England a virtual 'leisure revolution' [which] involved, amongst other things, three important social developments: a growth in the quantity of free time available, a growing array of new ways to fill the increasing hours of leisure time and associated changes in habits of spending on recreational activities. (1977: 1)

Moreover, time became increasingly compartmentalised into clearly defined and delimited work and leisure hours (Bailey 1987: 4). Thus, the frequent Victorian laments about acceleration and time-scarcity paradoxically coincide with anxious middle-class concerns about the spread of leisure and the proper use of such free time. Once it has become clearly divorced from labour, leisure is empty time that needs to be filled and Victorian moral authorities were very concerned that such empty time should be filled usefully. Heidi Liedke suggests that 'idleness, as emptiness or the state of being free/empty from anything, is shocking and evokes resentment in a society that is striving to become a capitalist clockwork society' (2018: 26). Even the arts are appropriated for such a leisure economy, with wide wide-reaching consequences: '[t]he museums, the public parks, the libraries, the musical life of the nation, the belief that leisure time should be spent in some improvement of self and society, all owe much to this movement which contemporaries came to call "rational recreation"' (Cunningham 1980: 90). In a society which increasingly understands time as a resource, no time should be idly wasted and even pleasure needs to pursue some useful aim.

Writing about the roots of this ideology in the eighteenth century, Sarah Jordan provides some useful thoughts on the emergence of the paradoxical situation, in which a sense of time-scarcity results directly from an increase of leisure. She points out that for the middle classes 'industriousness had become a value that could entitle them to social prestige and respect. Thus idleness posed a threat to one's status and self-definition, as well as a threat to the larger society' (2003: 18). However, this involves a crucial contradiction:

> the middle classes, in aspiring to join the gentry, were using their indus-triousness to leave a class known for its industry and join a class which by definition was idle. Idleness, therefore, was somehow the desired reward for hard work, the ultimate attainment in social status, while it was also viewed as deeply threatening, to the self and to the nation. (18)

Jordan's observations help to highlight the deep roots of the gospel of work in bourgeois ideology, as well as the essential aspirational nature of this gospel. In particular in the hands of the rational rec-reation movement and in the booming Victorian popular conduct book and advice literature, Carlyle's panegyric of work becomes what J. F. C. Harrison has called 'the Victorian gospel of success' (1957). In the context of an ideology of industriousness which turns not only work, but success through work into the single purpose of a worthy human life, the more leisure time there is, the stronger is the potential threat of idleness and the more imperative is the need to fill such empty time profitably.[3]

The problem poetry faces therefore seems to be not so much the actual lack of time for reading (though this is what contemporar-ies like to claim). Instead, there are two features of the temporal logic underlying a gospel of success that appear to be inhospitable to poetry, and to lyric poetry especially. These are, on the one hand, poetry's association with idle contemplation and disinterestedness, which seemed increasingly out of place in the Victorian present. On the other hand, the basic temporal structure of the gospel of success follows the logic of continual progress. In success literature like Samuel Smiles's immensely popular *Self-Help* (1859), success is the result of unceasing application, never a status that is achieved.

It depends on a belief in causal relations between present actions (work) and future results (success). A remarkable passage from John Henry Newman's *The Mission of the Benedictine Order* (1858) suggests the challenge such a sense of time as progressive development may pose to a Victorian understanding of the nature of poetry. Newman refers to Virgil's pastoral ideal and implicitly contrasts it to the Victorian present:

> Repose, intellectual and moral, is that quality of country life which he [Virgil] selects for his praises; and effort, bustle, and excitement is that quality of a town life which he abhors. Such a life, – living for the day without solicitude of the morrow, without plans or objects, even holy ones; here below; working, not (so to say) by the piece, but as hired by the hour; sowing the ground with the certainty, according to the promise, of reaping; reading or writing this present week without the consequent necessity of reading or writing during the next; dwelling among one's own people without distant ties; taking each new day as a whole in itself, an addition, not a implement, to the past; and doing works which cannot be cut short, for they are complete in every portion of them, – such a life may be called emphatically Virgilian. They, on the contrary, whose duty lies in what may be called undertakings, in science and system, in sustained efforts of the intellect or elaborate processes of action, [. . .] have a noble and meritorious mission, but not so a poetical one. (2011: 75–6)

The Virgilian poet lives in the present, without projecting his life into the future, without ambition. His life is plotless, in so far as it does not develop as a project; it does not throw itself into the future, its present merely extends but brings no alteration to the rhythms of life. He is not idle, but his work is not aspirational. It sustains but does not look for future increase or profit. The life of self-help which Smiles advocates, in contrast, is decidedly the kind of life of 'sustained efforts of the intellect or elaborate processes of action' which seemed to Newman to be unpoetical.

The primary literary form the nineteenth century favoured for the representation of elaborate processes of action was undoubtedly the novel. Tina Young Choi and Barbara Leckie have pointed to the importance of narrative form to Smiles's project: 'Smiles enlists narrative as a tool to instil in his readers the belief that positive outcomes follow causally – if slowly, sometimes taking years if not generations to come to fruition – from good habits' (2018: 574). They go on to argue that the Victorian novel 'with its multiple volumes and instalments, its temporally extended plots, and its transcendent, omniscient narratives', was particularly well suited for the representation 'of the traceable causalities unavailable in other accounts' (2018: 575), and thus strongly resonated with the kind of self-help ideology propagated by Smiles and others. This correlates with Peter Brooks's influential claim in *Reading for the Plot* (1984) that '[i]t may in fact be a defining characteristic of the modern novel (as of bourgeois society) that it takes aspiration, getting ahead, seriously, [. . .] and thus makes ambition the vehicle and emblem of Eros, that which totalizes the world as possession and progress' (39). Ambition and novelistic narrative go hand in hand.[4]

For poetry, however, I would like to suggest, such a pervasive ideology of success posed not only ideological, but also formal challenges. The attention poetry draws to its own language as well as its dependence on structures of repetition tends to counteract the dynamics of narrative desire, even in narrative poetry where the forward drive of plot is always at least conditioned and often checked by what Brian McHale has called the countermeasurement of poetic segmentivity. McHale argues that '[p]oetry is that form of discourse that depends crucially on segmentation, on *spacing*, in its production of meaning' and goes on to point out that this 'spacing' can also be understood metaphorically as the equivalent of 'pause, silence, or the beginning or end of a recurrent pattern' (2009: 14–15) – precisely that moment of pause for which, according to Dobson, there seemed to be decreasing patience in the Victorian world. I will draw further on McHale's useful intervention for the more general thoughts on poetic temporality which I develop in my final chapter. At this point, I merely want to note that verse, in contrast to prose, structurally depends both on interruption and on repetition: repetition of sounds in rhyme, assonance and consonance; repetition of metrical structure, of pauses; recurrence of words; of syntax, line and stanza structures; of refrains.

Of course, as Monika Fludernik and Miriam Nandi's edited collection tracing idleness in English literature serves well to show, idleness 'is a contested, equivocal term and a varied complex phenomena', which has, throughout history 'tended to draw [. . .] the anger and moral indignation of various apostles of thrift, industry and the work ethic' (Fludernik and Nandi 2014: 5–6). They also note that '[l]iterature itself both in its production and reception [. . .] provides a paradigmatic analogue for the practices and enjoyments of creative leisure' (2014: 4). While these general observations are doubtlessly correct, I want to insist on the importance of genre specificity in the Victorian context. The temporal regime implied in the

Victorian ideology of success, I suggest, poses a double challenge to poetry, both moral and formal. This comes particularly to the fore in poems which explicitly engage with idleness or inaction.

In this chapter, then, I focus on the way idleness features in Victorian poems as both morally condemnable and vitally important for poetic production. Taking my cue from Fludernik and Nandi's insistence that questions of gender and class are crucial to considerations of idleness (2014: 6), I will show that the problem of idleness takes very different shapes if regarded from the perspective of the working classes or of women. To conclude this chapter, I focus on the work of Christina Rossetti to illustrate how a religiously rooted understanding of time may undercut the only apparently straightforward opposition between aesthetic idleness and bourgeois industriousness. The challenge to poetry by a time regime which constantly projects itself towards a future, whose logic is progressive and which is suspicious not only of idleness, but of pause, silence and rest, is even more fundamental than the issues raised concerning poetry's subject matter or its truth status. It partly underpins, but also extends beyond the genre innovations which were my subject in the previous chapter. Dobson's poem, which I have quoted above, serves well to illustrate that the issue of idleness touches upon core conditions of poetic production, reception and form as perceived by the Victorians and was clearly a matter of serious concern for poets at the time.

Idle Singers, Idle Songs – The Birth of Poetry from the Spirit of Idleness

As the nineteenth century progresses, the association of aesthetic contemplation and poetic production with idleness comes into conflict with an increasingly dominant time regime, which condemns idleness as unproductive waste. Richard Adelman has argued that for the Romantic poets (he specifically refers to Cowper, Wordsworth, Coleridge, Keats and Shelley), 'idle aesthetic contemplation is the condition of all poetic creativity' (2018: 46). While both Adelman (2011) and Willard Spiegelman (1995) convincingly demonstrate that, on closer inspection, the Romantics' attitude and depictions of idleness are often fraught with ambivalence, dangers and conflicts, the association of poetic inspiration and production with idle contemplation was firmly lodged in the Victorian imagination. However, in a society in which a Carlylean gospel of work can be identified as 'one of the primary currents of [. . .] thought', idleness had little justification (Adelman 2018: 81).[5] As Matthew Arnold put it in *Culture and Anarchy* (1869), though with more than a pinch of sarcasm: 'It cannot but acutely try a tender conscience to be accused, in a practical country like ours, of keeping aloof from the work and hope of a multitude of earnest-hearted men, and of merely toying with poetry and aesthetics' (1993: 99–100). When bourgeois middle-class values of industry, self-realisation and active pursuit of progress turn into dominant social norms, contemplative idleness as the basis of the production and reception of poetry becomes increasingly fraught with moral objections.

Perhaps a little too quickly, Liedke concludes from this that '[i]n Victorian England, idleness was anachronistic, happening "against" other, dominant, concepts and their respective value for society' (2018: 25). She thereby implies a progressive timeline in which industrious behaviour is somehow more advanced than idleness. In a similar vein, commenting on poems by Tennyson, Arnold and Hopkins, Adelman comes to the conclusion that 'meditative poetry, which was the bastion and constant celebrant of aesthetic consciousness at the beginning of the century, has become that category's opponent and sometimes its mourner. [. . .] such states are consistently configured – in these examples of mid-Victorian thought – as the antitheses of correct, mature, civilized life' (2018: 113). These comments are not unjustified but a closer scrutiny of the role of idleness in a broader sample of Victorian poetry may serve to complicate the issue and helps to avoid both the kind of progressive logic Liedke's argument risks falling prey to and the generalisation which Adelman courts. Indeed, Adelman's rather limited text selection lets him underestimate, I think, both the variety of poetic responses to the issue and its gravity. Poetic considerations of the worth and justification of idleness, as we will see, often turn into considerations of the worth and justification of poetry itself. Indeed, even the poems Adelman does discuss can be seen to point in that direction. For instance, as I have had occasion to discuss in Chapter 1, Matthew Arnold, Adelman's foremost example of a nostalgic attitude towards idleness, repeatedly voices his opinion that the present age is unpoetical and eventually stops writing poetry altogether.

Adelman takes Tennyson's 'The Lotos-Eaters' as paradigmatic of the kind of rejection of idleness on moral grounds he wants to highlight, calling the poem 'a kind of touchstone for later Tennyson and for mainstream Victorian values' (2018: 101). The poem certainly serves this purpose well. As its title suggests, it takes up an episode from the *Odyssey*, in which the ship reaches the isle of the lotos-eaters.

Under the influence of the lotos fruit, the mariners decide to stay, since 'Most weary seem'd the sea, weary the oar, / Weary the wandering fields of barren foam' (ll. 41–2). Tired of 'ever climbing up the climbing wave' (l. 95), the mariners are seduced by the pleasure of the lotos and the beauty of the land into turning their backs on their former lives, and they propose to 'swear an oath, and keep it with an equal mind, / In the hollow Lotos-land to live and lie reclined / On the hills like Gods together, careless of mankind' (ll. 153–5). Adelman comments:

> In 'The Lotos-Eaters' [. . .] intense passivity becomes not a truthful and powerful engagement with the world's sensuousness, but a giving in to sensuality and also – perhaps more importantly considering the development of conceptions of idleness in the second half of the century – a giving in to one's inner anxieties and moral weaknesses. (2018: 101)

Indeed, such a reading is further substantiated by the fact that Tennyson significantly revised an earlier version of the poem, published in *Poems, Chiefly Lyrical* (1830) for his *Poems* (1842), to the effect that the poem's moral objection to idleness became much more pronounced. While the earlier version can be read to render a (albeit tentative) positive image of the mariners' decision, the revisions seem to suggest Tennyson's 'increasing alignment with the sensibility of his age' (Grob 1964: 118; see also Riede 2005: 57; Sanford Russell 2015).

It is easy to see Tennyson's revisions to the poem as the result of an increasing anxiety towards idleness. But they also intensify the poet's quandary. After all, the life the mariners propose to lead on the island is a life of aesthetic appreciation:

How sweet it were, hearing the downward stream,
With half-shut eyes ever to seem
Falling asleep in a half-dream!
To dream and dream, like yonder amber light,
Which will not leave the myrrh-bush on the height;
To hear each other's whisper'd speech;
Eating the Lotos day by day,
To watch the crisping ripples on the beach,
And tender curving lines of creamy spray;
To lend our hearts and spirits wholly
To the influence of mild-minded melancholy;
To muse and brood and live again in memory,
With those old faces of our infancy
Heap'd over with a mound of grass,
Two handfuls of white dust, shut in an urn of brass! (ll. 99–113)

The mariners reject their active life of labour for a life of aesthetic contemplation and sensual appreciation, a life of dreams, memories, melancholy musings and mourning of the dead. If these lines condemn the mariners, such condemnation can hardly seem whole-hearted, coming from a poet who has a notorious 'fixation on the past, on the days that are no more' (Tucker 1983: 9) and who stylised perpetual mourning into a fount of his poetic production. Notably, to the lotos-eating mariners, 'the gushing of the wave / Far away did seem to mourn and rave / On alien shores' (ll. 31–3). What may sound like an alienating experience is in fact a highly poetic one, indicated by the words 'far, far away', which, as Tennyson acknowledged, played a key role for him. Nor has this escaped the attention of the critics. David G. Riede notes that 'the stanza suggests [. . .] that the lotos inspires poetic apprehension akin to Tennyson's own' (2005: 57). It seems that a moral rejection of the mariners' decision would amount to a rejection of an aesthetically aware, poetic life.

As critics have not failed to point out, the subject of the poem 'lends itself readily to moral amplification as a fable of the artist who becomes enamored of poesy and loses all sense of responsibility to the world of men' (Grob 1964: 120). But the mariners' song is a direct result of their resolve to remain on the island. Their voices constitute the better part of the poem precisely because they now are idle enough to sing. And their lines are poetry par excellence; Tennyson musters all his remarkable sense of poetic musicality to make the mariners' song appealing. Indeed, contemporary reviewers singled the poem out for being 'rich in striking and appropriate imagery, and [. . .] sung to a rhythm which is music itself' ('The Poetry of Alfred Tennyson' 1845: 28). Moreover, even in spite of the revisions introduced to the 1842 version, reviewers could show decided sympathy for the mariners. The reviewer for *The British Quarterly Review*, for example, writes: 'It is no objection to this charming little poem, but an additional merit, that it is not necessary to have eaten of the lotos to sympathize with the strain of feeling which it so beautifully describes' ('Art. II *Poems*. By Alfred Tennyson' 1845: 55). In rejecting idleness, then, the poem would seem to be rejecting poetry itself.

One might object that this is an inadmissible generalisation, that what is rejected is not poetry *tout court*, but what has been retrospectively interpreted as an early form of Aestheticism (Leighton 2002: 58); that is, a sort of lyric poetry that withdraws into an aesthetic realm, and claims its autonomous distance from the busy whirl of the world. After all, 'The Lotos-Eaters' itself juxtaposes two kinds of poetic

genres, beginning as it does with five Spenserian stanzas which offer
a frame tale in the epic mode, before leading into the choric song of
the mariners. Thus, presumably, the epic or other more narrative or
less aesthetically rarefied modes of poetry – modes of poetry which
indeed would come to play an increasing role in Tennyson's later poetic
production – might be able to offer an alternative to the objection-
able idle Epicureanism of the mariners here associated with the lyric.
In her discussion of the 1832 version of the poem, Beatrice Sanford
Russell explores the juxtaposition of Spenserian frame and choric song
but intriguingly turns the underlying moral on its head. She reads the
poem as an example of Tennyson's 'shift away from acquisitive plots of
desire and ambition, writing in their stead narratives organized around
blank, eventless stretches of lived experience'. Indeed, she glosses this
as Tennyson's 'attempt [. . .] to write a counterhistory to supplement
the dominant Western histories of action and acquisition' (2015: 378).
Rather than casting this as a juxtaposition of two kinds of narrative,
however, as Sanford Russell does here, I would suggest that what is
juxtaposed is plot-driven narrative on the one hand and plotless song
on the other. The choric song of the mariners is not an eventless narrative. It is not narrative at all, but a dramatised lyric. Whichever genre
one might choose to see favoured in a reading of the poem, their juxtaposition clearly associates narrative with action ('Courage!' is the
poem's first word) and lyric with a 'poetics of inaction' (Sanford Russell
2015: 380). A narrative plot of ambition is pitched against a plotless,
lyric experience of the present, while dramatic distance invites a reader's judgement. Idleness thus turns into a question of poetic form, in
which a rejection or an endorsement of idleness implies a rejection or
an endorsement of particular poetic forms.

This may seem to confirm the suspicion that it is not poetry as
such which is rejected with a moral condemnation of idleness, but a
particular kind of poetry, namely an Aestheticist lyric *avant la lettre*.
However, things become rather more complex if one looks beyond
'The Lotos-Eaters' to other poems by Tennyson. After all, Tennyson
repeatedly returns to scenes of idleness as directly conducive to poetic
production and reception of all kinds. 'The Epic' (1842) features a
friendly Christmas gathering in which the poet reads from his work
(see Chapter 1); *The Princess* (1847) is the result of an idle afternoon,
in which a group of friends creates the story as a 'Seven-headed monster
[. . .] only made to kill / Time' (ll. 200–1); and even 'Ulysses' (1842),
that paradigmatic call to action and in many ways a companion piece
to 'The Lotos-Eaters', is the result of an idle state the speaker is impatient of.[6] And to return once more to 'The Lotos-Eaters', even this poem

plays a doubly paradoxical role. On the one hand, it amply provides the very seductiveness of poetic language which it condemns. On the other hand, precisely by addressing itself to the question 'of a poet's involvement in the external world of politics and labour, or his retreat into an isolated aesthetic that pretends to itself that it has no relation to the world beyond' (O'Gorman 2004: 67), it engages with this external world even as it appears to withdraw from it. The very act of withdrawal throws the poem into the middle of an ongoing social and aesthetic debate.

This debate clearly concerned poets deeply and often finds explicit expression in the poetry of the period. Adelman, for his part, concludes that '[p]oetry in this period should thus be seen to claim, time and again, that the Romantic model of passivity is unsustainable, unworldly and self-indulgent' (2018: 100). But a broader view on poems partaking in this debate shows that this assessment cannot stand without qualification. In fact, the lotos-eaters could become a symbol of resistance to the haste of contemporary life even for such a mainstream poet as Martin Farquhar Tupper, author of the immensely popular quintessence of early Victorian morals *Proverbial Philosophy* (1838). In 'Railway Times' (1855) Tupper laments, like many of his contemporaries, the 'rapid days, electric hours' (l.1), the 'Niagara-life' (l. 25) in which there is 'No rest' and 'We speed along, as if "too late" / Were the great terror of the times' (l. 26; ll. 31–2). In this context, a reference to Tennyson's poem turns into a nostalgic celebration of lotos-eating as a desirable alternative: 'The lotus-eaters all are dead; / There is no nook for quiet thought' (ll. 33–4). But Tupper is not merely nostalgic, lamenting an anachronistic state that has no place in the modern world. Instead, he actively advises pursuing an alternative course, beyond 'hot competing strife' (l. 41): 'my counsel is, keep still; / They do not drown who lie afloat' (ll. 49–50). It is striking and illustrative of the utter conventionality of the poem that for all this heralding of idleness, Tupper nonetheless reverts to a logic of success in the concluding lines, in which the course he advises is praised as the one which will ultimately lead to success in life:

he that stands aloof from strife,
Calmly resolved to thread the maze,
Shall quell to his Success in life
The riot of these rapid days. (ll. 53–6)

My point here is that Tupper's lament is not an exception running against 'mainstream Victorian values' which Adelman sees expressed in Tennyson's much more complex and contradictory 'The Lotos-Eaters', but rather that its praise of idleness is utterly conventional, part of a poetic commonplace that is scarcely less prevalent than the condemnation Adelman diagnoses.

If unreserved and explicit praise of idleness remains fairly rare, a note frequently struck by Victorian poems seems to be not so much moral condemnation, but rather a somewhat defensive endorsement, like that expressed in Allingham's epigram which serves as the epi-graph for this chapter, or the kind of deep ambiguity which we have seen to characterise Tennyson's poetry. Both of these stances do attest to a prevalent perception that poetic idleness is morally questionable; a perception against which poets stake their claims.

William Michael Rossetti's 'Fancies at Leisure', for instance, a group of nine poems in two parts published in the second and third issue of *The Germ* in 1850, includes a poem called 'Sheer Waste' which asks: 'Is it a little thing to lie down here / Beside the water, looking into it / And see there grass and fallen leaves interknit' (ll. 1–3)? The poem goes on to describe a scene of idleness in nature, full of minute descriptions of sense impressions. Intriguingly, a second-person address is used throughout, emphatically offering the poem as an experience to the reader to be appropriated or re-inhabited. The sense of idleness in the poem is extreme, almost oppressive:

> The sun's heat now is painful. Scarce can you
> Move, and even less lie still. You shuffle then,
> Poised on your arms, again to shade. Again
> There comes a pleasant laxness on you. When
> You have done enough of nothing, you will go. (ll. 36–40)

Nothing is done, nothing is achieved in this poem. What little move-ment there is, prompted by brief bodily discomfort, is emphatically repetitive ('again [. . .]. Again', l. 38), passive and aimless. This extremity of idleness is not invoked in order to condemn it, however, but to insist on the value even of the sheer waste the title announces it to be. The poem's final stanza returns to the opening question only to imply a negative answer:

> Some hours perhaps have passed. Say not you fling
> These hours or such-like recklessly away.
> Seeing the grass and sun and children, say,
> Is not this something more than idle play,
> Than careless waste? Is it a little thing? (ll. 41–5)

Commenting on this text, John Holmes has remarked:

> Rossetti's poem may seem to revel in laziness, yet it asks us to consider whether it is in fact a 'sheer waste' of time, a mere 'little thing' to spend an afternoon lounging in a park. 'Sheer Waste' may seem indolent, but it is dense with observations. (2018: 39)

Exploring the role of science in Pre-Raphaelism, Holmes goes on to suggest that what the poem series 'Fancies at Leisure' explores is leisure as 'a starting point for examining the world around us and the processes and value of perception and observation' (39). What appears to be idleness, in other words, is in fact not idle at all, but the application of scientific methods of observation.

Holmes's reading is persuasive, but one might remark that the sort of observation celebrated in the poem has no directly pragmatic function, not even that of gaining knowledge. Nature (such as the behaviour of damselflies) is observed closely in the poem, but with a sense of appreciation rather than probing curiosity. Moreover, the poem can be profitably set into the wider context of the problematic association between idleness and poetry. After all, one of the results of the idle play described in the poem is clearly the poem itself, as well as the entire group Rossetti chose to call 'Fancies at Leisure'. If one can take Holmes's reading to suggest that the answer to the poem's question should be 'no, it is not a little thing, it is science', the answer might well also be 'no, it is not a little thing, it is poetry'. I would thus qualify Holmes's observation that 'the very idea of leisure in these poems is a marker of their modernity' (39), by adding that it is not leisure per se that marks the poem as modern, but its defensiveness in arguing for the validity of idle contemplation.

William Michael's brother, Dante Gabriel, opted for the pleasure of a lotos-eater both with similar explicitness and a similar need for justification:

IDLE BLESSEDNESS
I know not how it is, I have the knack,
In lazy moods, of seeking no excuse;
But holding that man's ease must be the juice
Of man's philosophy, I give the sack
To thought, and lounge at shuffle on the track
Of what employment seems of the least use:
And in such ways I find a constant sluice
For drowzy humours. Be thou loth to rack

And hack thy brain for thought, which may lurk there
Or may not. Without pain of thought, the eyes
Can see, the ears can hear, the sultry mouth
Can taste the summer's favour. Towards the South
Let earth sway round, while this my body lies
In warmth, and has the sun on face and hair.[7]

Composed in 1849 as a *bout rimé* but only published posthumously, this sonnet endorses sensuous pleasure in idleness, explicitly rejecting even the activity of the brain which might lead to poetic creation. The speaker is utterly passive to the point where the identity of the voice established in the octet threatens to dissolve in the sestet into separate bodily parts: eyes, ears, mouth, face, hair. This dissolving is experienced as wholly pleasurable and takes the form of a recommendation with the imperative in line 8. The beginning of the poem, however, is defensive. Though the speaker claims to be 'seeking no excuse' (l. 2), an excuse is precisely what is offered in the next two lines, which suggest that there is, after all, a sort of practical use to idleness: it serves as a 'sluice / For drowzy humours' (ll. 7–8) – that is, it has health benefits. In addition, present idleness becomes the seed for future thought (and, one may infer, poetry). Moreover, the opening words of the poem, 'I know not how it is', are both apologetic and somewhat disingenuous. On the one hand, they suggest that the speaker might be talking about a personal idiosyncrasy, or even a failure in his or her nature, which lies beyond the speaker's control. On the other hand, the poem provides motivations and reasons for this knack for idleness and indeed goes on to recommend it. Thus, the following thirteen lines, by giving a precise shape to the 'knack', belie the profession of ignorance voiced in the first.

'Idle Blessedness' talks about idle moments as a possibility, not as an experienced present. In 'Autumn Idleness', written a year later, Rossetti evokes an idle moment itself and concludes on a much more troubled note.

AUTUMN IDLENESS
This sunlight shames November where he grieves
In dead red leaves, and will not let him shun
The day, though bough with bough be over-run.
But with a blessing every glade receives
High salutation; while from hillock-eaves
The deer gaze calling, dappled white and dun,
As if, being foresters of old, the sun
Had marked them with the shade of forest-leaves.

Here dawn to-day unveiled her magic glass;
Here noon now gives the thirst and takes the dew;
Till eve bring rest when other good things pass.
And here the lost hours the lost hours renew
While I still lead my shadow o'er the grass,
Nor know, for longing, that which I should do.

Reading these two sonnets next to each other suggests that the latter
gives flesh to the abstract contentions of 'Idle Blessedness', by providing the direct experience which was lacking from the other poem.
The opening deictic 'This' creates immediacy, and the experience that
follows is developed in the sensuous terms outlined in the previous
sonnet: vivid visual impressions (the eye), the warmth and glory of
the sun (sun on face and hair), the calling deer (the ears). The sestet lays even stronger emphasis both on the present and presence of
experience with its insistent deictics, 'here', 'to-day' and 'now'. To
this point the poem emphasises sensuous impressions in a realisation
of the kind of passive receptivity of disintegrated identity praised in
'Idle Blessedness'. However, shifting the scene from summer to late
autumn raises the temporal stakes of the idle waste of time. The
speaker only appears directly in the final two lines, and together with
the appearance of this sense of identity, moral condemnation enters
the poem. Thus, intriguingly, the later poem reverses the trajectory
of the earlier one, from 'I know not how it is' to 'Nor know, for longing, that which I should do'. This seems to amount to a rejection of
idle inactivity and a longing for action.

However, in the light of the earlier poem, a different reading of
this final line emerges. Instead of glossing it as saying, 'I long to
do something, but do not know what', one could read it to mean
'because I am longing, I do not know what I should do'. The line
would then suggest that one should stop longing, for then one would
be able to enjoy the moment passively, as 'Idle Blessedness' had suggested. In this reading, it would be precisely the intrusion of the 'I'
who cannot stop to rack and hack his or her brain, in search of a
thought that might or might not be there, which disturbs the potentially idyllic experience of time passing without aim or use. Much
depends on how line 12 is understood. Is the emphasis here on loss,
that is, on the inutility and waste of spending one's time dreaming
of the past? Do the lost hours recall and re-enact other lost hours,
maximising the loss in fruitless repetition? Or is the emphasis on
renewal, in which the double loss turns out to equal gain? Moreover,
once 'Autumn Idleness' has taken its place as sonnet LXIX in the

1881 version of *The House of Life*, does this line not seem to recall the 'dead deathless hour' of the introductory sonnet?[8] The renewal of lost hours would then turn out to be at the heart of the poetic project the introductory sonnet had laid out.

Indeed, the line also serves as a hinge between two different concepts of time that govern the sestet. In the first tercet, the passage of time is described in terms of the change from dawn (the past), to noon (the present), to evening (the future). These are not merely empty markers of time, however. Each is qualitatively different and each brings something to the day. They have a direct effect on experience. In line 12, emptiness and fullness stand in an uneasy relation. If the hours are lost, it seems to follow that they must have been empty of meaningful experience. But the line also suggests that they were filled with the memory of other lost hours. With the next line, then, the speaker effectively turns into a sundial, leading his or her shadow over the grass. Any such measurement, however, inevitably imposes homogeneity on time and neglects experience. It is the precondition for the possibility of experiencing time as empty, which leads, in the poem, directly to the anxious need to fill it with activity. Since the poem has dwelt so extensively on the beauty of the experience in its octet and on the gifts of time in the first three lines of the sestet, this emptying out of experience in measurement and the moral concern arising from it amount indeed to a kind of loss. To read the poem in this way is to suggest that the hours only begin to appear lost to the speaker due to the intrusion of an instrumental time regime that construes time as empty and in need of being filled by activity. Instead of taking the poem as an example of Adelman's claim that Victorian poetry condemns idleness, I suggest it can be seen to be providing a subtle critique which sets out to show what is lost in submitting to the dominant time regime, namely a qualitative understanding of time based in sensual experience. And once again, one of the implied victims of this loss is the very sentiment that was conducive to the creation of the poem in the first place.

If the Rossettis, in these lyric poems, take a rather defensive stance, William Morris, in the 'Apology' which prefaces his massive story cycle in verse *The Earthly Paradise* (1868–70), brazenly proclaims the idleness and inutility of the work that is to follow.

> Of Heaven or Hell I have no power to sing,
> I cannot ease the burden of your fears,
> Or make quick-coming death a little thing,
> Or bring again the pleasure of past years,
> Nor for my words shall ye forget your tears,

Or hope again for aught that I can say,
The idle singer of an empty day.

But rather, when aweary of your mirth,
From full hearts still unsatisfied ye sigh,
And, feeling kindly unto all the earth,
Grudge every minute as it passes by,
Made the more mindful that the sweet days die—
—Remember me a little then I pray,
The idle singer of an empty day.

The heavy trouble, the bewildering care
That weighs us down who live and earn our bread,
These idle verses have no power to bear;
So let me sing of names remembered,
Because they, living not, can ne'er be dead,
Or long time take their memory quite away
From us poor singers of an empty day.

Dreamer of dreams, born out of my due time,
Why should I strive to set the crooked straight?
Let it suffice me that my murmuring rhyme
Beats with light wing against the ivory gate,
Telling a tale not too importunate
To those who in the sleepy region stay,
Lulled by the singer of an empty day. (Morris 2002: 'Apology' ll. 1–28)

Florence Boos, in the introduction to her edition of the poem, reads
the speaker's stance in these lines to be ironic (2002: 6), but I think it is
possible to take them at face value. Rejecting all semblance of usefulness in the first stanza's accumulation of negations, both this poetry's
source and its aim are idle. Strikingly, the suggestion here is not that
the poem is a means to fill and kill empty time, as in Tennyson's *The
Princess*. The poem is not meant to make us forget time but rather
it should make our appreciation of time's passing keener. Nor does
it offer escape from daily care. Indeed, it can only be appreciated by
those who already dwell in the 'sleepy region' (l. 27) of mirthful leisure.
Here, too, we can find the familiar suggestion that such idle dreaming is
anachronistic, but the poem's defiance of the perceived hostility of the
spirit of the time to the 'Dreamer of dreams' (l. 22) is both nonchalant
and breath-taking. With 'Let it suffice me' (l. 24) the poet declares his
independence from the judgement of the world, as long as he himself
is content with his work. But, after all, the 'murmuring rhyme' (l. 24)
that follows, encompassing twenty-five verse narratives with more

than 40,000 lines of verse in total and filling eventually four consider-
able volumes, asks its reader for a massive time commitment.

If the poems discussed so far seem to associate idleness with lyric
form and experience in particular, in *The Early Paradise* idleness is a
feature of poetic narrative. This is not the plot-driven narrative of the
nineteenth-century novel, however. The poem does not promise novelty, but 'names remembered' (l. 18). It retells familiar tales, it thrives
on repetition. Its collection of stories is purely episodic and cyclical,
offering little to no development in its frame tale which would give
the overall poem the directionality of a plot. Thus, the tales are idle
in that their telling leads to no result, they fulfil no ambition. Indeed,
they are the result of ambition thwarted and exposed as vain. Twice
removed both historically and geographically from the Victorian
present, the stories which compose the cycle are told partly by the
members of a group of fourteenth-century Norsemen, who, after
a long odyssey in search of the earthly paradise in which everyone
would be immortal, have eventually come to an island far in the west
on which they find remnants of the ancient Greek civilisation, kept
alive over generations by erstwhile refugees. The old Norsemen are
befriended by the elders of that isle and

> in their times of idleness and ease
> They told of poets' vain imaginings,
> And memories vague of half-forgotten things,
> Not true or false, but sweet to think upon. ('March', ll. 62–5)

The two groups then resolve to hold two feasts per month, one at
the beginning and one at the end, at each of which they alternately
tell a story from their cultural tradition. Thus, each story is framed
by reference both to the passing of the seasons and to the idle feast-
ing which culminates in the telling of the stories. The Norsemen's
account of their journey in the prologue, for its part, is a paradigmatic case of a narrative of restless pursuit, but it is clearly misguided
and doomed to fail. The Norsemen find a semblance of contentment
only when they, in their old age, have given up the quest and enjoy
the aimless life of idle storytelling on the western island.

The speaker of the 'Apology' can thus be taken at face value, not
only because the poem responds to the wider idleness debate, but also
because the complex narrative framing of the story cycle constantly
repeats this insistence on idle narration. As if that were not enough,
some of the tales themselves feature further instances of idle storytelling. The most striking case is the tale 'The Land East of the Sun and

West of the Moon', told at the end of September – a tale, notably, which Frederick Kirchhoff calls 'Morris' most complex account of the creative process' (1980: 238). It begins with a man called Gregory the Stargazer, who dreams of a king's Christmas feast to which a stranger comes, who begins to tell a version of the swan maiden story which takes up the main part of the tale. Two further narrative levels are therewith added to the already complex embedding of the cycle's tales and all of them recall the idle dreaming the 'Apology' found so little reason to be apologetic about. Moreover, much emphasis is laid on the indolence of the protagonist of the embedded story. The youngest of three sons, he is introduced by the following lines:

> But slothful was the youngest one,
> A loiterer in the spring-tide sun,
> A do-nought by the fire-side
> From end to end of winter-tide,
>
> And wont in summer heats to go
> About the garden to and fro,
> Plucking the flowers from bough and stalk;
> And muttering oft amid his walk
> Old rhymes that few men understood. (ll. 117–25)

The poem is not content to merely call him idle but draws this characteristic out over nine lines and three seasons. Moreover, once again, idleness is directly associated with a proclivity for poetry. If the familiar folk tale set-up now leads us to expect that the son's idleness will result in grief and misfortune, we soon find that we are mistaken. Indeed, it is precisely his idleness, that is, his ability to sleep through the day that allows him to succeed where his industrious brothers fail, overcome by the weariness of their daily toil. The youngest son manages to stay awake to see the fairy women who haunt his father's meadow. This meeting, while leading to some hardships before the happy ending, eventually brings unimaginable bliss to the young idler. Far from being punished, his idleness is richly rewarded. Moreover, when we return to the frame tale at the end of the story, we are told that Gregory the Stargazer, still under the influence of his dream, no longer joins in with the work of his fellows.

> *He stood by as they launched the boat,*
> *And little did their labour note.*
> *And set no hand thereto at all;*
> *Until an awe on these did fall;* (ll. 3333–6)

Gregory is not condemned for his dreaming and idleness, but rather gains the respect of his comrades. We are further told that '*From all men would he go apart / In woods and meads, and deal by art / With his returning memory*' (ll. 3351–3). Idly wandering Gregory, that is, turns his idle dreams into poetry: '*His weary heart a while to soothe / He wove all into verses smooth*' (ll. 3355–6). The final lines of the tale then play on the double meaning of idle, as both indolence and vanity: '*—Well, e'en so all the tale is said / How twain grew one and came to bliss— / Woe's me an idle dream it is!*' (ll. 3365–6). Coming at the conclusion of a tale full of the benefits of idle dreaming this exclamation of woe is highly ambiguous. As idleness is very much presented as an ideal throughout the poem, the final line seems rather suggestive of a pun. The speaker expresses woe because the bliss experienced in the story is not available in reality and perhaps also because this is an ideal dream of the benefits of idle dreaming.

I take it as a sign for the continuing virulence of these issues, beyond the narrow Pre-Raphaelite circle from which most of my examples were drawn, that Augusta Webster takes them up in *Portraits* (1870).[9] As the short author's note to the 1893 edition makes clear, this collection was meant to follow some unified conception, though this, as Webster demurs, 'has never been completely carried out' (1893 n.pag.). While Webster nowhere specifies her intention, it is not difficult to see that she set herself to addressing what she must have felt to be pertinent contemporary issues. Her monologues raise gender questions like prostitution, the dependence of women on their husbands and the contradictory ideals of women's roles, but also address religious doubt, conflicts between work and family commitments, and the traumatisation of soldiers returning from the Crimean War. In one of her monologues, Webster addresses the issue of idleness directly, and in familiar terms. The speaker of 'In an Almshouse', an old, nearly blind and impoverished scholar and poet, muses nostalgically that the sort of slow contemplative wisdom to which he has devoted his life has become anachronistic. Like Morris's idle singer, who is 'born out of [his] time' (Morris 2002: 'Apology' l. 21), Webster's speaker 'came out of date' (l. 151):

Wise with the old-world wisdom grown unapt
To this changed morrow, for the lesson now
Is to accept to live one with to do—
The wisest wisdom plainly in this stir,
This over-crowding, this hot hurrying on,
That make a tempest of our modern days.

> This anxious age is driven half mad with work,
> It bids us all work, work: no need, no room,
> For contemplating sages counting life
> A time allowed for solving problems in
> And its own self a problem to be solved;
> On in the rush, or be swept out of sight,
> On in the rush, and find your place, and work. (2000: ll. 160–72)

The 'hot hurrying on [. . .] of our modern days' (ll. 164–5) with its gospel of work and success in which life turns into a race with a goal to win has little time for idleness, for contemplation, and, so one may assume, for poetry. Of course, typically for a dramatic monologue, the reader is invited to critically observe and judge the speaker of Webster's poem, who might strike one as rather pathetic, blaming the age for his own failure to seize the moment – an attitude, incidentally, which Webster singles out for explicit criticism in 'Waiting to be Ready', one of the essays in her collection *A Housewife's Opinions* (1879). The scholar in the almshouse himself admits to this failing. He likens himself to

> a late sleeper in the morn,
> That with a drowsy logic lulls himself,
> Chiding his tardiness on their delay
> Who will not come to tell him it is time. (ll. 139–42)

Webster's speaker is no Romantic rebel against the zeitgeist; he does not chafe against it, nor even reject it. He merely fails to suit it and placidly accepts his life as a failure.

And yet, despite blindness and poverty and his regrets for having lived his life in vain, the poem presents the old man as contented, even happy. He is receptive to 'The joy of present beauty' (l. 22) of the summer evening and even 'look[s] back very kindly on [his] life' (l. 201). For him,

> Life grows mere rest –
> I sit apart and I am done with the world,
> No hopes, no fears, no changes; I have lost
> All share in aims and duties (ll. 302–5)

This loss is also a gain. To the extent that the old man accepts the spirit of the age, which calls for productive work and constant improvement, he deems his life a failure. But precisely in so far as he resists this spirit, he finds a quiet sort of happiness. The poem concludes with a homely scene of care, as the old man's thoughts are interrupted by a child, who comes to him asking for 'The story about

Jesus' (l. 443). The old man's leisure, a result of what the world (and he himself) perceives as the failure of his life, thus opens a space for human warmth, religious instruction and intergenerational care. Whether the reader understands the life of Webster's speaker to have been a failure and his contentment to be pathetic thus depends entirely on whether the reader endorses the ideology of work which leads to such judgements in the first place.

Instead of a wholesale moralistic condemnation of idleness, the poems I have considered range from being openly defensive to maintaining at least a deeply ambivalent stance. Adelman, too, concedes that 'idleness and aesthetic consciousness retain the trace of their earlier positive and even revolutionary associations' (2018: 113), but, in his view, this is merely a utopian trace, overwhelmed by the general condemnation he perceives in the poems he studies. However, the examples I have discussed suggest that idleness continued to concern poets, primarily because they continued to associate it with poetry itself. A defence of idleness becomes, again and again, at a fundamental level a defence of poetry.

Weary Lives – Idleness as Utopia and Prison

It must have already struck my reader that both gender and class play an important role in these issues. While not all the speakers of the poems I have discussed so far in this chapter are explicitly gendered, implicitly they are predominantly male and none of the authors belong to the working class. Concerns about the relation between idleness and poetry seem to be predominantly middle-class concerns.

Reasons for this may be found deep in the ideological construction of idleness. For one, the working classes could appropriate the gospel of work to establish a moral high ground against the other, idler classes. In such cases, idleness is strictly condemned as a serious threat to working-class aspirations to respectability. The working classes are defined by their labour, and class-pride could build on it. Thus, the paradox Jordan has identified as afflicting the eighteenth-century middle-class attitudes towards idleness, which lies in upholding industriousness with the ultimate aim of joining the higher idle classes, is repeated and perhaps amplified for the Victorian working classes. Correspondingly, Benjamin Kohlmann notes:

> [s]ome of the harshest indictments of idleness occur in Victorian working-class autobiographies, a fact that is hardly surprising since most of

these working-class authors had only been able to achieve social rise and respectability by adopting some version of Victorian middle-class work ethic. (2014: 204)

If you managed to glean enough education for yourself to become a published working-class poet, idleness is unlikely to have featured large in your life. Moreover, Fabienne Moine remarks that, even if they resisted the ideology of work, there are several reasons why working-class poets would hesitate to challenge it openly in their poetry: their dependence on patronage to publish; the necessity to maintain the goodwill of their employers; perhaps simply a wish to write poetry that offers an escape from, rather than reflection of, their lives (Moine 2018: § 27). That working-class poets could easily come under the suspicion of lacking sufficient industry is well illustrated by the example, discussed at some length by Kohlmann, of the poet-carpenter John Overs, who published his work under the patronage of Charles Dickens. As Kohlmann points out, Dickens's preface to Overs's poems is at pains to justify the carpenter's poetic production as salutary and to ward off the spectre of the 'irresponsibly idle worker [which] hovers over [not only] this scene of working-class writing' (2014: 197).

That labour was unceasing for the working classes was nonetheless a frequent criticism. 'Shall ye be *unceasing* drudges?' asks Eliza Cook in her 'A Song for the Workers' (2000 [1853]: l. 21) and laments that such relentless labour will stifle the mind:

Shall we bar the brain from thinking
Of aught else than work and woe?
[. . .]
Shall we strive to shut out Reason
Knowledge, Liberty, and Health? (ll. 41–2, 45–6)

Deprived of rest and pleasure, Cook's workers are also deprived of their 'Spirit-light' (l. 47), their soul and even their humanity. At the same time, Cook's call for 'a juster lot' may lend some substance to the widespread middle-class worry that too much idleness might make the working classes rebellious. Nonetheless, middle-class authors also focus on the absence of idleness in poems which expose and attack the poor working conditions at the time, most famously Thomas Hood's 'The Song of the Shirt' (1843) and Elizabeth Barrett Browning's 'The Cry of the Children' (1844). Pertinently, in lacking idleness, Barrett Browning's children also lack the faculty of aesthetic appreciation. They cannot care for the beauty of nature: 'If we cared for any meadows, it were merely / To drop down in them and sleep' and to their eyes 'The reddest flower would look as pale as snow' (ll. 67–8; 72). Deprived of idleness by the constant demands of the machine, the poem implies, their souls are perilously impoverished. The seamstress of Hood's poem similarly yearns for 'one short hour! / A respite however brief' in order to 'breathe the breath / Of the cowslip and primrose sweet,' but finds herself with 'No blessed leisure for Love or Hope, / But only time for Grief!' (ll. 73–4; 65–6; 75–6). From this perspective, the mariners' refusal to return to their toil in Tennyson's 'The Lotos-Eaters', rather than being a passive withdrawal, might look more like an active rebellion against oppressive social forces. As Sanford Russell remarks, 'this is more of a sit-in than just a sit-down; the one thing the mariners do not seem to lack is will' (2015: 385).[10]

There is no sense of ambivalence about the blessedness of ease in these poems, since the forces that prevent idleness are entirely external. Where such praise of idleness emerges from a middle-class perspective, it seems to be informed by ideas of aesthetic education in which a major concern is that a lack of idleness will prevent the working classes from developing aesthetic appreciation. From a working-class perspective, however, things could look differently. Take 'A Lay of the Tambour Frame' (1868), by Scottish working-class poet Janet Hamilton. This poem also emphasises the cruel relentlessness of the toil of the woman worker but denounces primarily her low wages and the fact that she is overlooked by the unions which support men. In contrast to the more positive perspective of the poets discussed above, idleness and leisure, for Hamilton, are ambivalent blessings. Leisure time, Hamilton suggests, will easily be misused by the working classes. For example, she repeatedly highlights the importance of keeping the Sabbath and not engaging in leisure activities like taking the newly introduced Sunday rail to the seaside (Hamilton 1880: 'Sunday Rail I' and 'Sunday Rail II'). This day of repose is not an idle day but should be spent in 'prayer and meditation' ('Sunday Rail II', l. 26). Idleness tends to feature in Hamilton's moral didactics as 'idle pleasure, sin and folly' ('Sunday Rail II', l. 48) and may easily lead to 'the plague o'intemperance' ('Rhymes for the Times III – 1865', l. 22). Incidentally, the introductory pieces to her memorial works are no less keen to emphasise that 'she neglected no domestic duty' than Dickens was in the case of Overs (Hamilton 1880: 14, 26). Rather than a blessing to be wished for, idleness emerges here as a potential threat to be avoided.

If idleness was either unavailable or considered unsalutary for the working classes, it was available in excess for women of higher social status. Webster claims in *A Housewife's Opinions*:

> many an anxious gentle woman would feel it rest to exchange her responsible inactivity for the bustling vigour of the notable managers who presided over unaesthetic homes in the days of roast beef hospitalities, and envies her cook and her housemaid their mechanical tasks with a beginning and an end to them. (1879: 282)

Indeed, the 'correct, mature, civilized life' Adelman speaks of is, of course, first and foremost the life of a man. In a study of gendered inequalities of dominant time regimes Patricia Murphy reminds us that 'Victorian perceptions of the natural order of time inconspicuously but emphatically stemmed from intrinsic masculinist biases that served to bolster inflexible gender boundaries' (2001: 23). An understanding of time which privileged a progressive narrative of actively pursued ambition marginalised the temporal experience of most middle-class women, who were barred from an active life. Already by the end of the eighteenth century, Jordan argues, middle-class women 'were often viewed as leisure personified' (2014: 114). Is it surprising then, that women seem to feel less social pressure to defend the idleness of their poetic activity? Indeed, would it be surprising if they did not even associate such activity with idleness as much as male poets do? After all, a man idling at poetry does so, at least in principle, at the cost of other possible employments and labours. Women from the higher social ranks who wrote poetry, however, would fill essentially empty hours. What counts as idleness for men amounts to activity for women.

For the same reason, the sense of (utopian or nostalgic) escape into idleness which emerges to some degree from all the poems above is often lacking in female figures of higher social rank. If, as we have seen, for male speakers and for the working classes idleness can be the *object* of (more or less guilty) desire, for women idleness is often the *cause* or the *result* of thwarted desire. Thus, idle women are typically depicted as waiting, mostly for an absent lover. The lament of the abandoned woman in fact constitutes a genre on its own, much fuelled by the poetry of Felicia Hemans and Letitia Elizabeth Landon (L.E.L.), but popular throughout the century. Unable to escape from idleness into action, waiting women are dependent on the activity of someone else, the man they are waiting for. Thus, instead of being liberating, inspiring and potentially creative, for women idleness and inactivity can easily turn into a trap.

Once again, it is Tennyson who gave this a lastingly iconic poetic shape with the Shakespearean-themed 'Mariana' (1830), a poem which clearly resonated strongly with his contemporaries. 'The very emblem of bored Victorian womanhood' (Maynard 2009: 6), physically and psychologically barred from interaction with the outside world, Mariana is completely immobilised both by her grief and by societal strictures. Indeed, in many ways 'Mariana' can be read as a female counterpart to 'The Lotos-Eaters', illustrating the different stakes involved in male and female idleness. Like the lotos-eaters, Mariana 'falls victim to a habit-forming, addictive, self-perpetuating associative pattern' (Armstrong 1993: 51), and as with the lotos-eaters this deeply affects her sensual perceptions. Both the lotos-eaters and Mariana find themselves isolated from the rest of the world, on the island or the moated grange, and they share a more or less explicit death wish. Both poems draw on and elaborate a literary source – in the case of 'Mariana' the reference is to Shakespeare's *Measure for Measure* – and in both cases this implicit embeddedness in a familiar plot serves to undermine or question the changelessness on which the poem itself insists. Odysseus will drag the mariners weeping from the island, Mariana will eventually be married off to Angelo. Within the poems, notably, no trace of such future developments is visible.

If these similarities are striking, the differences between the poems are even more so. Having partaken of the lotos fruit, the mariners choose to stay on the island. They willingly reject their lives of ceaseless labour and let themselves be seduced by the sensual pleasures of their natural surroundings. Cutting their ties with and rejecting their obligations to the outside world, they choose the life of Epicurean gods, lulled and entertained but no longer touched by human woes. Critics have argued that 'those who taste the lotos find themselves estranged even from those of their fellows who have shared this experience' to the point at which '[t]here is an almost total failure of external communication' (Grob 1964: 123), since the mariners' senses turn inward and 'if his fellow spake, / His voice was thin, as voices from the grave' (ll. 33–4). But such a reading ignores that their song is emphatically communal as 'all at once they sang' (l. 44). Their song is a choric song, which insistently reiterates the first-person plural pronoun. Mariana's isolation, in contrast, is not a matter of choice, but of social coercion. As Armstrong notices, the numerous barriers which confine her are 'man-made, cunningly constructed through the material fabric of the house she inhabits, the enclosed spaces in which she is confined' (1993: 13). Thus, her removal from

the world is not an act of liberation, as it seems to be at least potentially for the mariners, but the result of suppression. For the mariners,
the 'land where all things always seem'd the same' offers rest and
peace ('Lotos-Eaters': l. 24), but for Mariana such changelessness
means despair: 'without hope of change, / In sleep she seem'd to walk
forlorn' (ll. 29–30). Both the mariners and Mariana cry out that they
are weary, but the mariners are weary of their labours and can choose
idleness. Mariana, in contrast, is weary of her idle waiting, but she
has no means of escape from this state on her own account. Waiting
is passive by definition. Moreover, Mariana's idleness does not serve
to heighten her aesthetic appreciation as it does for the mariners,
but rather dulls her senses: 'The sparrow's chirrup on the roof, /
The slow clock ticking, and the sound / Which to the wooing wind
aloof / The poplar made, did all confound / Her sense' (ll. 73–7).
No matter what she hears and sees, she is locked within the constant burden of her grief. Thus, while the mariners' decision to stay
on the island leads to the rich sensuality of the choric song with its
varied rhythms and different line and stanza structures which resist
the stricter Spenserian stanzas of the poem's introductory section,
'Mariana' features seven highly uniform stanzas. Each of the stanzas consists of eight tetrameter lines referring to Mariana's environment or circumstances and each stanza concludes with a refrain that
remains the same with only slight variations throughout the poem:
'She only said, "My life is dreary, / He cometh not," she said; / She
said, "I am aweary, aweary, / I would that I were dead!"' (ll. 9–12).
When the mariners speak, they sing and their song is an enchant-
ing celebration of the sensuous power of poetic language; Mariana,
in her grange, is reduced to a barrenly monotonous repetition from
which the poem offers no escape. Barely bearable in their monotony,
these repetitions evoke the boredom they speak of.

In a similarly striking illustration of the gender logic shaping views
on idleness, Christina Rossetti's poem 'The Prince's Progress' combines a condemnation of the idle man with a commendation of the
patiently waiting woman.[11] This fairy-tale allegory tells a *Pilgrim's
Progress* gone wrong, in which the prince is too tardy and negligent
to reach his princess in time. In spite of the title's focus on the Prince,
the poem opens with a description of the waiting Princess:

> Till all sweet gums and juices flow,
> Till the blossom of blossoms blow,
> The long hours go and come and go,
> The bride she sleepeth, waketh, sleepeth,

Waiting for one whose coming is slow: –
Hark! the bride weepeth.

'How long shall I wait, come heat come rime?' –
'Till the strong Prince comes, who must come in time'
(Her women say), 'there's a mountain to climb,
A river to ford. Sleep, dream and sleep:
Sleep' (they say): 'we've muffled the chime,
Better dream than weep.'(ll. 1–12)

Rather like Mariana, but still with some hope, the Princess is reduced to waiting, sleeping and weeping through the 'long hours that go and come and go' (l. 3). The Princess is not alone, however. Her women assure her that the prince 'must come' and that he is 'strong' (l. 8). But as soon as we encounter the Prince in the following stanza, the women's words are ironically undercut:

In his world-end palace the strong Prince sat,
Taking his ease on cushion and mat,
Close at hand lay his staff and his hat.
'When wilt thou start? the bride waits, O youth.'–
'Now the moon's at full; I tarried for that,
Now I start in truth. (ll. 13–18)

The 'strong Prince' (l. 8) is by no means climbing a mountain or fording a river, but idly sitting in his comfortable palace and clearly procrastinating. We soon learn that he is 'Strong of limb if of purpose weak' (l. 47). Though he proclaims his intention to 'start in truth', the next stanza again shows his reluctance to set off:

'But tell me first, true voice of my doom,
Of my veiled bride in her maiden bloom;
Keeps she watch through glare and through gloom,
Watch for me asleep and awake?' (ll. 19–22)

Instead of hurrying to his princess to relieve her of her gloomy watch, the Prince seems to take a self-indulgent pleasure in imagining her patiently longing for him. The stanza structure, too, serves to emphasise the Prince's indecisiveness. If the first three lines drive forward by sharing a rhyme sound, the embracing rhyme that follows introduces a more halting counter-movement by making the reader wait longer for the return of the rhyme. While metrically far less varied than Rossetti's 'Goblin Market', the poem's tetrameter lines freely combine iambs and anapaests, while the shorter concluding line of each stanza varies in length taking two or three feet, frequently giving it the quality of an epigrammatic commentary on the preceding stanza and suggesting the finality of a rhythm cut short. From the very beginning, the poem thus juxtaposes an irresolute quest narrative with the romanticised epitome of lyric existence of the Princess, emphasising rhythmic changelessness. If the plot dynamics of the quest proceed but haltingly as the prince lets himself be distracted again and again, the lyric intensity of the Princess's dreamlike state amounts to a prison.

The Prince eventually does start, but his journey is soon interrupted. Seeing a milkmaid with her pail, 'The Prince, who had journeyed at least a mile, / Grew athirst at the sight' (ll. 59–60). The poem goes on to treat the Prince with similar sarcasm throughout, often, like in the lines just quoted, by appropriating the Prince's perspective to expose his self-indulgence. When the milkmaid asks him to stay 'one idle day' (l. 82) at her side, he again proves weak of resolve and apt to find excuses for himself:

> Loth to stay, but to leave her slack,
> He half turned away, then he quite turned back:
> For courtesy's sake he could not lack
> To redeem his own royal pledge;
> Ahead too the windy heaven lowered black
> With a fire-cloven edge. (ll. 85–90)

By focalising these lines through the Prince, the poem shows both his lack of resolve and the irony of his self-indulgent logic, which counts his recent casual pledge to the milkmaid higher than his lifelong pledge to the Princess, and takes the approaching storm not for a warning to hurry on, but for a reason to linger, because it suits his idle inclination to 'stretch[. . .] his length in the apple-tree shade' (l. 91).

After several further delays, the Prince eventually does arrive at the palace of his bride, just in time to meet her funeral train.[12] The poem concludes with the 'bride-song' turned dirge, sung by the Princess's attendant women (l. 473). In this song, the halting rhythms of the sestets which had governed the poem so far are replaced by ten-line stanzas in which more regularly iambic rhymeless tetrameters alternate with di- and trimeter lines, all five of which share the same rhyme sound, a metrical form which approximates that of traditional hymns. Like the choric song of the mariners which supplants the epic introduction in 'The Lotos-Eaters', the uneven narrative progress of the Prince's journey thus concludes in a choric lyric.

The women's song berates him for his tardiness, praises the Princess for her long-suffering patience and suggests that she has finally found rest and release in death. The gendering of idleness comes vividly to the fore here. The voices begin by accusing the Prince: 'Too late for love, too late for joy, / Too late, too late! / You loitered on the road too long, / You trifled at the gate' (ll. 475–8). While the Prince should have hurried towards his bride, the passively waiting Princess is praised precisely for never showing hurry:

> We never heard her speak in haste
> Her tones were sweet,
> And modulated just so much
> As it was meet:
> Her heart sat silent through the noise
> And concourse of the street.
> There was no hurry in her hands,
> No hurry in her feet;
> There was no bliss drew nigh to her,
> That she might run to greet. (ll. 515–24)

In the context of the poem's insistence on the Prince's failure to show appropriate haste in meeting his bliss, this praise of the princess is not without irony. Indeed, it has been suggested that the Princess is by no means the paragon of virtues which the fairy-tale context may imply. Taking into account the poem's scriptural symbolism, Dawn Henwood, for example, has argued that 'the Bride can be held morally responsible for the barrenness of her own existence and, ultimately, for her own destruction' (1997: 90). However, it seems to me that instead of condemning the Princess, the poem subtly points to the destructive irony of gender ideals, which praise utter idle passivity as devoted waiting in a woman while condemning it as indolence in the man. After all, the Princess is 'enchanted' (l. 479) and 'Spell-bound' (l. 23), that is, she is under some external coercion which the poem emphasises but whose source it never specifies. Indeed, the suggestion is that she is spell-bound for the Prince's sake; she is under compulsion to wait for him, imprisoned in her 'one white room' (l. 23), with her female attendants seconding as jailors. Moreover, both the Prince and the Princess are constantly admonished to adhere to their prescribed roles by choric voices, a community of others which imposes its moral values on the narrative. The tragedy appears to be that the Prince does not satisfy such demands, while the Princess satisfies them only too well. Upholding idleness as a female virtue clearly has destructive consequences in this case, as the sleeping beauty finds a logical culmination in the dead Princess.

Thus, 'The Prince's Progress', for all the apparent simplicity of its moral and even beyond its rather baffling religious symbolism, suggests a critique of the social underpinnings of its fairy-tale dichotomy. In its version of the abandoned woman theme, the Prince is neither hero nor villain, he is neither 'more [n]or less than a man', merely a weak human being:

> He did what a young man can,
> Spoke of toil and an arduous way –
> Toil to-morrow, while golden ran
> The sands of to-day.' (ll. 357–60)

If this involves a critique of idleness, the more serious critique seems to be suggested by the fate of the Princess, who for all that she is enchanted cannot escape time and wastes her life in her useless wait: a critique of the logic of the narrative quest, which offers the passive woman as a prize for the achieving, ambitious man.

A critique of the social forces which condemn women to idleness emerges more or less directly from other abandoned women poems of the period, too. Instead of the ease and pleasure idleness offers to the male speakers discussed above, for women idleness rarely seems conducive to poetic creation but rather tends to involve silencing and (self-)destruction. As we have seen in the previous chapter, Webster's 'Circe', for example, welcomes even the havoc threatening her island by the approaching storm, if it would but 'bring [her] change, / Breaking the sickly sweet monotony' (ll. 31–2). Circe is 'evidently yet another nineteenth-century woman begging for that most elusive of rights: the right of experience' (Leighton 1992: 195), even if that experience is destructive.

As is often the case for Webster, the force of her criticism is amplified by means of the poem's intertextual relations. Featuring an idle ruler who is waiting for a lover in a paradisiacal island setting from which she longs to escape, this poem responds to Tennyson's 'Mariana', 'The Lotos-Eaters' and 'Ulysses' all at the same time. Whereas the lotos-eaters resolve to live the life of Epicurean gods 'careless of mankind' ('Lotos-Eaters' l. 155), this is precisely the life Circe longs to leave behind:

> What fate is mine, who, far apart from pains
> And fears and turmoils of the cross-grained world,
> Dwell like a lonely god in a charmed isle
> Where I am first and only, and, like one

Who should love poisonous savours more than mead,
Long for a tempest on me and grow sick
Of rest and of divine free carelessness!
Oh me, I am a woman, not a god; (ll. 58–65)

In the 1842 version of 'The Lotos-Eaters' the mariners are morally condemned for hubristically longing for the life of Epicurean gods. Circe lives such a life but longs to escape from it. Indeed, the poem seems to suggest that such an idle life is not compatible with humanity. After all, the mariners who are stranded on Circe's island may remind one of Tennyson's lotos-eating specimens. First they praise their survival and remember their homes with affection, then 'they will feel their ease / [. . .] Tasting delight of rest and revelling / [. . .] and they'll talk / How good it is to house in palaces / Out of the storms and struggles' (ll. 149–57). However, instead of making them godlike, as Tennyson's mariners hope, such a life of idleness awakens their baser instincts: 'Then the next day the beast in them will wake' (l. 159). They will become irritable, aggressive and conceited; they'll turn into thieves, drunkards, lechers and gluttons. The idle life on Circe's island does not suit human beings. It is a life fit only for gods or animals.

If this is a critique of idleness it also involves a subtler critique along similarly gendered lines as that developed in 'The Prince's Progress'. As a woman, Circe longs for the only kind of change and escape from the monotony of her life which Victorian gender ideals promised to women: she is waiting for a lover to come. But in hoping for the arrival of a lover the change Circe longs for would at best exchange one kind of imprisonment for another. The poem makes this clear when Circe impersonates her imagined lover, gazing narcissistically at her reflection in a pool. After apostrophising her own beauty in a catalogue of similes reminiscent of Petrarchan love poetry, she addresses her reflected image:

Should I be so your lover as I am,
Drinking an exquisite joy to watch you thus
In all a hundred changes through the day.
But that I love you for him till he comes,
But that my beauty means his loving it? (ll. 126–30)

Circe disregards the 'hundred changes through the day' her present clearly offers, preferring to project a lover who would only confirm and fix her image in the stasis she professedly wishes to escape. Showing her to impersonate her lover, and to thus prefigure the situation she longs for, the poem suggests that the fulfilment of her wishes would amount to a perpetuation of precisely the condition she wants to escape. She imagines that the lover she longs for in order to feel like a woman would set her up as a goddess. While for the lotos-eating mariners there is a real and moral choice between an idle or an active life, for women there seems to be merely the chance of exchanging one kind of idle life for another.

For women, the arrival of a lover or of death promises the only possibility for change in an idle life. In fact, this often amount to more or less the same thing. In her poem 'Over!' (1880) Anne Evans exemplifies this with chilling sarcasm:

> A knight came prancing on his way,
> And across the path a lady lay:
> 'Stoop a little and hear me speak!'
> Then, 'You are strong, and I am weak:
>   Ride over me now, and kill me.'
>
> He opened wide his gay blue eyes,
> Like one o'ermastered by surprise;
> His cheek and brow grew burning red,
> 'Long looked-for, come at last,' she said,
>   'Ride over me now, and kill me.'
>
> Then softly spoke the knight, and smiled:
> 'Fair maiden, whence this mood so wild?'
> 'Smile on,' said she, 'my reign is o'er,
> But do my bidding yet once more:
>   Ride over me now, and kill me.'
>
> He smote his steed of dapple-gray,
> And lightly cleared her where she lay;
> But still, as he sped on amain,
> She murmured ever, 'Turn again:
>   Ride over me now, and kill me.'

While the poem draws on the traditional quest plot, it immediately proceeds to subvert it. The rescue the lady is asking for is a release from life, and the 'prancing' (l. 1), 'gay' (l. 6) and smiling knight seems unwilling or unable to take this demand seriously. The irony of this short piece lies in its exposure of the logic underlying the romance quest, in which the role of the woman is generally reduced to passivity and suffering. For the lady in the poem, the 'Long looked-for' (l. 9) arrival of the knight and potential lover amounts to a wish for self-annihilation. The poem can thus count as a prime example of Elizabeth Bronfen's claim that eighteenth- and nineteenth-century female literary characters find in suicide 'a revitalising self-assertion in death against the lethal self-alienation in life' (1992: 153). By making this death-wish explicit, however, and addressing it to the arriving knight, the lady brings the unspoken out into the open, disturbing the ideological surface of the romance. It renders its resolution impossible, since that depends on the illusion that the knight serves the lady's happiness and the woman's self-sacrifice is to her own good. The repetitive insistence of the lady's implacably reiterated death wish in this poem interrupts a narrative logic of ambition. The knight, however, is free to ride 'lightly' on (l. 17), ignoring both the plight and the command of the woman who, Mariana-like, remains bound to her passive suffering and her constant refrain, dependent on male assistance even in her longing for death.

Indeed, with the exception of Circe, who is granted her own powerful voice while she is still hoping for the future, waiting women are often deprived of a voice or reduced to incessant repetitions and lamentations. Insistently repetitive direct-speech refrains are one of the most prominent features recurring in these poems. Instead of potentially enabling poetic production, idleness effectively silences these waiting women. To the male speakers of the first part of this chapter, idleness, while morally dubious, offered a creatively productive escape from the logic of acquisition and the ideology of success. In poems about the working classes it could feature as a utopian space of respite from relentless labour. For middle- and upper-class women it spells mainly frustrated desire and a condition from which only death promises release.

'There's nothing new under the sun' – Time and Faith in Christina Rossetti's Poetry

If I now turn to a closer consideration of Christina Rossetti's work, I do so to avoid a misrepresentation I have been courting. I have so far followed Adelman, Jordan and Liedke in their arguments, seeing the source of the moral rejection of idleness in a bourgeois ideology of success through constant application, exemplified in the success literature of the likes of Samuel Smiles. Following that logic, it would hardly seem surprising that idleness should emerge as a site of anxious negotiation of and resistance to the ideology of success in the work of male, middle-class poets; that it would be projected as utopian desire onto the working classes; and that it would be felt as a stifling restriction of agency in the poetry of middle-class women, who were excluded from most professions. In the remainder of this chapter, I want to unsettle this straightforward story by suggesting that among the Victorians the ideology of success, while on the rise, was still jostling for hegemony with other temporal logics, particularly religious ones, in which work and idleness may have rather different connotations and valences.[13]

Christina Rossetti's work provides a particularly rich source for an exploration of such an alternative. She was recognised and valued by her contemporaries primarily as a devotional poet, and her poetry clearly spoke to the religious sensibilities of her time. As the example of 'The Prince's Progress' has already suggested, time and its proper use was an issue of central importance to her, and it remained so with remarkable consistency for much of her life. Indeed, the kind of firm rejection of idleness in both genders which marks 'The Prince's Progress' reappears frequently in Rossetti's poetry. 'Man's life is but a working day / Whose tasks are set aright' she writes in the entry for 11 July of *Time Flies: A Reading Diary* (1886: 162), but any doubt that she uses 'Man' here as a universal term encompassing both genders is easily dispelled by looking at the numerous other instances in which she returns to the topic. If Rossetti rejects idleness, however, she does so on grounds that are diametrically opposed to those of the gospel of success and that eventually serve to blur the boundaries between work and idleness, rest and toil.[14]

A good starting point for an exploration of these issues is 'In the Willow Shade', published in 1881 in her collection *A Pageant and Other Poems*, which has its speaker lounging like the Prince in a tree shade, 'While fancies upon fancies solaced me, / Some true, and some were false' (ll. 3–4). The poem thus opens with the familiar trope of creative idleness but immediately strikes a warning note in suggesting the falseness of some of the arising fancies. Moreover, the speaker is all too aware of being guilty of idleness:

I loiter on a mossy bed
With half my work undone;

My work undone, that should be done
At once with all my might;
For after the long day and lingering sun
Comes the unworking night. (ll. 47–52)

Here, as in 'The Prince's Progress', the idler is unable to decipher the signs of nature: the singing birds rising to the sky, the shivering leaves of the willow tree and, above all, the oncoming nightfall in which 'The world drooped murmuring like a thing that grieves' (l. 63). Instead of the kind of communion with nature that we saw being celebrated in the idleness poems of her brothers, Rossetti's speaker is left feeling cold and lonely, alienated from nature and with unanswered questions:

> I rose to go, and felt the chill,
> And shivered as I went;
> Yet shivering wondered, and I wonder still,
> What more that willow meant. (ll. 65–8)

In 'Pastime', another poem from the same collection, the condemnation of idleness is even more explicit:

> A boat amid the ripples, drifting, rocking,
> Two idle people, without pause or aim;
> While in the ominous west there gathers darkness
> Flushed with flame.
>
> A haycock in a hayfield backing, lapping,
> Two drowsy people pillowed round about;
> While in the ominous west across the darkness
> Flame leaps out.
>
> Better a wrecked life than a life so aimless,
> Better a wrecked life than a life so soft;
> The ominous west glooms thundering, with its fire
> Lit aloft.

Like the Prince with the milkmaid under the apple tree, the idle people in this poem fail to realise the warning of the gathering thunderstorm. They lack agency so completely that no verbs are assigned to them in the syntactic structures of the stanzas. Movement and action are granted solely to the inanimate objects around them, so that the latter seem to be more truly alive than the human beings. It is important to note, however, that the rejection of idleness in this case does not follow a bourgeois logic of acquisition or ambition. If the narrative of 'The Prince's Progress' could still be read as ambition thwarted and opportunity missed, in 'Pastime' a rejection of idleness does not promise happiness and a better life. Though the poem strikingly echoes Webster's Circe, who welcomes the destructiveness of the storm as an escape from her all too pleasant and aimless life, Circe ultimately hopes for the excitement and fulfilment of love. 'Pastime', however, maintains that any life, even a life of suffering, would be preferable to a life of idle pleasure. It promises no gain from rejecting idleness but maintains that a life so soft and aimless is hardly a life at all.

Moreover, reading 'The Prince's Progress', 'Pastime' and 'In a Willow Shade' next to each other draws attention to their similar though subtly different characterisations and condemnations. From this comparison, the speaker of 'In a Willow Shade' can emerge in a more positive light. Both the Prince and the idle people in 'Pastime' either ignore the divine signs of nature or give them a self-serving interpretation. The speaker of 'In a Willow Shade', however, while she cannot figure out what the willow wants to say, is at least sensitive to nature's voice and indeed it seems that her questioning of her natural surroundings is precisely what makes her aware of her lack of duty:

> O silvery weeping willow tree
> With all leaves shivering,
> Have you no purpose but to shadow me
> Beside this rippled spring? ('In the Willow Shade' ll. 29–32)

Once she begins to ask such questions, she is forced out of the self-centred dreaming of the first stanzas into an appreciation of nature's otherness. Questioning the tree's purpose leads her to the realisation of her own fault. Her idleness is, to this extent, a positively productive idleness. After all, while I have emphasised above that the first stanza judges some of her fancies arising from her idle dreams to be false, one would be equally justified in pointing out that some of the fancies are supposedly true. Moreover, the speaker's questions in the poem equal those of the reader. Just as the speaker is wondering about the purpose of the willow, the reader is left to puzzle over the meaning of the various nature images in the poem.

One image which seems unequivocal in its meaning is the falling of night. Like the storm gathering in the west in 'The Prince's Progress' and 'Pastime', nightfall in Rossetti's poems generally points to the temporal horizon which, for Rossetti, always limits and qualifies human ambition: death and, ultimately, the Final Judgment. Where there is a sense, in Rossetti's poetry, that time is short and should not be wasted, it is consequently not with earthly success or material gain in view, but in the hope of spiritual fulfilment and eternal rest. In the 18 September entry of *Time Flies*, Rossetti strikes a note of particular urgency: 'We misappropriate time, we lose time, we waste time, we kill time. We do anything and everything with time, except redeem time. Yet time is short and swift and never returns. Time flies' (1886: 220). Time flies, but what we need to do with it, according to Rossetti, is not to instrumentalise it, to use it to gain wealth, social standing or success, but rather to 'redeem' it. Such redemption, one might almost think, might lie precisely in not *doing* anything with time, but in contemplating it, as *Time Flies* in fact invites its readers to do daily. As Rossetti admonishes us in the entry for the next day, we should not 'think lightly' of time.

Moreover, Rossetti's reminder that time is swift bears little resemblance to the complaints of contemporaries like Dobson. This is particularly apparent in poems in which Rossetti turns the secular logic of acceleration on its head. While her contemporaries are lamenting the increasing haste and a sense of the lack of time, in *Time Flies* Rossetti could strike a different tone:

> Our life is long—Not so, wise Angels say
> Who watch us waste it, trembling while they weigh
> Against eternity one squandered day.
>
> Our life is long—Not so, the Saints protest,
> Filled full of consolation and of rest:
> 'Short ill, long good, one long unending best.'
>
> Our life is long—Christ's word sounds different:
> 'Night cometh: no more work when day is spent.'
> Repent and work today, work and repent. (1886: p. 228, ll. 1–9)

The temporal logic Rossetti develops in this poem is so strikingly different from the gospel of success delineated above that it should give us pause. If the ideology of success maintains that time is valuable because it is a limited resource which should be used wisely to ensure gain, Rossetti maintains that 'we', that is, all human beings, generally and falsely consider our life long. Her angels, however, are no celestial versions of Samuel Smiles, exhorting us to put every moment to use in striving for success. Rather, they lament that we do not realise time's proper relation to eternity. There seems little doubt that, in the eyes of the angels, striving for worldly success amounts to squandering time. Moreover, with the next two stanzas, Rossetti turns the temporal logic of worldly ambition further on its head. If the first stanza can be read as a version of the *carpe diem* trope, the argument of the second stanza has shifted radically. The complacency expressed by 'Our life is long' in the first stanza turns into a lament in the second and third stanza, in which these same words express a complaint about the length of life with its pain and suffering and the responses of Jesus and the Saints offer the hope for a speedy end. Life may be but a working day, but the implication is not primarily one of admonishment and an urging to action, but rather a consolation and a hope: the toil and suffering of life is necessary but brief, and eternal rest, 'one long unending best' (l. 6) is awaiting us.

Thus, for Christina Rossetti, work does not and cannot lead in any worldly sense to success or improvement, because her outlook on life is firmly religious and anti-materialist. If we need to work in this world, it is not with the aim to achieve anything, not to gain wealth, power, fame or success. Rather, our work is our suffering, and it is our suffering that will earn us the promised rest in death. But by redefining life itself as work and suffering, the distinction between labour and idleness threatens to become blurred. Thus, in her sonnet 'Where neither Rust nor Moth Doth Corrupt',[15] published in her final collection, *Verses*, in 1894, rest itself is redefined as toil:

> Nerve us with patience, Lord, to toil or rest,
> Toiling at rest on our allotted level;
> Unsnared, unscared by world or flesh or devil,
> Fulfilling the good Will of Thy behest;
> Not careful here to hoard, not here to revel;
> But waiting for our treasure and our zest
> Beyond the fading splendour of the west,
> Beyond this deathstruck life and deathlier evil.
> Not with the sparrow building here a house:
> But with the swallow tabernacling so
> As still to poise alert to rise and go
> On eager wings with wing-outspeeding wills
> Beyond earth's gourds and past her almond boughs,
> Past utmost bound of the everlasting hills.

The Christian life is a life of waiting patiently in readiness, like the Princess waiting for her Prince, but it is also a life of constant work in which even resting is a kind of toil. As Joshua Taft notes about the sonnet, '[b]y redefining patience as a means to help with toil and by classifying rest as its own sort of labor, the poem makes it clear that active work forms a key part of any Christian life – even the seemingly restful ones' (322). In the context of Rossetti's devotional poetry, neither idleness nor work can be understood along the lines of a more secular logic of worldly success. But Rossetti's emphatic rejection of the world, 'this deathstruck life and deathlier evil' (l. 8), does not lead into idle passivity but into an active hope, and 'wing-outspeeding wills' (l. 12).

From the devotional perspective developed in Christina Rossetti's poetry, then, the logic of the gospel of success as well as the concomitant gender and class distinctions break down. For Rossetti, all Christians, whether male or female, of whatever class, are living a life of toil and toilsome rest, and all are waiting Mariana-like both for death and the divine love, weary of their life. Work is a Christian duty, but if idleness is condemnable, it is so not in itself, but because the idlers in Rossetti's poems ignore the signs of divine guidance. Indeed, idleness itself can sometimes be God's will, as her poem 'Weary in Well-Doing' (1866) emphasises:

> I would have gone; God bade me stay:
> I would have worked; God bade me rest.
> He broke my will from day to day,
> He read my yearnings unexpressed
> And said them nay.
>
> Now I would stay; God bids me go:
> Now I would rest; God bids me work.
> He breaks my heart tossed to and fro,
> My soul is wrung with doubts that lurk
> And vex it so.
>
> I go, Lord, where Thou sendest me;
> Day after day I plod and moil:
> But, Christ my God, when will it be
> That I may let alone my toil
> And rest with Thee?

Such work and toil are clearly not restricted to that of an earning profession, or to any sense of pragmatic self-improvement, but rather need to be conceived of much more broadly, to the point that the question of what would count as undue idleness becomes difficult to answer.

It is therefore perhaps no wonder that the moral stance of Rossetti's answer to Tennyson's 'The Lotos-Eaters' should be so difficult to decipher. 'Lotus-Eaters: Ulysses to Penelope',[16] the manuscript of which dates from 1847, revisits Tennyson's poem,[17] giving voice not to the lotos-eating mariners, but to Ulysses himself. While this shift in perspective might lead one to expect a clear moral condemnation, this is far from the case. Instead, Ulysses' description of the lotos-eaters is surprisingly non-judgemental:

> In a far-distant land they dwell,
> Incomprehensible,
> Who love the shadow more than light,
> More than the sun the moon,
> Cool evening more than noon,
> Pale silver more than gold that glitters bright. (ll. 1–6)

If a moral judgement could be construed from the lotos-eaters' preference for shadows, it is by no means a clear-cut one. After all, a preference for silver over brightly glittering gold could also imply a rejection of superficiality and of the kind of imperialist and acquisitive logic Ulysses himself conceivably stands for. This is a land of twilight, but the cloud which constantly hangs over it, though dark, is bountiful rather than threatening, and the island's inhabitants live in harmony, even in love with it. The river that flows through the land makes such a 'sleepy sound' (l. 21) that 'Those who will not listen, hear not; / But if one is wakeful, fear not; / It shall lull him to repose, / Bringing back the dream's [*sic*] of youth' (ll. 23–6). These lines imply that far from being compulsive, the dreamy existence of the lotos-eaters is a sensitive act of will, involving close attention to and appreciation of their natural surroundings. As Adam Colman puts it, '[t]hey are, like Tennyson's eaters, not mindless, but affectively attentive' (2019: 123). Only those who will listen will find the repose and the inspiration offered by the river's 'drowsy noise' (l. 22). Considering the importance that attentiveness to nature assumes elsewhere in Rossetti's poetry, this capacity seems to recommend rather than to condemn the island's inhabitants.

Colman reads Rossetti's poem together with Tennyson's 'The Lotos-Eaters' as poems about addiction, but what is particularly striking about Rossetti's Tennysonian echo is the way she draws attention away from the state of mind of the lotos-eaters, emphasising their surroundings instead. Beyond its title, lotos eating is never explicitly mentioned in the poem, nor in fact is any other sort of consumption.

> Hemlock groweth, poppy bloweth
> In the fields where no man moweth;
> And the vine is full of wine
> And are full of milk the kine,
> And the hares are all secure,

And the birds are wild no more,
And the forest-trees wax old,
And winds stir, or hot, or cold,
And yet no man taketh care,
All things resting everywhere. (ll. 27–36)

This is a land of milk and honey, but in a poem whose title emphasises the act of eating, the total absence of consumption is striking. Rossetti's lotos-eaters seem to live symbiotically and in a loving relationship with their environment. They 'love' the shadow (l. 3), and 'love' their cloud (l. 12), and no one seems to exploit nature, even for sustenance. Man takes no care of the island, but the implied objection to man's idleness is muffled, if not entirely muted, by the poem's continuing focus on the land. Because man takes no care, does not mow, or hunt, or cut down trees, nature is profuse, blooming and in harmony. Thus, in the poem's final line, it is not only the lotos-eaters who are resting, but all things everywhere. Is this a condemnation of man's idleness? Or a celebration of nature, relieved of man's destructive ambition? The phonetic richness of these lines with their internal rhymes, assonances and consonances, the lulling trochaic metre of the consistently rhyming couplets, as well as the accumulation of anaphoric parallelisms, all adding up to their intense sensual appeal, suggest the latter to me. Put into the mouth of Ulysses addressing Penelope, these lines are full of longing, rather than clear-cut condemnation. Indeed, the poem highlights its keyword by granting it a line of its own: 'Incomprehensible' (l. 2). To the constantly striving and ambitious Ulysses the land as much as the life of the lotos-eaters is, despite its alien nature, apparently enticing. As an echo from Tennyson, who was so clearly troubled by the moral implications of the lotos-eaters, Rossetti's poem remains remarkably ambiguous in its moral judgement. Instead, she provides a glimpse of a utopian land, in which all human agency and with it all moral judgement seem suspended.

One thing all these examples (and there would have been many more to choose from) serve to highlight is that Rossetti's characteristic use of repetition, which critics unfailingly comment on, extends beyond the bounds of the individual poem. Her poetry is an echo chamber. Again and again and throughout her life, she returns to similar concerns, often in similar wording and with similar imagery. Repetition within her poems often serves not so much as a confirmation but offers revisions and reinterpretations and 'produces a sense of openness and irresolution' (Connor 1984: 422), as in the example of the anaphoric phrase 'Our life is long' above. In the same way, repetition between poems serves frequently to destabilise rather than to solidify meaning. Her version of the story of the lotos-eaters, for example, suspends judgement where Tennyson invites it. Or, in another echo, 'In the Willow Shade' revisits the Prince loitering beneath the apple tree, but the shift from narrative to lyric unsettles any easy condemnation of the Prince, as readers are invited to take the speaker's position and therewith the blame themselves. 'Weary in Well-Doing' allows one to see more clearly that it is not idleness as such that poems like 'The Prince's Progress', 'In the Willow Shade' and 'Pastime' condemn, but rather blindness and deafness to God's command. In its repetitiveness, its continuous circling of the same topics and its frequent reuse of images and phrases, Rossetti's entire poetic production resists a developmental narrative and seems indebted to the first verses of Ecclesiastes, verses which Rossetti repeatedly reuses in her poems: 'The thing that hath been, it is that which shall be; and that which is done is that which shall be done: and there is no new thing under the sun' (King James Version 1:9).

While strongly teleological in its eschatology and aspirational in its hope for redemption, Rossetti's religious understanding of time is emphatically not progressive. It comes close to the Virgilian poetic life outlined by Newman above, full of work, but taking each day as a whole. Indeed, from Rossetti's eschatological perspective, any long-term planning is misguided in view of the always immanent apocalypse. Thus the irony in the title of 'The Prince's Progress' is not only that the Prince signally fails in his quest, but that the entire conception of progress underlying the poem is misguided. The problem seems to be that the Prince thinks that it would be enough merely to travel to the Princess to gain her, instead of endeavouring to live a life worthy of her love. In this sense, the Prince makes no progress at all throughout the poem. He is as idle, indecisive and weak when he finally reaches the Princess's palace as he was at the outset of the poem. As we have seen, Rossetti does sometimes strike a tone of temporal urgency, as also in the second sonnet of her sequence *Later Life* (1881), in which she likens life to a race and exhorts, 'Let us today while it is called today / Set out, if utmost speed may yet avail –' (ll. 9–10). Yet, this is a race whose urgency derives not from the condition of modernity, but from the fallenness of the human condition. Railways seem to be far from Rossetti's mind. The goal of this race lies not in the future but in eternity, and it cannot be achieved by human endeavour, only by divine grace.

Conclusion: The Timeless Realm of an Idle Lyric

What women's voices and in particular Christina Rossetti's devotional poetry allow us to see, is that the perceptible defensiveness of male poets, who renegotiate the relationship between poetry and idleness in tension with an allegedly inimical spirit of the age, is a self-made problem, one that has been given perhaps disproportional attention due to the long pervasive sidelining or silencing of other voices. It is, moreover, a problem that is exacerbated by an attempt to hold on to an ideal of poetic timelessness in an Aesthetics of Self-sufficient Form. As poetry tries to escape from time into form, it also escapes from the active world into a lotos-eating realm of idle contemplation, but this, as Adelman has suggested, is a privileged realm of 'the select few who possess the necessary knowledge and sensibility to perform aesthetic contemplation' (2018: 129), that is, to understand the intricacies of formal self-sufficiency. Meanwhile, the self-sufficient easily tips into the idle, in both senses of the word.

I take it to be a sign of the enduring influence of the Aesthetics of Self-sufficient Form and the role an idealised conception of the lyric plays in it that Theodor Adorno, in his 1957 address 'On Lyric Poetry and Society', should anticipate criticism to his topic in the following terms:

> The most delicate, the most fragile thing that exists is to be encroached upon and brought into conjunction with bustle and commotion, when part of the ideal of lyric poetry, at least in its traditional sense, is to remain unaffected by bustle and commotion. [. . .] Can anyone, you will ask, but a man who is insensitive to the Muse talk about lyric poetry and society? (2014: 339)

As poetic timelessness is redefined as remoteness from the practical realm of everyday concerns – 'free from the coercion of reigning practices, of utility, of the relentless pressures of self-preservation', as Adorno puts it (340) – poetry's purview is radically restricted and literary history becomes blind both to the cultural processes which have helped this particular definition of poetry to its temporary dominance and to the prolific alternative trajectories poets have always taken and will continue to pursue.

While recent scholarship has done much to redress the latter, its interest has rarely extended to an interrogation of the historical processes that help to shape the concepts we still use. Even Virginia Jackson and Yopie Prins (2014), in their historically informed critique of the concept of the lyric, content themselves with questioning the applicability and usefulness of the category 'lyric' but offer little speculation on the reasons for its emergence and success. As I have argued throughout, I take changing temporal concepts and perceptions, like the suspicion towards and ambiguity with regard to idleness I have addressed in this chapter, to be central to these conceptual shifts in the definition of poetry as well as in the importance of the lyric to this definition. Before I attempt to draw the different strands I have followed in these pages together in my concluding chapter, I want to add one final piece to the puzzle, by directly addressing what I have so far only touched on occasionally and in passing: poetry's very own timekeeper, the rhythmically alternating beats of poetic metre.

Notes

1. As Ehnes notes, this only applies to poetry. Novels and non-fiction do not similarly suffer from periodical publication. Poetry's claims to durability are doubtlessly part of the reason.
2. Even the railway was conducive to an increase in reading, suggests Pamela Horn, 'as travellers spent the enforced idleness of a railway journey reading rather than merely staring out of the window' (2014: 304). This railway reading, however, seems to have consisted predominantly of novels, while poetry failed to profit from it.
3. Hartmut Rosa has elucidated the further developments of this ideology, noting that, once it is firmly in place, every time-saving measure that is introduced leads not to more available leisure, but merely to further acceleration, as the freed time has to be immediately put to further use (2005).
4. Such an aspirational ideology resonated in particular with the genre of the *Bildungsroman* and changed the way the aim and process of education were understood. See Anne-Julia Zwierlein (2009: esp. 19–34), whose study also demonstrates the pervasiveness of such narratives of development and success beyond literature, by tracing similar plot structures in Victorian constructions of scientific knowledge.
5. For the centrality of the gospel of work for the Victorian worldview, see also Newsome (1997: 73–4); Lowerson and Myerscough (1977: 7).
6. Indeed, Ulysses' call for action could be condemned on precisely the same moral grounds as the lotos-eaters' wish for a life 'careless of mankind' and their decision not to return to their wives and families, since he proposes to leave his family and his kingdom, looking for death, or indeed, for the paradise of the 'Happy Isles' (l. 63). Ulysses' need for action and the mariners' idleness thus raise very similar moral questions.

7. This sonnet is not included in McGann's edition of Rossetti's poems, but can be accessed on McGann's invaluable online archive, www.rossettiarchive.org.

8. Jerome McGann's notes to the sonnet in the *Rossetti Archive* aptly comment that a 'major problem in reading the sonnet concerns the bibliographical context in which it is read. There are at least three: the original compositorial context; the context of its placement in the "Sonnets for Pictures and Other Sonnets" section in the 1870 volume; and the context of its position in *The House of Life*' (2008).

9. Webster herself, of course, had close personal connections to the Rossettis; William Michael wrote an introduction to her posthumously published sonnet sequence *Mother and Daughter* (1895).

10. In a similar vein, Isobel Armstrong calls this poem 'Tennyson's most intense critique of oppression' (1993: 86). However, she sees nothing positive in the mariners' idleness. Instead, she suggests that the critique lies in putting the blame for the mariners' decision on the oppressive world of labour they want to escape from. Reading the poem, as is her wont, as a double poem, she argues that '[i]n one reading a passive consciousness is the *result* of eating the Lotos. In the second reading exhaustion *causes* the addictive need to forget [. . .] Behind the second reading is the cruelty of work, brute, mindless labour. This reading considers the conditions which *constitute* consciousness, volition and labour in passive terms, the conditions which force the need for the Lotos upon the mariners, and which necessitate the exhausted, semi-conscious reverie of forgetting, the longing for mindless life' (1993: 87). However, I have been suggesting here that the mariners' life is scarcely mindless. After all, it is full of aesthetic appreciation and produces an eminently poetical and musical song. Instead of a double poem, 'The Lotos-Eaters' is in that sense a triple poem at least, and not as clearly dismissive of idleness as Armstrong suggests.

11. All line references to Christina Rossetti's poems are to the Oxford World's Classics edition of *Poems and Prose*, edited by Simon Humphries (2008), unless otherwise indicated.

12. The more detailed unfolding of the Prince's quest is, of course, important for any allegorical reading, but less so for my purposes. For a fuller account of the poem, see Henwood (1997); D'Amico (1999: 67–93).

13. Jerome Bump has suggested that '[o]ur experience and understanding of Victorian religious discourse would be greatly enhanced by increasing our awareness of the complexity of their sense of time' and that our bias for linear temporal thinking hampers our awareness of temporal alternatives, important at the time (2004: 27). Bump's focus lies on what he calls the 'Victorian Radicals' G. M. Hopkins, E. B. Pusey and F. M. Müller, for which the case plays out somewhat differently than in Christina Rossetti's work, which I am concerned with here. One aspect of such an increased awareness, relevant to Christina Rossetti's work,

which I lack the space to explore further concerns devotional reading practises; see Jones (2022).

14. In stressing the difference between Rossetti's engagement with devotional time and the time pressures apparently felt by many of her male peers, I disagree with Krista Lysack's reading of Rossetti's *Time Flies* as an attempt to 'create an experience of time that coordinates modern, industrial rhythms with the eternal time traditionally registered by liturgy' (2013: 465). Lysack's reading is thought-provoking, and she is correct in stating that *Time Flies* is centrally concerned with 'the synchronization of earthly and heavenly time' (464). But earthly time, I argue, is precisely not understood by Rossetti in terms of industrial time, nor is the latter simply coterminous with clock-time or calendrical time. Such a short-circuiting, I believe, fails to sufficiently account for a temporal complexity that cannot be reduced to simple binaries. It also remains blind to the heterogeneity of parallel, and sometimes conflicting Victorian temporal concepts. A focus on Rossetti's take on idleness helps to tease out some of this complexity.

15. This poem is not included in Humphries's collection of Rossetti's *Poems and Prose* and is listed separately in the list of references.

16. This poem is not included in Humphries's collection of Rossetti's *Poems and Prose* and is listed separately in the list of references.

17. Indeed, Adam Colman mentions that the manuscript of the poem carries the subtitle 'an echo from Tennyson' (2019: 122). The poem was not published during Rossetti's lifetime.

Chapter 4

Hearing Time in Metre – Prosody between Abstraction, Mechanism and Embodiment

In 1923, in the midst of Modernism and the triumphal progression of free-verse forms, Alice Meynell published 'The English Metres', a poem which Meredith Martin has called 'an ode to English metrical freedom at the same time that it is an elegy' for a kind of metrical understanding that Meynell felt to be on the wane (2012: 203):

The rooted liberty of flowers in breeze
    Is theirs, by national luck impulsive, terse,
Tethered, uncaptured, rules obeyed 'at ease,'
    Time-strengthened laws of verse.

Or they are like our seasons that admit
    Inflexion, not infraction: Autumn hoar,
Winter more tender than our thoughts of it,
    But a year's steadfast four;

Redundant syllables of Summer rain,
    And displaced accents of authentic Spring;
Spondaic clouds above a gusty plain
    With dactyls on the wing.

Not Common Law, but Equity, is theirs—
    Our metres; play and agile foot askance,
And distant, beckoning, blithely rhyming pairs,
    Unknown to classic France;

Unknown to Italy. Ay, count, collate,
    Latins! with eye foreseeing on the time,
And numbered fingers, and approaching fate
    On the appropriate rhyme.

Nay, nobly our grave measures are decreed:
    Heroic, Alexandrine with the stay,
Deliberate; or else like him whose speed
    Did outrun Peter, urgent in the break of day.

Meynell's poem was composed towards the end of a period of intense prosodic debates about the nature of English metre and helps to show why these debates mattered so deeply to those involved. For the Victorians, prosody was by no means an arcane and dry subtopic of critical enquiry. Critics like Yopie Prins, Meredith Martin, Jason David Hall, Joseph Phelan, Jason H. Rudy and others have done much recently to show how metre 'mattered in more ways, and to more people, than most of us, from our twenty-first-century vantage point, readily appreciate' (Hall 2011: 1). In a pioneering article that helped to spark renewed interest in the field, Prins noted that 'the publication of historical surveys and theoretical treatises on meter rose dramatically throughout the Victorian period' (2000: 89), an increase which further fired up the central prosodic controversies.

Building on the work of these scholars, I maintain that what Victorians thought about metre can tell us something about the way they thought about time. Though poetry, as we have seen in the previous chapters, may have been variously associated with timelessness, Victorian metrical theorists were alive to the way metre relates to time. Poetry, proposes E. S. Dallas in his *Poetics* (1852), 'will bring out the idea of Time by the use of timed or measured words' (Dallas 1852: 157). In effect, he argues, 'metre in its simplest form [is] time heard' (164). Proposing to take this contention seriously, I argue that Victorian prosodic debates are shaped by the changing conceptions of time which I am concerned with throughout this study. In this chapter, I will first outline some of the central issues debated among Victorian metrical theorists, especially concerning the difference between quantitative verse and accentual-syllabic versification. I then turn to the work of Coventry Patmore, not only because his theories were later identified as pivotal, but also because he has attracted significant attention within recent scholarship. Considering his metrical theory in the context of changing temporal concepts, I argue, throws a new light on problems with his theories which recent critics have controversially debated. This perspective shows in stark relief the dependence of Patmore's metrical ideas on newly dominant temporal concepts. In a second step, I turn from theory to practise to consider one specific metrical challenge Victorian poets faced: how to react to the powerfully rhythmical experience of railway travel. Though these two parts of my argument may initially seem only tangentially related, they coalesce in the complex and difficult negotiations of the relationship between bodies and machines, regularity and flexibility, submission and resistance, all of which occur within and speak to a wider cultural process of abstraction, in which mechanically regulated abstract time is juxtaposed to the time of individual, embodied experience.

Why did metre matter so deeply to the Victorians, however? For one, poetry retained an exceptionally high cultural status throughout much of the nineteenth century. When one can think it a 'truism that "the condition of poetry is a matter of public concern"' (D.C.L. 1873: 261), it should, perhaps, be no surprise that the form of poetry emerges as a matter of serious contention. Moreover, poetic scansion formed a cornerstone of the kind of classicist education that most British public-school children underwent and was thus by no means a specialist topic, but rather one with which any educated person was thoroughly acquainted. But beyond this, Meynell's poem may perhaps help to suggest why metrical problems could fire up heated discussions: poetic metres were understood to express particular features of a national spirit. A correct understanding of English metre thus promised a correct understanding of British national character. It clearly matters that Meynell's metres are English in explicit contrast to French and Italian, and even to Latin verse. They are taken to be as much part of British nature as its climate. Moreover, Meynell stresses both liberty and law, indeed liberty through law, and her legal references make clear that she understands this principle to govern not only English verse, but also the English nation.

Notably, however, Meynell refers to the terminology of Greek poetic feet, as if they were native to the English language, native even to English climate and soil. They correspond to what appear to be characteristically English seasons (mild winters, wet summers). And yet, Meynell glosses over a prosodic problem that had divided critics for almost a century: the applicability of the Greek foot system to English verse. Ancient Greek verse worked on fundamentally different principles than English verse. The Classical metres were quantitative, that is, different feet described various kinds of combinations of long and short syllables, instead of the alternation of stressed and unstressed syllables that governs metrical recurrence in the English language. While the Victorians generally considered the Classical models to be of importance to English culture, not everyone was willing to accept this 'foreign' element as essential and native. What was ultimately at stake in the prosodic debates was thus a sense of English national identity and of the relative importance of the classics, on the one hand, and the Anglo-Saxon heritage, on the other, in shaping that identity.[1] The history and the peculiarity of English metre were understood to reflect the history and peculiarity of the English national character, and a correct understanding of English metres could become synonymous with correct patriotic feeling.

Both Martin and Hall have shown the roots of this debate to lie in nineteenth-century education. Versification in Classical languages was an essential element of Victorian education, and with the extension of the school system ever more children were trained in Classical prosody. Generations of boys spent their schooldays constructing Greek and Latin verses according to prescribed metrical schemata into which syllables with the appropriate quantity needed to be fit, sometimes regardless of the sense. They were taught to consider the problem of true or false quantities earnestly and excessively and to understand prosody was an essential qualification to count as an educated gentleman.[2] Such an education, Michael D. Hurley suggests, 'would surely have encouraged a unique *habitus* of hearing', which promotes sound and rhythm as fundamental to poetic shaping, perhaps above and beyond the semantic import (Hurley 2013: 24). Moreover, this sort of prosodic training was widely held to be conducive to forming firm and refined characters as well as producing disciplined and upright men and good soldiers (Martin 2012: 122). At the same time, the nineteenth century saw wide-ranging educational reforms in which the Classical languages were gradually unsettled from their classroom monopoly and began to be replaced by the study of English literature. In such an ideological setting, in which metre is not only charged with expressing the national character but also with disciplining the future soldier, disagreements about the nature of English metre are clearly no minor matter. Indeed, Martin traces the various ways in which metre comes to stand 'for a host of evolving cultural concerns, including class mobility, imperialism, masculinity, labor, education, the role of classical and philological institutions, freedom, patriotism, national identification, and high art versus low art' (Martin 2012: 4).

English versification, however, turned out to be a tricky business, and the prosodic debates of the nineteenth century were hard-pressed to give it the kind of disciplinary order the classics had provided. The disagreements between different prosodists were various and sometimes subtle, but the central difficulty they endeavoured to resolve was the question how English metre should be marked or measured. Did it follow quantitative rules like the Greek and Latin verse every educated Victorian had learned to scan according to alternating long and short syllables? Was it marked by beats and alliteration like Anglo-Saxon verse? Does the metrical beat, or ictus, depend on accent, stress, tone, length or some combination of all these? Are there English equivalents of metrical 'feet'? What is the relation between metre and rhythm? What kinds of licences are allowable in metrical verse of any of these kinds? Again, Meynell's poem points to some of the difficulties involved, as well as the ideological charge underlying the issue in her oxymoronic attempts to balance liberty and law: her metres have 'rooted liberty' (l. 1), they are both 'tethered' and 'uncaptured' (l. 3), both 'terse' (l. 2) and 'redundant' (l. 9) or 'displaced' (l. 10), both 'Time-strengthened' (l. 4) and 'impulsive' (l. 2), both 'grave' (l. 21) and playful (l. 14). She derides the close adherence to fixed numbers and rhymes in French and Italian syllabic verse ('Ay, count, collate / Latins!'; l. 18) but ironically chooses the alexandrine – a French form if ever there was one – to celebrate as English.

Beyond such national ideologies, however, there is another aspect of metre which Meynell's poem serves to highlight: different metres shape time differently. Metre is markedly cast in temporal terms in the poem. The laws of verse are calcified time, strengthened by their history; the different metrical feet are associated with the cyclical progression of the seasons; different kinds of metrical feet bring their own kind of movement with them: blowing in gusts, flying on wings, moving gravely, pausing deliberately, or running swiftly. The poem attempts to merge a historical understanding of metre as 'Time-strengthened' (l. 4) and the contingent result of 'national luck' (l. 2) with a naturalised account of metre's cyclical eternity, turning metre's 'steadfast four' (l. 8) into a natural constant (though her mention of the spondee in the next stanza directly raises the question of which four metrical feet she might be referring to). And yet, they are not bound by the historical precedent of 'Common Law' but can find ever new expression and application in individual cases ('Equity', l. 13). Finally, the poem rejects the kind of time-counting ascribed to the Latins, a type of temporal awareness which is associated in the poem with a belief in fate and thus a future that is foreseeable and predetermined. The alternative, it seems, lies in the free, though rooted movement of the English metres, emerging from history but adaptable to an open future and moving 'urgent in the break of day' (l. 24). The compromises Meynell attempts to strike here between nature and history, between law and freedom, between strict time-counting and flexible movement, between rule and interpretation reveal fault-lines which run all the way through Victorian theories of versification.

From that perspective, the Victorian 'prosody wars' (Martin 2011) can be understood not only as a disagreement over national characteristics, but also as a clash between various ways of conceiving and measuring time. From the debates around English quantities to what T. S. Omond heralded as the 'new prosody' (1921: 166), associated primarily with Coventry Patmore, I argue that perspectives on the prosodical debates of the Victorians can be fruitfully refracted through the context of an increasing establishment of what Walter Benjamin, in his 'Theses on the Philosophy of History' (1940), so influentially termed 'homogeneous, empty time' (1999: 254): an increasing precision of mechanical means of timekeeping and an ever more extensive and prescriptive temporal structuring of daily life. The abstraction of the concept of metre which we see emerging with the new prosody, I contend, is part and parcel of a wider process of increasing differentiation, in which a public, objective time is juxtaposed to a private, subjective time. If metre is time heard, the endless debates about metre also reflect some of the complexities of temporal concepts. Metre, it turns out, invariably oscillates between objective law and subjective perception, between organicism and mechanism, in spite of all effort to pin it down – exemplified in Meynell's contradictory double symbolism of natural growth and established legal system. Even if one restricts one's focus to temporal aspects only, metre emerges as a highly complex nodal point for processes of abstraction and differentiation which are difficult to untangle and never entirely conclusive. Indeed, in his study of eighteenth-century prosody, Marcus Tomalin (2020) has shown that such complexities, and especially oscillations between organicism and the machinic, pre-date Victorian discussions, and in a sense, my contribution can be read as a continuation to the story he tells (which concludes with a focus on the prosodic work of Joshua Steele). I also argue, however, that the Victorian version of this debate takes a specific form, which is dependent on a dualistic understanding of time that only gains dominance in the course of the nineteenth century.

Towards Abstraction – Metre and Rhythm

If one opens an introduction into English studies these days and looks for the chapter on versification, one is likely to find the authors careful to distinguish between metre and rhythm. To take a random example, Lee Spinks sets up his chapter on 'Metre and Rhythm' in *The Edinburgh Introduction to Studying English Literature* (2014), 'by making a key distinction between our two terms, metre and rhythm':

> By metre, I mean the definitive patterned stress-shape of a poem (the way its beats are organised into a coherent and repeatable form such as iambic pentameter [. . .] or trochaic verse), while by rhythm I mean the sound or shapes that this metrical pattern creates as the poem unfolds during the time of our reading. (47)

Metre, that is, is the abstract rule, an '*organising principle*' of '*strictly-patterned regularity, that can be counted and named*' in the words of Derek Attridge's introduction to poetic rhythm (1995: 7), which Spinks refers to. Rhythm, in contrast, is the actual flow of words in a line, a '*flexible* [. . .] *movement and countermovement*' of textual '*energy*' which is '*complicated by constant variations and local inflections*' (Attridge 1995: 3). Musical time signatures and the rhythm of the notes that fill the empty regular grid of the bars is often used as an analogy. Metre somehow has to arise from the line (after all, where else is it to come from?), but nonetheless it has no material existence within the line. Its strict regularity is only an idealised, abstract pattern, having its place in the mind, not in the sensual phenomenon of a line's succession of sounds. In this chapter I want to question this common distinction between metrical rule and rhythmical realisation by interrogating the conditions of its historical emergence.

That this abstraction has its roots in the nineteenth century has already been noted some decades ago by Dennis Taylor. According to Taylor, the 'important distinction between two orders of discourse, talk about the metre and talk about a given line's rhythm, was not yet clearly made' in the eighteenth century (1988: 13). Before the nineteenth century prosodic discussion tended to use the terms 'metre', 'rhythm' and 'measure' interchangeably, or where they did not, metre and rhythm mostly referred to different aspects of a poetic line, namely quantity and accent. In the nineteenth century, however, metre came to be increasingly understood as accentual and thus metre and rhythm had to be newly differentiated. Thus, Taylor explains, prosodists in the nineteenth century began to maintain that metre 'does specify number and accent-placement of syllables, but on a level not identical with any particular manifestation' (Taylor 1988: 13). Metre and rhythm were both understood to depend on the placement of accents, but the first was conceptualised as the ideal, the latter as the individual instance.

Notwithstanding his awareness of the way metrical theory is 'peculiarly dependent on analogies and world views' and thus culturally conditioned (1988: 9), Taylor interprets this as an advance in understanding: 'a gradual achievement in placing the law of metre at the right level of abstraction' (13). This is where I beg to differ. In fact, I argue, this process of abstraction is part of a broader, historically specific cultural phenomenon, a symptom of a change in the dominant conceptualisation of time, which resulted in a split into a mechanically regular objective time on the one hand, and a subjective, flexible and embodied time on the other. From a critical historical perspective, this process of separation and abstraction can no longer be understood as part of a progressive narrative of intellectual advance, but rather emerges an act of purification of the kind which Bruno Latour (1993) has suggested to be foundational for what he calls the 'modern constitution': the attempt to impose a separation between nature and culture on a hybrid object. In the case of time (and, as we will see, metre), indeed, this separation is complicated from the beginning by the fact that the assignation to the cultural or natural sphere respectively is particularly unstable. 'Objective' time is natural, in that it is generally understood to be the kind of time all nature is subject to, though it is measured by machines and associated with scientifically established natural laws. At the same time, it is cultural – a socially constructed system which governs human behaviour. 'Subjective' time is cultural in that it arises from individual perception, which is necessarily shaped by culture. At the same time, it is associated with the involuntary physiological processes of the body and its natural rhythms.

To begin to trace how these entanglements reflect on metrical discussions and in order to understand the processes of abstraction and purification at issue, we need to first take a step back and consider more closely one of the fundamental problems in Victorian prosody: the relation between the Anglo-Saxon and Classical influences on English versification, or, more simply, the question of quantity versus accent. As we will see, apart from all the other factors that played into the controversy around this issue (nationalistic, educational, disciplinary and others), accent and quantity also carried different notions of time.

Quantity versus accent

Verse in Classical languages, according to the Victorian consensus, was scanned based on quantity; that is, its metrical patterns depend on the combination of syllables of different lengths. However, this system is not directly transferable to the modern English language, in which syllables do not have fixed quantities. Or rather, the question whether quantities exist in English was a matter of contention. At the same time, the nineteenth century saw influential scholarship on Anglo-Saxon verse, whose entirely different metrical principles, based on alliteration and accent, were only beginning to be understood. Much of the Victorian prosodic debate revolves around the question how much respective weight is given these different influences in the understanding of English metre. In order to illustrate the differences between these systems of versification and to begin to draw out the ways in which this relates to concepts of time, I turn to the explanations offered by G. W. Hegel in his *Aesthetics: Lectures on Fine Arts*, held between 1818 and 1829 and later published as a transcript by one of his students, Heinrich Gustav Hotho. I draw on the German writer in this context because his description of the difference between Classical quantitative and modern accentual or syllabic prosody develops significantly broad philosophical implications, including references to the different ideas of time that underlie these verse systems. Moreover, his views influenced the Victorian discussion, and Coventry Patmore in particular. While no full English translation of Hegel's *Aesthetics* was available in the nineteenth century, Patmore apparently read Hotho's transcript of Hegel's lectures in the French translation by M. Ch. Bénard, published in 1840–52, and he drew heavily on Hegel's ideas for his prosodic work (Roth 1961: 56–7).[3]

Hegel distinguishes between rhythmical versification (that is, quantitative verse), rhyme (alliterative verse) and modern attempts to combine the two. Classical rhythmic versification, Hegel explains, follows a number of main principles:

> First, the fixed tempo of the syllables in their simple difference between long and short and the numerous ways of fitting them together in specific relations and metres.
>
> Secondly, the enlivenment of rhythm by accent, caesura, and the opposition between verbal and verse-accentuation.
>
> Thirdly, the euphony of word-sounds that can be produced within this movement of verse, without their being drawn together into rhymes.

(α) The chief thing in rhythm is not sound picked out and isolated as such but temporal duration and movement. Its simple starting-point is (αα) the natural length and shortness of syllables. (1975: 1014–15)

Temporal measure in this system arises naturally from the length of the syllables. It is constituted by duration and movement, and every sound matters equally in establishing the rhythm. The sound of the language alone is rhythmical, since, in contrast to accent and stress, which give emphasis to important words or syllables, the quantity of syllables is entirely independent from semantics. Thus, 'the sense of the words is entirely fused with the sensuous element of sound and temporal duration' (1975: 1022). Moreover, this movement allows for a multiplicity of rhythms to establish themselves simultaneously. Hegel insists on the difference of poetic and musical time measure, as the former does not require 'an absolutely fixed measure of time for its communication and progress' which would assert 'the element of time [. . .] more preponderantly than the whole nature of poetry allows' (1017). The reason for this difference lies in the semantic import of language. Since poetry works not with sounds alone like music, but with words that establish meaning, it does not need to follow a strict beat but can shape its own time. Instead of depending on a single beat, Hegel argues, Classical verse achieves its rhythmic beauty by a complex interaction of diverse rhythms established individually by quantity, by verse-accent, by the placement of caesuras and by word-accent. What is essential to this concept of metre is the interaction of multiple rhythms, none of which takes precedence. In this 'polyrhythmia', as Isobel Armstrong calls it, 'the various rhythms are not alternatives or rivals'. Glossing on Hegel, she goes on to explain that these various rhythms 'ask the listener to orchestrate them, and the act of orchestration creates meaning' (2011b: 32). As Hegel was painfully aware, though, such active readerly orchestration is a skill mostly lost to modern readers: 'to make the beauty of the rhythm audible is a matter of great difficulty for our modern ear' (1975: 1019).

Rhymed verse, according to Hegel, loses most of this complexity. In modern languages like German and English quantities are uncertain because syllables are lengthened by stress and the accent lies usually on the word root. But without a stable metrical order based on the duration of syllables the whole Classical system collapses. Rhyme is '[t]he one possible compensation offered for this loss' (1975: 1027), but Hegel argues that it needs to draw much more attention to itself than Classical harmonies: 'in contrast to the all-pervasive euphony of rhythm, rhyme is an isolated, emphasized, and exclusive sound', '[it] is a thumping sound that does not need so finely cultivated an ear as Greek versification necessitates' (1028). The difference between quantitative and rhymed verse thus plays out as a difference in temporal shape. Once verse depends on rhyme, time no longer develops as a continually unfolding duration, but as a (more or less regular) recurrence of a sound. Whatever happens between these recurrences is no longer in itself expressive of time passing: rhyme depends on 'a mere drawing of the mind's and ear's memory to a recurrence of the same or associated sounds and meanings' (1028). A kind of verse that depends solely on alliteration, assonance or rhyme has no regular time measure, as varying amounts of time could pass before the recurrence of the rhyme sound. It depends entirely on rhyme for its structure. Consequently, Hegel opines that French and Italian syllabic verse lacks rhythm and metre, since counting syllables which have no stable quantity does not give a measure of time.

German (and, since they function similarly, one may add English) verse, however, attempts a unification of rhyme and rhythm. It does so, claims Hegel, by making the rhythm of metrical accent, caesura and word-accent coincide. According to Hegel, this results in an 'as it were more ponderous accentuation'. In order to counter the strong impulse of rhyme, metre needs to make itself equally conspicuous:

> But since it is not the quantitative natural difference of syllables and its variety that is to be systematized and made dominant, in the matter of this time-relation recourse can be had only to the identical repetition of the same time-measure, with the result that here the beat begins to be asserted far more strongly than is permissible in the rhythmic system. (1975: 1033)

Instead of the complex heterogeneity of rhythmic relations in Classical versification, in which every sound contributes to temporal duration and movement, the modern unification of rhythm and rhyme depends on a system of identical repetition, the regular recurrence of beats or rhyme sounds. Like in the striking of a clock, it is only the beats that count.

Armstrong's insightful discussion of these passages from the *Aesthetics* helps to illuminate what she calls the 'great epistemological myth' which Hegel develops in these pages (Armstrong 2011a: 127). There is a perceptible narrative of loss and decline underlying Hegel's characterisation of Classical rhythmic and what he terms 'Romantic' and Armstrong calls 'Post-Christian' rhyming verse. Romantic verse has not only lost much of the subtlety of rhythmic versification. 'Consciousness', Armstrong glosses, 'is now founded, not on a joyful and plastic corporeality that lives with the sensuous interplay of body and mind, but on a split between spirit and sensuous world' (131). Sound, and thus the materiality of language, is no longer coequal with sense, but subordinated to it. This has implications for the different kinds of temporal experiences that are juxtaposed. Armstrong summarises Hegel's view on Classical verse thus:

> The myth being evolved here, then, is that the joyous freedom and plasticity of Classical poetry comes about because it is, first, constituted by mobility: it is movement. Second, it *re-makes time itself* as music cannot, and third it *lives in unalienated time.* (131)

The rhythmic time of quantitative verse knows no differentiation into objective and subjective time, no abstract regular beat to which the sound of the words need to submit. As Armstrong puts it elsewhere, 'classical prosody, by virtue of its infinite capacity for varying metrical feet and quantity, can, unlike music, which is committed to the pace of temporality, actually remake time' (2011b: 34). Time in metrical rhyme, in contrast, is abstracted as the recurring beat of the ictus. Rhyme and ictus empty other rhythmical elements of meaning. The caesura, for example, which in Classical verse established a rhythm of its own right, 'becomes an abstract, empty pause' (Armstrong 2011a: 132). With this, Armstrong suggests, '[w]e are nearing Benjamin's cycles of empty, homogeneous time' (133). At the same time, precisely this split between materiality and spirit allows for more freedom of expression. Romantic art, Hegel avers, 'is so concentrated in itself that it strips away the, as it were, corporeal side of the language and in what remains emphasizes only that wherein the spiritual *meaning* lies for the purpose of communication, and leaves the rest alone as insignificant by-play' (1975: 1023). This seems to allow for more freedom, but Armstrong points out that abstraction is the prerequisite of manipulation: 'inherent in rhyme is the culture's readiness for exploitation and consumption. Once materiality is split off, isolated as a separate element, and experienced as an independent entity, it can be separately used and exploited' (2011a: 134). Thus, the move from Classical quantitative verse to rhyme is already framed as a step towards abstraction and purification, in which body and soul, materiality and spirit are separated.

Of course, as Armstrong repeatedly insists, Hegel's characterisation of these different verse systems is ideological and may well be disputed.[4] Nonetheless, Hegel's account of versification, both in its ideological underpinnings and in its contradictions, sets the scene for an exploration of the centrality of temporal concepts for prosodic discussion in the nineteenth century. Similar issues of embodiment versus abstraction, regularity versus modulation, freedom versus restriction, artificiality versus natural expression arise again and again in the metrical theory of the period which I examine below.

In the mid-nineteenth century, debates about English quantities were fired particularly by the work of translation, that is, by the question how to adequately imitate the movements of the Homeric hexameter in English. Joseph Phelan, who traces the fate of the nineteenth-century English hexameter in detail, remarks that 'the fashion for English hexameters did not endure much beyond the 1860s' (2012: 45), and serious advocacy of English quantitative metre did not survive much longer. In 1883 *The Saturday Review* could declare this particular debate to be not only concluded, but fundamentally deluded, commenting summarily:

> Hot controversy has raged as to whether long and short or accented and unaccented syllables should be considered as the primary elements of the English metrical foot. Victory appears to have declared for the school which puts accent in the place of quantity; but the controversy was rather about terms than facts. No sane man ever pronounced English verse by the ancient rules of quantity; and, on the other hand, those who classify by accents are fain to call many syllables accented whose sole claim to that honour is given by their length. ('Rhythm': 270)

Yet, such a victory for accent could do little to abate the discussion, and the *Saturday Review* article serves to suggest some of the reasons. For one, the question whether there is something like an English metrical foot at all was another heatedly debated issue.[5] The existence of the English foot was primarily contested by those who called for a return to the Anglo-Saxon alliterative and purely accentual verse which counts only beats, not syllables, and thus knows no fixed metrical unit. The most influential work to advocate Anglo-Saxon metres was Edwin Guest's *The History of English Rhythms* – first published in 1838 and influentially republished by Walter Skeat in 1883 – in which Guest contrasts 'accentual metre' with 'temporal metre' (Classical quantity, or Hegel's 'rhythm'), and claims that 'no temporal rhythms are to be found in our literature' (1883: 169).

The second contested question the *Saturday Review* article points to is that accent itself continued to be a troubled concept, since it remained difficult to ascertain how *exactly* the beat in a metrical line was marked and the relation between metrical stress and word stress continued to be controversial.[6] Finally, the article's title, significantly, is 'Rhythm',[7] a term that came to stand in an increasingly complex relationship with metre.[8] In quantitative verse, if one follows Hegel's elucidation, metre is one rhythmical element among others, contributing to the polyrhythm of the line in dialogue with accent, caesura and euphony. In accentual-syllabic verse – that is, verse which counts both accents and syllables – in contrast, both metre and rhythm are associated with the placing of accents and thus the difference between the two needs to be newly conceptualised. Tellingly, the *Saturday Review* article discusses rhythm not only in verse, but also in prose, arguing that short rhythmical sections in prose 'are closely analogous to classical feet' while the

> longer groups owe their rhythmical character to the regular beat which falls on each strong syllable – each of these is, within the section, separated from its neighbour by a constant time-interval. If we were to employ musical notation to express the time occupied in delivery, each strong syllable would begin a fresh bar. (1883: 270)

Such an emphasis on the regularity of the time-interval as well as the reference to musical notation marks shows the article to be indebted to a new sort of prosodic orthodoxy, the so-called 'new prosody' which gained ground in the second half of the nineteenth century.

The new prosody

T. S. Omond credited the 'new prosodists' of the second half of the nineteenth century with beginning to establish 'more rational and real methods of scansion' (1921: 166). As the *Saturday Review* article quoted above serves to suggest, the new prosodic approach could negotiate between quantity and accent by subordinating both to a more abstract scheme of underlying metrical beat. While no longer 'temporal' in the sense that Guest had used the term, the new prosodic theory reintroduced time as a crucial factor. However, instead of depending on varying lengths of syllables, this understanding of metre posited a regular underlying beat, marking off invariable time-intervals – a sort of fixity that Hegel had still considered inimical to poetry. Phelan points to the importance a supposed analogy between music and poetry played for the promotion of this new conceptualisation of metre (2012: 15–44; see also Taylor 1988: 14–15). The metrical line was understood to follow a fixed time signature and be divisible into bars, like music. At the same time, this analogy helped to conceptualise a fundamental difference between metre (the musical time signature) and rhythm (the rhythm of the notes filling the bars). The 'musical prosodists' also variously experimented with the elements of musical notation to clarify relations between metre and rhythm in a line. Such notation attempts to abstract the sound of language entirely from words and to standardise metrical effects.[9]

This theory found its most lastingly influential Victorian expression in Coventry Patmore's review essay 'English Metrical Critics' (1857), which was republished in slightly revised form as his 'Essay on English Metrical Law' several times over the course of his life. According to Omond, Patmore 'was sometimes less original than he fancied', but he 'voiced ideas that were in the air' (1921: 171), and his essay has been a touchpoint for the revived interest in Victorian prosody over the last decades. Patmore's position, then, is interesting precisely because what he proposes is new but not original. If he voices 'ideas that were in the air', the question remains why new ideas about metre arose at this specific time. Jason David Hall provides a convincing answer when he points out that Patmore's essay is 'framed by and exhibit[s] signs of the standardizing impulses associated generally with the machine age' (2017: 17). 'Patmore and his contemporaries', Hall maintains,

> could not have failed to notice the systematizing force of machine-regulated homogeneous time, which governed the setting of clocks in homes and public spaces, controlled factory production, enabled the transmission of telegrams, and coordinated travel by omnibus, canal barge, and train. (2017: 23)

Discussing Patmore's essay in the context of the spread of the railway system and the *'reification* of meter' in the Morse code of telegraph communication, Hall suggests that '[i]t is hardly surprising, [. . .] that a new metrics, just beginning to coalesce as the age of railway travel was itself getting up to speed, should incorporate elements of this widespread spatio-temporal experience of machine culture' (2017: 26). We can trace the growing influence of concepts of time in the endeavours of the new prosody, which projects time as an abstract spatialised grid, measurable by invariable, regular beats and external to the body of verse – a spatialisation which becomes palpable in Patmore's comparison of the ictus to 'a post in a chain railing, [which] shall mark the end of one space, and the commencement of another' (1857: 136).

Most important in this context is Patmore's insistence on the isochrony of the time-intervals between the beats that mark the metrical ictus, that is, the exactly equal distance between those railing posts. He credits Joshua Steele's *Prosodia Rationalis* (1779) with 'having propounded more fully than had hitherto been done, the true view of metre, as being primarily based upon isochronous division by ictuses or accents' (1857: 128). This principle of isochrony is a recurring idea in the work of the musical prosodists and it had radical consequences: it got rid of syllable counting, since the number of syllables between accents could vary, as long as the interval remained regular, and it understood pauses to be integral elements of the line (Phelan 2012: 17). Thus, it could be perceived as uncommonly flexible (as is also demonstrated by Patmore's own attempt to put his prosodic theory into practice in his later collection *The Unknown Eros* (1877), which features highly irregular metres) and simultaneously as severely constricting.[10] While Patmore seems to lean towards accent as prime marker of the ictus – for example when he speaks of '[m]etre, in the primary degree of a simple series of isochronous intervals, marked by accents' (1857: 132) – later in the text he 'attributes to [metre] the function of marking, *by whatever means*, certain isochronous intervals' (136). Thus, how metre marks time no longer matters. What matters is that it marks time. 'Metre implies something measured,' Patmore maintains, calling this 'a truism', but what is measured 'is the time occupied in the delivery of a series of words.' This, one might think, comes close to the Classical way of measuring verse by the length of syllables, but Patmore disagrees: 'time measured implies something that measures, *and is therefore itself unmeasured*; an argument before which those who hold that English accent and long quantity are identical must bow' (1857: 136). In unpacking this argument, we get to the core of the temporal concepts involved in this view of metre. The syllabic quantities of Classical metre produce certain time-lengths in their specific combinations of long and short syllables. Time, as it were, is embodied and brought forth by the metrical flow of the verse. Isochronous metre, in contrast, moves according to a fixed regular interval marked by a constant beat.

Time is thus external to the verse; what matters is not time as such, but merely the regularity of the beat. Moreover, and crucially, Patmore goes on to claim:

> this all-important [. . .] time-beater [. . .] *has no material and external existence at all*, but has its place in the mind, which craves measure in everything, and, whereever the idea of measure is uncontradicted, delights in marking it with an imaginary 'beat'. (1857: 136)

Metre is not embodied in the durational and phonetic movement of the words, but superimposed on the verse, as a rule against which the line is measured.[11]

Valuing this increasing abstraction as a seminal step, Taylor argues that this conceptualisation of metre allows Patmore and his contemporaries to reintroduce the principle of polyrhythm which Hegel had presumed lost with the ancient quantitative metres; a polyrhythm based on the interaction 'between the pattern set up by the accentual-syllabic metre and the normal speech rhythm' (Taylor 1988: 28). Taylor does not seem to note the striking difference of such a principle of polyrhythm to that which Hegel describes for quantitative verse. According to Hegel, ancient polyrhythm developed in the interaction of various rhythmic elements of a line, all of whose movements are assumed to be simultaneously audible to the practised ear. The polyrhythm theorised by Patmore, in contrast, is the tension between ideal and realisation, between law and life, between artifice and 'normal speech'. The tension between the two cannot be heard, but only mentally ideated. Poetic harmony is no longer the sensuous effect of interweaving of various rhythmic elements, but, in Patmore's striking metaphor, metrical law provides the 'bonds' which poetic language 'should always seem to *feel*, though not to *suffer from*' (1857: 131). Instead of true polyrhythm, in which different more or less flexible rhythms interact, the tension between rhythm and metre, as conceptualised by Patmore, is a hierarchical one of rule and deviation.

Others have already associated these prosodic debates with 'a larger cultural pattern in Victorian England, a turn toward abstraction' (Prins 2000: 108; see also Hall 2017: 5 and *passim*). The rule of metre emerges as the ideal of precise temporal measurement. What we can see here, then, is the effect of a fundamental split in the concept of time, separated into an embodied, flexible and subjective temporal movement on the one hand, and an abstract, exact and objective temporal measure on the other, a 'double-consciousness' which, Hall argues, characterised the modern experience of railway travel, since 'to move by the modern machine was to possess at once an awareness of the regular, periodic spacing of guide-time [that is, the railway time-tables] and the quite possibly messy pacing of lived-time – and, of course, also the slippages between the two' (2017: 26). But what is remarkable in Patmore's metrical system is the way it clearly reveals the ruptures within its own logic of abstraction. The move towards abstraction, which others have noticed and Taylor has lauded, is in fact ridden with contradictions, which emerge in particular in the ambiguous position of the natural.

This comes most clearly to the fore in Patmore's central assumption that a 'natural' craving of 'measure in everything' should find expression as isochrony, that is, perfectly regular time-intervals. That the human mind should naturally crave exact measure, as Patmore maintained, does seem a rather daring claim. After all, few organic time-intervals are truly isochronous. In so far, Patmore's word choice is revealing: apart from prosodic discussions, the term 'isochrony' is used primarily in connection with the movement of pendulums, in particular in clocks. Isochronous movement is essential to mechanical timekeeping, and that truly isochronous beats were probably most familiar to Patmore's contemporaries in the form of ticking clocks is suggested not least by the way clocks continue to turn up as examples in prosodic treatises.[12] The mind Patmore imagines, it seems, is a mind which has absorbed mechanical rhythms, to the point of 'craving' their perfect regularity.

The importance of the musical analogy to the new prosodists is also telling in this regard. After all, the nineteenth century was only beginning to see exactly timed music with the spread of the use of the metronome, patented in 1815 by Johann Maelzel, whose sometime collaborator Ludwig van Beethoven was the first composer to include metronome marks in his compositions. As Alexander Evan Bonus explains, the mechanically regular time kept by the metronome was by no means unanimously welcomed. Rather, contemporary critics and composers (Bonus cites Liszt, Brahms, Wagner and Saint-Saëns among others) complained that the mechanical regularity of the metronome robbed musicians of their expressivity. Inconsistent with 'traditional aesthetics of musical time', for many, 'the ticking of Maelzel's metronome, while failing to project the subjective, sensory qualities of musical movement, more accurately reflected the stark mechanical rhythm propelling the Industrial Age'. The acceptance of the metronome as the standard timekeeper for music, according to Bonus, thus 'reflects a drastic aesthetic paradigm shift in modernity, a *metronomic turn*' as 'proponents of a scientifically oriented view of time and motion, one diametrically opposed to past aesthetics, regarded automatic metronomes as being both beneficial and necessary indicators of accurate, efficient, and "normal" personal behaviour' (Bonus 2014). Music, from which prosodists derived the isochronous principle, was thus itself in the process of becoming governed by an abstract mechanical time-beater.

That mechanical exactitude is by no means the only way to think about metrical regularity becomes apparent when comparing Patmore's insistence on abstract isochrony with Dallas's comments on the nature of metrical time: '[Time's] real value with every man', says Dallas, 'is subjective, what is long to one being short to another [. . .]. The measure of time, therefore, which the imagination will provide, is not a uniform beat, like that of a clock, but one like the pulse, varying according to circumstances' (1852: 160–1). The time that Dallas hears in metre is thus a flexible, subjective time, embodied in the verse rhythms and dependent on the reader. In contrast, Patmore's concept of metre sits uneasily between embodiment and abstraction. As a formal feature of verse it belongs to what Patmore, with Hegel, considers to be 'the corporeal element' of poetry (as opposed to the 'spiritual' element of poetic subject). At the same time, metre is the formal 'law' which governs the 'life' of poetic content (Patmore 1857: 130) and it is entirely immaterial, marked only by the 'mind, which craves measure'. It is independent of the verse rhythm (or 'music', as Patmore prefers), which derives beauty from varieties of tone (137). At this point, Patmore strikingly brings in the example of a ticking clock to claim that its regular beating is perceived as *rhythmical* (as opposed to metrical) merely because we imagine a difference in tone in subsequent beats which are in truth monotones. This not only illustrates once again the difference Patmore establishes between metre (the regular ticking) and rhythm (the imagined variation in tone), but also tantalisingly reverses the prior association of metre with the mind and rhythm with the body. In the ticking of the clock, what we *hear* is the regular, metrical beat, what we *imagine* is the rhythmic variation. Moreover, Patmore was very aware of the fact that actual voicings of verse differ and that the 'fashion [. . .] to seek expression at too great an expense of law [. . .] would ill bear us out in our assertion of the metrical isochronism in English'. Once verse is embodied, in the sense of spoken, the abstract law of metre threatens to disappear. In fact, after having forcefully argued for isochrony, Patmore concedes that 'the equality of metrical intervals between accent and accent is no more than general and approximate' (1857: 140) and maintains:

> the marking of the measure by the recurrent ictus may be occasionally remitted, the position of the ictus altered, or its place supplied by a pause, without the least offence to a cultivated ear, which rather delights in, than objects to, such remission, inversion, or omission. (141)

Such flexibility, it seems, must threaten to undermine the entire premise of Patmore's theory. It can only be maintained because the notion of precise and regular time measuring is assumed to be so deeply ingrained in the mind that departures from metre's regular beat fail to unsettle it. The metrical metronome, once set running, goes on ticking, no matter which modulations of tones and rhythm fill the interval between the beats.

The distinction between physiological, flexible rhythm and intellectual, isochronous metre, however, should prove difficult to maintain, within Patmore's essay and beyond. Some have suggested that Patmore's apparent anxiety to locate metre in the mind, not the body, needs to be understood in its specific context, as a reaction against the overly physiological theories of his prosodic predecessors – by dismissing attempts to theorise accent with reference to the way the human speech organs produce sounds, Phelan argues, 'Patmore frees English metrical theory from its physiological fixation' (2012: 29) – or as a rejection of the emphatically physiological poetics associated with the Spasmodic poets (Rudy 2009: 114). While the Spasmodic poets were long regarded as little more than a minor aberrance of little consequence for Victorian poetry, their importance for an understanding of Victorian concepts of rhythm and metre has been stressed in recent studies (Blair 2006: 94–100; Rudy 2009). The Spasmodics believed that 'the pulsations of verse might have affective and organic properties' (Blair 2006: 19). They developed what Rudy calls a '*rhythmic epistemology*', that is, a 'poetic theory that holds that poetry transmits knowledge and feeling primarily through rhythm, rather than through words or other formal structures' (2009: 80; 79). According to this theory, poetic rhythms directly affect their readers, somatically working on their emotions. It is worth noting here as an aside that this Spasmodic theory is not unrelated to the attempts to justify poetry's timeless appeal in the face of an awareness of historical change which I have discussed in Chapter 1. The bodily rhythms poetry was assumed to be in sympathy with were presumably universal and permanent. As Rudy explains, the poet can thus be figured as 'something of a scientist of human nature, crafting verses to elicit through physiological association patterns of universal thought and feeling' (2009: 87). Nonetheless, it was the spectre of such a direct bodily effect of rhythm beyond conscious control which allegedly led Patmore to emphasise his eminently cerebral, controlled and controlling metrical law.

But, for all that, Patmore does not leave the body behind. In fact, some scholars have argued that the supposed opposition between body and mind in Patmore's essay, as well as in Victorian prosody more generally, is merely a retrospective construction of recent criticism (Harrington 2007; Jones 2016). For one, Patmore draws on Hegel who, as we have seen, contrasted the spirituality of poetry's content with the materiality of its language. For Hegel, metre as an effect of sound was therefore associated with the corporeality of verse. Patmore's gloss on Hegel already introduces a slippage between the two:

> Art must have a body as well as a soul; and the higher and purer the spiritual, the more powerful and unmistakeable should be the corporeal element; – in other words, the more vigorous and various the life, the more stringent and elaborate must be the law. (1857: 130)

In this gloss, Patmore equates the life with the soul and the law with the body, but his terms imply a slippage which is easily missed. As Blair has noticed, the juxtaposition of 'life' and 'law' in verse 'suggests the inference that its physical impulses are subdued by principles of order imposed by a higher power' (2006: 87). Thus, even an attentive reader like Rudy could misunderstand this passage to imply that Patmore 'locates the true experience of poetry in meter and relegates to the sidelines "the corporeal element," rhythmic sensation' (2009: 115). This, however, is not the case. Instead, Patmore's reference to Hegel initially locates metre clearly within the corporeal material of language. The step towards abstraction and immateriality is made only later in the essay.

Another element which serves to entangle the corporeal and the abstract in Patmore's text is the influence of a Victorian commonplace, which justifies the existence of verse by arguing that it is rooted in the body and is the natural expression of passion or strong emotion. 'Rhythm', G. H. Lewes writes in a typical instance of this view, 'is not a thing invented by man, but a thing *evolved* from him, and it is not merely the accidental form, but the only possible form of poetry; for there is a rhythm of feeling correspondent in the human soul' (1842a: 13). In some form or another, this claim rears its head insistently across Victorian discussions and justifications of verse. Even Patmore, to whose endeavour to locate metre in the intellect, not the physiological processes of the body, this commonplace arguably stands in some tension, apparently felt its truth and importance too powerfully to deny it. He professes to be 'writing under the conviction that the musical and metrical expression of emotion is an instinct, and not an artifice. Were the vulgar and infantine delight in rhythm insufficient to justify that conviction, history itself would prove it.' 'Metre', he further maintains, 'in the primary degree of a simple series of isochronous intervals, marked by accents, is as natural to spoken language as an even pace is natural to walking' (1857: 132). In such claims, Patmore sounds intriguingly similar to the Spasmodic poet Sydney Dobell, who, in a lecture held in the same year that Patmore published his review, would establish a principle of regular time intervals on a purely physiological basis. The body, Dobell argues, is subject to rhythmic ordering, in particular through the pulse, whose rhythm he understands to be perfectly regular: 'The interval of time between every healthy heart-throb is precisely equal to that of the throb itself.' '[E]very portion of the incessant vital action of the system,' Dobell suggests, 'is keeping measured dance to that great *beater of time*', and thus poetical utterance 'must occur in a succession bearing proportional relations to a time marked by a series of equal intervals, that is, to the time beaten by a healthy heart' (Dobell 1876 [1857]: 24). If Patmore wants to find his 'all-important *time-beater*' in the mind, Dobell locates it squarely in the physiological processes of the body.

These matters are further complicated by the fact that the distinction between the organic and the mechanical was a highly contested issue for the Victorians, as the work of both Blair and Hall amply illustrates. Blair argues that the pulse could 'serve [. . .] as a model for rhythm in that it always involves the possibility of variation from the steady beat, the deviation from a set metrical pattern on which poetic rhythm depends.' And yet, she notes, 'in nineteenth-century literature, there is an evident anxiety that the heartbeat might be purely mechanical, equivalent to the ticking of a clock or other repetitive, "methodical" action, that it might not be responsive to emotion' (2006: 63–4). Hall pursues this further, illustrating the way in which prosodic discourse was informed by '[t]he nineteenth-century understanding of the human as machine [as] experimental, materialist methods began to redefine the various motive forces of the human organism and the mechanical properties, functions and outputs associated with them' (2017: 167). From such perspectives the dichotomy between machine and organism collapses.

What this goes to suggests is that the increasingly materialist outlook of the nineteenth century also made a distinction between mind and body like the one often ascribed to Patmore's essay difficult to maintain. This surfaces in Dobell's lecture, which goes a decisive step further by situating its physiological claims in the context of contemporary scientific work on light and sound waves. Recent scientific studies, says Dobell, 'have shown to what a wonderful extent vibrations are propagated through matter, and when once set in motion are repeated by sympathetic and other action in innumerable reflexes, each bearing computable relations to the original impulse.' Thus, 'the two great sources of bodily sensation – sound and light – are already shown to be results of undulations' and the body is therefore singularly conditioned towards rhythmic principles (1876 [1857]: 23). Such analogies became increasingly popular with the scientific advances in wave theory. Rhythm could be understood not only as based in primitive (that is, 'natural' and physiological) human life, but also as a fundamental principle of the cosmos. In *The Science of English Verse* (1880), Lanier similarly draws on science to detect rhythm everywhere, on a scale ranging from the cosmic 'spiral distribution of the remote nebulae' via 'the great tides in the sea, the great trade-winds in the air', to various life forms, whether 'sweet long grasses in running brooks', 'the lungs of man, the heart of the beast' or 'the cilia of the animalcule' (1894 [1880]: 248). '[R]hythm', writes Lanier,

> not only [. . .] appears as perhaps the widest artistic instinct in man: it would seem to be a universal principle throughout nature. Perhaps every one, in these days, is more or less familiar with the complete way in which modern physical science has reduced all that enormous and complex mass of phenomena which we call physical nature to a series of motions. Older conceptions of substance as opposed to form have resolved themselves into the general conception of force producing motion in certain modes. (1894 [1880]: 247)

This scientific generalised principle of rhythmic motion threatens to undermine distinctions between law and life, movement and bond. Regular rhythm, instead of being imposed by the mind, emerges as a fundamental principle, a natural law that is beyond human control. At the same time, to find rhythm in everything is an act of scientific abstraction ('physical science has reduced . . .') and thus an abstract pattern human minds impose on 'that enormous and complex mass of phenomena we call physical nature'. It remains unspecified how much variation this universal law would allow for in any individual instance. Moreover, it depends on precise mechanical means of measurement, without which many of the rhythmic undulations Lanier mentions would not be perceivable. The question whether the universal principle of rhythm Lanier wants to establish is mechanical or organic, material or abstract, involuntary or willed, precise or variable is unanswerable.

In view of such equivocations, the distinction between material, embodied rhythm and abstract, immaterial metre which Taylor heralded as the main achievement of the new prosody, is difficult to maintain. Instead of an advance in knowledge, offering a more sophisticated or more accurate understanding of prosody, it emerges as one of the processes of abstraction that took hold in industrialised societies, mirroring the concomitant split between concepts of embodied, private and subjective and abstract, public and objective time. But a closer look at the distinction between metre and rhythm established in the new prosody shows all too well that the modern work of purification – which, according to Latour (1993), aims to keep apart the realms of nature and culture, body and mind – is doomed to fail in face of the hybrid networks it wants to contain. Ironically enough, today's prosody has generally maintained Patmore's distinction between metre and rhythm, in which one is the law and the other the manifestation, but nonetheless sticks to the metrical foot. Pure isochrony, as Patmore's irregular odes in *The Unknown Eros* (1877) demonstrate, allows for much more varied rhythms (though it remains questionable whether these odes really do follow an isochronous metrical pattern). But beyond the question of isochrony versus metrical foot, the new prosody suggests that metrical thinking faced a new challenge in the perfect and therefore monotonous regularity of the machine.

Mechanical Beats

Notwithstanding tendencies, particularly in scientific discourse, to understand the body in terms of a machine, in the lived experience of many Victorians, the incongruity between mechanic and organic rhythms became part of a daily reality and often a serious concern. Victorian literature, Herbert L. Sussman summarily claims, 'consistently suggests that the rhythms of the machine are unnatural and, as such, destructive' (1968: 4). As a result of industrialisation and the factory system, mechanical regularity particularly affected the working classes, who had to adjust the rhythms of their labour and their lives to the exigencies of the relentless machine. The strain this puts on the human system became a frequent literary topic, both in fiction and poetry, which sympathised with the situation of the workers.[13]

While the novel has been identified as an important site of 'boundary mapping between "the machinery, human and metal"' (Pettitt 2012: 559) at a time in which industrial technology became a pervasive presence in everyday life,[14] poetry, I want to maintain, is particularly attuned to the *rhythmic* interactions that are at issue here. In contrast to prose fiction, Kirstie Blair points out, 'poetry, through its rhythms, can more easily showcase [a] "machine time" versus "human time" distinction' (2014: 36). And yet, metre fulfils a paradoxical role in the negotiation between the body and the machine, as both the most 'mechanical' and the most somatically effective aspect of verse, both a law imposed on language and an effect that has its necessary foundation in the physiological experience of the body and the sounds the body's vocal system produces. Machine rhythms prove so powerful precisely because they are so eminently physical, overpowering human will by taking control of their bodies.

I want to explore this complicated rhythmical nexus of machine, human body and verse further by focusing on the machine ensemble which influenced Victorian life rhythms most broadly, across all social classes: the railway. There are many reasons for this choice. For one, the railway fundamentally influenced Victorian concepts of time. I have already referred to Hall's argument that the railway imposed a 'double-consciousness' of time on travellers, which abetted the movement towards abstract regularity in new prosody. The railway, as Wolfgang Schivelbusch has impressively shown, radically transformed travel experience and destroyed traditional time–space relations (2014 [1977]: 33–44). By introducing timetables which had to be kept precisely, the railway further transformed the organisation of social time:

> their riders [. . .] found their entire consciousness of time altered by the requirements and opportunities of a railway world. [. . .] Train schedules opened new possibilities for appointments, for work done within time limits, for long-distance comings and goings, hence for ordering of movement and multiplication of activity. (Landes 1983: 285)

Beyond these radical transformations of conceptions of time, travelling on a railway was also an intensely rhythmical experience, a first-hand encounter between body and machine for all those who did not handle machines to earn their living. The experience of travelling on the railway exposed passengers to a new kind of mechanical rhythm. Early railway lines were not entirely continuous, since small gaps had to be kept between the rails, to allow the steel to expand and contract in changing temperatures without damage to the lines. This added a further rhythmic vibration to the rhythm of the steam engine itself, a vibration that was not only heard, but felt with the entire body. Indeed, continual exposure to this vibration caused pathological symptoms in railway workers, especially engineers, who spend long hours on engines with no or very little buffering (Schivelbusch 2014 [1977]: 114). With the spread of the railway, mechanically regular rhythms were not merely an abstract ideal but became, for many Victorians, a physiologically experienced reality. Finally, the Victorians themselves understood the railway to be symbolic of their age, an emblem of industrialised progress par excellence. Its interaction with human or natural rhythms was therefore viewed with much ambiguity, criticised by some, lauded by others, a matter of equal fascination and dread.

Railway rhythms

That verbal rhythm could be exploited effectively in literary representations of the railway even in prose was clearly realised by Charles Dickens. In his description of a delirious railway journey of Paul Dombey in *Dombey and Son* (1846–8), the railway's inexorable rhythmic drive becomes audible, while at the same time serving a metaphorical purpose, becoming 'the type of the triumphant monster, Death' which drags 'living creatures of all classes, ages, and degrees behind it':

> Away, with a shriek, and a roar, and a rattle, from the town, burrowing among the dwellings of men and making the streets hum, flashing out into the meadows for a moment, mining in through the damp earth, booming on in darkness and heavy air, bursting out again into the sunny day so bright and wide; away, with a shriek, and a roar, and a rattle, through the fields, through the woods, through the corn, through the hay, through the chalk, through the mould, through the clay, through the rock, among objects close at hand and almost in the grasp, ever flying from the traveller, and a deceitful distance ever moving slowly within him: like as in the track of the remorseless monster, Death! (1848: 200)

I quote only the first of four paragraphs that continue in this vein, in order to note that Dickens's prose draws on many rhythmical registers to achieve the somatic pull of this description. The section opens with a refrain consisting of driving anapaests, emphasised by means of polysyndeton and alliteration, which subsides into more uncertain, though highly alliterative prose rhythms with 'burrowing', only to emerge again (like the train from the tunnel) with the return of the refrain, this time to be sustained throughout much of the remaining paragraph, with its insistently anaphoric structures ('through the . . .'). Rhymes and half-rhymes make the rhythmic pyrotechnics of the passage even more audible (day, away, hay, clay; bright, wide). The end of the paragraph introduces a further refrain, which is repeated at the end of each of the following paragraphs. The point I would like to stress is that the appeal of this passage is primarily rhythmical. It does not describe the effect of the journey on Dombey but rather attempts to somatically convey the way the railway's rhythm overpowers his senses to the point of hallucination. Nonetheless, one might note a suspicion about this rhythmical power in the way Dickens's prose continually shies away from the rhythmical pull on which the passage's effect depends. There is something decidedly gothic and threatening about the power of rhythm here, and it should be noted that later in the novel the railway serves as an avenger, killing the main villain in another hallucinatory encounter.

In view of this powerful rhythmical potential of the railway, it is quite striking that the railway should have become the main symbol and shorthand in the debates about poetry's ability or inability to address the contemporary world which I have traced in detail in Chapter 1. The railway was invoked by both sides, as either eminently poetical or eminently unpoetical. An article in Charles Dickens's journal *Household Words* in June 1855 summarises the perceived antithesis between poetry and railways nicely:

> what can there be of the poetical, or even of the picturesque, element in a Railway? Trunk lines, branch-lines, loop-lines, and sidings; cuttings, embankments, gradients, curves and inclines; points, switches, sleepers, fog-signals, and turn-tables; locomotives, break-vans, buffers, tenders, and whistles; platforms, tunnels, tubes, goods-sheds, return-tickets, axle-grease, cattle-trains, pilot-engines, time-tables, and coal-trucks: all these are eminently prosaic matter-of-fact things, determined, measured and maintained by line and rule, by the chapter and verse of printed regulations and bye-laws [. . .]. Is there any poetry in Railway time – the atrociously matter-of-fact system of calculation that has corrupted the half-past two o'clock of the old watchman into two-thirty? [. . .] How the deuce (I put words into my opponent's mouths) are you

to get any poetry out of that dreariest combination of straight lines, a railroad: – straight rails, straight posts, straight wires, straight stations, and straight termini. ('Poetry on the Railway': 415)

The article tantalisingly plays with a hint of metrical form in its long enumeration, beginning with a perceptible trochaic rhythm ('**Trunk** lines, **branch**-lines, **loop**-lines, and **sid**ings') only to turn to the almost tongue-twisting compound words which conclude the list, as if to play out the argument in form as well as content. Like poetry, the railway is measured in lines and verses, but its 'combination of straight lines' is dreary, one might surmise, not only in its 'prosaic matter-of-fact things', but also in its endless recurrence of the same: 'straight rails, straight posts, straight wires, straight stations, and straight termini', repetition without variation. As a social as well as physical experience, then, the mechanical regularity of railway rhythms could be experienced as excessive. As it were, its perfectly regular beat is precisely what makes the railway so decidedly unpoetical.

In contrast, others opined that the modern world knows nothing as eminently poetical as the steam engine. A comment published in 1844 in the *Chambers's Edinburgh Journal*, for example, lauded the steam engine thus:

> Stand amid its ponderous beams and bars, wheels and cylinders, and watch their unceasing play; how regular and how powerful! [. . .] How exquisitely complete is every detail! – how subordinate every part towards the one great end! – how every little bar and screw fit and work together! [. . .] It is one complete piece of harmony – an iron essay upon unity of design and execution. There is a deep poetry in the steam-engine. ('The Poetry of a Steam Engine': 336)

The steam engine is a created piece of regular, rhythmic harmony, of unity of form and purpose, in which the parts are subordinate to the whole. It is, one might say, in effect the material embodiment of a poem. In the context of the *'rhythmical epistemology'* underlying Spasmodic poetic theory but circulating widely in Victorian prosodic discourse, which maintained that rhythm could communicate 'knowledge and feeling through physiological pulses' (Rudy 2009: 80), the overwhelming rhythmical experience of railway travel could be understood to affect both body and mind in ways similar to, but much more powerful than, metrical poetry. Either way, the railway poses a peculiar challenge to poetry. It is either, as a utilitarian modern machine, deeply prosaic and inimical to poetical feeling, or it is in itself almost too ideally poetical.

Victorian poets were no doubt fully aware of the role the railway played in these debates. Thus, mentions of railways in Victorian poetry are usually programmatic. In the remainder of this chapter, I explore some poetic reactions to the overpowering inherent rhythmicality of the railway, arguing that it is both a source of fascination and perceived as a threat to the more variable rhythms of the poetic voice. What is ultimately at stake here is the relationship between humans and machines, the complex ways in which this intersects with issues of will and body, as well as the ability of poetry to address that relationship. As we will see, these questions hinge on the issue of metre and rhythm explored in the first part of this chapter.

A poem which addresses the debate around the railway's poetic potential directly is Augusta Webster's dramatic monologue 'Coming Home' from *Portraits* (1871). The speaker is a soldier, returning home presumably from the Crimean War. The poem sets out with a precise attention to punctuality, which exemplifies the double time consciousness of railway travel:

> Five minutes here, and they must steal two more!
> Shameful! Here have I been five mortal years
> And not seen home nor one dear kindred face,
> And these abominable slugs, this guard,
> This driver, porters – what are they about? –
> Keep us here motionless, two minutes, three. –
> Aha! at last! (ll. 1–7)

Impatient for the train to carry him home after a five-year absence, the soldier has clearly studied the timetable and is annoyed by a delay. The machine is supposed to be working with precision, but the humans working the machine are 'abominable slugs' (l. 4), stealing minutes. While these blank-verse lines scan fairly easily, the soldier's impatience becomes rhythmically audible in that most lines above could take additional stresses for emphasis, slowing the metre down (the first line, for example, could take two extrametrical stresses: '**Five** **mín**utes **here**, and **they** must **steal** *two* more!'). Once the machine is in motion again, the soldier's indignation changes to exhilaration:

> Good! We shall check our minutes;
> We're flying after them, like a mad wind
> Chasing the leaves it has tossed on in front.
> Oh glorious wild speed, what giants' play!
> And there are men who tell us poetry
> Is dead where railways come! Maybe 'tis true,

I'm a bad judge, I've had scant reading time
And little will to read . . . and certainly
I've not found railways in what verse I know:
But there's a whizz and whirr as trains go by,
A bullet-like indomitable rush
And then all's done, which makes me often think
One of those men who found out poetry,
And had to write the things just that they saw,
Would have made some of their fine crashing lines
That stir one like the marches one knows best,
And the enemy knows best, with trains in them
As easily as chariots.
                          Anyhow
I've poetry and music too to-day
In the very clatter: it goes 'Home, home, home'. (ll. 7–26)

The ambiguities and ironies in the lines attributed to Webster's illiterate soldier bring out some of the issues of the debate around the poetry of railways nicely. On the one hand, of course, the poem contradicts by its own performance the opinion that 'poetry / is dead where railways come' (ll. 11–12). There might be few railways in the verse the soldier knows but, like him, the audience of the poem might hear a hint of 'verse' in the 'whirr as trains go by' (ll. 15–16). Incidentally, line 17 demonstrates well the role that quantity may still play in shaping a poem's rhythmic effects, as the indomitable rush of the line's delivery depends on its use of predominantly short syllables, with no caesura.

On the other hand, the poem's rhythmically varied blank verse is surely far from the kind of 'fine crashing lines' (l. 21) the soldier imagines as appropriate to the rhythm of the railway. The song the railway sings for him personally is indicative of machine monotony as much as of the single-mindedness of the speaker: 'Home, home, home' (l. 27). Indeed, the poem suggests that the 'fine crashing lines' the soldier imagines are the beats of martial marches, compelling rhythms that are supposed to conduct soldiers in mechanic efficiency (and the trochaic inversions at the beginning of line 9 and line 21 even make it possible to hear a faint echo of the driving dactyls of Tennyson's 'Charge of the Light Brigade' underlying the iambic pentameter). Webster here seems to anticipate a process which was to gain traction, according to Martin, at the turn of the twentieth century: the disciplinary and particularly patriotic use of metre in the education of future soldiers, which Martin associates in particular with the immense success of Henry Newbolt (Martin 2012: 122–44). Like the soldiers in Newbolt's poem 'The Toy Band' – on which

Martin comments that they 'are an unthinking, automaton audience, reanimated only by the "penny drum" and urged to fight despite their physical limitations' (Martin 2012: 127) – Webster's soldier has little will and agency of his own. From early childhood, he has been told: 'No whying, boy, but do what you are bid' (l. 142), a rule which, according to his mother, 'Made the best heroes and best Christians, too' (l. 149). As a soldier, his 'deeds / Have been to just be one among us all / Doing what we were bidden as we could' like a cog in a wheel (ll. 114–16), and he cannot even interpret or tell his own experience. Instead, he hopes to understand what happened retrospectively, being told by others: 'I shall make them [the military actions] better out in print, / And learn in our snug study what I saw / Among the rush and smoke' (l. 131–3). There is something very machine-like in his personal philosophy: 'To say things as I see them, going straight; / Just as a plain man's life does, tramping on / The way that lies before one, with no whys' (ll. 137–9). The railway that conveys him home and whose stops and starts he must suffer passively seems an apt image for his life, which has carried him forward on a track he has done little to influence.

Railway rhythms, then, might be compelling and produce dutiful soldiers (Webster's speaker has earned a Victoria Cross for bravery). But at least from today's perspective the underlying criticism of the poem seems obvious. Symbolic of the soldier's submission and lack of agency, the railway rhythms threaten to be stupefying, and to turn human beings into little more than obedient machines. And this is the final turn of the screw: perhaps poetry about railways is impossible after all, because the railway's compelling rhythm, if imitated, would entirely dominate the sense and thus produce marching songs, but no poetry.

After all, in spite of its setting, the poem is not really a poem about the railway. After the poem's opening lines, the soldier's thoughts turn to his family, projecting his arrival and merging past with present. Despite the rapid movement of the train and the fact that the railway is a common symbol for progress and change, the soldier, obviously changed himself by the experience of war, nonetheless hopes to return to an unchanged home. The main irony of the poem, then, is that the soldier misjudges the effect of the railway, both in its rhythms and as a harbinger of change. This irony is reinforced by Webster's characteristically varied blank-verse rhythms, which for the most part resist falling into a regular beat and feature frequent strong caesuras and abrupt turns of mind and phrase. Instead of 'going straight', the soldier's thoughts continually break off, or turn in on themselves. Indeed, the straight-forward three strong beats of the railway rhythm of 'home, home, home' intrude as a metrically foreign body into the flow of Webster's pentameter.

Blank verse, as the most versatile, almost prosaic metre could thus serve to address and simultaneously resist railway rhythms, in poems in which their rhythmic pull is perceived to be threatening and overpowering. Elizabeth Barrett Browning offers a vivid example in *Aurora Leigh* (1850), in which the eponymous heroine hears in the train's incessant noise the clamour of her cousin Romney's marriage bells, which haunt her imagination:

> The next day, we took the train to Italy
> And fled on southward in the roar of steam.
> The marriage-bells of Romney must be loud,
> To sound so clear through all! I was not well;
> And truly, though the truth is like a jest,
> I could not choose but fancy, half the way,
> I stood alone i' the belfry, fifty bells
> Of naked iron, mad with merriment,
> (As one who laughs and cannot stop himself)
> All clanking at me, in me, over me,
> Until I shrieked a shriek I could not hear,
> And swooned with noise, – but still, along my swoon,
> Was 'ware the baffled changes backward rang,
> Prepared, at each emerging sense, to beat
> And crash it out with clangour. (Book VII, ll. 395–409)

An escalation of the soldier's single-minded 'Home, home, home', the monotonous railway rhythm threatens to beat all sense out of Aurora, replacing it with monomaniac madness. To a degree, she appears to merge with the railway, as her shriek echoes the shriek of steam and her body submits to its rhythmic beat. Aurora's very sense of self is threatened by the railway's overpowering rhythmic dislocations: 'I struggled for the posture of my soul / In upright consciousness of place and time' (Book VII, ll. 410–17). The poem's own metre, however, establishes an individual voice against the overriding rhythms it only describes, but does not imitate. There is some increased regularity in the somewhat unusual frequency of end-stopped lines in this passage of *Aurora Leigh*, but otherwise Barrett Browning's subtle blank-verse rhythms resist the threatening dominance of the railway beat. It is in the rhythmic qualities of the passage, then, that the poetic voice preserves its integrity and continues to stage its own agency.

If the railway is an almost gothic threat to the poetic self and voice in *Aurora Leigh*, its threat is understood to be of a different kind in Dante Gabriel Rossetti's verse epistle travelogue, 'A Trip to Paris and Belgium', addressed to his brother, William Michael, chronicling a journey he undertook in 1849 with William Holman Hunt. The letters contain both blank verse and sonnets, but the descriptions of train travel mostly make use of the former, while the latter form is employed chiefly in local sketches and meditations. As John Holmes comments, blank verse offers Rossetti 'syntactic and rhythmical fluidity, [but] it limits the potential of onomatopoeic effects, such as the use of rhythm to imitate the rhythmic quality of train travel itself' (2018: 36). In fact, what the letters have to say about the effect of railway rhythms suggests that this is may be an act of deliberate resistance:

> A heavy clamour that fills up the brain
> Like thought grown burdensome; and in the ears
> Speed that seems striving to o'ertake itself;
> And in the pulses torpid life, which shakes
> As water to a stir of wind beneath. ('On the Road', ll. 30–4)

The railway rhythm is stupefying, numbing the senses. It overpowers the body's physiological pulses, which can only passively react to the external stimulus. Subduing life and action, this overpowering rhythm makes thought burdensome and verse impossible. Moreover, both the rhythm and the journey experience are monotonous, emptied of life and poetry: 'Nothing to write of, and no good in verse' (l. 60). At times, though, there is some excitement in the rush of speed, which Rossetti duly notes and effectively conveys:

> We are upon the road. The thin swift moon
> Runs with the running clouds that are the sky,
> And with the running water runs – at whiles
> Weak 'neath the film and heavy growth of reeds.
> The country swims with motion. Time itself
> Is consciously beside us, and perceived. ('Antwerp to Ghent', ll. 7–12)

The initial excitement at the universal motion as everything seems to run along with the train, however, soon begins to transform into a kind of boredom, as the difference between moon, clouds, sky, water and country becomes imperceptible, the only thing perceived being motion, or 'Time itself' (l. 11). The excitement of speed wears off, leaving only a dull haze:

> The darkness is a tumult. We tear on,
> The roll behind us and the cry before,
> Constantly, in a lull of intense speed
> And thunder. Any other sound is known
> Merely by sight. The shrubs, the trees your eye
> Scans for their growth, are far along in haze. (ll. 15–20)

The very intensity of speed and noise lulls and dulls the senses; sounds and sight can hardly be distinguished and merge into each other. The poem's last lines thus summarise the impressions of the journey in the most general terms: 'Wind and steam and speed / And clamour and the night' (ll. 25–6).

Though Rossetti is clearly not in principle opposed to poetry on railways, the sonnet which follows this blank-verse description questions the poetic potential of railway travel fundamentally:

> BETWEEN GHENT AND BRUGES (Wednesday night, 24 October)
> Ah yes, exactly so; but when a man
> Has trundled out of England into France
> And half through Belgium, always in this prance
> Of steam, and still has stuck to his first plan –
> Blank verse or sonnets; and as he began
> Would end; – why, even the blankest verse may chance
> To falter in default of circumstance,
> And even the sonnet miss its mystic span.
> Trees will be trees, grass, pools merely pools,
> Unto the end of time and Belgium – points
> Of fact which Poets (very abject fools)
> Get scent of – once their epithets grown tame
> And scarce. Even to these foreign rails – my joints
> Begin to find their jolting much the same.

The result of railway poetry, as much as railway travel, seems to be boredom. Not only are differences effaced and perceptions merged into the blur of motion, not only does the fleeting view of the landscape prevent individual trees, meadows and pools to catch the attention; the poet also seems to have become bored with his own plan to produce blank verses and sonnets. While the poem is careful to resist the metrical regularity of the sonnet, in particular through its heavy use of enjambments, the placing of the word 'joints' (l. 13), which serves, as it were, as a joint for the rhyme sounds as well as for the lines, suggests that the monotonous jolting of the railway rhythm may have infiltrated not only the physical but also the poetical 'joints' of the poet. Railway poetry, thus the suggestion, might not be impossible, but struggles to be anything else than soporific.

But not all poets were averse to exploring the rhythmical appeal of railways more mimetically in their verse. Elizabeth Rundle Charles was the daughter of an MP and an author best known for her religious writing and hymns, but her poem 'A Journey on the South-Devon Railway' offers an interesting contrast to Rossetti's blank-verse railway boredom, with its juxtaposition of the quiet, stately rhythms of nature with the haste and clatter of the railway. Each of the poem's four stanzas follows the same logic, juxtaposing tranquil scenes of pastoral idyll with the rush of the passing train. This is the first stanza, along with my suggestion for scansion:

> The **young oak casts** its delicate **shadow**
> Over the **still** and **emerald meadow**;
> The **sheep** are **cropping** the **fresh** spring **grass**,
> And **never raise** their **heads** as we **pass**;
> The **cattle** are **taking** their **noon**-day **rest**,
> And **chewing** the **cud** with a **lazy zest**,
> Or **bathing** their **feet** in the reedy **pool**
> **Switch** their **tails** in the shadows **cool**;
> But a**way**, a**way**, we **may** not **stay**,
> **Panting** and **puffing**, and **snorting** and **starting**,
> And **shrieking** and **crying**, and **madly flying**,
> **On** and **on**, there's a **race** to be **run** and a **goal** to be **won** ere the **set** of
> the **sun**. (ll. 1–12)

The poem sets off at a leisurely pace with a tetrameter combination of iambs and anapaests which varies in most lines. The couplets emphasise stillness and rest. The intrusion of the railway, which enters with line 9, comes as an explosion of noise and rhythmic speed. There's a rhyme-word on every beat in line 9, followed by the dactylic polysyndeton of the next two lines, in which the conjunctions and present participles further hammer in the rhythm established by alliterations. The stanza hurries on into the double-length of its last line, consisting entirely of monosyllables, in which the beats are again emphasised by means of internal rhymes and alliterations. Note that the effect of acceleration is achieved primarily by the interaction between metre and internal rhyme or repetition in these lines but that their rhythmical regularity is foot based, as metrical feet vary much less than in the opening lines. There is exuberance in these rhythmic fireworks, this

poetic celebration of railway beats. But the exhilaration palls somewhat as these lines are repeated as a refrain at the end of each of the
poem's four stanzas. The beginning of each stanza presents a variety of different scenes of rural quietude and beauty, but the railway
lines remain exactly the same throughout. For all their emphasis on
movement in contrast to the quiet stillness of the rural scenes, they
are the ones that threaten to become monotonous in their unvaried
repetition, merely a variation on Rossetti's boredom with the ever
same jolting of the train. And yet Charles's railway rhythms inexora-
bly and relentlessly carry the speaker and the reader with them. The
poem thus juxtaposes rural and railway rhythms in what might be
read as a subtle scepticism, which acknowledges and embodies the
rhythmic appeal of the railway, while at the same time suggesting the
limitation that lies in its invariance.

Singing engines – the railway songs of Alexander Anderson

A fascination with and exploration of the rhythmic and poetic appeal
of the railway even more strongly governs the final work I want to
address in this context: the Scottish poet Alexander Anderson's collection *Songs of the Rail* (1878). In contrast to the other poets I have mentioned, Anderson had first-hand experience of the rail as of a labourer
on the line, a fact he does much to market, publishing his poetry under
the moniker of 'Surfaceman' and introducing himself to his readers as
'A worker on the rail, where, day by day, / The engine storms along'
who sends the reader 'from out the "four-feet way," / This book of
railway song' ('To my Readers', ll. 1–2; 75–6).[15] Anderson's collection
provides a more extensive and more intimate representation of the
railway than the previous examples I have discussed and it turns the
question of the possibility of railway poetry on its head.

Anderson repeatedly suggests that his poetry is unable to catch
the music of the engine, even where it lets the engine speak itself:

> There is one brown fellow among them who sings
> The terrible sweep of my limb;
> The fool! dare he mimic this music of mine,
> And such pitiful music in him? ('The Song of the Engine' ll. 61–4)

There is irony in this topos of poetical modesty, in which the poet
lends the engine a decidedly human voice to deny the adequacy of
such human approximation to its music. Nonetheless, Anderson so
consistently exalts the machine that these lines can also be taken

at face value: human poetic rhythms cannot approach the superior music of the machine. Elsewhere, though, the engine's 'mad lyric' (l. 8) is more conciliatory, calling on the poet to set its pulses to music, to 'Sing the nerve and toil within' it ('On the Engine in the Night-Time' l. 41), and Anderson suggests that, even if his own poetry fails, the future might still bring a poet 'whose fire / Shall place on his wild, rough page / The spirit that lurks and forever works / In the breast of this mighty age' ('The Spirit of the Times' ll. 73–6). Despite the compelling power of its own rhythm, the engine needs the human voice to interpret it, to lend it sense and to articulate its prophecy. Indeed, Anderson's poems repeatedly insist that it is frail man who 'help[s] to keep / [the engine's] footsteps a little in place' ('The Engine', ll. 17–18) and 'Keeps the iron will within him pulsing to a proper tone' ('On the Engine in the Night-Time' l. 26). It is man who ultimately controls the engine's rhythm. However, Anderson's consistent personification of the engine lends it an agency which always threatens to exceed and throw off human control, to break out of its proper rhythm, an event which, as Anderson knows too well, often has deadly consequences. From Anderson's perspective as a worker on the line, the machine's rhythm might be relentless and terrifying, but even more terrifying is the prospect that it may break down, an event which usually spells disaster.

There is rivalry and potential conflict in this pitching of human against machine as well as a troubling question about agency and control. In a rare recent discussion of Anderson's poetry along with that of another Scottish railway poet, William Aiken, Kirstie Blair has highlighted this conflict, drawing attention to the ballads in the poets' respective collections, which focus almost exclusively on fatal, or near-fatal accidents. She reads this as a subtle criticism, an awareness of the incompatibility of machine and human rhythms:

> Anderson and Aitken set the rhythms of their verse by the mechanical beat of the train and celebrate its 'iron pulses,' but they also counterpoint the pulse of the rails with the fragile and easily damaged rhythms of the human body, and comment trenchantly on the impossibility of expecting human physiology to withstand the stress and strain of relentless industrial rhythm. (2014: 36)

Blair is correct to note the centrality of death in the narratives of *The Songs of the Rail*, deaths which are frequently caused by the attempt of the engine-drivers to avoid delays and stick to their schedule. And yet, if the collection is read in its entirety, Anderson's insistent praise of progress and the role of the railway within it tends to make the tragic narratives in the collection sound like lamentable, but necessary sacrifices. On a first perusal, Anderson's poetry can strike one as almost painfully optimistic about the role of the labourer in shaping a bright future:

> in them is the sure seed from which the ages yet to be,
> Rising up with great broad sickle, shall reap all its golden grain;
> Then the kindlier thought and nobler use of manhood shall be free,
> And be brighter from the struggle such a sunny height to gain.
>
> ('A Song of Progress' ll. 49–52)

This might sound like a late-Chartist call to arms and class struggle, but Anderson concludes with the dutiful exhortation to return to work: 'Back to honest pick and shovel, and to daily task again – / Back with nobler thoughts within me, all the higher aims to cheer' (ll. 61–2). The railway, in particular, is heralded repeatedly as a harbinger of progress; it is 'the type of the soul of this age' ('Song of the Engine' l. 99) which is 'Ever from the front of progress leading onward human things' ('On the Engine by Night' l. 28). Machine rhythms might be dangerous to the individual human body, but they are also the ones which Anderson repeatedly hails as heralding progress and with it, universal peace and brotherhood.

I therefore want to pursue a different perspective from that developed by Blair. In fact, instead of pitching human against machine rhythms, Anderson's poems intriguingly blur the difference between human and machine. Blair herself notes Anderson's consistent personification of the engine, which becomes often 'interchangeable with [. . .] the (male) working-class poet' (Blair 2014: 9). This is not merely a passing trope, but a consistent and full-fleshed personification: In 'The Engine', for example, the machine throbs with life: he has 'a heart of fire, and a soul of steel' (l. 7), 'muscles' (l. 10), 'sinews' (l. 99) and 'limb[s]' (l. 8); he breathes, looks, talks and sings, and 'shrieks in his smoky glee' (l. 40). The engine's rhythm is a throbbing and pulsing, 'the beat of his fire-fed breast' (l. 97); and his movement, rather than being mechanically regular, 'flashes, and stretches, and strives' (l. 39). Tellingly, the comparison Anderson uses most often is that to Frankenstein's monster. While not human, the monster is decidedly organic, and Anderson's insistent use of this comparison carries all the multiple ambiguities of Mary Shelley's creation. Anderson expresses both fascination with and fear of the engine, and suggests that, while it serves human aims, it may also become an uncontrollable threat to human society. It presents a humanly created force that exceeds human control. But Frankenstein's monster becomes destructive because it is mistreated, and in associating the engine with the monster, Anderson appears to express sympathy with its plight.

This personification of the engine gains particular importance because Anderson's poems repeatedly suggest similarities between human and machine toil. For the workers, there is a 'voiceless measure ranging through our toiling days' ('A Song of Labour' l. 272) and the rhythms of the engine are of the same kind of constant toil: 'I rush to the cities of men / With a load I lay down like a slave at their feet, / Then turn and come backward again' ('Song of the Engine' ll. 10–12). In fact, the rhythms seem to be symbiotic, as the engine sings:

> I send through the city's wild heart shocks of life,
> But to feel them come back like a wave;
> I loom broad and swart in wild traffic's rough mart,
> I kneel to men like a slave. ('Song of the Engine' ll. 81–3)

In 'A Song of Labour', which in metre and tone recalls Tennyson's 'Locksley Hall', machine and human sounds and toil seem to merge as the machines sing a 'triumphal hymn' of the modern age:

> Hearken! as the world rolls onward with a slow and toiling sound,
> All their voices swell and mingle in triumphal hymns around,
> Come they from the dash of paddles urging through the spray and foam,
> Freights of earnest bosoms outward, freights of smiling faces home;
> From the lunge of pistons working scant of room to breathe and pant,
> Yet like slaves do all the feats their ever-cunning masters want;
> From the whirring of the spindle in the hot and dusty room,
> From the mazes of the wheel, and from the complicated loom,
> From the furnace belching outward molten forms at their desire,
> Like Enceladus upspringing through his hill of smoke and fire:
> Mighty sounds are these, but mightier rush with everlasting hail
> From the thunder of the engine and the clanking of the rail.
> Ah! the monster that shall mould and make the coming cycles strong –
> Shame on me that could desert the inspiration of my song! (ll. 257–70)

Intriguingly, this paean on machines both effaces and subtly hints at the human beings working them. By personifying the machines, calling them slaves, panting with scant breathing space in hot and dusty rooms at the bid of their masters, the distinction between human worker and machine is dizzyingly blurred as these lines seem to sound two notes at once: praise of the machine and criticism of working conditions. The potential critique seems to retract with the return to the song's 'inspiration' (l. 270), the railway. The speaker resolves to

> rise from out my weakness as he flares along my view,
> And I deem that I am mighty in the labour others do;
> For the Frankensteins who made him part by part and limb by limb
> Had the same soul beating in them as my own at seeing him. (ll. 287–90)

This results in a return to the call on his fellow labourers to go to their work – 'Arm to arm, then, lay the metals, let him roll along the rods' (l. 291) – a refrain reiterated several times in the poem. And yet, much ambiguity remains. Is this a submission to machines, or a call to arms?

Anderson's poems allow for a reading which does not juxtapose machines and workers, but rather uses the engine as a metaphor for both the power of human labour force and for their future liberation. Thus 'A Song of Labour' culminates in a vision of the future in which the engine escapes from its serfdom:

> But to them, our larger fellows of the ages yet to be,
> He shall rise, as gods are statured, huge of limb, and broad and free;
> [. . .]
> While through all their fret and hurry he, the monster of our song,
> Like a wild earth-bound Immortal shall in thunder flash along,
> Clasping all things in his vigour, as a serpent flings his coil,
> Labour's mightiest Epic rolling through the panting heart of Toil.
> (ll. 313–20)

It is not machine and human rhythms that are in conflict in these poems. Rather, the poems depict a struggle between submission to rule and a will for freedom which both workers and engine share. The engine, for all its might, is bound to the lines laid out for him, but there is a force in him which could wreak havoc if loosened from its restrictions. The analogy to the working class is suggestive and clearly deliberate. In strong contrast to the way the railway figured in Webster's 'Coming Home', in which it suggested submission, mechanical automatism and loss of agency, Anderson draws on the visceral power of railway rhythms to stir passion and action.

Another obvious analogy is that to lines of verse and the bounds of metre. Since Anderson associates the engine so closely with the poet, the following lines become potentially self-referential:

> The coward, he dare not slip from the line,
> That is guiding his feet beneath,
> For his soul would burst from him in gushes of flame,
> Like a sword drawn in haste from its sheath. ('On the Engine Again'
> ll. 61–4)

The martial simile of the final line is particularly striking, as is the self-referential suggestion that invites an investigation of Anderson's own adherence to the line that guides his feet, to the metres that bind his poetry. Blair draws attention to the notable influence of Tennyson's poetry on Anderson, who chooses the metre of 'Locksley Hall' for several of his poems.[16] She argues that this metrical evocation of Tennyson's lines 'Let the great world spin forever in the ringing grooves of change' ('Locksley Hall' l. 182) – in which he famously mistook railway lines for grooves – 'makes it clear that the rhythms of the poem [Blair specifically talks about Anderson's 'A Song of Labour'] embody the beat and throb of this new mechanical power' (2009: 294). To me, however, another aspect of Tennyson's poem seems to be even more important for Anderson's choice of the metre. After all, Anderson favours it for those of his poems which develop distinctly prophetic visions of the future. To understand Anderson's use of the metre, the more important reference lines from 'Locksley Hall' may thus well be 'When I dipt into the future far as human eye could see; / Saw the Vision of the world and all the wonder that would be.—' ('Locksley Hall' ll. 15–16), lines which Anderson's poems repeatedly echo in sense as well as rhythm. Moreover, in several of the poems in which Anderson employs this metre, he changes the rhyme scheme from Tennyson's couplets to alternating rhymes. This delay of rhyme in long verse lines serves rather to subdue the rhythm, working against the driving energy often attributed to Tennyson's use of the metre. In contrast, the poems in the collection which most directly address the engine and give voice to its rhythms tend to choose more variable metres, with shorter lines and more frequent rhymes and show a decided preference for the alternating tetra- and trimeters of the ballad stanza. Moreover, they employ this popular form in all its metrical freedom, constantly mixing iambs and anapaests. Thus, far from metrically suggesting machine regularity, the voice of the engine is rhythmically variable, but also closely associated with the voice of the people. In fact, the most irregular stanza form to be found in the collection is that of a poem in which the engine speaks directly with the poet, 'What the Engine Says'. I quote the first two stanzas, highlighting stresses as I hear them:

> **What** does the **mighty** engine **say,**
> **Rolling along**
> **Swift** and **strong,**
> **Slow** or **fast** as his **driver** may,
> **Hour** by **hour,** and **day** by **day,**
> His **swarthy side**
> A**glow** with **pride,**
> And his **muscles** of **sinewy steel** ablaze?
> **This** is **what** the engine **says:**
>
> **First** his **breath** gives a **sudden snort,**
> As **if** a **spasm** had **cut** it **short,**
> Then with **one** wild **note**
> To **clear** his **throat,**
> He **fumes** and **whistles**—'**Get out** of my **way,**
> **What** are you **standing** there for—**say?**
> Fling **shovel** and **pick**
> A**way** from you, **quick!**
> Ere my **gleaming limbs** with **out**-reaching **clutch**
> **Draw** you **into** your **death** with a **single touch.**
> For **what** care **I** for a **puppet** or **two,**
> A **little** over **five feet** like **you?**['] (ll. 1–21)

These stanzas combine tetra- and dimeters in an irregular pattern, with no consistent rhyme scheme, though mostly in rhyming couplets, and with syllable counts ranging from three to eleven per line. Iambs and anapaests are freely mixed with frequent catalexis, and scarcely any two subsequent lines follow the same rhythmical pattern, making the applicability of the metrical vocabulary of feet to such lines questionable. Nonetheless, a perceptible beat is driving these stanzas, emphasised by the heavily end-stopped lines and strong rhymes, and abetted by the fact that the dimeters, or two-stress lines usually (though not always) come in pairs and thus rhythmically equal the four beats of the poem's other lines. Moreover, the poem heavily employs assonance and consonance to draw its lines further together phonetically. There is no need here to hear metre beating abstractly in the mind: it pulses perceptibly through the lines. If these are machine rhythms, they are not monotonous, nor are they juxtaposed to human rhythms. The engine rolls along, yet not in mechanical regularity, but sometimes fast, sometimes slow. It snorts, clears its throat and stops short in a 'spasm' (l. 11) – a word choice which carries associations with the physiological poetics of the Spasmodics. Railway rhythms seemed to pose a danger to the poetic voice and self in the work by the middle-class poets I have discussed above. In *The Songs of the Rail* they become invigorating, physiologically stirring and even potentially revolutionary.

In view of these observations, Blair's argument that *The Songs of the Rail* pitches human against machine rhythm needs to be adjusted. A conflict of times indeed plays out, in particular in the collection's ballads, in which accidents often happen because the trains are pressed to keep time, regardless of weather conditions, personal frailties or mechanical failure. But this is not a conflict between human being and machine, but rather one between an embodied time and rhythm that the worker shares with the machine and an abstract time of railway schedule, the law that binds their bodies. This abstract time is imposed on them, not by the machine itself, but by the human and social power system in which they operate.

All the more remarkably, the posthumous collection of Anderson's poems, published in 1912, includes a poem that strikes a much more reactionary and conventional tone. 'Is there any room for the poet / In this nineteenth-century time' ('No Room for the Poet' ll. 1–2), Anderson asks, and answers in the negative. 'In the hurry of life and its battle / And the tramp and clangour of feet' (ll. 7–8), no one listens any longer to poetic feet, to the 'the cadence / That rises and sinks and falls' (ll. 13–14). The sound of poetry is drowned out by the sound of modern technology. The world 'hears the ring of the railway, / The moan of the wind on the wire, / The groan of the torture of monsters / In the coils of the pythons of fire' (ll. 17–20). Thus, the singing of the poet has become futile:

> It is naught then, this harping and piping,
>> If it sounds it can only be heard
> As one hears in the lull of the tempest
>> The lone low cry of a bird.

> There is no room for the poet
>> In this nineteenth century time,
> For the earth has grown up into manhood,
>> And has turned its back upon rhyme. (ll. 33–40)

If his *Songs for the Rail* had still held out the hope for an epic poet of the age, in this later poem, the poet is merely a musical singer whose lone cry recalls Tennyson's recurring simile of the linnet singing in grief. Since Anderson reduces poetry to its sounds, its music, and gives up its empowering association with the machine, opting instead for a much more conventional natural trope, poetry has become irrelevant and is easily drowned in the noise of the modern world. Giving up on higher claims for poetic insight, the poem concludes with the familiar commonplace that poetry has no room in the modern world, which is characterised as mature and sober and thus has no patience for childish rhyme. If this is an indictment of the modern age, it also suggests a disillusionment with a poetry that contents itself with its own formal beauty. Read together with the hopeful *Songs for the Rail* it also reads as a bitter comment on the poet's own younger self, who hoped his poetry would be heard and who could still conceive of a poetry that would be invigorated, rather than drowned out, by the din of the railway.

Conclusion – Metre's Demise

'If life is not always poetical, it is at least metrical,' wrote Meynell, a close acquaintance of Patmore, in her essay 'The Rhythm of Life' (1892b: 1). But as her use of organic and seasonal metaphors in 'The English Metres', which I discussed at the beginning of this chapter, also suggests, for Meynell there is nothing abstract, nor mechanically regular, in metre, and her interchangeable use of metre and rhythm is telling. In contrast to the prosodists featuring in the first part of this chapter, Meynell is not interested in establishing a system. Indeed, metre, in the sense she uses in her essay, resists systematic abstraction. It is synonymous with periodicity but escapes precise measurement: 'Distances are not gauged, ellipses not measured, velocities not ascertained, times not known.' Only 'the recurrence is sure' (1892b: 1). Though she locates life's metricality in 'the mental experience of man', the mind she talks of is not abstract, aloof, but emphatically embodied. Its 'tides' (1) are those of emotions, like happiness, suffering, gaiety, remorse, delight and love, and she adds the even more directly physiological examples of disease and 'the rhythmic pangs of maternity' to the list (6). For Meynell, no less than for Dobell and Lanier, this rhythmicality connects us to the cosmic order. However, understood as the mere fact of inevitable recurrence 'keeping no man knows what trysts with Time' (Meynell 1892b: 3), Meynell's view of metre is not only indistinguishable from rhythm, it also does not depend on any sense of regularity, and rejects mechanical measurement for the intuitions of the embodied mind. Meynell's cosmos is rhythmic, but not regular. As Prins has noted, for all Meynell's respect for Patmore's work, there is an implicit critique of his law of metre in this, since rhythm is felt naturally rather than imposed on the body of verse as restraining bounds (Prins 2005: 269). Meynell makes this criticism explicit in an essay on 'Mr. Coventry Patmore's Odes', in which she doubts the applicability of his metrical theories to his own poetical practise in *The Unknown Eros*, maintaining that '[l]iberal verse, dramatic, narrative, meditative, can surely be bound by no time measures', which only apply to 'cradle verse and march-marking verse' (1892a: 94–5). Although Meynell uses 'metrical' and 'rhythmical' synonymously in 'The Rhythms of Life', the basis on which she resists the idea of an isochronous beat becomes clear: it is regular, while life and nature, in which poetry is rooted like the flower in the ground, is irregular; it is measurable, while life (and poetry) resists measurement; it is simple and easy, while poetry is complex and sophisticated; it is compelling and restrictive, while poetry is 'liberal'. At the end of the century, Meynell's thought thus offers an alternative to the movement towards abstraction and mechanisation which increasingly governed prosodic discourse and troubled poets in their engagement with machines. Her persistent commitment to metrical forms, at a time in which other poets turned increasingly to free verse, may find one of its reasons in this more organic conception of metre. For her, metre is no mechanical bond that needs to be shattered, no rule against which she has to assert the freedom of her poetic voice.

Critics have repeatedly and rightly warned against constructing teleological narratives of prosodic debates which suggest a culmination in the development of Modernist free verse (Harrington 2007: 337; Phelan 2012: 134–80). And yet, in view of the material I have discussed in this chapter, I believe it is possible to see a combination of theoretical, historical and cultural factors which helped prepare the ground for the demise of metre and the rise of free verse. Broader processes of abstraction, which were influenced, if not driven, by technological innovations like the railway and the telegraph, which familiarised abstract concepts of time and made precise timekeeping a matter of daily importance, prepared the ground for the conceptual separation of abstract, regular metre and embodied, flexible rhythm. Metre thus easily became associated with mechanical regularity, and with the strictures the increasing precision of timing put on ever larger

parts of modern life, while rhythm could be idealised as a more natural
and holistic experience of spatio-temporal relations, subversive of the
increasing technological regularity of modernity (Salgaro and Vangi
2016: 11–21). Metrical precision, being dependent on machines, could
easily be reduced to them. Thus, famously, Ezra Pound, H. D. and
Richard Allington pitched themselves against regularity and agreed 'to
compose in the sequence of the musical phrase, not in sequence of a
metronome' (Pound 1918: 95), and Ford Madox Ford, looking back
at his personal experience of Victorian poets reading their poetry,
remarked in 1911: 'And it went on and on – and on! A long, rolling
stream of words no-one would ever use, to endless monotonous, polysyllabic, unchanging rhythms, in which rhymes went unmeaningly by
like the telegraph posts, every fifty yards, of a railway journey' (1964:
157). The Modernist turn from metre to rhythm, I thus suggest, stands
in the context of what Stephen Kern discusses as '[t]he thrust of the
age [. . .] to affirm the reality of private time against that of a single
public time and to define its nature as heterogeneous, fluid, and revers-
ible' (2003 [1983]: 34). In that widest sense, the railway indeed might
have been inimical – not to poetry but to metrical verse.

If there is a teleological necessity in these developments, it encompasses wider cultural and conceptual processes, in which thinking
about metre, and about literature more generally, is embedded. I do
not share Taylor's view of this as a narrative of progress. Rather, as
should have become clear from the poetic examples I have discussed
in this chapter, with the loss of a strong rhythmicality poetry loses a
means of expression which, as the Victorians never tired of emphasising, can speak to our bodies as much as to our minds.[17] From
the blank-verse resistance to the overpowering railway rhythms in
the work of Barrett Browning and Dante Gabriel Rossetti, to the
rhythmic impetus of Charles's railway lines and the invigorating and
potentially incendiary power of Anderson's railway songs, metre
offered a powerful mode of expression which mediates between
mind and body, intellectual challenge and somatic appeal, and which
allows the temporal structure of poems to be felt and heard.

Notes

1. Joseph Phelan provides an overview of these lively debates (2009; especially Chapter II on the English hexameter and Chapter III on the influence of alliterative verse traditions). Martin brilliantly interrogates the
   national sensibilities involved in pitching 'foreign' Classical feet against
   'native' Anglo-Saxon metres (2012: 109–12).

2. See Hall (2017) for a fascinating discussion of this didactic practice and its wider cultural implications (61–110).
3. More generally, Taylor notes that '[t]ranslations of Hegel into English coincided with the rise of the new prosody' (1988: 28). While Michael D. Hurley calls Hegel 'the most influential disputant for Victorian verse theorists' (Hurley 2013: 25), his presence in the debate beyond Patmore is not as obvious as this might suggest.
4. Armstrong herself offers a beautiful reading of modern polyrhythmics in Tennyson's 'Break, Break, Break' in contestation of Hegel's assertion that polyrhythmics have become impossible in modern verse (Armstrong 2011b).
5. See Meredith Martin's discussion of the role of George Saintsbury in the establishment of the English foot (2011); see also Taylor (1988: 39–40).
6. Phelan helpfully clarifies the involved ambiguities: '"Accent" (or "ictus" or "arsis") refers to the extra attention or emphasis given to a syllable by virtue of its position within the metrical schema. "Stress" is sometimes used as a synonym for this; but it is also used to signify the emphasis given to a particular syllable in a polysyllabic word, and to the emphasis acquired by a syllable as a result of its place within a sentence or paragraph' (2012: 9).
7. The article is at least partly prompted by the republication of Guest's *History of English Rhythms*.
8. The intriguing career of the concept of rhythm, which came to increasing prominence in the course of the nineteenth century, is mapped by Janine Wellmann (2017) for the German context and by Ewan Jones (forthcoming) for the British context. Jones goes so far as to claim 'that the concept of rhythm that has come to seem second nature to speakers of English emerged only across the nineteenth century'.
9. See Phelan's chapter on musical prosody (2012: 15–44), but also Prins's fascinating discussion of different musical notations and settings for Tennyson's poem 'Break, Break, Break' (2011).
10. See also Tomalin's comments on the reception of Joshua Steele's prosody, which make a similar point (2020: 73).
11. Phelan's discussion of the difference between Patmore's ideas and those of Gerald Manley Hopkins shows illuminatingly that such abstraction was neither inevitable nor necessarily immediately understood by contemporaries. Phelan points out that Hopkins understood his metrical innovations to rely on the tension between a 'time-rhythm' and a 'beat-rhythm'. Beat does not mark time for him, but the actual duration of pronunciation (time-rhythm) counterpoints with the placing of the accents (beat-rhythm). Both are palpable aspects of the verse line, not abstract idealisations of the mind. The writers' 'shared use of largely musical and accentual vocabulary', Phelan notes, 'lead[...] to a certain amount of mutual incomprehension when they finally met and began

to correspond in 1882; they felt that they ought to be in agreement, and were rather puzzled to discover they were not' (2012: 129).

12. As I will discuss below, both Patmore and Dallas mention clocks, as does William Whewell in his discussion of rhythm in *The Philosophy of Inductive Science* (1840: vol. 1, 134) and, towards the close of the century, Sydney Lanier, in his elaborate theory of musical prosody (1894: 63). For earlier references to clocks and pendulums in prosodic theory, see Tomalin (2020: 68–73).

13. One of the best-known examples is Elizabeth Barrett Browning's protest poem 'The Cry of the Children' (1843). Herbert Tucker has brilliantly identified the means by which this poem establishes a 'precociously laboring, mechanically driven, metronomically merciless prosody', pitching human against machine in its form as well as its content (2006: 88). The poem appeals to the reader's sentiment, not only through its depiction of the children's plight, but also somatically, in the compulsions, subversions and palpitations of its metre.

14. Rich scholarly work has focused on the novel as a site for grappling with and renegotiating human–machine interactions; see, for example, Gallagher (1985), Daly (2004), Ketabgian (2011).

15. All line references are to the 1881 edition of Anderson's *Songs of the Rail*.

16. Elsewhere, Blair discusses the importance of Tennyson for Victorian working-class poets more generally, in which 'Locksley Hall' figures centrally (2009).

17. Amittai F. Aviram regards the shift towards unmetrical poetry as 'a trend away from poetry and toward prose narrative or exposition; away from the rhythmic pleasures of the body and toward its repression in social discourse; away from the transsubjective effect of rhythm and toward the expression of the individual, socially constructed self' (1994: 4). In the endeavour to get rid of the self-imposed bonds of mechanical metre, the bodily connection to a rhythmic cosmos manifest in Meynell's image of the maternal body is effaced.

Chapter 5

Of Time and Poetry – Towards a Theory of Poetic Temporality

It has been my wager throughout this book that a focus on the way changing temporal regimes influence the practice and theory of poetry in the nineteenth century can help to develop a better understanding of the condition of poetry, not only in that historical period, but also in our own day. My main contestation has been that the wide-ranging changes to dominant temporal concepts over the nineteenth century posed a challenge to received conceptions of poetry and to poetic practice. This historical perspective, I propose, helps to understand the genealogy of some of the conceptual architecture we can see in place today.

In this final chapter, I depart from the historical perspective which has directed my investigation to this point. Instead, I want to build on the insights of the previous chapters to gain some theoretical leverage on the problem of poetic time. Throughout, I strongly resist the critical position that poetry, or more particularly the lyric, is timeless. In a first step, I revisit and bring into conversation key arguments of the previous chapters to highlight the conceptual shifts which gave credibility to a claim for lyric timelessness in the first place. In the course of this discussion, I will have occasion to comment on the fraught problem of a definition of the lyric, its relation to poetry more generally, as well as its supposed opposition to narrative. Finally, I distinguish different analytical levels of poetic temporality, with the aim of providing a critical framework that is flexible enough to help approach the issue of temporality in a wide range of poetry, lending it purchase beyond the comparatively narrow historical bounds of the Victorian age and its poetic production.

Diachronic Timelessness

That poetry is timeless is a claim of long standing. As I have shown (in Chapter 1 and *passim*), however, in the course of the nineteenth century what was meant by this claim underwent a significant shift. Victorians often celebrate the timelessness of poetry based on its supposed access to eternal, indeed, divine truths, in what I have been calling an Aesthetics of Eternal Essence. The underlying concept of poetry is very broad, to the degree that, somewhat tautologically, everything which promises a glimpse of divine truths could be called poetic. Most certainly, this aesthetic claim for poetic timelessness did not privilege the lyric form, but rather looked to dramatic and epic poetry (or, indeed, to biblical language) for its prime examples. However, with the increasing importance of change as a central cultural paradigm and with the rise of science, which replaced intimations of divine truth with the mechanisms and facts of natural laws, the Aesthetics of Eternal Essence gradually lost its power to convince. No longer committed to an aesthetics based on eternal truths or divine guarantees, poets found various ways to respond to and integrate change, not only in the topics they addressed, but also in the new or renewed poetic forms they used. In Chapter 2, I considered the poetic sequence, the dramatic monologue and the verse novel as poetic forms that offered ways to navigate the temporal tensions and reconfigurations Victorian concepts of poetry were facing.

Poetic timelessness was not necessarily relinquished, however, but rather shifted grounds. It found a new incarnation in an Aestheticist elevation of form over content. In what I have called the Aesthetics of Self-sufficient Form, time is dissolved in the self-referentiality of poetic spacetime. The poem thus can be framed as timeless because its essence lies in itself, in its internal language relations, which are not subject to change over time. Tucker, who introduced the term 'poetic spacetime', notes that it is no coincidence that elaborate constructions of poetic spacetime abound in Victorian poetry:

> The overdetermined, redundantly patterned verbal designs that adorn, and congest, our anthologies bespoke a serious attempt to construct a venue for poetry's survival: an attempt grounded in the conviction that the poetics of spacetime had a healing and quickening task to perform in modern culture. (1997: 278)

Beyond the sanative function Tucker identifies, however, the creation of a self-sufficient poetic spacetime allows poetry to maintain claims to timelessness by means of a formal perfection that characterises lyric forms in particular. 'Thus,' Sharon Cameron writes, 'the lyric is seen as immortal not so much because it has, unlike the writer, no death to survive, but rather because it is complete/completed in and of itself, transcending mortal/temporal limits in the very structure of its articulation' (1979: 197). Indeed, by turning in on itself and apparently turning its back on the world, the lyric poem could maintain even a remnant of the universalising claims of the Aesthetics of Eternal Essence. This is the premise on which, well into the twentieth century, we have seen Theodor Adorno rely, when he maintains in his deliberations 'On Lyric Poetry and Society', first published in 1957, that 'the ideal of lyric poetry, at least in its traditional sense, is to remain unaffected by bustle and commotion' (2014: 339). He further claims that 'the substance of a poem is not merely an expression of individual impulses and experiences. Those become a matter of art only when they come to participate in something universal by virtue of the specificity they acquire in being given aesthetic form' (340). The individual experience expressed has no claims to universality or to timelessness. Rather, it is the aesthetic form which carries the whole burden of the poem's claim to transcendence. At the same time, as I have argued in Chapter 3, with its concerted removal from the 'bustle and commotion' of quotidian, everyday reality, poetry's association with idleness became both a strength and a threat in the context of a society in which pragmatism and a gospel of success increasingly took hold.

As my reference to Adorno and Cameron may have already served to suggest, the shift from timeless essence to timeless form abetted another conceptual shift that was already well under way: the increasing identification of poetry with the lyric. Tucker notes that '[t]he reflexive, self-referential function of poetry strengthens as the prosodic system thickens; in other words, poetic spacetime becomes more or less roomy in proportion as its versification is enriched or depleted' (1997: 275–6), and in a footnote he calls this 'a set of commonplaces about lyric [!] poetics' (276n5). The short, densely crafted lyric is particularly suited to create the self-sufficient poetic spacetime effect Tucker refers to. It is thus no surprise that the poems he goes on to discuss include several sonnets (Rossetti's sonnet on the sonnet among them) and other 'stanzaic poems' (278).

The historical process of 'lyricisation' in which poetry increasingly became identified with the lyric as its most essential form has been well documented, in particular in the context of the so-called 'new lyric studies' spearheaded by Virginia Jackson. Jackson, together with Yopie Prins, calls for a resistance to what they term 'lyric' reading, a kind of reading which remains blind to historical as well as generic difference and which they target in particular as 'a project modern literary criticism took from the nineteenth century and made its own' (Jackson and Prins 2014: 2). In contrast, I emphasise that this process of lyricisation needs to be seen as part and parcel of the reconfiguration of poetic concepts and poetry's temporal relations which I have traced in these pages. Because poetry increasingly sought to claim timelessness through form rather than through subject matter, the highly crafted short poem came to replace the long and bulgy epic as poetic paradigm. Lyricisation on the one hand and the shift from an Aesthetics of Eternal Essence to an Aesthetics of Self-sufficient Form on the other are thus, if not quite the same, certainly closely intertwined processes.

While the highly structured intricate poetic form on which poetic spacetime relies according to Tucker no longer has a prominent place in a contemporary understanding of poetry, the association between the lyric and timelessness has survived, albeit in changed form. These days, it is mainly understood in terms of a supposed fundamental distinction between a (temporal) narrative and a (atemporal) lyric mode. To understand the underlying logic of this development, I suggest, one needs to take into account the increasingly close association of time with narrative, for which the lyric then comes to function as a logically necessary atemporal counterpart.

The dominance of narrative

I have already referred to the argument that the prominence of an ideology of success in the nineteenth century gave preference to a conception of time which found a particularly amenable form in the novel (in Chapter 3). The basic narrative dynamic Peter Brooks identifies is that of ambition, which he sees fully realised in the nineteenth-century novel. While he understands this narrative dynamic of plot to be in principle transhistorical, he also suggests that

> there have been some historical moments at which plot has assumed a greater importance than at others, moments in which cultures have seemed to develop an unquenchable thirst for plots and to seek the expression of central individual and collective meanings through narrative design. From sometime in the mid-eighteenth century through to the mid-twentieth century, Western societies appear to have felt an extraordinary need or desire for plots, whether in fiction, history, philosophy, or any of the social sciences [. . .]. As Voltaire announced and then the Romantics confirmed, history replaces theology as the key discourse and central imagination in that historical explanation becomes nearly a necessary factor of any thought about human society [. . .]. (1984: 5–6)

Time, as one might paraphrase Brooks, becomes increasingly thought of in terms of history, and history implies narrative in the sense of plot; that is, a retrospective coherent ordering of a sequence of events in chains of cause and effect. Jerome Buckley proposes that this sense of time marks an entry into a 'modern world': 'The notion of public time, or history, as the medium of organic growth and fundamental change, rather than simply additive succession, was essentially new. Objects hitherto apparently stable had begun to lose their old solidity' (1976: 59). These observations agree with Michel Foucault's argument that the underlying epistemic conditions of knowledge and thought saw a fundamental change at the beginning of the nineteenth century:

> the theory of representation disappears as the universal foundation of all possible orders; [. . .] a profound historicity penetrates into the heart of things, isolates and defines them in their own coherence, imposes upon them the forms of order implied by the continuity of time [. . .]. ([1966] 2018: xxv)

This epistemological change from representation to history, I argue, implies the ascendance of a particular concept of time, namely one that thinks of time specifically in terms of historical development. Reinhart Koselleck speaks in this context of a 'temporalisation of history' (1979: 19). History and time subsequently become almost synonymous terms. The writing of history, conversely, implies a retrospectively selective ordering of events in causal sequences. In other words, an epistemology based on history privileges a concept of time that is aligned with the process of narrative emplotment. As I will go on to argue, however, such exclusive alignment of time with narrative makes us unreceptive to alternative temporalities.

Consequently, narrative concepts of time dominate much of the important work on aesthetic time done recently. For example, in the context of a recent German research cluster on 'aesthetic temporalities' (Ästhetische Eigenzeiten), which is centrally concerned with the way aesthetic form both shapes and is shaped by time, that is, how temporal concepts both inform and emerge from aesthetic objects (Gamper and Hühn 2014: 15–16; Gamper and Geulen 2016: 7–9), Dirk Oschmann proposes that 'the modern sense of time and the modern sense of form emerge in parallel' (2016a: 42; my translation). He argues that what is particularly modern in this is precisely the interrelation between time and form, in which thinking about form becomes thinking about time (43). Developing this idea further, however, Oschmann quickly turns to the novel, pointing to a long critical agreement according to which, compared to other genres, the novel has 'most leeway for the shaping of time' and even that it 'has an affinity with time itself' (40; my translation). The central place his discussion grants to considerations of genre as formations of and in time is thus biased towards narrative genres and largely neglects the question of how the modern temporalisation of form comes into play in poetry.[1]

What Oschmann helps to suggest, nonetheless, is that the con-catenation of time, form and narrative, which found its expression in the novel, can be located historically. It is only by neglecting this historical dimension that Paul Ricœur, in his magisterial three-vol-ume *Time and Narrative* (1983–5), can claim that 'time becomes human time to the extent that it is organized after the manner of a narrative; narrative, in turn, is meaningful to the extent that it por-trays the features of temporal experience' (1990: vol. 1, 3); or, even more strongly: 'there can be no thought about time without narrated time' (vol. 3, 241). In a three-way dialogue between the phenome-nology of time, literary criticism and the theory of history, Ricœur proposes that narrative, and in particular the activity of emplotment, is uniquely placed to help address, and to a degree redress, the apo-rias of time.

Ricœur draws a close connection and interaction between narra-tive, history and time, and the influence of his work has been sub-stantial. But is narrative really the *only* possible way to think time? Ricœur's own approach, in fact, raises some doubts on this issue. After all, Ricœur bases his theoretical framework on texts which do not discuss narrative, but rather poetry and drama respectively. For his conception of emplotment, he draws on Aristotle's *Poetics*, jus-tifying his neglect of the specificity of the dramatic genre for which Aristotle's concept was developed by equating narrative with the activity of emplotment and arguing that he can ignore the 'how' of presentation, since his focus lies exclusively on the 'what' (vol. 1, 35–7). In Volume 2 of *Time and Narrative*, however, Ricœur's argu-ment relies heavily on features specific to narrative representation. Moreover, the three literary texts he discusses at some length at this point are not only all novels, but indeed were all published nearly contemporaneously, and thus exemplify the narrative aesthetic of a particular historical moment: Marcel Proust's *À la recherche du temps perdu* (1913–27), Thomas Mann's *Der Zauberberg* (1924) and

Virginia Woolf's *Mrs Dalloway* (1925). Ricœur shows his awareness of such objections in the conclusion of Volume 2 where he asks:

> The distinction between utterance and statement, then the stress placed on the dialectic between the narrator's discourse and that of the character, and finally the fact that I concentrate at the end on point of view and narrative voice – do not all these aspects indicate a preference for the diegetic mode? (154)

He attempts to answer this objection by suggesting that, with an 'enriched' notion of plot, these narratological categories might also be made applicable to dramatic texts, in the hope 'that concentrating on the novel represents simply a de facto restriction, the obverse of that practiced by Aristotle to the benefit of the tragic *muthos*'. However, as he freely admits, this is an assertion for which 'proof is missing in the present work' (154). Yet, he did not remain the only one to consider drama in terms of narrative. Since both share features like fictional world-making, plot, characters and setting, and because novels in particular habitually rely heavily on dramatic elements like extended dialogues, some narratologists have declared narrative and drama to be 'structurally similar' (Morgan 2009: 12), with the lyric as the odd one out.[2] What such an equation of narrative and dramatic representation overlooks, however, is precisely a difference in their temporal structure. As I have argued in Chapter 2 and am going to elaborate below, while both drama and narrative share the causal progression of a plot, narrative time is essentially retrospective, allowing for different kinds of temporal manipulation. Drama, in contrast, which is understood to be at least nominally meant for performance, necessarily unfolds as a present process. Dramatic time may develop according to the logic of its own fictional world – it may be 'compressed, accelerated, slowed' (Wagner 2018: 58) – but, as Bruce Wilshire has noted, '[h]owever strange or remote be the "time" of the play's world, it can be enacted only within the time in which the actors and audience agree to be gathered together within the theatre's space' (1982: 22). Dramatic time is thus marked by temporal difference in coincidence. For the audience it unfolds as the experience of a present in the present, but one that is different from their own.

Even more pertinent for my purposes, the second touchstone for Ricœur is Augustine's meditation on time in Book XI of his *Confessions*. Ricœur discusses this text in detail to draw out the aporias of time and to promote Augustine's conception of a *distentio animi* as the fundamentally human experience of time. Towards the end of his speculations, Augustine draws on the example of the recitation of a psalm to illustrate his insight into the nature of temporal experience:

> Suppose I am about to recite a psalm which I know. Before I begin, my expectation is directed towards the whole. But when I have begun, the verses from it which I take into the past become the object of memory. The life of this act of mine is stretched in two ways, into my memory because of the words I have already said and into my expectation because of those which I am about to say. But my attention is on what is present: by that the future is transferred to become the past. As the action advances further and further, the shorter the expectation and the longer the memory, until all expectation is consumed, the entire action is finished, and it has passed into the memory. What occurs in the psalm as a whole occurs in its particular pieces and individual syllables. The same is true of a longer action in which perhaps that psalm is a part. It is also valid of the entire life of an individual person, where all actions are parts of a whole, and of the total history of 'the sons of men' (Ps. 30:20) where all human lives are but parts. (1991 [c. 397–400]: 243)

Commenting on this passage, Ricœur claims that '[t]he entire province of narrative is laid out here in its potentiality, from the simple poem, to the story of an entire life, to universal history' (1990: vol. 1, 22). I have quoted from Augustine at length, however, precisely because this passage seems to me to suggest, on the contrary, a conception of time that is far from narrative. After all, Augustine's *canticus* is not a narrative, but rather a chant or song, a structure that has been committed to memory in its entirety and that depends for its progression not on a logic of cause and effect, but rather on repetition and modulation within a structure that relies on the mirroring of micro-level and macro-level, that is, in which every part is a reflection of the order of the whole. Such structuring is characteristic of poetic production, and verse in particular, but it is rare in narrative. I would thus argue that it matters that Augustine's example is a poem or song. Instead of concluding from Augustine's reference to individual life and history that his poem belongs to the 'province of narrative', to me it seems more appropriate to read 'life' and 'history' here in terms of poetry. In fact, Augustine's analogy only works on the premise that both life and history are as predictable and fixed in their course as the psalm is – they are a part of the whole that is God's eternity.

Such a concept of time, however, seems rather different from, perhaps even diametrically opposed to, the solution narrative brings to what Ricœur calls the first aporia of temporality: the relationship between the time of the self and the time of the world. This relationship is troubled because 'the physical definition of time by itself is incapable of accounting for the psychological conditions for the apprehensions of this time' (vol. 3, 244). The time of the self and the time of the world seem incommensurable. Ricœur proposes that the 'bridge' narrative time 'set[s] over the breach speculation constantly opens between phenomenological time and cosmological time' (vol. 3, 244) is narrative identity, which 'does illustrate in a useful way the interplay of history and narrative in the refiguration of a time that is itself indivisibly phenomenological time and cosmological time' (vol. 3, 248). In other words, the stories we tell about ourselves connect our individual experience to a collective narrative, drawing on both history and experience to construct our identity. Such narrative identity, notably, is an artificial construct. The interweaving of history and fiction which is so central to Ricœur's argument about the workings of narrative allows for various ways of emplotment and so 'it is always possible to weave different, even opposed, plots about our lives' (vol. 3, 248). In Augustine's metaphor, however, every word in the poem and every action in life or history finds its form and its meaning solely with regard to the whole and is already contained within eternity. It has its fixed place and meaning and has a predetermined role to play. If Ricœur's narrative weaving and unweaving of the self attempts to bridge difference, Augustine emphasises similarity. The psalm is both contained in and serves as an equivalent of a human life, and even history in its entirety.

A similar incompatibility arises from Ricœur's claims about narrative's response to what he calls the second aporia of temporality, that of totality and totalisation. At the heart of this aporia lies the discrepancy between the thought of time as singular and unified and that of time in its three ecstasies of past, present and future. According to Ricœur, the poetics of narrative 'opposed a firm but costly refusal to the ambition of thought to bring about a totalization of history entirely permeable to the light of concepts, and recapitulated in the eternal present of absolute knowledge' (vol. 3, 255). Precisely such a totalisation in eternity, however, clearly underpins Augustine's metaphor – although, being divine, it cannot be a human 'ambition of thought' but is reserved to God.

I have dwelt on these contradictions, not because I want to question the validity of Ricœur's conclusions about the way a narrative poetics productively engages with these temporal aporias. Rather, I want to emphasise that narrative provides just one possibility, and not the only way to figure and engage with time. Indeed, Ricœur himself eventually admits to the limits of the narrative paradigm and speculates on other possibilities. In the final pages of the third volume of *Time and Narrative*, he concedes: 'There comes a moment, in a work devoted to the power of narrative to elevate time to language, where we must admit that narrative is not the whole story and that time can be spoken of in other ways, because, even for narrative, it remains inscrutable' (vol. 3, 272). Tantalisingly, he goes on to suggest that '[i]t is not for narrative art to deplore the brevity of life, the conflict between love and death, the vastness of a universe that pays no attention to our lament'. Rather, it is '[l]yric poetry' which 'gives a voice, which is also a song, to this fundamental element', namely, 'the misery of humanity handed over to the erosion of time' (273). However, these brief final comments and qualifications are eclipsed by the force of his main arguments, which were taken up widely and enthusiastically. Once Ricœur had established the connection of history, time and narrative so masterfully, speaking of time in literature could easily become synonymous with speaking of time in narrative.

In fact, Ricœur also explores the mechanism with which the connection between narrative and time becomes mutually informative and reinforcing. He introduces a three-level concept of mimesis to describe how narratives shape experience and how their configurations feed back into the reader's conceptualisations. If narrative thus offers a powerful response to the aporetics of temporality, this response in turn comes to shape readers' concepts of time. Narrative texts train their readers to understand time along narrative lines and, what is more, the specific shapes narrative takes, for example in the novel, feed back into the way readers conceptualise time.

Timeless? Poetry?

This productive cycle of mutual reinforcement may be the reason for the striking lack of attention for non-narrative temporal formations in today's criticism. Once time is closely associated with narrative dynamics (tacitly subsuming dramatic forms), temporal narrative can be pitched against the supposedly timeless generic other of lyric poetry. Instead of contrasting timeless poetry with the temporality of other genres, however, I maintain that different literary forms and indeed different individual texts shape time differently, and that these differences can be productively investigated. Indeed, claims for a particular affinity to time have been made at one point or another for all the major genres. For instance, Matthew Wagner praises theatre as 'that unique activity that allows for contradictory modes of time and temporal experience to exist simultaneously' and foregrounds 'the way in which performance echoes and even amplifies the rhythms and cycles of life' (2018: 69, 61). Meanwhile, Susan Stewart has argued that (lyric) poetry is particularly attuned to time:

> As first-person expression in measured language, lyric poetry lends significant – that is, shared and memorable – form to the inner consciousness that is time itself. The most obvious facts of lyric practice – lyric as first-person expression and lyric as the most musical of literary forms – are the most interesting here. (2002: 42)

One of the few recent critics who address the issue of poetic time, Stewart pertinently contends that 'lyric's first-person, subjective, and emotional rendition of time is built through processes of incremental repetition, progression, and return. In this sense, lyric can both oppose, and go beyond other models of sequential and chronological time' (198). Moreover, the lyric, as Frieder von Ammon has noted, is thematically centrally concerned with time: 'Among all literary genres, it is the lyric, it seems, in which the phenomenon "time" has been and continues to be most extensively and emphatically treated as a topic' (2020: 235; my translation). The task that would seem to emerge from these observations is to find a way to describe the specific temporal structures shaped by different literary forms.

I thus maintain the importance of a distinctly formalist engagement with the question of the relation of genre, and poetry in particular, to time, taking my cue from Gamper and Geulen, who propose that '"form" inheres in or is inscribed on the object as a non-propositional, non-discursive dimension of culturally determined time-knowledge' and call for interpretive practices which 'clarify how this time-knowledge relates to discursive stories as well as to formal time structure' (2016: 9; my translation). In other words, a consideration of the way literary form shapes time needs to take into view formal as well as semantic aspects and should consider their interrelations.

It is both a result and a further exacerbating factor of the prominence of narrative time that both dramatic time and poetic time have been comparatively neglected topics in literary criticism. While there has recently been some increased interest in the question of time and performance (Grant, McNeilly and Veerapen 2015; Rabey 2016; Wiles 2014), poetic time is only beginning to be consistently theorised.[3] Such a theory would offer ways to better understand and analytically grasp intuitions about poetic time. Do they all point to the same kind of temporal structure, or do they denote different temporal possibilities of poetry? On which level of the text are they put to work – syntactic, semantic, pragmatic, or pervading all these? What is the relation of these temporal structures to narrative, dramatic and lyric modes in poetry?

A notable exception to the lack of interest in poetic time structures is Sharon Cameron's study of Emily Dickinson's poetry, *Lyric Time*, which sensitively engages with the temporal complexities of Dickinson's work and argues that its 'idiosyncrasies are really only exaggerations of those features that distinguish the lyric as a genre' (1979: 201). In making this claim, however, Cameron offers only what she calls 'a prolegomenon to a thorough study of the question' of lyric time, without aiming to develop a differentiated system of analysis. Moreover, her conception of lyric time is heavily invested in an Aesthetics of Self-sufficient Form and she repeatedly speaks of a 'temporal collapse' in the lyric poem (134), of the poetic 'post-mortem of temporality' (163) and of the poem as 'a necessary "time-out"' (90). Cameron's exclusive interest in the poetic genre of the lyric and her focus on the poetry of one particular poet shape and restrict her ideas about time in poetry.

Much more recently, Rüdiger Zymner (2020) and Frieder von Ammon (2020) have each made suggestions for categories of lyric time analysis. Von Ammon suggests four categories which he calls historical time (*geschichtliche Zeit* – the time of the poem's composition), poetic time (*Gedichtzeit* – time structure and length of the poem), thematic time (*thematische Zeit* – time as topic) and mimetic time (*gedichtete Zeit* – in analogy to narrated time, the duration of events portrayed in the poem). If these categories are very broad, Zymner's list of 'time-givers' is very fine-grained, including, for example, orthography, tenses and grammatical structures, as well as metre and themes. In both cases, the specificity of these categories to the lyric remains unclear, however. With the sole exception of metre, which is not applicable to all poems, they seem to be applicable to any sort of text. Moreover, like for Cameron, these scholars' interest lies in short lyric poems exclusively. In contrast, I aim to develop a terminology that considers the specificity of poetic time structures and is, at the same time, flexible enough to address aspects of temporality in a broad range of different kinds of poem.

Before I turn to this task, however, I need to address directly one problem which such a project faces: the lack of consensus about a definition of poetry. Attempts to define poetry or the lyric continually struggle and stumble over the sheer historical variety and ambiguity

228 Time and Timelessness in Victorian Poetry

in the application of these terms.[4] The shift in the meaning of poetic timelessness I have been tracing in these pages is just one of the aspects that play into this. As Scott Brewster remarks, 'for such an apparently "timeless" and "universal" literary category, lyric is remarkably time-bound, and its generic classification cannot be dissociated from historical shifts in the use of the term' (2009: 11). It may seem important to first establish the nature of one's research object, before one can begin to build a theoretical structure. Nonetheless, it is both surprising and regrettable that much theorisation of poetry has restricted itself almost exclusively to the question of definition. After all, definitions are always a treacherous business and easily become the bone of contention in largely fruitless debates. The success of narratology, I believe, should teach us that such debates are not altogether unavoidable. Most foundational narratology unapologetically developed purely synchronic concepts, often based primarily on the aesthetics of the Modern(ist) novel.[5] Genette (1980), for instance, develops his ground-breaking system of narrative analysis largely on the basis of a single novel: Marcel Proust's *À la recherche du temps perdu*. He clearly did not feel hampered by the consideration that his categories would be of very limited use for the analysis of, say, a fairy tale or a graphic novel, nor does his system lose its use value only because it fails to encompass all conceivable narrative possibilities (for example, he does not account for second-person narration). Of course, this synchronic perspective limits the applicability of Genette's work. But it does not invalidate it. Moreover, if theorists of the lyric habitually complain about the difficulty of defining their research object, the definition of narrative, too, is by no means incontestable or uncontested.[6]

In some attempts to rethink the nature of narrative, the boundaries to poetry and even to the lyric in fact become somewhat blurred. In her influential proposal for a *Natural Narratology* (1996), Monika Fludernik, for instance, questions the centrality that plot usually plays in definitions of narrative and suggests a radical redefinition along cognitive lines. For Fludernik, the essential aspect of narrative is what she calls 'experientiality', which 'can be aligned with actantial frames, but [. . .] also correlates with the evocation of consciousness or with the representation of a speaker role' and 'reflects a cognitive schema of embodiedness that relates to human existence and human concerns' (1996: 12–13). This leads Fludernik also to question the constitutive centrality of temporality to narrative: 'It is not temporality *per se* that "makes" narrative; or if so, that temporality relates more to the reading process than to the context of the story' (1996: 21). Temporality is important to narrative, in Fludernik's conception, but only in so far as it is a basic quality of experience. The 'radical elimination of plot from [Fludernik's] definition of narrative' has significant consequences for the demarcation of narrative proper (1996: 13). As Jan Alber has noted, if narrative is redefined on the basis of experientiality, sidelining traditional narrative categories like plot, action, character, 'almost every poem qualifies as a narrative' (2002: 69). In fact, Fludernik herself notes that '[n]arrativization in poetry is widespread indeed' (1996: 309) and she concedes in response to Alber's criticism that 'the line between narrative and poetry [. . .] may be fragile' (2018: 343). The difference she senses between narrative and much poetry is based in particular on her insistence that experientiality depends on specificity: 'Much that *appears* to be narrative in poetry does not actually qualify as such because it does not concern specific fictional personae but posits a hypothetical or allegorical scenario' (1996: 354). Moreover, she notes that 'timeless or habitual situations do not trigger narrative dynamics, just as narratives cannot have everybody (or no one in particular) as their protagonist' (1996: 29). If this is granted, lyric poetry's investment in iterability and the gnomic runs counter to experientiality and therewith narrativity. Finally, poetry tends to foreground language over representation, the poetic over referential, conative or emotive functions of communication: 'Where language has become pure language, disembodied from speaker, context and reference, human experience and narrativization by means of human experience recede into the background' (Fludernik 1996: 310). The difference between lyric poetry and narrative, one might gloss from the perspective of my discussion, depends on the former's performative eventfulness, which is appropriated into the present of reading. Narrative represents an experience, lyric poetry endeavours to be an experience.

Even if such a reframing of narratology may be open to a consideration of poetry, however, I will not proceed from the assumption that narratological categories will be able to adequately handle poetic specificity. Instead, I want to turn to poetry itself, developing categories of analysis that acquire particular pertinence for poetry but might well turn out to be helpful in thinking about narrative or drama, too. Since I aim to provide ways to think about poetic, that is, not merely lyric, temporality, I will draw on narratological and dramatic concepts of time where appropriate.

Poetic Temporality

An approach to poetic temporality, I suggest, needs to take account of three different levels, each of which I will develop further below: 1. mediation (pragmatic level); 2. representational content (semantic level); 3. language (syntactic level). It is on the level of mediation that the differentiations I introduced in Chapter 2 between narrative, dramatic and lyric temporal structures become pertinent. Poetic mediation, I argue, can establish different kinds of 'presents', be they narrative, dramatic or lyric, each of which implies different temporal relations between the moment of utterance, the referential dimension of the utterance and the reader or audience. On the level of representational content or the semantic level of the utterance, thinking about time in poetry differs significantly from the perhaps more familiar concerns of temporal narrative analysis: what is relevant is not the (supposed) order of events (that is, the question of chronology), but the kinds of time that a text evokes. What I propose here is that time can be productively investigated in ways analogous to (and intertwined with) spatial setting. In other words, poetry can help to foreground the importance of a semiotics of time – it can reveal ways in which time features on the representational level of texts beyond issues of chronology. The third level, that of poetic language itself, is the most fundamental. After all, poetic form highlights specific ways to shape language in time. What poetry may draw particular attention to, then, is that language does not simply happen in time in a necessarily linear fashion, but rather that all language (including prose) always shapes certain kinds of temporal experience. Poetry can help to highlight that the temporality of language is not simply a given structure, shared by all texts, but takes form in a multitude of different ways in individual texts of whatever genre.

Level of mediation

In Chapter 2 I have distinguished three different temporal structures as possibilities for poetic communication and have called them narrative, dramatic and lyric. There are three points I want to emphasise before I recapitulate and refine the central propositions put forward earlier. Firstly, these three temporal possibilities on the level of mediation intersect but are not synonymous with distinctions between different poetic genres. While some poetic genres might be typically characterised by a particular temporal logic of mediation (ballads are mostly narrative, dramatic monologues dramatic, hymns lyric), most poetic genres allow for different kinds of mediation. In fact, my second point is that, as I have argued in Chapter 2, these three temporal possibilities often combine and merge or clash in individual poems. Lastly, it is important to insist again that they are at least partly determined by reception, in so far as an individual poem can give cues for different ways of parsing its underlying temporal structure.

To illustrate my points, I will draw all my examples for the different kinds of mediation below from a single work: Dante Gabriel Rossetti's sonnet sequence *The House of Life* (1881).[7] This may seem to narrow the import of the theory, but my claim for its applicability could hardly by wider: I contend that the terminology and perspective I offer here could be made productive for the analysis not only of any kind of poem, but indeed, any type of literary text. Rossetti's sequence will here serve the purpose Proust's novel has served for Genette's narratological system. Apart from offering a multitude of poems with very different kinds of mediation – all of which, being sonnets, are conveniently short and can therefore be quoted in full – *The House of Life* is intensely concerned with time throughout. It may thus well count as an equivalent to those novels favoured by narratological analysis of temporal structures which Ricœur called 'tales about time'. In *The House of Life*, no less than in Proust's *Recherche* or Woolf's *Mrs Dalloway*, 'it is the very experience of time that is at stake in these structural transformations' (Ricœur 1990: vol. 2, 101).

Narrative time

I have previously defined narrative time as a temporal structure that depends on the act of narration, that is, on the *retrospective emplotment* of events (see Chapter 2). It is thus a doubled time, one that involves the temporal order of the narrated events (*énoncé*) as well as the temporality of narration (*énunciation*). The narrated events are represented, and this representation takes various temporal shapes, which Gérard Genette (1980) has differentiated into the categories of order, frequency and duration. Order designates the relation between the represented sequence of story events and the sequence of their representation, frequency refers to the number of times an event is narrated, and duration to the time taken up by the story event relative to the length of its narration. Clearly, all three of these Genettian categories depend on the act of retrospective temporal shaping, in which the duality of narrative time can come fully into play. Narration is free to manipulate order, frequency and duration because it is representation. The moment of narration can be – though it does not have to be – shared by the reader, but the reader does not share the temporality of the depicted events or situation. Since manipulations of order and frequency require a certain length, they are comparatively rare in short narratives. For (short) poetry, narrative temporality develops mainly in the tension between story time and discourse time, that is, in manipulations of duration on the one hand, and in the tension between the moment of narration and the narrated moment on the other. One needs to keep in mind, though, that mediation is not the only, nor in fact the most important, level of temporal manipulation in poetry. Even very simple poetic narratives may develop further temporal complexities on the semiotic level or the level of language (I will return to this point below).

In Rossetti's sonnet sequence, the Willowwood group (sonnets XLIX, L, LI and LII) provides the best example of the development of a narrative temporal logic. This suite of sonnets proceeds to narrate a little scene, which is set out in the first of the sonnets:

> I sat with Love upon a woodside well,
> Leaning across the water, I and he;
> Nor ever did he speak nor looked at me,
> But touched his lute wherein was audible
> The certain secret thing he had to tell:
> Only our mirrored eyes met silently
> In the low wave; and that sound came to be
> The passionate voice I knew; and my tears fell.
>
> And at their fall, his eyes beneath grew hers;
> And with his foot and with his wing-feathers
> He swept the spring that watered my heart's drouth.
> Then the dark ripples spread to waving hair,
> And as I stooped, her own lips rising there
> Bubbled with brimming kisses at my mouth.

Unmistakeably, and from its first line, this poem establishes a narrative voice, recounting past events. If the octet establishes the setting, the sestet narrates a series of events, in the most basic narrative mode of the 'and then'. The main event in the poem is paradigmatically narrative: a metamorphosis; that is, a process that turns one thing into another and therefore necessarily unfolds in time. The fulfilment offered with the kiss in the final line of this sonnet turns transitory, however, precisely because the narrative continues. It is further developed in chronological sequence over the course of the following three sonnets that comprise the Willowwood group.

A narrative temporality emerges in these sonnets not merely because of their use of past tense. Rather it depends on the way in which the temporality of the depicted scene is mediated through its narrative description, that is, the relation between the different temporalities of *sujet* and *fabula*, and the way the sonnets in the group vary and shape this difference in what Genette calls duration. After the scene established in the first sonnet, the second sonnet introduces another event, as Love begins to sing. But the sonnet then pauses to consider the thoughts and visions that Love's song evokes in the speaker. The duration established through this extension of the time of narration becomes oppressive as the blissfully brimming kisses of the first sonnet turn sinister and necrophiliac: 'alive from the abyss / Clung the soul-wrung implacable close kiss' (L, ll. 11–12). The third sonnet in the group is Love's song itself, all in direct speech, and thus the story time of the second sonnet (whose first line announces the commencement of Love's song) and the third sonnet coincide. As the narrative voice leaves it unclear whether this is a scene, a pause or a stretch, the kiss, extending over all four sonnets and only finally unclosing in the last one, is painfully prolonged.

But whether this is a moment of bliss or horror, extended as it may be, it necessarily ends in narrative retrospect. The fourth sonnet emphasises this further by not only telling us what happens but also what the speaker retained from the experience in retrospection; that is, the sonnet straddles the narrated time and the time of narration. This emphasis on retrospective assessment, marked by a shift to present tense in the final sonnet, is effective precisely because it withdraws the interpretation and knowledgeable hindsight its retrospective narrative perspective promises:

> So when the song died did the kiss unclose;
> And her face fell back drowned, and was as grey
> As its grey eyes; and if it ever may
> Meet mine again I know not if Love knows.
>
> Only I know that I leaned low and drank
> A long draught from the water where she sank,
> Her breath and all her tears and all her soul:
> And as I leaned, I know I felt Love's face
> Pressed on my neck with moan of pity and grace,
> Till both our heads were in his aureole. (LII, ll. 5–14)

Instead of having gained a retrospective insight into the meaning of the events, what the speaker knows is merely what happened.

His retrospection gives him no further insight, only further knowledge of transience and further experience of loss. Thus, while the use of past tense is not a prerequisite for the establishment of a narrative temporality, the past tense is an important feature of this particular sonnet group: it exacerbates and emphasises the loss with which the whole group is concerned, by putting even this fleeting encounter with the past itself into the past of memory and by emphasising the uniqueness of the event: the retrospective point of view of the speaker indicates that he has not seen the face of his beloved again. Narrative retrospection thus offers no solution to the riddle posed by the poems' vision but emphasises the passage of time. Indeed, the only things that endure are ignorance and loss.

Dramatic time

Such retrospection is not available in dramatic time. As I have said before (see Chapter 2), the dramatic temporal structure shares the unfolding of its present with the reader or audience, although it unfolds as a different present, one the reader or audience is witness to. Dramatic mediation involves presentation, not representation; it 'demands that the viewer follow the continuity of an action in succession as if it were occurring at the present moment, step by step, minute by minute, and event by event, from beginning to end' (Stewart 1978: 15). The dramatic present is in constant flux; it is 'always only a passage, a phase of an unfolding time which is constituted as a temporal flow' (Ingarden 1968: 142; my translation). Clearly, this somewhat restricts the kinds of temporal manipulation available to dramatic texts. Manipulations of order and, to some degree, frequency would, in theory, be possible for a dramatic text, but they are used comparatively rarely since they are difficult to frame without a narrative commentary. As far as manipulations of duration are concerned, drama can condense or stretch the represented time to a degree, but such manipulations will always stand in some tension with the audience's experience of a passing present of representation (Pfister 2001: 369–74). While in a drama there is usually a difference between the timespan of what is represented (*gespielte Zeit*) and the time of presentation (*Spielzeit*), this difference is mostly due to ellipsis (Stewart 1978: 25–6). Thus, instead of order, frequency and duration, the temporal dynamics of a dramatic text are generally determined by processes of selection, combination and the pacing of scenes.[8] Like narrative temporality, dramatic temporality involves a sense of successively unfolding events, however. In contrast to the theatrical possibilities open to drama, poetry, of course, must imply continuity of action entirely through language. In other words, dramatically mediated poetry presents a fictional speech act, addressed to an auditor or in soliloquy, but overheard by the reader or audience. Although this sounds like John Stuart Mill's definition of poetry as 'overheard' (2005 [1833]: 565–6), the thrust of my argument is somewhat different: my emphasis is on the *specificity* of dramatic address as clearly defined in its fictional situation, its speaker and its addressee.

As the middle term between narrative and lyric temporality, dramatic temporality thus defined admittedly has fuzzy boundaries. How much eventfulness is required for a dramatic event? How much specificity is necessary to establish a dramatic speaker or situation? In poetry, dramatic versus lyric mediation is thus a question of degree, not of kind. It is helpful in this context to recall Jonathan Culler's concept of triangulated address, the 'characteristic indirection' to which his 'account of the lyric grants major importance [. . .]: addressing the audience of readers by addressing or pretending to address someone or something else' (2018: 8). Arguably, such triangulated address structures dramatic (perhaps even narrative) utterances as much as lyric ones, in so far as any literary text ultimately addresses a public audience. But here, once again, specificity and thus the degree of indirection become important. In a dramatically mediated text, the audience becomes witness to an utterance, by someone to someone else; that is, an utterance that is rooted in action. This distancing of speaker and addressee from the audience is precisely what is at stake in the dramatic monologue.

The dramatic monologue is the paradigmatic example of a dramatically mediated poem, but I have also suggested (in Chapter 2) that dramatic mediation can emerge as a secondary effect from the combination of poems into sequences, in which the individual poems turn into dramatic events and serve to cumulatively specify speaker, addressee and communicative situation. I have also maintained that *The House of Life* resists such specificity, by constantly changing its subject position and point of view. Nonetheless, individual poems of the sequence develop different degrees of dramatic potential, although none of them is a pure case. Sonnet X, 'The Portrait', provides one of the clearest examples of distinctly dramatic elements within the sequence:

> O Lord of all compassionate control,
> O Love! let this my lady's picture glow
> Under my hand to praise her name, and show
> Even of her inner self the perfect whole:
> That he who seeks her beauty's furthest goal,
> Beyond the light that the sweet glances throw

And refluent wave of the sweet smile, may know
The very sky and sea-line of her soul.

Lo! it is done. Above the enthroning throat
The mouth's mould testifies of voice and kiss,
The shadowed eyes remember and foresee.
Her face is made her shrine. Let all men note
That in all years (O Love, thy gift is this!)
They that would look on her must come to me.

This address to personified Love establishes unmistakeably a specific situation, that of a painter in the process of painting the portrait of his lover. It involves a succession of events, or of speech acts as the portrait is finished in the interval between the octet and the sestet. It thus combines two moments and two speech acts in succession, establishing a minimal plot. While an address to Love is certainly fanciful, the octet is still construable as a likely utterance of a speaker, addressing a higher power in form of a prayer. Both speaker and addressee are thus clearly defined and, initially at least, relatively stable. But, as I have said before, none of the sonnets of *The House of Life* offer an example of pure dramatic mediation. In this poem, the dramatic structure of the octet turns lyric with the sestet. After all, there is no dramatic motivation for the description of the portrait offered in lines 9–13. The description serves as a substitute for the portrait in language and would not be necessary in a dramatic situation, in which the portrait itself would be present.[9] Instead, the portrait is summoned into the reader's present. With this, the structure of address has become permeable, with Love no longer featuring as the primary addressee. Indeed, the sestet goes on to make this permeability of address explicit, when it expands its audience to 'all men' (l. 12) in 'all years' (l. 13), relegating the direct address to Love to a parenthetical insertion (l. 13). This is the characteristic hubris of the lyric voice which claims to address everyone, every time the lyric poem is read, as each reading makes this utterance present. In effect, lyric address is substituted for the dramatic situation with which the sonnet set out, and it is only in the structure of this lyric address that the poem's possessive claims are able to maintain their hold. Whoever wants to look on the portrait evoked by these lines must indeed come to the poem.

Lyric time

As this might already serve to indicate, in contrast to both narrative and dramatic mediation, the lyric mode of mediation is characterised by a singular temporal structure, in which the lyric present not only parallels the present of reading but is identical with it. Moreover, in a lyrically mediated text the distinctions between speaker, addressee and audience become unstable, enabling a potential doubling of roles, speaker/audience or addressee/audience. As William Waters suggested, '[lyric] poetry [. . .] enacts – for us, as readers, now – not so much a stable communicative situation as a chronic hesitation, a faltering, between monologue and dialogue, between "talking about" and "talking to", third and second person, indifference to interlocutors and the yearning to have one' (2003: 7). Waters thus speaks of the lyric poem as 'an underspecified communicative act', in which it becomes difficult to answer the question '[w]ho is speaking (or writing), to whom, in what context?' (2003: 8). In a ritual performative gesture, the lyric becomes an event in each reading, in which it claims neither to represent, nor to present, but to be. Thus, the lyric temporal structure is eminently self-referential. Sonnet X itself is the portrait, as signifier and signified coincide temporally. This way of understanding the specific temporal structure of the lyric goes beyond Hempfer's attempt to define the lyric as the 'simultaneity or coinciding of speech situation [*Sprechsituation*] and represented situation [*besprochene Situation*]' (Hempfer 2014: 31–2; my translation). Taking its cue from Culler's and Greene's intuition about the ritualistic character of the lyric, my conception of lyric temporality involves not only the simultaneity of speech act and represented situation but finds its full realisation in the simultaneity of speech situation, represented situation and the moment of reception.

It does not follow from this, though, that the lyric mode allows for no temporal complexity. On the contrary, I would even argue that, in short poems, lyric mediation often allows for more complex temporal structures than narrative or dramatic forms. If dramatic time depends on succession and narrative time on retrospection, and thus both rely largely on extension for complexity, the lyric condenses time in the moment of reception. Time in the lyric does not unfold in succession, but folds into layers. Cameron, too, highlights the importance of this process of temporal condensation for the lyric:

> Although lyric verbs often record temporal change, they also collapse their progressions so that movement is not consecutive but is rather heaped or layered. This stacking up of movement, temporal forays cut off from linear progression and treated instead as if they were vertically additive [. . .], is quite opposite to the way in which meaning 'unfolds' in novels or in the drama. The least mimetic of all art forms, the lyric

compresses rather than imitates life; it will withstand the outrage of any complexity for the sake of being able to present sequence as if it were a unity. (1979: 240–1)

Cameron herself does not develop the implications of this idea beyond suggesting that '[p]erhaps it would be more accurate to say that its [the lyric poem's] meanings are spatial rather than temporal' (1979: 196). Extension and horizontality, however, are spatial metaphors, and no less so than compression and verticality. Instead of understanding such temporal compression as a resistance to time and a turn to space, as Cameron tends to do, I would follow Jessica Wiskus's intuition in thinking of this 'not as time stopped, but as time reoriented, for a reorientation does not imply a cessation of motion but rather reverberation along a perpendicular axis' (2006: 190).

Beyond such vague formulations, however, I suggest that such compression, or vertical time structure, is no less amenable to description and analysis than the horizontal unfolding of narrative or dramatic sequence. Nor, indeed, is it the only possibility within lyric mediation. In a tantalisingly brief footnote on poetic temporality in his 'Pragmasemiotics of Poetry' Andreas Mahler suggests that there are three logical temporal possibilities for poems: 'If the situation of enunciation' is 'the *hic-et-nunc* of the utterance, its object (the situation of the enounced [. . .]) is either the same situation or another one [. . .]. If the object of speaking is no situation at all, the poem, remains, of course, atemporal'. Mahler calls the first type 'homochronous', the second 'heterochronous' and goes on to draw on Genette to suggest that 'the textual occurrence [. . .] of a diegetic situation [. . .] can be "singulative" (1 or n occurrences of 1 or n situations), "iterative" (1 occurrence of n situations), or "repetitive" (n occurrences of 1 situation)' (2006: 246). While logically convincing, this treatment of poetic temporality needs further nuancing. After all, a frequent temporal structure of poems contrasts a present with a past moment and would thus have to be considered both homochronous and heterochronous. Moreover, for reasons that should by now have become sufficiently clear, I believe it is potentially misleading to call any kind of poem 'atemporal'. Finally, a transferral of Genettian categories to the discussion of lyrically mediated poetry, as I understand it here, does not work, since repetitive representations of situations are only an option in heterochronous (and thus narrative) poems. Starting from my premise that lyric time is marked by the performative coinciding of the situation of enunciation, enounced and reception (and is thus doubly homochronous, to adapt Mahler's terms), a closer look at the temporal complexity of such poems reveals differences that emerge within and occasionally cut across Mahler's distinctions. Within the lyric present, I suggest, there are different ways in which temporality can be layered. To clarify this, I would like to distinguish three basic options of temporal layering typical for the lyric: lyrically mediated poems which depict no specific event at all have 'zero' temporal layers (Mahler, as we have seen, calls such poems 'atemporal'); poems which focus on and highlight a single event are 'singulative'; poems which evoke a habitual or recurring situation are 'iterative' or 'durative'.

Poems with zero temporal layering do not depict any specific event at all. They are not mimetic, but discursive; they do not construct a particular moment, neither of utterance nor of reference. A typical sentence structure of zero layering is the gnomic constative of the type of 'A sonnet is a moment's monument'. Zero temporal layering is very frequent in lyric poetry, but is not the only, nor even necessarily the most typical temporal structure of lyric texts. Note, for example, that Rossetti's introductory sonnet is zero-layered in this sense, but the kind of sonnet it advocates demands a temporal reference to a moment. Nor does it seem correct to speak of zero temporal layering as atemporal or timeless. In fact, such poems can be intensely concerned with time, as Rossetti's sonnet on the sonnet clearly demonstrates (see my comments in the Introduction). After all, a poem with zero temporal layers can be closely concerned with time on the semantic as well as the language level (see below). To illustrate this further with another example from Rossetti's sequence, one which is somewhat less directly self-referential or metapoetic than the introductory sonnet and that favours the rhetorical question rather than the constative utterance, let me turn to sonnet LXII, 'The Soul's Sphere':

> Some prisoned moon in steep cloud-fastnesses,—
> Throned queen and thralled; some dying sun whose pyre
> Blazed with momentous memorable fire;—
> Who hath not yearned and fed his heart with these?
> Who, sleepless, hath not anguished to appease
> Tragical shadow's realm of sound and sight
> Conjectured in the lamentable night? . . .
> Lo! the soul's sphere of infinite images!
>
> What sense shall count them? Whether it forecast
> The rose-winged hours that flutter in the van
> Of Love's unquestioning unrevealèd span,—
> Visions of golden futures: or that last
> Wild pageant of the accumulated past
> That clangs and flashes for a drowning man.

This poem asserts not a moment or a sequence in time, but proposes the wide applicability of its statements, suggested by its rhetorical questions. Its statements claim truth independent of the moment of their utterance. In this, zero temporal layering comes closest to the timelessness that has been claimed for the lyric, a kind of timelessness, however, that this sort of lyric shares with any discursive text that makes general truth claims. But, like in the introductory sonnet to *The House of Life*, the celebration of the imagination in sonnet LXII is concerned closely with the former's relationship to time. This becomes particularly prominent in the sestet, although the poem's concern with time cannot be analytically grasped on the level of mediation and will have to wait for the discussion of the semantic and language levels below. It is further worth adding that, although I have called this sonnet less directly metapoetical than the proem of the sequence, it too is highly self-reflective. After all, the 'infinite images' (l. 8) of the soul find their partial equivalent in the individual sonnets of the sequence, which constantly hover between the 'rose-winged hours' (l. 10) of love and the 'wild pageant' (l. 13) of the dying man. Though zero-layered in itself, the sonnet thus emphasises temporal relationships between the individual sonnets of the sequence.

The *singulative poem* picks out and highlights a single moment. This is the type which best realises Rossetti's demand for the sonnet to become 'a moment's monument'. As I have argued before, fairly few of the sonnets that make up *The House of Life* in fact fall clearly into this category. Moreover, in most cases the singular moment serves as the nucleus around which complex temporal relations revolve. In Rossetti's sequence, the attempt to truly exempt the moment from temporal flux is shown to be fraught with difficulties and aporias.

The fullest attempt is made in sonnet XIV, 'Youth's Spring-Tribute', which struggles hard to keep past and future at bay:

> On this sweet bank your head thrice sweet and dear
> I lay, and spread your hair on either side,
> And see the newborn woodflowers bashful-eyed
> Look through the golden tresses here and there.
> On these debateable borders of the year
> Spring's foot half falters; scarce she yet may know
> The leafless blackthorn-blossom from the snow;
> And through her bowers the wind's way still is clear.
>
> But April's sun strikes down the glades to-day;
> So shut your eyes upturned, and feel my kiss

Creep, as the Spring now thrills through every spray,
Up your warm throat to your warm lips: for this
Is even the hour of Love's sworn suitservice,
With whom cold hearts are counted castaway.

The poem insists on its evocation of the present moment with its emphatic accumulation of temporal and spatial deictics ('this' l. 1, 'these' l. 5, 'to-day' l. 9, 'now' l. 11, 'this' l. 12), and the imperatives in the sestet. The moment is not only evoked and described but embodied through vivid reference to sensual experience. While this poetic moment has specificity, it is lyric, not dramatic, because it cannot be construed as an actual utterance addressed to the lover within the situation it describes, nor even as an internal monologue of the speaker. The nature of its address is typically unstable, as the supposed address to the lover merges with the evocation of the situation for the reader. In fact, the situation it evokes would seem to preclude the actual utterance of the poem (after all, the speaker can hardly speak and kiss at the same time). But the poem's very refusal to look beyond the moment becomes conspicuous. By emphasising its 'now' in 'even the hour' (l. 13) of loving embrace, the poem cannot prevent, but rather invites a sense of transience. This is strengthened by the contrast between the warmth of the kiss and the coldness of the hearts introduced with the final line, a contrast which invites a temporal construal. What is warm now may be cold tomorrow. Moreover, the very structure of lyric address necessarily points beyond the moment it evokes, since it draws attention to the verbal construction of a present moment in which its utterance itself has no place. The moment, the hour, may be preserved in the sonnet, a moment's monument indeed, but only precariously, and only as a moment that can be invoked because it has passed.

This precariousness of the singular moment emerges even more explicitly from sonnet XIX, 'Silent Noon'. This sonnet sets out from a very similar premise as sonnet XIV:

Your hands lie open in the long fresh grass, –
The finger-points look through like rosy blooms:
Your eyes smile peace. The pasture gleams and glooms
'Neath billowing skies that scatter and amass.
All round our nest, far as the eye can pass,
Are golden kingcup-fields with silver edge
Where the cow-parsley skirts the hawthorn-hedge.
'Tis visible silence, still as the hour-glass.

Deep in the sun-searched growths the dragon-fly
Hangs like a blue thread loosened from the sky: –
So this wing'd hour is dropt to us from above.
Oh! clasp we to our hearts, for deathless dower,
This close-companioned inarticulate hour
When twofold silence was the song of love.

The vivid particularity of visual details of the octet evokes a specific situation, very similar to that of sonnet XIV. This hour of stilled time is like a divine gift to the lovers, dropped on them from above, and the 'deathless dower' (l. 12) here harks back both semantically and phonetically to the 'dead deathless hour' of Rossetti's introductory sonnet. But the twist comes with the final two lines and the shift to past tense: 'This close-companioned inarticulate hour / When the twofold silence was the song of love'. The point here is not only that the immortal hour has passed. It is that the last line nostalgically looks back to the moment when no song was necessary, only silent communion. Instead of granting eternity to the moment, by its very existence the sonnet is replacing, indeed destroying, the evoked blissful silence by its own words, and the poem clearly suggests that this is rather a poor substitution. The sonnet thus plays with its own impossibility (how to sing silence). At the same time, the song becomes necessary precisely because the lovers fail to clasp the 'inarticulate hour' close. The moment of bliss needs to enter into song to be preserved, but by doing so it falls victim to the fundamental temporality of language, which poetry can never escape. The deathless moment is a moment of visual impression and spatial expansion, but necessarily silent since language happens in time and is therefore always a reminder of transience. 'Silent Noon' thus directly contradicts Rossetti's introductory poem. If the proem suggests that it is the art of the sonnet that elevates the moment into eternity, 'Silent Noon' suggests that poetry parasitically feeds off and destroys the timelessness of the moment's bliss.

Both 'Youth's Spring-Tribute' and 'Silent Noon' attempt to isolate their 'deathless' moment from the flux of time, but more frequently, the singular moment serves as the nucleus from which and around which multiple temporal relations evolve. As Cameron puts it so vividly, a lyric poem can 'push its way into the dimensions of the moment, pry apart its walls and reveal the discovered space there to be as complex as the long corridors of historical or narrative time' (1979: 204). Sonnet LXIX, 'Autumn Idleness', which I have discussed in Chapter 3, would be one example of this, as the idle moment is both extended into the near past and beset by present and future uncertainty. The sonnet which follows it in the sequence, sonnet LXX, 'The Hill Summit', illustrates this layering strategy even better:

> This feast-day of the sun, his altar there
> In the broad west has blazed for vesper-song;
> And I have loitered in the vale too long
> And gaze now a belated worshipper.
> Yet may I not forget that I was 'ware,
> So journeying, of his face at intervals
> Transfigured where the fringed horizon falls, –
> A fiery bush with coruscating hair.
>
>   And now that I have climbed and won this height,
> I must tread downward through the sloping shade
> And travel the bewildered tracks till night.
> Yet for this hour I still may here be stayed
> And see the gold air and the silver fade
> And the last bird fly into the last light.

The journey, a recurring image in Rossetti's sequence, is condensed in the present moment on top of the hill. The temporal movement is not simply one from past remembrance (loitering in the vale) to future expectation (treading downward), but develops a complex rhythm. The poem thus perfectly illustrates Cameron's claim that 'the lyric[. . .] travel[s] backwards and forwards restlessly over the same ground', a feature which serves to 'unhinge time from its fixtures' (1979: 241). The first two lines evoke the sunset which the traveller has just missed, line 3 provides the reason, by looking further into the past of the traveller's journey through the vale. Line 4, then, first puts us in the present moment and location of the hill summit, the 'now' which is already temporally conditioned in being 'belated' (l. 4). The second quatrain commences to bridge the present and the past in emphasising the function of memory ('I may not forget', l. 5), returning not to a single moment but to the process and progression of the journey in the course of which the traveller has seen the sunset intermittently. The sestet places us again more firmly into the present moment only to veer off directly, with its second line, into future expectation, referring to the continuation of the trip. Only the final tercet serves exclusively to evoke the present moment; and yet, this present moment is one of marked transience, of fading light and disappearing birds, merely a brief pause before the continuation of the journey and the onset of night. Instead of taking a moment out of time, the poem becomes a monument to temporal flux and transience. Still, this temporal flux is not simply a sequence, not only because of the interweaving of temporal layers, but also, because the present moment is charged with these past and future times. Diverse temporal layers are compressed in the present moment, which is entirely conditioned by them. What the poem thus develops is not a replacement of one temporal moment with another in a progressive development of plot, but a simultaneity of temporal layers, all of which are suffused with one another and derive their meaning only from their interrelation. It is precisely this temporal richness which renders the moment both significant and beautiful.

The *iterative* or *durative poem* refers not to a particular moment, but a certain kind of moment or event. Such poems either concern an event that happens repeatedly or name a certain state of being which has an unspecified duration. Next to the multiple temporal layers which can be present in the singular moment, the iterative or durative mode provides another possibility for what Cameron has called the 'pluralistic' vision of the lyric: 'the perception of many moments distilled into one' (1979: 207). This mode makes explicit what always remains a latent possibility in the general iterability of lyric mediation. As with the singulative structure, iterative and durative poems can have varying numbers of temporal layers and thus develop varying degrees of temporal complexity. Sonnet XXI, 'Love-Sweetness', for example, has a fairly simple temporal structure:

Sweet dimness of her loosened hair's downfall
About thy face; her sweet hands round thy head
In gracious fostering union garlanded;
Her tremulous smiles; her glances' sweet recall
Of love; her murmuring sighs memorial;
Her mouth's culled sweetness by thy kisses shed
On cheeks and neck and eyelids, and so led
Back to her mouth which answers there for all:—

What sweeter than these things, except the thing
In lacking which all these would lose their sweet:—
The confident heart's still fervour: the swift beat
And soft subsidence of the spirit's wing,
Then when it feels, in cloud-girt wayfaring,
The breath of kindred plumes against its feet?

As in sonnets XIV and XIX, the octet of this poem evokes a scene, an encounter with the lover, vividly and sensuously. However, the indirection of the second-person address as well as the lack of specificity which would mark this situation as unique suggests its iterability. What is described is not a particular encounter, not a specific moment, but a generic situation; the sweetness of 'these things' (l. 9) is a sweetness not tasted once, but repeatedly; even, such might be the implication of the lack of specificity of the description, a sweetness that might be tasted with different lovers, as long as the conditions set in the sestet are met. The second-person address emphasises the appropriability of the described scene, which is offered as an experience available, in principle and through the poem itself, not exclusively to a specific addressee, but rather to every 'you'.

Such iterative temporal layering, in which several, similar moments are condensed into the lyric present can develop significant temporal complexity, as in sonnet XXVIII, 'Soul-Light':

> What other woman could be loved like you,
> Or how of you should love possess his fill?
> After the fulness of all rapture, still,—
> As at the end of some deep avenue
> A tender glamour of day,—there comes to view
> Far in your eyes a yet more hungering thrill,—
> Such fire as Love's soul-winnowing hands distil
> Even from his inmost ark of light and dew.
>
> And as the traveller triumphs with the sun,
> Glorying in heat's mid-height, yet startide brings
> Wonder new-born, and still fresh transport springs
> From limpid lambent hours of day begun;—
> Even so, through eyes and voice, your soul doth move
> My soul with changeful light of infinite love.

Within the mode of iteration, this sonnet encompasses and projects a series of changes, both in the post-coital moment it sets out from and in the extended simile it develops, introducing the image of the journey in connection with the progression of the day (an image which, as we have seen, is taken up again in 'The Hill Summit'). The rhetorical question the poem begins with already opens a diachronic as well as a synchronic perspective, as the question is not only whether any other woman is thus loved, but also whether any other woman could ever be thus loved, while the second part of the question emphasises this temporal aspect even further: the speaker cannot imagine himself ever satiated with his love for the addressee. The moment the poem chooses to highlight is the moment after the 'fulness of rapture' (l. 3), that is, a moment explicitly determined by what came before and what the future promises. Instead of celebrating the moment itself, the poem is thus, as it were, distended between the fullness of the past and the expectation of future bliss. Within this distended iterative moment, the poem condenses all the 'changeful light of infinite love' (l. 14) which it tropes in terms of both bodily movement through space and the progression of the day.

To consider the different temporal structures made possible by different kinds of mediation is thus a first step to approach the diversity of temporal premises of poetic texts. The suspension of the moment, vertical time, simultaneity of multiple temporalities, iterability, gnomic utterance – aspects of the lyric which have often been highlighted – should, I suggest, be understood as a range of temporal possibilities the lyric mediation offers. Nor should they blind one to an appreciation of dramatic and narrative temporalities in poems. Rather than narrowing down definitions and speaking of lyric and poetic time as something with a unified structure that could easily be opposed to, say, narrative time, my endeavour is to provide ways to address variability and complexity. But mediation is only one level of temporal shaping of poetic texts. A fuller account of poetic time needs further to address the semiotics of time as well as the temporality inherent in the materiality of language.

Semiotics of time

If I speak of a semiotics of time, I propose to analyse the temporal references of a given poem along analogous lines as the analysis of spatial setting. Such a separation of temporal from spatial setting for the sake of analysis still acknowledges their fundamental unity, as spatial and temporal relations constantly interact in the literary text (as, for example, in the journey topos used repeatedly by Rossetti in the poems discussed above). In order to understand the chronotopic shape of a text (*pace* Bakhtin), attention needs to be paid to both its spatial and its temporal aspects, but so far, a differentiated analytical framework for the latter is lacking.[10] Drawing loosely on Jurij Lotman's work on spatial semantics (1977), one can distinguish four aspects of spatial meaning in a literary text: geographical, topographical, topological and semantic. Geographical features situate a space within a relational geographic field, be it with reference to real-world geography, or with reference to the wider geography of a fictional world. They place a setting on a real or a fictional map. Topographical features distinguish between different kinds of spaces (for example city, bedroom, hill summit). Topological features denote the relative qualities of a setting, like inside versus outside, high versus low, centre versus margin, and so on. Finally, such different spatial features accrue different kinds of semantic import, some of which are historically and culturally determined and some of which may be developed within the individual text. Thus, individual spaces or spatial features can be charged with meanings like dangerous or safe, they can be gendered, or associated with particular fictional characters or sets of characters, and so on. I would argue that a closely analogous framework may help to investigate temporal references of literary texts, focusing on what I call historical, chronographical, chronorelational and semantic features respectively.

1. *Historical:* in analogy to the location of a place within a geographical space, temporal references in a literary text can be historically located, situating the text in relation to some real-world historical moment. Alternatively, a literary text might establish its own time frame within which the events referred to are temporally embedded. Historical features of time references thus define events in relation to an established chronology.
2. *Chronographical:* in analogy with the topography of literary space, one could speak of the chronography of literary time, which would take different kinds of time into view (for example different seasons, different passages of human life, like childhood or age, different times of the day, future/present/past, and so on).
3. *Chronorelational:* parallel to topology, and to avoid the misleading term 'chronology', one may, perhaps, speak of chronorelational features, which refer to relative temporal aspects like fast or slow, long or brief, new/young or old, eternal or transient, and so on.
4. *Semantic:* finally, all of these aspects can be semantically charged in various ways, both conventionally and specifically by the text in which they occur. Childhood, for example, conventionally implies happiness, innocence and affinity with nature at least since the Romantics, but individual texts may work with or against this semantic charge.

This conceptual framework, I propose, is broadly applicable to all literary texts, not just poetry. Yet, it is especially helpful to highlight temporal concerns even in such apparently 'timeless' texts as lyric poems with zero temporal layers. To illustrate this, let me return again to sonnet LXII, 'The Soul's Sphere', which I have already briefly discussed above. The sonnet's title draws on a spatial metaphor which embraces both the poem's alleged theme and, self-referentially, the sonnet itself. A sphere is a perfectly round form with clearly defined boundaries. In its perfect wholeness it shows a significant family resemblance to the idea of the well-wrought urn which was later to become a defining metaphor for the formalist version of the Aesthetics of Self-sufficient Form. Moreover, the sphere is a container: it contains the (infinite, immortal) soul – the perfect form is thus filled with perfect timelessness. Instead of delivering the title's promise of containment and timelessness, however, the poem immediately begins to put the image of the self-contained sphere into question and to steep it in temporality. It does so by setting temporal semantics to play in productive tensions.

The first quatrain evokes two images: the moon, imprisoned in 'steep cloud-fastnesses' (l. 1) and the 'dying sun'. With these images, the octet establishes a chronographical imagery of the diurnal cycle which it continues to adhere to with the reference to the 'lamentable night' of the second quatrain (l. 7). In their accumulation, these images emphasise, chronorelationally, the cyclical and continual movement of the heavenly bodies and therewith the succession of day and night. Semantically, however, the poem at first seeks to resist this connotation. The moon is 'prisoned' and 'thralled', the sun is 'dying', lying on a 'pyre / Blazed with momentous memorable fire' (ll. 3–4). Movement, in particular the movement of time, is restrained and locked in the image with which the yearning heart of line 4 is fed. In a semantic and phonetic echo of the introductory sonnet, these images freeze a moment into a memorial. And nonetheless, as is the case for the introductory sonnet, this freezing cannot escape time; indeed, temporal passage is inscribed deeply into the images themselves. The sun's fire is 'momentous' (l. 3), present for only a moment, and it depends on the sun's 'dying' (l. 2), a process that cannot be translated into a timeless state. The moon's cloudy prison, too, is as short-lived as it is insubstantial, and the 'cloud-fastnesses' (l. 1), for all their apparent hold on the moon, also hint at the speed of cloud movement and thus at the transience of the apparent imprisonment.

If the first quatrain projects images that endeavour to still time in order to feed the heart's yearning, the next quatrain turns this yearning into its opposite. In the 'sleepless' night, one hopes to stop the flow of images that prevents rest, 'to appease / Tragical shadow's realm of sound and sight' (ll. 5–6). The chronorelational implications of diurnal periodicity which the first quatrain seems to resist would here be welcomed, but the wished-for passing of the night is prevented, not by the timelessness of the image or sphere, but by the continual succession of images themselves: 'Lo! the soul's sphere of infinite images!' (l. 8). The sphere is anything but timeless. If John Keats's urn famously freezes its series of images on its surface into a timeless 'Cold Pastoral' which will outlive generations ('Ode on a Grecian Urn' ll. 45–7), the soul's sphere is the opposite: it is an infinite succession of images, extending in and through time.

This idea is emphasised and further developed in the sestet. 'What sense shall count them?' (l. 9) the sestet asks and makes clear that such counting would be a question of succession, not simultaneity, and that it embraces 'Visions of golden futures' (l. 12) as well as 'that last / Wild pageant of the accumulated past / That clangs and flashes for a drowning man' (ll. 12–14). Chronographically, the sestet thus leaves the diurnal cycle behind and turns to the course of a human life. In terms of chronorelations, this is a significant shift. The dying sun of the octet holds out the expectation of the sun's eventual return in the morning, for all the endless-seeming sleepless night. The drowning man with whom the poem concludes holds out no such promise. The individual human life, with its hopeful expectations and its regrets, is irremediably linear in its temporal progression. Moreover, the images of stilled time with which the poem began are replaced in the sestet with temporal projections of the future and of the past. The soul's sphere, rather than being a serene form of timeless stillness – a promise the prisoned moon still seemed to hold – emerges from this poem as a teeming hotpot of whirling temporality.

In highlighting the complex interactions between the different levels of the semiotics of time, the categories I have introduced above can thus help to sharpen critical perspective when addressing poems. In particular because of the widely prevalent prejudice about lyric timelessness, temporal semantics might easily be neglected, especially in poems which initially seem to confirm the prejudice. The worth of the framework thus lies entirely in its promise as a heuristic tool which makes temporal aspects of poems (or, indeed, any literary text) more easily available for investigation and interpretation.

Poetic language

As much as an individual poem might aim to escape from time, its medium is irremediably temporal. No poem can avoid this kind of temporality as long as it still involves language which needs to be processed by the reader in time – although some concrete poetry may approach, or even cross the border into, pictorial art. As Cameron notes, language cannot escape temporality, and she discerns a 'crucial relationship between the ability to speak at all and an indispensable sense of time' (1979: 20). Thus, her discussion of lyric time is premised on the basic assumption that 'the relationship between the parts of a poem is inevitably a temporal relationship' (18). Language, and literary language in particular, not only unfolds in time but also gives shape to time in specific ways. That is, on the level of language use itself, even before entering questions of reference, address or rhetoric, texts take temporal forms. Poetry is the genre in which this level of temporal shaping comes most prominently to the fore, because, as Roman Jakobson (1960) has argued, in poetic language the poetic function dominates; that is, poetic language self-referentially draws attention to the poem's own linguistic realisation. Moreover, Jakobson anchors the poetic function of language in structures of repetition (or parallelism); that is, in a structural principle that emphasises temporality.[11] One should not lose sight of the fact that all language necessarily shapes time in some way. Poetry, however, is particularly suited for letting language's processes of giving form to time take centre stage.

What I am aiming at here is the specificity of poetic language, that is, verse. However, I would like to insist that this perspective does not juxtapose the form of verse to an alleged formlessness of prose. Rather, I agree with Susan Wolfson who points out:

> prose, too, involves form, but the modalities – macro-structures of plot or argument, medial structuring in paragraphs, local syntaxes and verbal patterns – do not confer the kind of discursive identity inscribed by poetic forms. Poetry is precisely, and inescapably, defined by its formed language and its formal commitments. (1997: 3)

Prose, too, shapes time in particular ways, regardless of its referential content, and prose, too, can develop very different senses of rhythm. Therefore, even with my focus on the role of verse, prose poetry is no contradiction in terms within my framework. Prose, free or metrical verse, specific line or stanza structures, punctuation or no punctuation, parataxis or hypotaxis: all these are stylistic decisions which will influence the kind of temporal shape a poem (or, for that matter, any kind of literary text) takes. And yet, if there is a fundamental difference between poetic and prosaic time structures, it would lie here: in the importance of recurrence (Jakobson's parallelism) in verse (*vertere* = to turn) and the emphasis on progression in prose (*proversus* = turning forward).

My proposition amounts to a different perspective on well-established practices of poetic criticism. Analysis of rhythmical and rhyme structure, as well as of the interplay of line and syntax, is a staple element in the interpretation of poems. Yet, what is rarely emphasised nowadays is that all this works in and with time; in fact, structures of repetition are frequently identified as central to the poetic illusion of timelessness (Schlaffer 2015: 84; Thain 2016: 62–3; Tucker 1997). Repetition, however, depends on temporal succession. What is resisted by poetic form then, as Schlaffer correctly notes, is 'physical time, which only runs in one direction, always onwards' (2015: 84; my translation), but his own comparison of poetic movement to a dance might have alerted him to the fact that poetic time follows a different logic, but one that is no less temporal. Repetitions of rhyme, rhythm, syntax and line structures give even the most 'timeless' poem (in whatever sense) a specific temporal signature. As I have demonstrated in Chapter 4, Victorians knew this well. 'Rhythm of any sort is impossible, except through the co-ordination of time,' noted Sydney Lanier (1894: 65), and, as we have seen, some forty years earlier E. S. Dallas put it even more pithily: 'metre in its simplest form [is] time heard' (1852: 164).

Of course, poetic practice has changed significantly over the course of the last 150 years, and metrical verse, which both Lanier and Dallas assumed to be essential to poetic composition, is no longer the norm for contemporary poetry. If a consideration of the temporal structure of poetic language aims to be flexible enough to embrace more recent forms of poetic production, its analytical categories need to be broadened. I would suggest that it is possible to discern three interconnected aspects of temporal shaping in poetic language: rhythm, rhyme and segmentivity. All three of these are, fundamentally, forms of repetition with variation. Rhythm is a repetition of beats or stresses, rhyme is a repetition of sounds, segmentivity is a repetition of pauses.

As I have argued in Chapter 4, I take the supposed difference between metre and rhythm to be the result of historically rooted processes of temporal abstraction. My understanding of rhythm, then, encompasses both regularity and variation, as rhythm presumes the presence of some sort of recognisable pattern of repetition, but has significant leeway for variation. Metrical poetry is simply defined by a comparatively regular rhythmic structure. In speaking of rhyme, I would like to marshal Valentine Cunningham's very broad definition as 'the repeating of verbal items of any and every kind. Of everything commonly included in "rhyme" – phrases, words, bits of words, the sounds repeated at the ends of lines – but also what's ordinarily separated out as alliteration (front-rhyme) and assonance (middle-rhyme)' as well as 'refrains, burdens' (2011: 59). As such, rhyme has a double temporal pull. As Veronica Alfonso notes, it 'combines progress and delay, anticipation and nostalgia; it may propel a sentence forward by predicting its own future reiterations, but it may also cue readers to recall and return to previous lines' (2017: 16). In contrast to Cunningham, however, I consider metre and stanza structures separately, the first under the aspect of rhythm, the latter as one element of segmentivity. I take the term 'segmentivity' from Brian McHale, who, in turn, elaborates on and fuses ideas developed by Rachel DuPlessis and John Shoptaw. Poetry, according to DuPlessis, depends on 'the ability to articulate and make meaning by selecting, deploying, and combining segments' and involves 'the creation of meaningful sequence by the negotiation of gap (line break, stanza break, page space)' (qtd in McHale 2009: 14). McHale brings DuPlessis's idea into fruitful conversation with Shoptaw's concept of countermeasure. With Shoptaw, McHale identifies different scales of poetic measure: the foot, the word, the phrase, the line, the sentence, the stanza, the poem section. These different measures, importantly, interact with each other: 'in many, perhaps most instances, measure at one level or scale is played off against measure at another level or scale' (McHale 2009: 17). Moreover, I would add, segmentivity also enters into a productive interplay with rhyme and rhythm. Rhythm and rhyme condition us to identify patterns and to expect a return of the same; they are what 'induces us to *lean forward* in anticipation of the completion of the pattern, or its repetition (the *next* foot, the *next* line, etc.), on the other side of the break' (McHale 2014: 285).[12] Segmentivity introduces this break; it provides the (infinitesimal) interruption that structures the pattern of return. Thus rhythm, rhyme and segmentivity depend on each other. They can interact in multiple ways in different kinds of texts (including prose or dramatic texts). Specific poetic forms often depend on set patterns of combination. Strict verse forms like the heroic couplet, for example, prescribe a pattern for rhythm (iambic pentameter), rhyme (end-rhymed couplets) and segmentivity on the scale of the phrase (end-stopped lines), although, of course, these still allow for complex interrelations and countermeasures on different scales of segmentivity, for rhythmic variation and internal rhyming.

If the interplay of these three elements is what Thain (albeit referring only to metre) has called 'poetry's self-conscious awareness of its existence in time', it is also what enables some lyric poems to establish the illusion of timelessness in the perfect form (2016: 55). Referring to the highly formalised verse of Parnassian poetry, Thain suggest that

> the high degree of internal patterning and complexity in these forms offers the potential for an illusion that, at a formal level, no time passes over the course of the poem. These short, strict-form structures seem to depend on holding together many images synchronically within the poem even though they appear textually in diachronic sequence. Rhyme, as well as rhythm, is often a key component in achieving this illusion, with end-rhymes across the length of the lyric asserting temporal identity. (2016: 62).

Such illusion of simultaneity, however, is not a necessary effect of formalised poetry, but only one of many possible poetic aims and achievements. After all, repetition can serve to emphasise variation and temporal diversity as much as sameness and temporal identity. The point is, then, that the effect of the interaction between rhythm, rhyme and segmentivity is not generally predictable; it is not 'theoretically invariant', as Tucker holds (1997: 276). Instead, it is differently realised in different poetic forms and even in individual poems.

Of course, critics and readers have always been aware of the capacity of rhythm, for example, to speed up or to slow down; the way in which enjambment, say, can bring the countermeasure of line and syntax into productive tension, hurrying a reader into the next line; how caesuras or rhythmical anomalies can seem to slow the poem down; or how rhyme can serve to create onward momentum across stanza breaks in forms like the *terza rima*, in which the desire for the return of the rhyme may drive the reader breathlessly onward. Even Alfonso, who insists on lyric's atemporality, shows herself sensitively aware of the way rhyme both presses forward and doubles back, or the 'start-and-restart' of stanzas or individual lines (2017: 16). Her emphasis on atemporality makes her description of these processes sound strangely pejorative, however. Rhyme 'may cause the verse to double back upon itself, undermining its efforts to advance toward new thoughts and new events'; stanzas 'generate memorably autonomous hesitations and suspensions that impede the arc of plot' and this 'internal discontinuity' is associated with a poem's alleged 'origins in frustrated action' and 'often prevent[s] it from sustaining a cohesive storyline' (2017: 16). 'Undermine', 'impede', 'prevent', 'frustrated': such descriptions pitch the lyric as a deviation against a norm of a 'cohesive' temporality of plot and ascribe an inherent value to the progressive logic of plot's infatuation with the ever new. To avoid such assignations, I want to draw attention to the way rhyme, rhythm and segmentivity are themselves essentially temporal features that should be considered as alternatives to, rather than deviations from, the time of plot or prose. I thus aim to emphasise, once again, that no poetry, not even lyric poetry, is generically timeless, but rather that a poem's temporal shaping well rewards close critical attention.

To briefly return to sonnet LXII, 'The Soul's Sphere', in this context, one might note that the forms of temporal movement the Italian sonnet form generally affords are largely determined by its asymmetry, its strong sense of segmentivity in the volta and the division between quatrains and tercets, and by the change in rhyme sounds from octet to sestet. In sonnet LXII, for example, Rossetti significantly varies the usual rhyme scheme of the octet from abbaabba to abba'a'b'b'a, with a and a' being half-rhymes based on consonance and b and b' half-rhymes based on assonance. As the return of the first rhyme-sound is delayed to the conclusion of the octet, the octet rounds into the sphere its last line evokes ('Lo! the soul's sphere of infinite images!'), trying to contain it like the sphere of the moon within its cloud-prison – the 'Throned queen and thralled' of line 2 – who is also hemmed in by the surrounding strong alliteration of 'throned' and 'thralled'. However, this self-containment of the octet then spills into the sestet, in which the images can no longer be restrained or fixed in a moment. The open vowel sounds of the rhymes in the sestet culminate in the assonances of the final tercet: 'that last / Wild pageant of the accumulated past / That clangs and flashes for a drowning man'. In these lines, the stressed return of the same vowel in its insistent repetition no longer establishes a return to an original moment or a 'temporal identity' (Thain 2016: 62), but rather the temporal succession of a returning beat, like a beating heart which stops abruptly with the end of the final verse line.

Conclusion – Imagining Poetic Time

Readers who pick up Rossetti's *The House of Life* taking his introductory sonnet by its word will likely either be disappointed in their expectation to find individual moments enshrined, or may fall back on dubious biographical explanations, searching in Rossetti's life for the singular moment they miss in the poems. Or, again, they might follow Carol Christ in arguing that Rossetti 'obscures the particularity of the moment in order to transcend it, to make it infinite' (1975: 111). A sustained look at time structures in the sequence, however, calls the Aesthetics of Self-sufficient Form promoted in the introductory sonnet into question. Instead of putting his own precepts into practice, presenting a series of moments, impearled and immortalised by art, *The House of Life* is exceptional in the temporal variety of its speaking positions, mixing them sometimes even within the same poem (as in the combination of dramatic and singulative lyric in 'A Portrait'). Moreover, those singular moments the sequence does celebrate are all made to feel the pressure of time (as we have seen, for example, in 'Silent Noon'). It is not the moment itself that matters. Rather than celebrating art's capacity to preserve 'as much of the instant as can be retained' (Conners 1982: 32) and presenting life as 'a series of moments to be experienced and then preserved for remembrance' (Conners 1982: 23), *The House of Life* offers sustained meditations on time and the way it can take shape in poetry. These are fragments shored up against the ruins, much more than an art confident of its ability to stop time. Moreover, in spite of the sonnets' insistent tendency to universalise, they refuse to set up a transcendent ideal (so often the focus of sonnet sequences). Nothing evades time. Eternal assurances (God, Love, Art, Beauty, the Soul, Identity . . .) all crumble under the pressure, not of the single sonnet, but of the mass of the entire, complex building of *The House of Life*.

Because of the importance of time to Rossetti's sequence, it lends itself well to the kind of temporal analysis I am promoting here. But my claims are of a more general nature. Like every literary text, poetry unfolds within time and itself gives shape to time. To overlook this is to underestimate the breadth of temporal possibilities that can emerge in aesthetic experience. Ines Detmers and Michael Ostheimer have recently proposed the term 'temporal imaginary' (*das temporale Imaginäre*), drawing on the work of Wolfgang Iser, Mikhail Bakhtin and Paul Ricœur in an endeavour to theoretically grasp the complex interplay between socially established time concepts, individually intuited time experience and aesthetic emergence of temporal forms. They draw up a catalogue of relevant questions that arise in this context:

> Where do societies derive their temporal concepts from? What forms
> the 'temporal clay' out of which social time figures are shaped (aestheti-
> cally)? How do cultural communities manage to collectivise, institution-
> alise and habituate time concepts? That is, how to do they achieve their
> shared recognition, implementation and internalisation? How can we

explain the social integration of successful time cultures? And inversely, how are time cultures and concepts which have become obsolete suspended? (2016: 15; my translation).

Clearly, these questions resonate with the kind of historical perspective with which I have approached Victorian poetry. In the course of this study, we have repeatedly seen how new time concepts invalidate and displace older time cultures, and I have argued throughout that these shifts are inextricably linked with questions of literary form and genre. It is therefore all the more regrettable that Detmers and Ostheimer immediately – that is, already in the third sentence of their introduction – specify that the only kind of aesthetic form they deem relevant to their discussion is narrative. Productive as their intervention may be for the closer analysis of narrative chronotopes, this restriction sets limits on any critical engagement with the important broader questions they raise. These can only begin to be answered if narrative in all the variability of its shapes is still recognised as merely one kind of, and not the only possible, way in which time is aesthetically conceived and shaped.

This recognition, I maintain, is not only necessary if we want to fully understand the 'temporal imaginary' and the way historically and culturally variable time concepts both shape and emerge from aesthetic forms. It is also prerequisite to a critical interrogation and extension of our own temporal preconceptions. Why have we become irresponsive to temporal formations that are not narrative? What are the consequences of this irresponsiveness? What could alternative temporal structures like those I have begun to trace in poetry teach us about different possibilities to shape our relationship to and experience of time? These are the questions which I hope an increased awareness of and attention to poetic time structures will help begin to address.

That these are timely questions in more than one sense emerges not least in the context of ecocriticism. 'The Anthropocene', Tobias Menely notes, 'is, after all, a name for a problem of time, of how we perceive, conceptualize, and give form to temporal heterogeneity in the interface between social systems and planetary systems' (2018: 85). In the context of literature, this environmental challenge to rethink time has been recognised partly as a challenge to narrative, including its dominant time structure. Thus, Amitav Ghosh rejects both the novelistic focus on the development and growth of an individual and, more broadly, the 'idea of a continuous and irreversible forward movement, led by an avant-garde, [which] has been one of the animating forces of the literary and artistic imagination since the start of the twentieth century' (Ghosh 2016: 79).[13] Meanwhile, poetry rises to new prominence, as it has been claimed that 'the true complexity of environmental issues has been perhaps easier to represent in new or revised forms of poetic practice than in prose forms like the novel, short story or the non-fiction essay, or in theatre' (Clark 2019: 59). A conception of poetry that considers it to be 'timeless' in any sense will hardly be able to adequately acknowledge its potential in addressing the most important challenge of our time. A better understanding of the various ways in which poems shape time might fruitfully begin to do so.

Notes

1. In another version of his article, it should be added, in which Oschmann pursues a broader argument about the historical moment at which time-consciousness and form-consciousness begin to interrelate, he still privileges the novel but also references poetry (2016b: 140–1). This bias appears to be endemic. None of the twenty-nine research projects belonging to the research cluster Ästhetische Eigenzeiten considers poetry centrally, and there is generally a clear tendency towards narratives in critical studies of time and literature. In a typical instance, narrative and narratological considerations feature prominently in Thomas Allen's recent Cambridge Critical Concepts volume on *Time and Literature* (2018) while poetry plays a much smaller role.
2. For a nuanced discussion of this issue, see Fludernik (1996: 349–56).
3. Richard Cureton, in his article with the promising title 'Rhythm, Temporality and "Inner Form"', published in *Style* in 2015, attempts to systematise poetic temporality. In its preference for groups of four, however, this proposal, for all its terminological complexity, merely baffles, as Cureton's accumulation of quadratic assignations become both increasingly arbitrary and increasingly constraining. Thus, in his system, 'the canonical lyric poem, which compared to the other literary genres is reflex of centroidal time, is stylistically organic, comedic, logical, synecdochic, rhymed, stanzaic, chiastic, copular, conjunctional, phrasal, adjectival, copular, modifying, present tense, 1st person, imperfective, subjunctive, exclamative, gendered, aspectual, reciprocal, and derivational, with a rise-fall intonation, a prosodic focus on tertiary stress and the clitic phrase, and an imagery that tends to focus on youth, Eden, growth, summer, noon, water, plants, and so forth – a very reasonable characterization' (2015: 98–9). I, for my part, remain unconvinced. Moreover, even if Cureton's categories were less whimsically

cumulative, they would have little heuristic value for the analysis of individual texts.

4. As Jackson and Prins have suggested, 'it may be the case that because we have come to think of all poetry as lyric, we have not really wanted a concise definition of lyric' (2014: 1). It is true that in recent years the endeavour to theorise the lyric has intensified, not only, but very markedly, among German scholars, who find themselves in an academic environment that is particularly amenable to attempts at systematic theorisation (see, for example, Hempfer 2014; Hühn and Kiefer 2005; Müller-Zettelmann 2000; Petzold 2012; Wolf 2005; Zymner 2013). Much of the discussion, however, revolves centrally around the problem of definition and demarcation of what is to be considered 'the lyric' to the exclusion of a further development of analytical tools. Klaus W. Hempfer (2014) provides a concise summary and pertinent critique of the most prominent recent German attempts at defining the lyric. In the Anglo-American context the debate has recently been dominated by the disagreement between those who, like Jonathan Culler, maintain that there is a transhistorical category of the lyric that bears theorisation and those who, like Virginia Jackson, stress the historical dimension in order to question the validity of the lyric as a genre *tout court*.

5. Monika Fludernik notes that Stanzel is an exception, since his narrative situations 'trace a historical development from the predominance of first-person narrative and authorial narrative to the invention of figural, i.e. reflectoral, narrative in the late nineteenth-century novel and its eventual hegemony in the Modernist canon' (1996: 314). In Stanzel's influence on narratology, this diachronic perspective is largely lost from view in favour of a synchronic application of this system of narrative situations. Of course, Fludernik herself also develops her radical redefinition of narrative on the basis of experientiality with a historical perspective in view.

6. See, for example, David Rudrum's argument that we should understand narrative as 'more a contextual than a textual property' (2005: 198). Of course, Stanley Fish had already said the same about poetry a couple of decades earlier (Fish 1980).

7. In an article version of this chapter published in German (Huber 2021), I apply the same analytical framework to sonnets by Rainer Maria Rilke.

8. I should emphasise again that I am speaking here of prototypical structures, which can be differently manipulated by different literary texts. Individual dramas may well include narrative temporal structures, just as individual poems may play equally with lyric, narrative and dramatic kinds of temporal mediation.

9. One might compare this to Browning's 'My Last Duchess'. In that poem, the description of the portrait is entirely embedded in, and motivated by, the dramatic situation the poem develops.

10. Pfister, who, in a different context, draws attention to the need to consider a semiotics of time in analogy to a semiotics of space in literary analysis discusses the former only cursorily, while devoting several sub-chapters to the latter (2001: 339–45; 367–9).

11. Intriguingly, Jakobson's most important source for this claim is the Victorian poet Gerald Manley Hopkins. As Holt Meyer points out, however, Jakobson's structuralist endeavour made him blind to cultural contexts, and in the case of Hopkins in particular, to the metaphysical charge of the poet's ideas about rhyme and rhythm (Meyer 2003). Instead of dissolving difference into a common principle of 'parallelism', the aim, I suggest, should be to begin from this common principle, in order to take into account culturally and historically determined charges of poetic forms.

12. McHale is particularly concerned with the interplay between poetic and narrative segmentivity, that is, the relation between poetic segments like the line, and narrative segments like events and point of view. On the role of segmentivity in drama, see Pfister (2001: 307–18).

13. See also Barri J. Gold (2021), who develops this argument in detail for the specific context of the nineteenth-century novel.

Works Cited

The Poet of the Age: A Satirical Poem with Introductory Remarks on the Decline of Poetry, and Critical Notes. 1842. London: Robert Hardwicke.

'The Poetry of a Steam-Engine.' 1844. *Chambers's Edinburgh Journal*, no. 21: 336.

'The Poetry of Alfred Tennyson.' 1845. *Chambers's Edinburgh Journal*, no. 80: 25–9.

'Art. II. – *Poems*. By Alfred Tennyson.' 1845. *The British Quarterly Review* 2 (3): 46–71.

'*Poems*. By Elizabeth Barrett.' 1845. *The British Quarterly Review* 2 (4): 337–52.

'Poetry in All Things.' 1846. *Chambers's Edinburgh Journal*, no. 118: 209–11.

'The Princess. A Medley.' 1848. *Examiner*, no. 2048: 20–1.

'Art. II – *The Roman: A Dramatic Poem*. By Sydney Yendys.' 1850. *The Eclectic Review* no. 27: 627–84.

'Poetry on the Railway.' 1855. *Household Words* 11 (271): 414–18.

'Aurora Leigh.' 1856. *Athenaeum* no. 1517: 1425–7.

'Robert Browning's Poems.' 1863. *The London Review of Politics, Society, Literature, Art, and Science* 1 (168): 310–11.

'Book Review.' 1881. *Athenaeum*, no. 2812: 361.

'Eugene Onéguine.' 1881. *Saturday Review of Politics, Literature, Science and Art* 52 (1352): 396–7.

'Rhythm.' 1883. *The Saturday Review* 55 (1427): 270–1.

Adam, Barbara. 2004. *Time*. Cambridge and Malden, MA: Polity.

Adelman, Richard. 2011. *Idleness, Contemplation and the Aesthetic, 1750–1830*. Cambridge: Cambridge University Press.

Adelman, Richard. 2018. *Idleness and Aesthetic Consciousness, 1815–1900*. Cambridge: Cambridge University Press.

Adorno, Theodor. 2014. 'On Lyric Poetry and Society.' [1957]. Translated by Shierry Weber Nicholson, in *the Lyric Theory Reader: A Critical Anthology*, edited by Virginia W. Jackson and Yopie Prins, 339–50. Baltimore, MD: Johns Hopkins University Press.

Alber, Jan. 2002. 'The "Moreness" or "Lessness" of "Natural" Narratology: Samuel Beckett's Lessness Reconsidered.' *Style* 36 (1): 54–75.

Alfano, Veronica. 2017. *The Lyric in Victorian Memory: Poetic Remembering and Forgetting from Tennyson to Housman*. Basingstoke: Palgrave Macmillan.

Allen, Thomas M., ed. 2018. *Time and Literature*. Cambridge: Cambridge University Press.

Allingham, William. 1867. 'On Poetry.' *Fraser's Magazine for Town and Country* 448 (75): 523–36.

Allingham, William. 1884. 'Is Idleness Indeed. . .' In *Blackberries: Picked Off Many Bushes*, 162. London: G. Philip & Son.

Altick, Richard. 1973. *Victorian People and Ideas*. London: WW Norton & Company.

Ammon, Frieder von. 2020. 'Zweierlei Zeit? Überlegungen zur Zeitstruktur von Gedichten.' In *Grundfragen der Lyrikologie 2: Begriffe, Methoden und Analysedimensionen*, edited by Claudia Hillebrandt, Sonja Klimek, Ralph Müller and Rüdiger Zymner, 235–50. Boston, MA: de Gruyter.

Anderson, Alexander. 1881. *Songs of the Rail*. [1878]. London: Simpkin, Marshall, & Co.

Anderson, Alexander. 1912. 'No Room for the Poet.' In *Later Poems of Alexander Anderson 'Surfaceman'*, edited by Alexander Brown, 240–1. Glasgow, Dalbeattie: Fraser, Asher Co. Limited.

Armstrong, Isobel, ed. 1972. *Victorian Scrutinies: Reviews of Poetry 1830–1870*. London: Athlone.

Armstrong, Isobel. 1993. *Victorian Poetry: Poetry, Poetics and Politics*. London: Routledge.

Armstrong, Isobel. 2011a. 'Hegel: The Time of Rhythm, the Time of Rhyme.' *Thinking Verse* vol. 1: 124–36.

Armstrong, Isobel. 2011b. 'Meter and Meaning.' In *Meter Matters: Verse Cultures of the Long Nineteenth Century*, edited by Jason D. Hall, 26–52. Athens, OH: Ohio University Press.

Arnold, Matthew. 1888. 'The Study of Poetry.' In *Essays in Criticism: Second Series*, 1–55. London: Macmillan.

Arnold, Matthew. 1968. *The Letters of Matthew Arnold to Arthur Hugh Clough*. Edited by Howard F. Lowry. Oxford: Clarendon Press.

Arnold, Matthew. 1979. *The Poems of Matthew Arnold*. 2nd edn. Edited by Kenneth Allott and Miriam F. Allott. London: Longman.

Arnold, Matthew. 2005. 'The Function of Criticism at the Present Time.' [1865]. In *The Broadview Anthology of Victorian Poetry and Poetic Theory*, edited by Thomas J. Collins and Vivienne Rundle, 616–32. Peterborough, Ont.: Broadview Press.

Assmann, Aleida. 2013. *Ist die Zeit aus den Fugen? Aufstieg und Fall des Zeitregimes der Moderne*. Munich: Hanser.

Attridge, Derek. 1995. *Poetic Rhythm: An Introduction*. Cambridge: Cambridge University Press.

Augustine. 1991. *Confessions* [c. 397–400]. Translated by Henry Chadwick. Oxford: Oxford University Press.

Aviram, Amittai. 1994. *Telling Rhythm: Body and Meaning in Poetry.* Ann Arbour, MI: University of Michigan Press.

Bagehot, Walter. 1862. 'Mr. Clough's Poems.' *The National Review* no. 30: 310–26.

Bailey, Peter. 1987. *Leisure and Class in Victorian England: Rational Recreation and the Contest for Control, 1830–1885.* London: Methuen.

Bain, Alexander. 1887. *On Teaching English: With Detailed Examples, and an Enquiry into the Definition of Poetry.* London: Longmans, Green, & Co.

Barlow, George. 1902–14a. 'Poetry and Science.' In *The Poetical Works.* 10 vols, 109–11. London: Glaisher.

Barlow, George. 1902–14b. 'The Gospel of Science.' In *The Poetical Works.* 10 vols, 171–6. London: Glaisher.

Bartky, Ian R. 2007. *One Time Fits All: The Campaigns for Global Uniformity.* Stanford, CA: Stanford University Press.

Baudelaire, Charles. 1964. 'The Painter of Modern Life.' [1863]. In *The Painter of Modern Life, and Other Essays*, edited and translated by Jonathan Mayne, 1–40. London: Phaidon Press.

Bedingfield, Richard. 1847. 'Ideal Poetry, and the Poetry of Drama.' *Richard Hood's Magazine* 8 (2): 142–5.

Beer, Gillian. 1983. *Darwin's Plot and Nineteenth-Century Fiction.* London: Routledge & Kegan Paul.

Benjamin, Walter. 1999. *Illuminations.* [1940]. Translated by H. Arendt. London: Random House.

Berger, Karol. 2002. *A Theory of Art.* Oxford: Oxford University Press.

Bies, Michael, Sean Franzel and Dirk Oschmann. 2017. 'Einleitung.' In *Flüchtigkeit der Moderne: Eigenzeiten des Ephemeren im langen 19. Jahrhundert*, edited by Michael Bies, Sean Franzel and Dirk Oschmann, 7–16. Hanover: Wehrhahn Verlag.

Billone, Amy Christine. 2007. *Little Songs: Women, Silence, and the Nineteenth-Century Sonnet.* Columbus, OH: Ohio State University Press.

Blair, Kirstie. 2006. *Victorian Poetry and the Culture of the Heart.* Oxford: Clarendon Press.

Blair, Kirstie. 2009. '"Men, my brothers, men the workers": Tennyson and the Victorian Working-Class Poets.' In *Tennyson Among the Poets*, edited by Robert Douglas-Fairhurst and Seamus Perry, 276–98. Oxford: Oxford University Press.

Blair, Kirstie. 2012. *Form and Faith in Victorian Poetry and Religion.* Oxford: Oxford University Press.

Blair, Kirstie. 2014. 'Inhuman Rhythms: Working-Class Railway Poets and the Measure of Industry.' *Victorian Review* 40 (1): 35–9.

Blake, Kathleen. 1986. 'Elizabeth Barrett Browning and Wordsworth: The Romantic Poet as a Woman.' *Victorian Poetry* 24 (4): 387–98.

Blasing, Mutlu Konuk. 2007. *Lyric Poetry: The Pain and the Pleasure of Words.* Princeton, NJ, and Woodstock: Princeton University Press.

Bonus, Alexander Evan. 'Metronome.' *Oxford Handbooks Online*. https://www.oxfordhandbooks.com/view/10.1093/oxfordhb/9780199935321.001.0001/oxfordhb-9780199935321-e-001. Accessed 28 April 2020.

Boos, Florence Saunders. 2002. 'General Introduction.' In *the Earthly Paradise*, edited by Florence S. Boos, 3–41. New York and London: Routledge.

Bradley, Andrew C. 1884. *The Study of Poetry: A Lecture*. London and Cambridge: Macmillan.

Bradley, Andrew C. 1901. *Poetry for Poetry's Sake: An Inaugural Lecture, Delivered on June 5, 1901*. Oxford: Clarendon Press.

Brewster, Scott. 2009. *Lyric*. London: Routledge.

Bristow, Joseph. 1995. '"Love, Let Us Be True to One Another": Matthew Arnold, Arthur Hugh Clough, and "Our Aqueous Ages".' *Literature & History* 4 (1): 27–49.

Bronfen, Elisabeth. 1992. *Over Her Dead Body: Death, Femininity and the Aesthetic*. Manchester: Manchester University Press.

Brooks, Peter. 1984. *Reading for the Plot: Design and Intention in Narrative*. Oxford: Clarendon Press.

Brown, Daniel. 2013. *The Poetry of Victorian Scientists: Style, Science and Nonsense*. Cambridge: Cambridge University Press.

Browning, Elizabeth Barrett and Robert Browning. 1991. *The Brownings' Correspondence*. Edited by Kelley Phillip and Scott Lewis. Winfield, KS: Wedgestone Press.

Browning, Robert. 1961. *The Ring and the Book*. [1868]. New York: Norton.

Brush, Stephen G. 1977. *The Temperature of History: Phases of Science and Culture in the Nineteenth Century*. New York: B. Franklin.

Buckler, William E. 1982. *On the Poetry of Matthew Arnold: Essays in Critical Reconstruction*. New York: New York University Press.

Buckley, Jerome H. 1966. *The Triumph of Time: A Study of the Victorian Concepts of Time, History, Progress and Decadence*. Cambridge, MA: Harvard University Press.

Bulwer Lytton, Edward Robert. 1868. 'A Man of Science or the Botanist's Grave.' In *Chronicles and Characters*. 2 vols, vol. 2, 317–35. London: Chapman and Hall.

Bump, Jerome. 2004. 'The Victorian Radicals: Time, Typology, and Ontology in Hopkins, Pusey, and Müller.' In *Victorian Religious Discourse: New Directions in Criticism*, edited by Jude V. Nixon, 27–49. New York and Basingstoke: Palgrave Macmillan.

Byron, Glennis. 2003. *Dramatic Monologue*. London: Routledge.

Cameron, Sharon. 1979. *Lyric Time: Dickinson and the Limits of Genre*. Baltimore, MD: Johns Hopkins University Press.

Campbell, Matthew. 2011. 'The Victorian Sonnet.' In *The Cambridge Companion to the Sonnet*, edited by A. D. Cousins and Peter Howarth, 204–24. Cambridge: Cambridge University Press.

Carroll, Joseph. 2004. *Literary Darwinism: Evolution, Human Nature, and Literature*. New York: Routledge.

Castoriadis, Cornelius. 1987. *The Imaginary Institution of Society*. [1975]. Translated by K. Blamey. Cambridge, MA: MIT Press.

Chapman, Alison. 2002. 'Sonnet and Sonnet Sequence.' In *A Companion to Victorian Poetry*, edited by Richard Cronin, Alison Chapman and Antony H. Harrison, 99–114. Malden, MA, and Oxford: Blackwell.

Chapman, Raymond. 1986. *The Sense of the Past in Victorian Literature*. London: Croom Helm.

Charles, Elizabeth Rundle. 1887. 'A Journey on the South-Devon Railway.' In *Songs Old and New*, 329–31. London: T. Nelson and Sons.

Choi, Tina Young, and Barbara Leckie. 2018. 'Slow Causality: The Function of Narrative in an Age of Climate Change.' *Victorian Studies* 60 (4): 565–87.

Christ, Carol T. 1975. *The Finer Optic: The Aesthetic of Particularity in Victorian Poetry*. New Haven, CT: Yale University Press.

Christ, Carol T. 1984. *Victorian and Modern Poetics*. Chicago, IL: University of Chicago Press.

Clark, Timothy. 2019. *The Value of Ecocriticism*. Cambridge: Cambridge University Press.

Clough, Arthur Hugh. 1869. '*Dispychus*.' In *The Poems and Prose Remains of Arthur Hugh Clough: With a Selection from His Letters and a Memoir*, edited by his Wife. 2 vols, 109–73. London: Macmillan and Co.

Clough, Arthur Hugh. 2003. *Selected Poems*. Edited by Shirley Chew. New York: Routledge.

Clough, Arthur Hugh. 2005. 'Recent English Poetry: A Review of Several Volumes of Poems by Alexander Smith, Matthew Arnold, and Others.' [1855]. In *The Broadview Anthology of Victorian Poetry and Poetic Theory*, edited by Thomas J. Collins and Vivienne Rundle, 582–97. Peterborough, Ont.: Broadview Press.

Clune, Michael W. 2018. 'Time and Aesthetics.' In *Time and Literature*, edited by Thomas M. Allen, 17–30. Cambridge: Cambridge University Press.

Coleridge, Samuel Taylor. 1907. 'Definition of Poetry.' [1836]. In *Coleridge's Essays & Lectures on Shakespeare & Some Other Old Poets & Dramatists*, edited by Ernest Rhys, 9–13. London: J. M. Dent & Sons.

Colley, Ann C. 1998. *Nostalgia and Recollection in Victorian Culture*. New York: St. Martin's Press.

Colman, Adam. 2019. *Drugs and the Addiction Aesthetic in Nineteenth-Century Literature*. Basingstoke: Palgrave Macmillan.

Connor, Steven. 1984. '"Speaking Likenesses": Language and Repetition in Christina Rossetti's "Goblin Market".' *Victorian Poetry* 22 (4): 439–48.

Cook, Eliza. 2000. 'A Song for the Workers.' In *The Victorians: An Anthology of Poetry & Poetics*, edited by Valentine Cunningham, 437–8. Oxford: Blackwell.

Craik, George L. 1863. *A Compendious History of English Literature and of the English Language: From the Norman Conquest, with Numerous Specimens.* 2 vols. New York: Charles Scribner.

Culler, A. Dwight. 1975. 'Monodrama and the Dramatic Monologue.' *PMLA* 90 (3): 366.

Culler, Jonathan D. 1981. 'Apostrophe.' In *The Pursuit of Signs: Semiotics, Literature, Deconstruction*, 135–54. London: Routledge & Kegan Paul.

Culler, Jonathan D. 2008. 'Why Lyric?' *PMLA* 123 (1): 201–6.

Culler, Jonathan D. 2018. *Theory of the Lyric.* Cambridge, MA: Harvard University Press.

Cunningham, Hugh. 1980. *Leisure in the Industrial Revolution, c. 1780–c. 1880.* London: Croom Helm.

Cunningham, Valentine. 2011. *Victorian Poetry Now: Poets, Poems, Poetics.* Oxford: Wiley-Blackwell.

Cureton, Richard. 2015. 'Rhythm, Temporality, and "Inner Form".' *Style* 49 (1): 78–109.

D. C. L. 1873. 'A Reply to the *Quarterly Review* on the Present State of English Poetry.' *The St. James's Magazine* (12): 261–71.

Dallas, Eneas Sweetland. 1852. *Poetics: An Essay on Poetry.* London: Smith, Elder, & Co.

Dallas, Eneas Sweetland. 2011. 'The Gay Science, 2 Vols. (London: Chapman & Hall, 1866), Vol. 1, pp. 3–6, 47–65, 68–72.' In *Negotiating Boundaries*, edited by Piers J. Hale. Victorian Literature and Science vol. 1, 95–108. London: Pickering & Chatto.

Daly, Nicholas. 2004. *Literature, Technology, and Modernity, 1860–2000.* Cambridge: Cambridge University Press.

D'Amico, Diane. 1999. *Christina Rossetti: Faith, Gender, and Time.* Baton Rouge, LA: Louisiana State University Press.

Daston, Lorraine, and Peter Galison. 2007. *Objectivity.* New York: Zone.

Dawson, Gowan, and Bernard V. Lightman. 2011. 'General Introduction.' In *Negotiating Boundaries*, edited by Piers J. Hale. Victorian Literature and Science vol. 1, vii–xix. London: Pickering & Chatto.

Detmers, Ines, and Michael Ostheimer. 2016. *Das temporale Imaginäre: Zum Chronotopos als Paradigma literaturästhetischer Eigenzeiten.* Hanover: Wehrhahn Verlag.

Dickens, Charles. 1848. *Dombey and Son.* London: Bradbury and Evans.

Dobell, Sydney. 1876. 'Lecture on "The Nature of Poetry".' [1857]. In *Thoughts on Art, Philosophy, and Religion: Selected from the Unpublished Papers of Sydney Dobell*, edited by John Nichol, 3–64. London: Smith, Elder, & Co.

Dobson, Austin. 1885. 'On the Hurry of This Time.' In *At the Sign of the Lyre.* London: Kegan Paul, Trench & Co.

Dubrow, Heather. 2006. 'The Interplay of Narrative and Lyric: Competition, Cooperation, and the Case of the Anticipatory Amalgam.' *Narrative* 14 (3): 254–71.

DuPlessis, Rachel Blau. 2006. *Blue Studios: Poetry and Its Cultural Work.* Tuscaloosa, AL: University of Alabama Press.

Ehnes, Caley. 2019. *Victorian Poetry and the Poetics of the Literary Periodical.* Edinburgh: Edinburgh University Press.

Erchinger, Philipp. 2018. *Artful Experiments: Ways of Knowing in Victorian Literature and Science.* Edinburgh: Edinburgh University Press.

Evans, Anne. 1998. 'Over!'. In *The Penguin Book of Victorian Verse*, edited by Daniel Karlin, 352. London and New York: Penguin Books.

Faas, Ekbert. 1988. *Retreat into the Mind: Victorian Poetry and the Rise of Psychiatry.* Princeton, NJ, and Oxford: Princeton University Press.

Felluga, Dino. 2002. 'Verse Novel.' In *A Companion to Victorian Poetry*, edited by Richard Cronin, Alison Chapman and Antony H. Harrison, 171–86. Malden, MA, and Oxford: Blackwell.

Felluga, Dino. 2018. 'A Sonnet is a Moment's Monument.' *COVE.* https://editions.covecollective.org/edition/sonnet/sonnet-moments-monument-1. Accessed 12 August 2020.

Ferguson, Trish. 2013. 'Introduction.' In *Victorian Time: Technologies, Standardizations, Catastrophes*, edited by Trish Ferguson, 1–15. Basingstoke: Palgrave Macmillan.

Fish, Stanley. 1980. 'How to Recognize a Poem When You See One.' In *Is There a Text in This Class? The Authority of Interpretive Communities*, 322–37. Cambridge, MA: Harvard University Press.

Flint, Kate. 1997. '". . . As a Rule, I Does Not Mean I": Personal Identity and the Victorian Woman Poet.' In *Rewriting the Self: Histories from the Renaissance to the Present*, edited by Roy Porter, 156–66. London: Routledge.

Fludernik, Monika. 1996. *Towards a 'Natural' Narratology.* London: Routledge.

Fludernik, Monika. 2005. 'Allegory, Metaphor, Scene and Expression: The Example of English Medieval and Early Modern Lyric Poetry.' In *Theory into Poetry: New Approaches to the Lyric*, edited by Eva Müller-Zettelmann and Margarete Rubik, 99–124. Amsterdam and New York: Rodopi.

Fludernik, Monika. 2018. 'Towards a "Natural" Narratology Twenty Years After.' *Partial Answers* 16 (2): 329–47.

Fludernik, Monika, and Miriam Nandi. 2014. 'Introduction.' In *Idleness, Indolence and Leisure in English Literature*, edited by Monika Fludernik and Miriam Nandi, 1–16. Basingstoke: Palgrave Macmillan.

Ford, Ford Madox. 1964. *Critical Writings of Ford Madox Ford.* Edited by Frank MacShane. Lincoln, NB: University of Nebraska Press.

Foucault, Michel. 2018. *The Order of Things: An Archaeology of the Human Sciences.* [1966]. London: Routledge.

Frye, Northrop. 1985. 'Approaching the Lyric.' In *Lyric Poetry: Beyond New Criticism*, edited by Chaviva Hošek and Patricia A. Parker, 31–7. Ithaca, NY: Cornell University Press.

Gallagher, Catherine. 1985. *The Industrial Reformation of English Fiction: Social Discourse and Narrative Form, 1832–1867*. Chicago, IL, and London: University of Chicago Press.

Gamper, Michael, et al., eds. 2016. *Zeit der Form – Formen der Zeit*. Hanover: Wehrhahn Verlag.

Gamper, Michael, and Eva Geulen. 2016. 'Einleitung.' In *Zeit der Form – Formen der Zeit*, edited by Michael Gamper et al., 7–16. Hanover: Wehrhahn Verlag.

Gamper, Michael, and Helmut Hühn. 2014. *Was sind Ästhetische Eigenzeiten?* Hanover: Wehrhahn Verlag.

Garnett, Richard. 1898. 'Introduction.' In *The Poems of Samuel Taylor Coleridge*, edited by Richard Garnett, xiii–lii. London: Lawrence & Bullen.

Garratt, Peter. 2010. *Victorian Empiricism: Self, Knowledge, and Reality in Ruskin, Bain, Lewes, Spencer, and George Eliot*. Madison, NJ: Fairleigh Dickinson University Press.

Genette, Gérard. 1980. *Narrative Discourse*. Translated by Jane E. Lewin. Oxford: Blackwell.

Ghosh, Amitav. 2016. *The Great Derangement: Climate Change and the Unthinkable*. Chicago, IL: University of Chicago Press.

Glendening, John. 2007. *The Evolutionary Imagination in Late-Victorian Novels: An Entangled Bank*. Aldershot: Ashgate.

Goethe, Johann Wolfgang von. 1827. *Werke: Noten und Abhandlungen zum besseren Verständnis des West-Östlichen Divans*. Stuttgart und Tübingen: J. G. Cotta'sche Buchhandlung.

Gold, Barri J. 2010. *ThermoPoetics: Energy in Victorian Literature and Science*. Cambridge, MA, and London: MIT Press.

Gold, Barri J. 2021. *Energy, Ecocriticism, and Nineteenth-Century Fiction: Novel Ecologies*. Cham: Palgrave Macmillan.

Gosse, Edmund. 1893. *Questions at Issue*. London: William Heinemann.

Gould, Stephen Jay. 1987. *Time's Arrow, Time's Cycle: Myth and Metaphor in the Discovery of Geological Time*. Cambridge, MA: Harvard University Press.

Grant, Stuart, Jodie McNeilly and Maeva Veerapen. 2015. *Performance and Temporalisation: Time Happens*. Basingstoke: Palgrave Macmillan.

Greene, Roland. 1991. *Post-Petrarchism: Origins and Innovations of the Western Lyric Sequence*. Princeton, NJ, and Oxford: Princeton University Press.

Grob, Alan. 1964. 'Tennyson's "The Lotos-Eaters": Two Versions of Art.' *Modern Philology* 62 (2): 118–29.

Grob, Alan. 2002. *A Longing Like Despair: Arnold's Poetry of Pessimism*. Newark, DE: University of Delaware Press.

Guest, Edwin. 1883. *A History of English Rhythms*. Edited by Walter W. Skeat. London: George Bell.

Haber, Francis C. 1972. 'The Darwinian Revolution in the Concept of Time.' In *The Study of Time*, edited by J. T. Fraser, Francis C. Haber and G. H. Müller, 383–401. Berlin, New York: Springer-Verlag.

Hall, Jason David. 2011. 'Introduction: A Great Multiplication of Meters.' In *Meter Matters: Verse Cultures of the Long Nineteenth Century*, edited by Jason D. Hall, 1–25. Athens, OH: Ohio University Press.

Hall, Jason David. 2017. *Nineteenth-Century Verse and Technology*. London: Palgrave Macmillan.

Hallam, Arthur Henry. 2005. 'On Some Characteristics of Modern Poetry.' [1831]. In *The Broadview Anthology of Victorian Poetry and Poetic Theory*, edited by Thomas J. Collins and Vivienne Rundle, 540–55. Peterborough, Ont.: Broadview Press.

Harrington, Emily. 2007. 'The Measure of Time: Rising and Falling in Victorian Meters.' *Literature Compass* 4 (1): 336–54.

Harrington, Emily. 2013. 'Augusta Webster: Time and the Lyric Ideal.' In *Oxford Handbook of Victorian Poetry*, edited by Matthew Bevis, 507–20. Oxford: Oxford University Press.

Harrington, Emily. 2014. *Second Person Singular: Late Victorian Women Poets and the Bonds of Verse*. Charlottesville, VA: University of Virginia Press.

Harrison, J. F. C. 1957. 'The Victorian Gospel of Success.' *Victorian Studies* 1 (2): 155–64.

Hegel, Georg Wilhelm Friedrich. 1975. *Aesthetics: Lectures on Fine Art*. Translated by T. M. Knox. Oxford: Oxford University Press.

Hempfer, Klaus W. 2014. *Lyrik: Skizze einer systematischen Theorie*. Stuttgart: Franz Steiner Verlag.

Henwood, Dawn. 1997. 'Christian Allegory and Subversive Poetics: Christina Rossetti's "Prince's Progress" Re-Examined.' *Victorian Poetry* 35 (1): 83–94.

Herbert, Christopher. 2001. *Victorian Relativity: Radical Thought and Scientific Discovery*. Chicago, IL: University of Chicago Press.

Hillebrandt, Claudia, Sonja Klimek, Ralph Müller and Rüdiger Zymner, eds. 2020. *Grundfragen der Lyrikologie 2: Begriffe, Methoden und Analysedimensionen*. Boston, MA: de Gruyter.

Holmes, Edmond. 1900. *What is Poetry?* London and New York: John Lane.

Holmes, John. 2005. *Dante Gabriel Rossetti and the Late Victorian Sonnet Sequence: Sexuality, Belief and the Self*. Aldershot: Ashgate.

Holmes, John. 2013. *Darwin's Bards: British and American Poetry in the Age of Evolution*. Edinburgh: Edinburgh University Press.

Holmes, John. 2018. *The Pre-Raphaelites and Science*. New Haven, CT: Yale University Press.

Hood, Thomas. 2000. 'The Song of the Shirt.' In *The Victorians: An Anthology of Poetry & Poetics*, edited by Valentine Cunningham, 63–5. Oxford: Blackwell.

Horn, Pamela. 2014. *Amusing the Victorians: Leisure, Pleasure and Play in Victorian Britain*. Stroud: Amberley.

Houston, Natalie M. 2003. 'Towards a New History: *Fin-de-Siècle* Women Poets and the Sonnet.' In *Victorian Women Poets*, edited by Alison Chapman, 154–64. Cambridge: D. S. Brewer.

Howe, Elisabeth A. 1996. *The Dramatic Monologue*. New York: Twayne.

Howse, Derek. 1997. *Greenwich Time and the Longitude*. London and Wappinger's Falls, NY: Philip Wilson and National Maritime Museum.

Huber, Irmtraud. 2019. 'Competing for Eternity: Tracing the Relation between Poetry and Science in Victorian Discourse.' *Journal of Literature and Science* 12 (1): 1–20.

Huber, Irmtraud. 2021. 'Zeitstrukturen im Gedicht.' *Poetica* 52 (3/4): 334–60.

Hudson, Maxim. 1910. *The Science of Poetry and the Philosophy of Language*. New York, NY: Funk & Wagnalls Company.

Hühn, Peter. 2016. *Facing Loss and Death: Narrative and Eventfulness in Lyric Poetry*. Berlin: de Gruyter.

Hühn, Peter, and Jens Kiefer, eds. 2005. *The Narratological Analysis of Lyric Poetry: Studies in English Poetry from the 16th to the 20th Century*. Translated by Alastair Matthews. Berlin and Boston, MA: de Gruyter.

Hühn, Peter, and Jörg Schönert. 2005. 'Introduction: The Theory and Methodology of the Narratological Analysis of Lyric Poetry.' In *The Narratological Analysis of Lyric Poetry: Studies in English Poetry from the 16th to the 20th Century*, edited by Peter Hühn and Jens Kiefer, 1–13. Berlin and Boston, MA: de Gruyter.

Hunt, Leigh. 1891. 'An Answer to the Question "What Is Poetry?".' In *Imagination and Fancy*, 1–61. London: Smith, Elder, & Co.

Hunt, Robert. 1850. *The Poetry of Science: Or the Studies of the Physical Phenomena of Nature*. [1848]. Boston, MA: Gould, Kendall, and Lincoln.

Hurley, Michael D. 2013. 'Rhythm.' In *Oxford Handbook of Victorian Poetry*, edited by Matthew Bevis, 19–35. Oxford: Oxford University Press.

Hylton, Stuart. 2007. *The Grand Experiment: The Birth of the Railway Age, 1820–1845*. Hersham: Ian Allan.

Ingarden, Roman. 1968. *Vom Erkennen des literarischen Kunstwerks*. Tübingen: Max Niemeyer Verlag.

Jackson, Virginia Walker. 2005. *Dickinson's Misery: A Theory of Lyric Reading*. Princeton, NJ: Princeton University Press.

Jackson, Virginia Walker, and Yopie Prins. 2014. 'General Introduction.' In *The Lyric Theory Reader: A Critical Anthology*, edited by Virginia W. Jackson and Yopie Prins, 1–8. Baltimore, MD: Johns Hopkins University Press.

Jakobson, Roman. 1960. 'Linguistics and Poetics.' In *Style in Language*, edited by Thomas A. Sebeok, 350–77. Cambridge, MA: MIT Press.

Jameson, Fredric. 1981. *The Political Unconscious: Narrative as a Socially Symbolic Act*. Ithaca, NY: Cornell University Press.

Jones, Darryl. 2013. '"Gone into Mourning . . . For the Death of the Sun": Victorians at the End of Time.' In *Victorian Time: Technologies, Standardizations, Catastrophes*, edited by Trish Ferguson, 178–95. Houndmills, Basingstoke and New York: Palgrave Macmillan.

Jones, Ewan. 2016. 'Coventry Patmore's Corpus', *ELH* 83 (3): 839–72.

Jones, Ewan. 2018. 'Thermodynamic Rhythm.' *Representations* 144 (1): 61–89.

Jones, Ewan. 2022. 'Poetic Vigil, Rhythmical Vigilance'. In *Zeiten der Wachsamkeit*, edited by Arndt Brendecke and Susanne Reichlin, 131–56. Berlin and Boston, MA: de Gruyter.

Jordan, Sarah. 2003. *The Anxieties of Idleness: Idleness in Eighteenth-Century British Literature and Culture*. Lewisburg, PA: Bucknell University Press.

Jordan, Sarah. 2014. 'Idleness, Class and Gender in the Long Eighteenth Century.' In *Idleness, Indolence and Leisure in English Literature*, edited by Monika Fludernik and Miriam Nandi, 107–28. Basingstoke: Palgrave Macmillan.

Keats, John. 2008. 'Ode to a Grecian Urn.' In *Romantic Poetry: An Annotated Anthology*, edited by Michael O'Neill and Charles Mahoney, 448–51. Maldon, MA, and Oxford: Blackwell.

Kempton, Adrian. 2018. *The Verse Novel in English: Origins, Growth and Expansion*. Oxford and New York: Peter Lang.

Kermode, Frank. 1967. *The Sense of an Ending: Studies in the Theory of Fiction*. New York: Oxford University Press.

Kern, Stephen. 2003 [1983]. *The Culture of Time and Space, 1880–1918*. Cambridge, MA: Harvard University Press.

Ketabgian, Tamara Siroone. 2011. *The Lives of Machines: The Industrial Imaginary in Victorian Literature and Culture*. Ann Arbor, MI: University of Michigan Press.

Kirchhoff, Frederick. 1980. 'The Aesthetic Discipline of the "Earthly Paradise".' *Victorian Poetry* 18 (3): 229–40.

Kohlmann, Benjamin. 2014. 'Versions of Working-Class Idleness: Non-Productivity and the Critique of Victorian Workaholism.' In *Idleness, Indolence and Leisure in English Literature*, edited by Monika Fludernik and Miriam Nandi, 195–214. Houndmills, Basingstoke: Palgrave Macmillan.

Koselleck, Reinhart. 1979. *Vergangene Zukunft: Zur Semantik geschichtlicher Zeiten*. Frankfurt am Main: Suhrkamp.

Koselleck, Reinhart, and Keith Tribe. 2005. *Futures Past: On the Semantics of Historical Time*. New York: Columbia University Press.

Landes, David S. 1983. *Revolution in Time: Clocks and the Making of the Modern World*. Cambridge, MA, and London: Belknap Press of Harvard University Press.

Langbaum, Robert. 1957. *The Poetry of Experience: The Dramatic Monologue in Modern Literary Tradition.* London: Chatto & Windus.

Lanier, Sidney. 1894. *The Science of English Verse.* [1880]. New York: Charles Scribner's Sons.

Latour, Bruno. 1993. *We Have Never Been Modern.* Translated by C. Porter. New York, London: Harvester Wheatsheaf.

Le Goff, Jacques. 1980. *Time, Work & Culture in the Middle Ages.* Chicago, IL: University of Chicago Press.

Leighton, Angela. 1992. *Victorian Women Poets: Writing against the Heart.*

Leighton, Angela. 2002. 'Touching Forms: Tennyson and Aestheticism.' *Essays in Criticism* 52 (1): 56–75.

Levine, Caroline. 2015. *Forms: Whole, Rhythm, Hierarchy, Network.* Princeton, NJ: Princeton University Press.

Levine, George. 1988. *Darwin and the Novelists: Patterns of Science in Victorian Fiction.* Cambridge, MA, and London: Harvard University Press.

Lewes, George Henry. 1842a. 'Article I.' *The British and Foreign Review* 13 (25): 1–49.

Lewes, George Henry. 1842b. 'The Roman Empire and Its Poets.' *Westminster Review* no. 38: 33–58.

Lewes, George Henry. 1879. *Problems of Life and Mind.* Boston, MA: Houghton, Osgood and Company.

Liedke, Heidi. 2018. *The Experience of Idling in Victorian Travel Texts, 1850–1901.* Cham: Palgrave Macmillan.

Lotman, Jurij. 1977. *The Structure of the Artistic Text.* Translated by Gail Lenhoff and Ronald Vroon. Ann Arbor, MI: University of Michigan.

Lowerson, John, and John Myerscough. 1977. *Time to Spare in Victorian England.* Hassocks: Harvester Press.

Luu, Helen. 2016. 'A Matter of Life and Death: The Auditor-Function of the Dramatic Monologue.' *Victorian Poetry* 54 (1): 19–38.

Lynch, Thomas Toke. 1853. *Essays on Some of the Forms of Literature.* London: Longmans.

Lysack, Krista. 2013. 'The Productions of Time: Keble, Rossetti, and Victorian Devotional Reading.' *Victorian Studies* 55 (3): 451.

McGann, Jerome. 'Autumn Idleness: Dante Gabriel Rossetti.' *The Rossetti Archive.* http://www.rossettiarchive.org/docs/2-1850.raw.html. Accessed 9 June 2020.

McGann, Jerome J. 2000. *Dante Gabriel Rossetti and the Game That Must Be Lost.* London and New Haven, CT: Yale University Press.

McHale, Brian. 2009. 'Beginning to Think about Narrative in Poetry.' *Narrative* 17 (1): 11–30.

Mahler, Andreas. 2006. 'Towards a Pragmasemiotics of Poetry.' *Poetica* 38 (3/4): 217–57.

Markovits, Stefanie. 2006. *The Crisis of Action in Nineteenth-Century English Literature.* Columbus, OH: Ohio State University Press.

Markovits, Stefanie. 2017. *The Victorian Verse-Novel: Aspiring to Life*. Oxford: Oxford University Press.

Marston, J. Westland. 1838. *Poetry as an Universal Nature*. London: W. Strange.

Martin, Meredith. 2011. 'Prosody Wars.' In *Meter Matters: Verse Cultures of the Long Nineteenth Century*, edited by Jason D. Hall, 237–61. Athens, OH: Ohio University Press.

Martin, Meredith. 2012. *The Rise and Fall of Meter: Poetry and English National Culture, 1860–1930*. Princeton, NJ: Princeton University Press.

Maynard, Lee Anna. 2009. *Beautiful Boredom: Idleness and Feminine Self-Realization in the Victorian Novel*. Jefferson, NC: McFarland.

Menely, Tobias. 2018. 'Ecologies of Time.' In *Time and Literature*, edited by Thomas M. Allen, 85–100. Cambridge: Cambridge University Press.

Meredith, George. 2004. 'Modern Love.' [1862]. In *Victorian Poetry: An Annotated Anthology*, edited by Francis O'Gorman, 328–49. Malden, MA, and Oxford: Blackwell.

Mermin, Dorothy. 1983. *The Audience in the Poem: Five Victorian Poets*. New Brunswick, NJ: Rutgers University Press.

Mermin, Dorothy. 1993. *Godiva's Ride: Women of Letters in England, 1830–1880*. Bloomington and Indianapolis, IN: Indiana University Press.

Meyer, Holt. 2003. 'G. M. Hopkins' Lyrik und Meta-Lyrik und/als die kulturelle Provokation der "poetic function of language" und der "message as such".' In *Roman Jakobsons Gedichtanalysen: Eine Herausforderung an die Philologien*, edited by Hendrik Birus, Sebastian Donat and Burkhard Meyer-Sickendiek, 196–231. Göttingen: Wallstein.

Meyerhoff, Hans. 1955. *Time in Literature*. Berkeley and Los Angeles, CA: University of California Press.

Meynell, Alice. 1892a. 'Mr. Coventry Patmore's Odes.' In *The Rhythm of Life: And Other Essays*, 89–96. London: John Lane.

Meynell, Alice. 1892b. 'The Rhythm of Life.' In *The Rhythm of Life: And Other Essays*, 1–6. London: John Lane.

Meynell, Alice. 1947. 'The English Metres.' In *The Poems of Alice Meynell, 1847–1923*, edited by Francis Meynell, 103. London: Hollis & Carter.

Mill, John Stuart. 1831. 'The Spirit of the Age: No. 1.' January 9. *Examiner* no. 1197: 20–1.

Mill, John Stuart. 1860. 'Thoughts on Poetry and Its Varieties: Part II.' *The Crayon* 7 (4): 123–8.

Mill, John Stuart. 2005. 'What is Poetry?' [1833]. In *The Broadview Anthology of Victorian Poetry and Poetic Theory*, edited by Thomas J. Collins and Vivienne Rundle, 562–70. Peterborough, Ont.: Broadview Press.

Miller, Christopher R. 2006. *The Invention of Evening: Perception and Time in Romantic Poetry*. Cambridge: Cambridge University Press.

Mitchell, Sally. 2009. *Daily Life in Victorian England.* 2nd edn. Westport, CT: Greenwood Press.

Moine, Fabienne. 2018. 'Voices in the Machine: Class, Subjectivity and Desire in Victorian Women's Factory Poems.' no. 87 Printemps. https://journals.openedition.org/cve/3550#text. Accessed 17 January 2021.

Moir, George. 1842. 'Poetry.' In *Encyclopaedia Britannica: Seventh Edition*, 140–73. Edinburgh: Adam and Charles Black.

Moore, Natasha. 2015. *Victorian Poetry and Modern Life: The Unpoetical Age.* London: Palgrave Macmillan.

Morgan, Monique R. 2009. *Narrative Means, Lyric Ends: Temporality in the Nineteenth-Century British Long Poem.* Columbus, OH: Ohio State University Press.

Morris, William. 2002. *The Earthly Paradise.* Edited by Florence S. Boos. New York and London: Routledge.

Moy, Olivia Loksing. 2018. 'Simian, Amphibian, and Able: Reevaluating Browning's Caliban.' *Victorian Poetry* 56 (4): 381–411.

Müller-Zettelmann, Eva. 2000. *Lyrik und Metalyrik: Theorie einer Gattung und ihrer Selbstspiegelung anhand von Beispielen aus der englisch- und deutschsprachigen Dichtkunst.* Heidelberg: Winter.

Müller-Zettelmann, Eva, and Margarete Rubik. 2005. 'Introduction.' In *Theory into Poetry: New Approaches to the Lyric*, edited by Eva Müller-Zettelmann and Margarete Rubik, 7–20. Amsterdam and New York: Rodopi.

Müller-Zettelmann, Eva, and Margarete Rubik, eds. 2005. *Theory into Poetry: New Approaches to the Lyric.* Amsterdam and New York: Rodopi.

Mumford, Lewis. 1946. *Technics and Civilisation.* London: Routledge.

Murphy, Patricia. 2001. *Time is of the Essence: Temporality, Gender, and the New Woman.* Albany, NY: State University of New York Press.

Najarian, James. 2013. 'Verse Versus the Novel.' In *The Oxford Handbook of the Victorian Novel*, edited by Lisa Rodensky, 589–605. Oxford: Oxford University Press.

Newman, Francis. 1858. 'Science of Things Outward.' In *Theism: Doctrinal and Practical*, 19–21. London: John Chapman.

Newman, John Henry. 2011. '"The Mission of the Benedictine Order", *Atlantis*, 1 (1858), pp. 1–4, 5, 16–18, 24–6, 32–4, 46–7.' In *Negotiating Boundaries*, edited by Piers J. Hale. Victorian Literature and Science vol. 1, 69–77. London: Pickering & Chatto.

Newsome, David. 1997. *The Victorian World Picture: Perceptions and Introspections in an Age of Change.* New Brunswick, NJ: Rutgers University Press.

Noel, Roden. 1876. '*Thoughts on Art, Philosophy, and Religion* by Sydney Dobell.' *The Academy* 20 May no. 211: 478–9.

Nowotny, Helga. 1994. *Time: The Modern and Postmodern Experience.* Cambridge and Cambridge, MA: Blackwell.

O'Gorman, Francis, ed. 2004. *Victorian Poetry: An Annotated Anthology.* Malden, MA, Oxford: Blackwell.

Omond, Thomas Stewart. 1921. *English Metrists: Being a Sketch of English Prosodical Criticism from Elizabethan Times to the Present Day.* Oxford: Clarendon Press.

Oschmann, Dirk. 2016a. 'Der Einbruch der Zeit in die Form: Englisch-deutscher Theorietransfer im 18. Jahrhundert.' In *Zeit der Form – Formen der Zeit*, edited by Michael Gamper, Eva Geulen, Johannes Grave, Andreas Langenohl, Ralf Simon and Sabine Zubarik, 37–62. Hanover: Wehrhahn Verlag.

Oschmann, Dirk. 2016b. 'Formbewusstsein als Zeitbewusstsein: Die Anfänge moderner Zeitpoetik im 18. Jahrhundert.' In *Critical Time in Modern German Literature and Culture*, edited by Dirk Göttsche, 129–43. Oxford: Peter Lang.

Palgrave, Francis T. 1886. 'Poetry Compared with the Other Fine Arts.' *The National Review* 7 (41): 634–48.

Pater, Walter. 1868. 'Art. II: Poems by William Morris.' *Westminster Review* 34 (2): 300–12.

Pater, Walter. 1998. *The Renaissance: Studies in Art and Poetry*. [1873]. 4th edn. Edited by Adam Phillips. Oxford: Oxford University Press.

Patmore, Coventry. 1857. 'English Metrical Critics.' *The North British Review* 27 (53): 127–61.

Parker, Joanne, and Corinna Wagner, eds. 2020. *The Oxford Handbook of Victorian Medievalism.* New York: Oxford University Press.

Pearsall, Cornelia D. J. 2000. 'The Dramatic Monologue.' In *The Cambridge Companion to Victorian Poetry*, edited by Joseph Bristow, 67–88. Cambridge: Cambridge University Press.

Pearsall, Cornelia D. J. 2008. *Tennyson's Rapture: Transformation in the Victorian Dramatic Monologue.* New York and Oxford: Oxford University Press.

Perkin, Harold James. 1971. *The Age of the Railway.* Newton Abbot: David & Charles.

Pettitt, Clare. 2012. '"The Annihilation of Space and Time": Literature and Technology.' In *The Cambridge History of Victorian Literature*, edited by Kate Flint, 550–72. Cambridge: Cambridge University Press.

Petzold, Jochen. 2012. *Sprechsituationen lyrischer Dichtung: Ein Beitrag zur Gattungstypologie.* Würzburg: Königshausen & Neumann.

Pfister, Manfred. 2001. *Das Drama: Theorie und Analyse.* 11th edn. Munich: W. Fink.

Phelan, Joseph. 2005. *The Nineteenth-Century Sonnet.* Basingstoke: Palgrave Macmillan.

Phelan, Joseph. 2012. *The Music of Verse: Metrical Experiment in Nineteenth-Century Poetry.* Houndmills, Basingstoke and New York: Palgrave Macmillan.

Plotz, Judith A. 1987. *Ideas of the Decline of Poetry: A Study in English Criticism from 1700 to 1830*. New York and London: Garland Publishing.

Powell, James Henry. 1853. *The Poetry of Feeling and the Poetry of Diction*. Aylesbury: Geo. De Frein.

Prins, Yopie. 2000. 'Victorian Meters.' In *The Cambridge Companion to Victorian Poetry*, edited by Joseph Bristow, 89–113. Cambridge: Cambridge University Press.

Prins, Yopie. 2005. 'Patmore's Law, Meynell's Rhythm.' In *The Fin-de-Siècle Poem: English Literary Culture and the 1890s*, edited by Joseph Bristow, 261–84. Athens, OH: Ohio University Press.

Prins, Yopie. 2011. '"Break, Break, Break" into Song.' In *Meter Matters: Verse Cultures of the Long Nineteenth Century*, edited by Jason D. Hall, 105–34. Athens, OH: Ohio University Press.

Rabey, David Ian. 2016. *Theatre, Time and Temporality: Melting Clocks and Snapped Elastics*. Bristol: Intellect.

Reeds, Eleanor. 2019. 'Voicing an Epic for the Age in *the Prelude* and *Aurora Leigh*.' *Victorian Poetry* 57 (2): 225–46.

Reinfandt, Christoph. 2003. *Romantische Kommunikation: Zur Kontinuität der Romantik in der Kultur der Moderne*. Heidelberg: Winter.

Rennie, Nicholas. 2005. *Speculating on the Moment: The Poetics of Time and Recurrence in Goethe, Leopardi, and Nietzsche*. Göttingen: Wallstein.

Richter, Virginia. 2011. *Literature after Darwin: Human Beasts in Western Fiction, 1859–1939*. Basingstoke: Palgrave Macmillan.

Ricœur, Paul. 1983–5. *Temps et récit*. Paris: Éditions du Seuil.

Ricœur, Paul. 1990. *Time and Narrative*. [1983–5]. Translated by K. McLaughlin and D. Pellauer. 3 vols. Chicago, IL: University of Chicago Press.

Riede, David G. 1992. *Dante Gabriel Rossetti Revisited*. New York: Maxwell Macmillan International.

Riede, David G. 2005. *Allegories of One's Own Mind: Melancholy in Victorian Poetry*. Columbus, OH: Ohio State University Press.

Rogers, Janine. 2015. *Unified Fields: Science and Literary Form*. Montreal: McGill-Queen's University Press.

Rohrbach, Emily. 2016. *Modernity's Mist: British Romanticism and the Poetics of Anticipation*. New York: Fordham University Press.

Rosa, Hartmut. 2005. *Beschleunigung: Die Veränderung der Zeitstrukturen in der Moderne*. Frankfurt am Main: Suhrkamp.

Rosa, Hartmut. 2013. *Social Acceleration: A New Theory of Modernity*. Translated by Jonathan Trejo-Mathys. New York: Columbia University Press.

Rosenberg, John D. 2005. *Elegy for an Age: The Presence of the Past in Victorian Literature*. London: Anthem Press.

Rossetti, Christina. 1990. 'The Lotus-Eaters: Ulysses to Penelope.' In *The Complete Poems of Christina Rossetti: A Variorum Edition*, edited by

Rebecca W. Crump, vol. 3, 144–5. Baton Rouge, LA, and London: Louisiana State University Press.

Rossetti, Christina. 1886. *Time Flies: A Reading Diary.* Boston, MA: Roberts Brothers.

Rossetti, Christina. 1894. 'Where Neither Rust Nor Moth Doth Corrupt.' In *Verses*, 8. London: Society for Promoting Christian Knowledge.

Rossetti, Christina. 2008. *Poems and Prose.* Edited by Simon Humphries. Oxford: Oxford University Press.

Rossetti, Dante Gabriel. 'Idle Blessedness.' [1849]. *The Rossetti Archive.* http://www.rossettiarchive.org/docs/26-1848.raw.html. Accessed 14 June 2020.

Rossetti, Dante Gabriel. 2003. *Collected Poetry and Prose.* Edited by Jerome McGann. New York: Yale University Press.

Rossetti, William Michael. 1849. 'Sheer Waste.' *The Germ* no. 2: 77–8.

Rossetti, William Michael. 1867–8. 'Mrs. Holmes Grey.' In *The Broadway Annual: A Miscellany of Original Literature in Poetry and Prose*, 449–59. London and New York: George Routledge and Sons.

Roth, Sister Mary Augustine, ed. 1961. *Coventry Patmore's 'Essay on English Metrical Law': A Critical Edition with a Commentary.* Washington, DC: The Catholic University of America Press.

Rubik, Margarete. 2005. 'In Deep Waters. Or: What's the Difference Between Drowning in Poetry and in Prose?' In *Theory into Poetry: New Approaches to the Lyric*, edited by Eva Müller-Zettelmann and Margarete Rubik, 189–206. Amsterdam and New York: Rodopi.

Rudrum, David. 2005. 'From Narrative Representation to Narrative Use: Towards the Limits of Definition.' *Narrative* 13 (2): 195–204.

Rudwick, M. J. S. 2014. *Earth's Deep History: How It was Discovered and Why It Matters.* Chicago, IL, and London: University of Chicago Press.

Rudy, Jason R. 2009. *Electric Meters: Victorian Physiological Poetics.* Athens, OH: Ohio University Press.

Salgaro, Massimo, and Michele Vangi. 2016. 'Der Mythos Rhythmus.' In *Mythos Rhythmus: Wissenschaft, Kunst und Literatur um 1900*, edited by Massimo Salgaro and Michele Vangi, 11–28. Stuttgart: Franz Steiner Verlag.

Sanford Russell, Beatrice. 2015. 'How to Exist Where You Are: A Lesson in Lotos-Eating.' *Victorian Poetry* 53 (4): 375–99.

Scheinberg, Cynthia. 1997. 'Recasting "Sympathy and Judgement": Amy Levy, Women Poets, and the Victorian Dramatic Monologue.' *Victorian Poetry* 35 (2): 173–92.

Schivelbusch, Wolfgang. 2014. *The Railway Journey: The Industrialization of Time and Space in the Nineteenth Century.* [1977]. Berkeley, CA: University of California Press.

Schlaffer, Heinz. 2015. *Geistersprache: Zweck und Mittel der Lyrik.* Stuttgart: Reclam.

Shairp, John Campbell. 1881. *Aspects of Poetry: Being Lectures Delivered at Oxford*. Oxford: Clarendon Press.

Shaw, W. David. 1987. *The Lucid Veil: Poetic Truth in the Victorian Age*. London: Athlone.

Shelley, Percy Bysshe. 2002. 'A Defence of Poetry.' [1840]. In *Shelley's Poetry and Prose: Authoritative Texts, Criticism*, edited by Neil Fraistat and Donald H. Reiman. 2nd edn, 509–35. New York and London: Norton.

Shoptaw, John. 1995. 'The Music of Construction: Measure and Polyphony in Ashbery and Bernstein.' In *Tribe of John: Ashbery and Contemporary Poetry*, edited by Susan Schultz, 211–57. Tuscaloosa: University of Alabama Press.

Simmons, Jack. 2009. *The Victorian Railway*. London: Thames & Hudson.

Slinn, Warwick E. 2002. 'Dramatic Monologue.' In *A Companion to Victorian Poetry*, edited by Richard Cronin, Alison Chapman and Antony H. Harrison, 80–98. Malden, MA, and Oxford: Blackwell.

Spiegelman, Willard. 1995. *Majestic Indolence: English Romantic Poetry and the Work of Art*. New York and Oxford: Oxford University Press.

Spinks, Lee. 2014. 'Metre and Rhythm.' In *The Edinburgh Introduction to Studying English Literature*, edited by Dermot Cavanagh, Alan Gillis, Michelle Keown, James Loxley and Randall Stevenson. 2nd edn, 47–56. Edinburgh: Edinburgh University Press.

Stainthorp, Clare. 2019. *Constance Naden: Scientist, Philosopher, Poet*. Oxford, Bern, Berlin and Vienna: Peter Lang.

Starzyk, Lawrence J. 1992. *The Dialogue of the Mind with Itself: Early Victorian Poetry and Poetics*. Calgary, Alb.: University of Calgary Press.

Steele, Timothy. 1990. *Missing Measures: Modern Poetry and the Revolt against Meter*. Fayetteville, AR: University of Arkansas Press.

Stewart, Susan. 2002. *Poetry and the Fate of the Senses*. Chicago, IL, and London: University of Chicago Press.

Stewart, Walter K. 1978. *Time Structure in Drama: Goethe's Sturm und Drang Plays*. Amsterdam: Rodopi.

Sussman, Herbert L. 1968. *Victorians and the Machine*. Cambridge, MA: Harvard University Press.

Swinburne, Algernon Charles. 1866. *Notes on Poems and Reviews*. London: J. C. Hotten.

Swinburne, Algernon Charles. 1870. 'The Poems of Dante Gabriel Rossetti.' *Fortnightly Review* 7 (41): 551–79.

Symonds, John Addington. 1882. *Animi Figura*. London: Smith, Elder, & Co.

Symonds, John Addington. 1884. *Vagabunduli Libellius*. London: Kegan Paul, Trench & Co.

Symonds, John Addington. 1907. 'On Some Principles of Criticism.' In *Essays Speculative and Suggestive*. [1890]. 3rd edn, 53–78. London: Smith, Elder, & Co.

Taft, Joshua. 2013. 'The Forms of Discipline: Christina Rossetti's Religious Verse.' *Victorian Poetry* 51 (3): 311–30.

Tate, Gregory. 2012. *The Poet's Mind: The Psychology of Victorian Poetry, 1830–1870.* Oxford: Oxford University Press.

Tate, Gregory. 2017. 'Poetry and Science.' In *The Routledge Research Companion to Nineteenth-Century British Literature and Science*, edited by John Holmes and Sharon Ruston, 101–14. London: Routledge.

Taylor, Dennis. 1988. *Hardy's Metres and Victorian Prosody: With a Metrical Appendix of Hardy's Stanza Forms.* Oxford: Clarendon Press.

Tennyson, Alfred. 2009. *The Major Works.* Edited by Adam Roberts. Oxford: Oxford University Press.

Tennyson, G. B. 1979. 'Tractarian Aesthetics: Analogy and Reserve in Keble and Newman.' *Victorian Newsletter* no. 55: 8–10.

Thain, Marion. 2016. *The Lyric Poem and Aestheticism: Forms of Modernity.* Edinburgh: Edinburgh University Press.

Thompson, E. P. 1967. 'Time, Work-Discipline, and Industrial Capitalism.' *Past and Present* no. 38: 56–97.

Tomalin, Marcus. 2020. *Telling the Time in British Literature, 1675–1830: Hours of Folly?* London: Routledge.

Tucker, Herbert F. 1983. 'Tennyson and the Measure of Doom.' *PMLA* 98 (1): 8–20.

Tucker, Herbert F. 1997. 'Of Monuments and Moments: Spacetime in Nineteenth-Century Poetry.' *Modern Language Quarterly* 58 (3): 269–97.

Tucker, Herbert F. 2006. 'Tactical Formalism: A Response to Caroline Levine.' *Victorian Studies* 49 (1): 85–93.

Tucker, Herbert F. 2007. 'Dramatic Monologue and the Overhearing of Lyric.' In *Robert Browning's Poetry: Authoritative Texts, Criticism*, edited by James F. Loucks and Andrew M. Stauffer. 2nd edn, 542–57. New York: Norton.

Tucker, Herbert F. 2008. *Epic: Britain's Heroic Muse, 1790–1910.* Oxford: Oxford University Press.

Tupper, Martin F. 1855. 'Railway Times.' In *Lyrics*, 16–19. London: Arthur Hall, Virtue & Co.

Tyndall, John. 2014. *Heat Considered as a Mode of Motion: Being a Course of Twelve Lectures Delivered at the Royal Institution of Great Britain in the Season of 1862.* [1862]. Cambridge: Cambridge University Press.

Tyndall, John. 2020. *The Poetry of John Tyndall.* Edited by Roland Jackson, Nicola Jackson and Daniel Brown. London: UCL Press.

van Remoortel, Marianne. 2011. *Lives of the Sonnet, 1787–1895: Genre, Gender and Criticism.* Farnham: Ashgate.

Veblen, Thorstein. 1998. *The Theory of the Leisure Class: An Economic Study of Institutions.* [1899]. Amherst, NY: Prometheus Books.

Wagner, Jennifer A. 1996. *A Moment's Monument: Revisionary Poetics and the Nineteenth-Century English Sonnet.* Madison, WI, London, and Cranbury, NJ: Fairleigh Dickinson University Press.

Wagner, Matthew. 2018. 'Time and Theatre.' In *Time and Literature*, edited by Thomas M. Allen, 57–71. Cambridge: Cambridge University Press.

Warren, Alba H. 1966. *English Poetic Theory, 1825–1865*. London: Frank Cass & Co. Ltd.

Wasserman, Earl R. 1959. *The Subtler Language: Critical Readings of Neoclassic and Romantic Poems*. Baltimore, MD: Johns Hopkins University Press.

Waters, William. 2003. *Poetry's Touch: On Lyric Address*. Ithaca, NY, and London: Cornell University Press.

Watts, Alaric Alexander. 1851. 'Egypt Unvisited. Suggested by Mr. David Roberts's Egyptian Sketches.' In *Lyrics of the Heart*, 269–70. London: Longman.

Watts, Theodore. 1885. 'Poetry.' In *Encyclopedia Britannica: PHY–PRO*. 9th edn. 24 vols, vol. 19, 256–72. New York: Charles Scribner's Sons.

Webster, Augusta. 1879. *A Housewife's Opinions*. London: Macmillan & Co.

Webster, Augusta. 2000. *Portraits and Other Poems*. Edited by Christine Sutphin. Peterborough, Ont., and Orchard Park, NY: Broadview Press.

Wellbery, David E. 1996. *The Specular Moment: Goethe's Early Lyric and the Beginnings of Romanticism*. Stanford, CA: Stanford University Press.

Wellmann, Janina. 2017. *The Form of Becoming: Embryology and the Epistemology of Rhythm 1760–1830*. Translated by K. Sturge. Brooklyn, NY: Zone Books.

Whewell, William. 1840. *Philosophy of the Inductive Sciences Founded upon Their History*. 2 vols. London: John W. Parker.

Wiles, David. 2014. *Theatre & Time*. Basingstoke: Palgrave Macmillan.

Williams, Raymond. 1997. 'Dominant, Residual, and Emergent.' In *Twentieth Century Literary Theory*, edited by K. M. Newton. 2nd edn, 235–9. Houndmills, Basingstoke: Macmillan.

Wilshire, Bruce W. 1982. *Role Playing and Identity: The Limits of Theatre as Metaphor*. Bloomington, IN: Indiana University Press.

Wiskus, Jessica. 2006. 'Inhabited Time: Couperin's *Passacaille*.' In *Logos of Phenomenology and Phenomenology of the Logos. Book Three: Logos of History – Logos of Life, Historicity, Time, Nature, Communication, Consciousness, Alterity, Culture*, edited by Anna-Teresa Tymieniecka, 177–93. Dordrecht: Springer Netherlands.

Wolf, Werner. 2005. 'The Lyric: Problems of Definition and a Proposal for Reconceptualisation.' In *Theory into Poetry: New Approaches to the Lyric*, edited by Eva Müller-Zettelmann and Margarete Rubik, 21–56. Amsterdam and New York: Rodopi.

Wolfson, Susan J. 1997. *Formal Charges: The Shaping of Poetry in British Romanticism*. Stanford, CA: Stanford University Press.

Wolmar, Christian. 2008. *Fire and Steam: A New History of the Railways in Britain*. London: Atlantic Books.

Wordsworth, William. 1974a. 'Essay, Supplementary to the Preface' [1815]. In *Wordsworth's Literary Criticism*, edited by W. J. B. Owen, 192–218. London and Boston, MA: Routledge & Kegan Paul.

Wordsworth, William. 1974b. 'Note to "The Thorn" (1800).' In *Wordsworth's Literary Criticism*, edited by W. J. B. Owen, 96–8. London and Boston, MA: Routledge & Kegan Paul.

Wordsworth, William. 1994. *Selected Poems*. Edited by Damian W. Davies. London: Everyman.

Wordsworth, William, and Samuel Taylor Coleridge. 1992. *Lyrical Ballads*. Edited by Michael Mason. London: Longman.

Wright, Lawrence. 1968. *Clockwork Man*. London: Elek Books.

Zemka, Sue. 2012. *Time and the Moment in Victorian Literature and Society*. Cambridge: Cambridge University Press.

Zettelmann, Eva. 2017. '*Discordia Concors*: Immersion and Artifice in the Lyric.' *Journal of Literary Theory* 11 (1): 136–48.

Zuckermann, Joanne P. 1971. 'Tennyson's *In Memoriam* as Love Poetry.' *Dalhousie Review* 51 (2): 202–17.

Zwierlein, Anne-Julia. 2009. *Der physiologische Bildungsroman im 19. Jahrhundert: Selbstformung, Leistungsethik und organischer Wandel in Naturwissenschaft und Literatur*. Heidelberg: Winter.

Zwierlein, Anne-Julia. 2015. 'Poetic Genres in the Victorian Age I: Post-Romantic Prose Narrative.' In *A History of British Poetry: Genres – Developments – Interpretations*, edited by Sibylle Baumbach, Birgit Neumann and Ansgar Nünning, 243–55. Trier: Wissenschaftlicher Verlag Trier.

Zymner, Rüdiger. 2013. *Funktionen der Lyrik*. Münster: mentis.

Zymner, Rüdiger. 2016. 'Lyrik und Zeit.' In *Schlüsselkonzepte und Anwendungen der kognitiven Literaturwissenschaft*, edited by Roman Mikuláš, 29–53. Münster: mentis.

Zymner, Rüdiger. 2020. 'Zeitgeber der Lyrik.' In *Grundfragen der Lyrikologie 2: Begriffe, Methoden und Analysedimensionen*, edited by Claudia Hillebrandt, Sonja Klimek, Ralph Müller and Rüdiger Zymner, 311–30. Boston, MA: de Gruyter.

Index

abstraction
of metre, 173–5, 179–88, 191,
192–3, 209, 211–12, 251
of time, 15–16, 19, 22, 26, 170, 173,
179, 183–5, 191, 210, 212, 251
scientific, 27, 53, 57, 190
acceleration, 15, 19–21, 24n, 26–7, 31,
36–7, 68n, 120–2, 158, 165n
address, lyric, 75, 83, 84, 86, 90–1, 94,
235–7, 241, 245
Adelman, Richard, 126–8, 131–2, 136,
142, 145, 154
Adorno, Theodor, 164, 218
Aestheticism, 6, 20, 49, 62, 63, 64n,
112, 129–31, 217
Aesthetics of Eternal Essence, 7–9, 14,
26, 36, 38, 45–6, 53, 56, 60, 63,
76, 77, 217–19
Aesthetics of Self-sufficient Form, 7–9,
15, 26, 60, 62–5, 88, 164, 217–19,
227, 248, 253, 255
Aesthetics of the Enduring Word, 7–9,
44
affect *see* emotion
Alfano, Veronica, 14, 23n, 88, 117n
Allingham, William, 30, 50, 67n, 120,
132
Anderson, Alexander, 203–11, 213
apostrophe *see* address
Armstrong, Isobel, 55–6, 146, 166n,
177–80, 214n
Arnold, Matthew, 27, 35–7, 39–41,
43–4, 64, 67n, 69n, 127
Culture and Anarchy, 127
'Dover Beach', 37–9
'Empedocles on Etna', 35
'Resignation: To Fausta', 37

'Stanzas from the Grande
Chartreuse', 27, 43
'Stanzas in Memory of the Author of
"Oberman"', 37
'The Scholar Gipsy', 37
atemporality *see* timelessness
Augustine, 222–4

Bailey, Peter, 17, 122
Bain, Alexander, 13, 18, 56
ballad, 10, 70–1, 204, 208, 210, 230
Barlow, George, 61–2
Barrett Browning, Elizabeth
Aurora Leigh, 43–7, 60, 70–1, 104,
110–12, 116, 199–200, 213
Sonnets from the Portuguese, 78, 85–7
'The Cry of the Children', 143–4
'The Runaway Slave at Pilgrim's
Point', 103
Baudelaire, Charles, 27
beat, 2, 165, 172, 174, 177–91, 195,
198–9, 202–5, 208–9, 251, 254
beauty, 13, 29, 30, 40, 46, 50, 51,62, 255
Benjamin, Walter, 173, 179
Bildungsroman, 80, 95, 165n
Blair, Kirstie, 51, 188–9, 192, 204–5,
208, 210
blank verse, 33, 46, 67n, 108–9,
196–202, 213
body, 22, 27, 45, 47, 55, 134, 170,
175, 179, 183–93, 196, 199–200,
204–5, 210–13, 228; *see also*
material
boredom, 99, 100–2, 147, 151–3,
200–3, 213
Bradley, Andrew C., 62, 121
Brooks, Peter, 73–4, 125, 219–20